ELIZABETH POSTUMA SIMCOE
1762-1850

POSTHUMA

A Biography

by Mary Beacock Fryer

D1253663

Design and Production:Andy Tong
Printing and Binding:Gagné Printing Ltd., Louiseville, Quebec, Canada

The publication of this book were made possible by support from several sources. The publisher wishes to acknowledge the generous assistance and ongoing support of **The Canada Council, The Book Publishing Industry Development Programme** of the **Department of Communications,** and **The Ontario Arts Council.**

J. Kirk Howard, Publisher

Canadian Cataloguing in Publication Data

Fryer, Mary Beacock, 1929-
  Elizabneth Posthuma Simcoe

Includes bibliographical references.
ISBN 1-55002-063-3 (bound). — ISBN 1-55002-064-1 (pbk.)

1. Simcoe, Elizabeth, 1762-1850. 2. Ontario - History - 1791-1841 - Biography.* 3. Ontario - Social life and customs. 4. England - Social life and customs - 19th century. I. Title.

FC3071.1.S5F78 1989   971.3'02'092   C89-090704-8   F1058.S7F78 1989

Dundurn Press Limited
2181 Queen Street East, Suite 301
Toronto, M4E 1E5
Canada

Dundurn Distribution Limited
73 Lime Walk
Headington, Oxford
EX3 7AD
England

ELIZABETH POSTUMA SIMCOE
1762-1850

A Biography

by Mary Beacock Fryer

DUNDURN PRESS
TORONTO & OXFORD
1989

CONTENTS

Introduction 7

PART I
THE HEIRESS 1762-1792

Chapter 1 A Very Special Child 9
Chapter 2 Early Life 13
Chapter 3 Hembury Fort House 19
Chapter 4 Wolford Lodge 26
Chapter 5 Departure for Canada 34

PART II
SOVERIGN LADY OF UPPER CANADA 1791-1796

Chapter 6 Winter at Quebec 1791-1792 46
Chapter 7 News from Home September 1791-June 1792 . 53
Chapter 8 Nature Untamed 59
Chapter 9 Winter in the Wilds 67
Chapter 10 Miss Burges Reports 1792-1793 76
Chapter 11 The Move to York 1793-1794 85
Chapter 12 Miss Burges and Mrs Graves
    May 1794-January 1795 95
Chapter 13 War Clouds May 1794-January 1795 103
Chapter 14 Mrs. Burges' "Commissions" 129
Chapter 15 The Season of 1795 138
Chapter 16 Julia 1795-1796 149
Chapter 17 End of the Tour of Duty 1796 157

PART III
PARTINGS: HUSBAND, SON, DEAREST FRIEND
1796-1813

Chapter 18 Return to Wolford Lodge.................. 167
Chapter 19 General Simcoe's Last Years 1803-1806..... 177
Chapter 20 Francis and Mary Anne 1812-1813......... 188

PART IV
HEAD OF THE FAMILY 1813-1850

Chapter 21 Fresh Interests 198
Chapter 22 The New Generation 1824-1826 205
Chapter 23 More Joy in Heaven 1827-1837 212
Chapter 24 Sir Francis and the Rebels of 1837 219
Chapter 25 The Church Builders.................... 226
Chapter 26 The Best Christian...................... 233

Notes 241
Bibliography....................................... 253
Appendix: The Simcoes' Genealogy by Hilary Arnold... 255
Index 267
Acknowledgements................................. 276

Illustrations

Elizabeth Posthuma Simcoe......................... 6
Elizabeth Simcoe's Sketches and Watercolours...... 113-128
Maps.. 41-45

Portrait of Elizabeth Simcoe by Mary Anne Burges

INTRODUCTION

Had she not spent five years in Upper Canada (now the Province of Ontario) as the wife of the first lieutenant governor, Elizabeth Simcoe's many diaries and letters would have been of interest mainly to her descendants. In Ontario today, and to a much less extent elsewhere, Elizabeth is best remembered for the record she wrote while in Canada for her family and close friends who remained in England, and for the informative water colour sketches she made of the country through which she travelled.

The first person to investigate Elizabeth Simcoe's life outside the province of Ontario was the newspaper publisher John Ross Robertson. His version of Mrs. Simcoe's diary was first published in 1911. Later authors, Marcus Van Steen and Mary Quayle Innis, accepted many of Robertson's assumptions and built upon them. In more recent years Hilary Arnold of York, England, became interested in Elizabeth Simcoe and did her own exploring. She found a different date and place of birth, and she has unearthed considerable information about Elizabeth's entire family, information that differs from the accepted version. Hilary has been very much my collaborator, and her lengthy genealogy on Mrs. Simcoe forms an impressive appendix to this work.

Edith Firth, formerly with the Metropolitan Toronto Library, contributed the account of Mrs. Simcoe to the *Dictionary of Canadian Biography*. She discovered that there are at least three versions of the Canadian diary; the first is short notes on which Elizabeth based the other two. The second she sent to Mrs. Ann Hunt, who was in charge of the children who were left in England; the third was for her dearest friend, Mary Anne Burges, in which she enlarged her detail on flora and fauna of Upper Canada. The version John Ross Robertson used was a combination of the latter two. Apparently some of the Simcoe family added details from Mary Anne Burges' version, because in places Elizabeth was answering specific questions which her friend had asked her. Of the two children who accompanied the Simcoes to Canada, Elizabeth says almost nothing about her daughter Sophia, except in her short notes or in letters to Mrs. Hunt and Miss Burges. The diary, as published by Robertson, has more detail about Francis, because Miss Burges asked Elizabeth to tell her about the boy. The parts relating to him have been added from the version Elizabeth sent her friend, probably by her daughters after Francis' premature death. Many sources other than Robertson's reveal more of Elizabeth Simcoe's life than the disclosures in her Canadian diaries — details on her early life, on the lives of her children while she was in Canada, and on her life and those of her children after the family had been reunited in England in 1796. One extensive collection is in the Devon Archives, and copies of this material are on microfilm in the National Archives of Canada in Ottawa. The other is the Ontario Archives' Simcoe Collection, which does not pertain to Canada.

The letters and diaries unveil a world that in some ways resembles that portrayed by Jane Austen, Elizabeth Simcoe's contemporary. Both women are formal in their way of addressing others. Elizabeth gives no indication that she ever called her husband John: she used his military or other rank. In his letters to Elizabeth, Simcoe addresses her as "My most Excellent & noble wife" or in similar phrases, but in one poem to her he calls her "Eliza".[1] Frustrating was the custom of all the Simcoes of referring to their friends and relatives only as Miss or Mrs. or Mr. or by a title, and rarely by given name. Only when writing to one's own children, or when omitting it would cause confusion, was the given name used. A notable departure from Jane Austen is the interest Elizabeth, her daughters and their friends took in international affairs, in politics, in news about well-known personalities of their day, and in the Church of England. In contrast, Austen's characters live in a much smaller world and are preoccupied mainly with domestic matters and match-making. Yet there was even a link between Mrs. Simcoe and Miss Austen. Both were acquainted with Lord and Lady Dorchester; the former was John Graves Simcoe's superior in Canada.[2]

Elizabeth reveals little of her inner self in her Canadian diaries, and not very much in her letters to friends and relatives. This is true, too, of the letters written by her children. The education all received schooled them in a particular form of letter-writing that was polite, informative, rarely emotional, and following rigid conventions. Mary Anne Burges' letters are much more personal; she relays most of the conversations used, while the others are based on sources. No conversation is invented.

The events of Elizabeth Simcoe's early life help explain her apparently cheerful acceptance of conditions of life and travel in the Upper Canada of the 1790s. Her life spanned four reigns, two of them remarkable for their longevity. Elizabeth was born in the early years of the reign of George III, lived through those of George IV and William IV, and she saw the first fourteen years of the Victorian era. In her youth she travelled by coach, chaise or on risky sailing ships. Before her death, steamships plied inland waters and oceans, and railways were extending their tentacles across England and North America. Always interested in anything new, she mentioned acquiring an "electric motor". She did not, as John Ross Robertson assumed, live in seclusion after the death of her husband. She was, by the standard of any era, a lively, involved, active person all her life. Yet she was the product of the late eighteenth century, and an early representative of the genteel woman who accompanied Britain's colonial administrators to the outposts of empire. What James Morris wrote of the Honourable Emily Eden in *Heaven's Command* applied equally well to the Elizabeth Simcoe of the Canadian years: "Her England is the England of the younger Pitt; her style is the style of Sheridan, Addison, and the cool amusing ladies of the age of reason."[3]

The same cannot be said of the man she married. John Graves Simcoe was an empire builder at a time when British politicians were still smarting over the the loss of one empire in America, and were not yet ready to found another that might also be lost. The self confidence to expand the empire was not to return until after the Napoleonic Wars, when Great Britain emerged as the strongest nation in the world. Even then, Britons remained suspicious of the concept of empire until well into Queen Victoria's reign.[4] Had Simcoe gone out as an administrator in the mid-nineteenth century, instead of at the end of the eighteenth, he would have been a great success. Born at a later time he might have been the epitome of the Victorian imperialist, but he was out of step in the 1790s when British politicians were not yet in an expansionist frame of mind.

PART I

THE HEIRESS
1762-1792

Chapter 1

A VERY SPECIAL CHILD

After Christmas day in 1761, Lieutenant-Colonel Thomas Gwillim prepared to leave his London home for Germany to take command of the 50th Regiment of Foot. For Gwillim this was a promotion and a new posting. Until 19 November he had been the major of the 7th Royal Fusiliers, which, like the 50th, was now stationed on the Continent. However, Gwillim had not been with the 7th for some time. He had been detached from that regiment in 1759 so that he could serve as a brigade-major under General James Wolfe on the expedition against Quebec. After the capture of Quebec, where Wolfe had been killed, Thomas had remained at the Canadian fortress until he was granted leave. Now that leave had come to an end, and he was looking forward to his new command with mixed feelings. Active duty gave the promise of further promotions, and the possibility of a title, but it also meant prolonged absence from Elizabeth.

Although they were not wealthy, both Thomas and Elizabeth stood to inherit considerable property. He was the heir to the manors of Old and New Court, Whitchurch, in Herefordshire. There his parents, Thomas and Elizabeth Gwillim, resided, with their two daughters, Elizabeth Sophia, then aged thirty-seven, and Henrietta Maria, thirty-four. In the meantime Thomas Junior held commissions in the army, as so many young men did until they were required to manage their properties. His wife had been born Elizabeth Spinckes at the family manor of All Saints' Aldwinkle, in Northamptonshire. In residence there were Elizabeth's younger sister Margaret, and their mother Jemima. Their father, Elmes Spinckes, had died in 1749. Aldwinkle would pass to Elizabeth and Margaret on the death of their mother.

As the name Gwillim implied, Thomas' ancestors were Welsh on his father's side. At the same time he had strong Northamptonshire connections. His mother had been Elizabeth Steward, whose sister, Jemima Steward, was the mother of his wife, Elizabeth Spinckes Gwillim. Thus the Gwillims were first cousins. Their marriage had taken place at St. Dubricius' Church, Whitchurch, on 14 January 1750. Although most marriages of the day were performed in the Church of England, theirs had particular significance. Both families could be described as high Tories, deeply committed to the principle of an established church as necessary for the state's welfare. In the minds of Thomas and Elizabeth Gwillim and their relations, the well-being of the Church of England and of the monarchy were interdependent. One could not be strong without the other. The families accepted regular church attendance, family prayers, and intensive study of the Bible and other religious writings as a natural part of daily life. In the same spirit they honoured the sovereign and a constitution that permitted only a limited franchise. The very word "democracy" was an anathema.

The Gwillims made a congenial couple; their one regret was that they had no children. If they had succeeded in having a child, it would have stood to inherit Old and New Court at Whitchurch and All Saints' Aldwinkle. Neither of Thomas' sisters, Elizabeth Sophia and Henrietta Maria, nor Elizabeth's sister, Margaret, had married. Elizabeth herself was thirty-eight, while her sister, Margaret Spinckes, was four years younger.[1] Thus the prospect of an heir to both estates seemed remote. In time, everyone assumed, the Aldwinkle and Whitchurch properties would be sold, and the assets divided among distant relatives or charities.

By early January 1762, Thomas Gwillim had left to join the 50th Regiment. His wife Elizabeth was joined at the London house by her sister Margaret who had come to keep her company. They passed the time visiting other town houses and entertaining, and they had long cultivated the friendship of women of intellect and education. A close friend of Margaret's was Mrs. Elizabeth Montagu, for whom the nickname "bluestocking" had been coined. Her house in Hill Street, Mayfair, was a Mecca for men and women of fashion who enjoyed lively, stimulating discussions. Mrs. Montagu held literary breakfasts and, evening assemblies which she called "conversation parties."[2]

The days passed pleasantly for Elizabeth and Margaret. Accustomed to Thomas' long absences, Elizabeth made a life of her own and had her own circle of friends. An independent nature was an asset for the wife of an army officer who was likely to be sent to some outpost or trouble spot where British interests were threatened. This time, Elizabeth thought that the separation might not be long. Much of the talk in London was about the impending signing of preliminary peace terms. What would be known as the Seven Years' War was nearly over. Everyone knew that France did not have the resources to continue the struggle much longer, and would soon be ready to sue for an end to hostilities. Elizabeth's mood was optimistic when, in late February, she received a melancholy message from the War Office.

Colonel Thomas Gwillim had died, of an unspecified cause, in Germany on 29 January 1762, and had been buried there with full military honours. For a moment Elizabeth felt that her heart had stopped. No matter how often she had comtemplated the prospect of losing her soldier-husband, when the moment came she felt stunned, hardly able to comprehend what she learned. For the moment she had Margaret to comfort her, but she must soon give up the London house. Now that Thomas would not be returning, she could not justify the expense of keeping a place in town. She would have to move, either to Whitchurch, to his family, or to her mother's home at Aldwinkle.

At Whitchurch, Thomas' parents and sisters took the news of his death philosophically. When a son was on active duty in wartime, one had to be prepared for such a loss, and to believe that he had not been sacrificed in vain. France had begun to sue for peace; England would be victorious and Thomas had done his part towards the victory. They deeply regretted that Thomas would not lie in the family tomb at St. Dubricius' Church; instead he had a soldier's grave in a distant land.

Whitchurch lay in the picturesque Wye Valley, with its high banks between which the river wound its way. Elizabeth adored the scenery and enjoyed the time she spent there. She may have gone to Whitchurch soon after she received the news of Thomas' death, to comfort his parents. If she did, she did not stay long. Ultimately she made her way to Aldwinkle for a special reason. She wanted to be with her own mother, even though she was thirty-eight years old, for, unlikely event, she was carrying a child.

How she found out is not known. She may have consulted a fashionable London physician, as was often done, or else she waited until she could talk with her mother. She might have shared her news with her sister Margaret, although a married woman was more likely to be candid with another married one. At some point after she closed up the London house, Elizabeth travelled to Aldwinkle, in the shallow valley of the Nene River, so much less picturesque than the Wye Valley where Whitchurch nestled. Her mood was blend of apprehension and elation. She was old to be having a first baby, but Thomas had left her a legacy more precious than anything money could buy. Thomas would live on in this child, of whose existence her firm religious faith told her he knew, though he could never learn about it on earth.

In the old stone house known as the Hall, close to All Saints' Church, Mrs. Spinckes gave her daughter the tenderest of care, seeing that she got plenty of rest and dainty meals, often served to her on a couch. Her mother could not banish the memory of the five children she had borne, of which only Elizabeth and Margaret had lived to maturity. Then there was the matter of Elizabeth's age, and whether she could survive a lying in. Childbirth was such a hazard. In her prayers the mother asked God to give her this grandchild, the only one she would ever hold, and to spare the life of her precious daughter.

When Mrs. Spinckes wrote to inform the Gwillims at Whitchurch of the coming birth, Miss Elizabeth Gwillim replied on behalf of her parents. Both were pleased, but a little pessimistic about the child's prospects on earth. Of their own six children, only their two daughters remained. The two youngest sons, Jasper and Elmes, had died as children, and one daughter, Anna Jemima, passed away at age twenty-one after contracting smallpox while on a visit to Aldwinkle.[3] And Thomas Junior, the eldest son, lay somewhere in Germany. Their prayers, Elizabeth Gwillim wrote, were for Thomas' widow, and for the tiny heir to Whitchurch and Aldwinkle.

By the third week in September, the air showed the chill of early autumn, and the trees near the Hall overlooking the River Nene were twinged with yellow. That week Elizabeth Spinckes Gwillim's labour pains began. What she suffered can only be imagined. The doubts of both families for the fate of the mother were all too well founded, those for the child groundless. Elizabeth lived only long enough to see her baby daughter; in a few hours she was dead. Margaret Spinckes had already sent for the wet nurse the family had hired, for the child was howling lustily and mouthing about in search of sustenance.

Margaret, who tended to put her own wants above the needs of others, was relieved that the newborn was a girl since she expected to be in charge of her. Margaret did not like small boys. The few with whom she had had contact had been too untidy and noisy. Mrs. Spinckes herself was happy that the child seemed strong as she tried to reconcile herself to the loss of the little girl's mother. Elizabeth Spinckes Gwillim, widow of Lieutenant-Colonel Thomas Gwillim and mother of the very special child, was buried at Aldwinkle on 23 September 1762.

Aunt and grandmother decided to call the baby Elizabeth Posthuma, in honour of the mother who had died giving her life, and in recognition of the infant's orphaned state. While the Gwillim and Spinckes families prayed that the child would survive to maturity, little did they suspect that she, whose chance of even being born was so unlikely, would live an active life for more than eighty-seven years and give birth to eleven children.

Chapter 2

EARLY LIFE

Margaret Spinckes has long been recognised as Elizabeth Posthuma Gwillim's mother-substitute, the woman who brought up the orphaned girl. Yet she had capable assistants in the child's Grandmother Spinckes, and her paternal aunts, Elizabeth and Henrietta Maria Gwillim, both of Whitchurch. Following the custom of the time, their niece wrote frequently in her diaries, and letter writing was a daily chore that kept her in touch with people at a distance, and even with those who lived close by. Many of Elizabeth Posthuma's letters and diaries are in the Devon Archives. These sources reveal that she had circles of friends in more than one place. The evidence suggests that she divided her time between Aldwinkle, her mother's home, and Whitchurch, her father's home. All her life Elizabeth was accustomed to feeling comfortable wherever she found herself.

That she had more than one place where she felt comfortable helps to account for the ease with which she adjusted to new surroundings in later life. Her Canadian journal shows that she was able to tolerate considerable discomfort without being unduly perturbed, provided her accommodation was clean. Having had roots in more than one place contributed to her flexibility and to her ability to adapt to new situations. Furthermore the warm reception she received at Aldwinkle and Whitchurch, where in each place loving family members awaited her, explains why, wherever she went, she assumed that she would be welcome and among friends. She was self-centred, but that was hardly her fault. She grew up having a decided sense of her own importance, as heiress to two families, and intensely proud of her descent from the ancient Gwillims and of their connections with mythical heros from the time of King Arthur. She was equally as proud of her mother's Northamptonshire forebears as of her Welsh heritage.

Servants, who treated her like royalty, played a part in developing Elizabeth's sense of her own worth and her place in society, which was high although not titled. The job of the servants was her care. A good nurse was the first necessity after the wet nurse had played her part. Grandmother's and Aunt Margaret's roles were mainly supervisory, although they took a more direct hand in the child's intellectual development. To them fell the responsibility of reading to the tiny girl, of explaining the meaning of new words, of seeing that concepts were grasped. Elizabeth was a rewarding child to teach, bright and quick. The nurse, too, was a supervisor, having under her command lesser minions to perform the drudgery. Doing the bidding of Grandmother and Aunt Margaret and the nurse was a tiny army of hirelings whom Elizabeth was conditioned to regard and treat as inferiors. With this attitude came the paternalistic one, that the aristocracy had a responsibility to care for the poor, and to guard their morals. These ideals, as well as the place in society of the sovereign, church, nobility and landed gentry, were instilled into the girl by everyone who came in contact with her.

She was small for her age, fine-boned and slender, with dark hair, typically Welsh in stature and colouring.[1] At Whitchurch these physical attributes endeared her to the Gwillim family and to all who saw the miracle child. Pride in her Welsh ancestry was nurtured, and she learned to treasure it. Her studies also embraced the Welsh language, and she attended church services in that tongue.[2]

The time spent at Whitchurch was beneficial to the child in other ways as well. Aunt Margaret Spinckes was artistic and an intellectual, but she was also erratic and given to changes in her objectives which tended to confuse her niece. Little is known about Elizabeth's Aunt Henrietta Maria Gwillim, but letters written by her sister, Aunt Elizabeth, reveal a down-to-earth, practical woman. She regarded common sense and reason as virtues. She was also a woman who took a lively interest in current events and who held strong political views, even though she was not enfranchised. Most women of her class believed in a limited franchise that denied many men the right to a say in how they were governed. A vote was not the right of everyone; government was the privilege of the élite. Men who stumped about at election time demanding a wider franchise were called "democrats" by Aunt Elizabeth and the other adults in young Elizabeth's world.

Aunt Elizabeth's feet-on-the-ground approach was an antidote for Aunt Margaret's whims. Aunt Margaret was the sort of person one had to learn to manage, and Aunt Elizabeth helped the young girl view the other's shifts of mood with equanimity. Very early, the child became adept at getting her own way.

Her first experience of a death in the family came in November 1766, when she was four years old. Her grandfather Gwillim was laid to rest in the family plot at Whitchurch.[3] Grandmother Gwillim lived less than a year after the demise of her husband, for she died in July 1767.[4] Afterwards, the two Gwillim aunts spent part of each year at Bath, the fashionable spa where the wealthy gathered to take the waters and enjoy themselves. Aunt Margaret, too, loved going to stay in Bath, and her young niece often accompanied her. Sometimes Grandmother Spinckes journeyed from Aldwinkle with them.

As the bright-eyed child grew, the time came for a governess to be chosen, to supervise the kind of education suitable for a girl of her social position. She was far too aristocratic to be sent to a day school. Boarding schools for girls existed, but as far as is known, Elizabeth was instructed at home, and her governess may have been a Miss Smith; in later years Margaret Graves recalled Elizabeth walking along the Wye River in Whitchurch with Miss Smith.[5] Possibly this governess was a young woman of good but not wealthy family, such as the daughter of a clergyman with limited private means, well educated but needing to earn her living. For a time the governess may have been French, or at least one who was versed in foreign languages. A young woman who spoke only English was not considered educated. Elizabeth was also expected to acquire skills that would make her a fine companion and hostess. A good education was important to a member of the leisured class, so that time could be passed to advantage in intellectual pursuits.

She was probably taught to play the pianoforte and to sing, but she never mentioned doing either. Her main references to music were to her enjoyment of the band of the Queen's Rangers playing near her quarters or on outings in Upper Canada. Art, however, was something at which she excelled. She learned to sketch well and to enhance her drawings with her watercolour brush, a talent encouraged by governesses and families alike. The ability to sketch realistic representations was a great asset, especially when travelling, to obtain a record of scenes visited. For the eighteenth century tourist, a sketch book, pencils and paint box were the equivalent of a camera. Thus considerable attention was paid to accuracy of representation. Friends loaned each other their drawings and made copies. Such a practice may seem uncreative by modern standards, but at the time copying was a way of acquiring a pleasing or informative picture. Another ladylike skill was needle work; hours were spent learning to embroider.

Elizabeth also had to learn deportment. A lady must be erect at all times. Slouching was not permitted; a straight spine and neck were considered essential for both men and women. A soldier's uniform included a leather stock around his neck, whose sharp edges would cut into his skin of he did not hold his head high. For the same purpose, a collar was placed on children, to ensure that if holding the head so erect was fatiguing, dropping it was painful. Short stays supported the upper back, to ease fatigue; these stays were more comfortable to wear than the long, tightly laced ones of the nineteenth century.

Daily life for Elizabeth did not mean all work, keeping straight, and filling her mind. Outdoor exercise was an regular habit, weather permitting. Long walks were the most logical — considered necessary for good health, and she had to become a competent horsewoman, for safety. Since many journeys were on horseback, the ability to stay on a horse was important, and especially difficult for women, who rode sidesaddle. At both Aldwinkle and Whitchurch, a pony was kept for Elizabeth's rides. A riding master gave her lessons, and if she rode out in the lanes she was accompanied by an aunt or a groom. Days were full, since everyone agreed that a child should never be idle. The best way to avoid mischief was constant activity and supervision. Elizabeth's childhood was rather solitary; her companions were nearly always adults, whether family members or teachers. Sons and daughters of the gentry of like rank were brought together occasionally for parties, but she could not form casual friendships with other children. The few who lived close to Aldwinkle and Whitchurch were children of servants and tenants, and not considered fit company for an heiress. In conversation and manners Elizabeth was a little adult, quite like the children Charles Dickens was to portray in the next century.

By the time she was six years old, Elizabeth had become fascinated by plants, and her governess was beginning to instruct her in botany, a life-long interest. The two often brought home plants to sketch and identify. She was learning the effects of elevation and exposure on plant life. Whenever a friend of the family visited another country, it was customary to return home with seeds of exotic plants. These Elizabeth and her governess would plant in various habitats to see in which they would thrive. From wild plants to cultivating foreign species, her interest turned to crops, and to the qualities of the soil which different crops required. This practical knowledge would serve her well when the time came for her to manage her own estate.

That same year a great change took place in Elizabeth's life. On 14 June 1769, at All Saint's Aldwinkle, her Aunt Margaret married Admiral Samuel Graves. The admiral was a widower with no children. He was then fifty-six and Margaret Spinckes was forty-two. They had become friends at Bath the previous winter. The marriage provided Elizabeth with two more homes, in addition to Aldwinkle and Whitchurch. The admiral owned Hembury Fort House, near Honiton, Devonshire, a country mansion named after an enormous pre-Roman Iron Age earthwork fortification with three outer rings. The admiral also kept a house in the parish of St. James, Westminster, which he used while visiting London.[6]

For Admiral Graves, Elizabeth was the daughter he had never had. Yet he and Aunt Margaret could not regard themselves as the girl's sole parents. She still had to be shared with her two aunts at Whitchurch and her Grandmother Spinckes at Aldwinkle. Elizabeth herself did not live full time with Aunt Margaret and her new uncle (whom she addressed as "Admiral", never as Uncle Samuel). Despite the change, both Elizabeth and Aunt Margaret continued spending considerable time at Aldwinkle, with visits to Whitchurch and Bath. The admiral was away at sea part of the time, and during his absences Hembury Fort House seemed too empty. Going visiting was a pleasant way of passing the time until Admiral Graves' tour of duty ended.

The year 1776, when Elizabeth was fourteen, was a sad one. In May her grandmother Spinckes died at Aldwinkle. Gradually Hembury Fort House became Elizabeth's main place of residence, with visits to Whitchurch, or to Bath when her Gwillim aunts were staying there. Elizabeth fell in love with the beautiful Devon landscape, which she grew to regard as her spiritual home. She roamed the rolling countryside, and the moor rising above the green fields with their underlayer of red sandy soil. She rode along the lanes and into the Blackdown Hills, and sometimes to the coastal village of Sidmouth—a resort where people of affluence went for holidays. Sidmouth lay nestled below the high red sandstone cliff, in a cleft where the River Sid entered the sea.

Part of each year was spent in London after her Aunt Margaret married Admiral Graves. There Elizabeth found a lifelong friend and kindred spirit in Mary Anne Burges. She was the youngest of three daughters; her older sisters were Caroline and Frances Anne. Their parents were George Burges, the comptroller general of customs for Scotland, and a Scotswoman, the Honourable Anne Somerville, a daughter of James, the 12th Lord Somerville. Mary Anne had been born in Edinburgh in 1763 while her father was employed there. Her family kept houses in London and in Bath. Her brother, James Bland Burges, was a lawyer and public servant.

The two girls soon became inseparable, and when Elizabeth went to spend time at Hembury Fort House in Devon, Mary Anne frequently accompanied her for extended visits. They rode ponies and went on long walks. Both were talented artists and they went on sketching trips together. The word "picturesque" occurs often in their correspondence. Each developed an eye for what would make an absorbing picture. They collected plant specimens, and took pride in preserving them in boxes. They often dressed alike, and they loved to stay up all night, reading to one another, or talking of their hopes and dreams. They called these night-long sessions "vigils".[7] Both were studying Spanish, and they often spoke and wrote notes in that language. Sometimes the pair went to visit Mary Anne's uncle, Hugh Somerville, her mother's brother, who lived at Fitzhead Court, in Somerset near Taunton. At the time of their early visits, Hugh was a widower with one son, John Southby, who was born in September 1765, and was not much younger than Elizabeth and Mary Anne.[8]

Like her friend, Mary Anne soon became enchanted with the Devon countryside. People seemed so much friendlier, and more genuine than those in London, and she decided that she would like to make her home in the beautiful county. Elizabeth, too, thought she would like to live in Devon, as long as she could make journeys to Northamptonshire and Herefordshire, and into Wales, her ancestral land. Both young women dreamed of a time when each would own her own home in Devon, homes within easy walking or riding distance, so that they could visit each other daily.

Elizabeth, one year older than Mary Anne, tended to be the leader. Where she was the more outgoing, Mary Anne was shy and nervous. Where Elizabeth's upbringing at the hands of adoring aunts encouraged self confidence, Mary Anne's in a larger family had left her burdened by self doubts. Like Elizabeth, Mary Anne was tiny, but where Elizabeth was slender and inclined to be wiry, Mary Anne tended to plumpness, which she decried. Mary Anne was the more dependent emotionally, inclined to consult Elizabeth about almost every aspect of her life. In many ways they were two compatible sisters. The relationship remained intense as long as both of them lived.

Elizabeth was destined to become well-known to the people of Ontario, Canada, while Mary Anne would make the more lasting impression in Britain. She rated a place in the *Dictionary of National Biography*. Elizabeth Posthuma Gwillim's future husband and youngest son were included in the *Dictionary*, but not Elizabeth herself. Mary Anne, who never married, became a distinguished author and student of botany and geology who collaborated with the Swiss scientist Jean André de Luc in some of his publications. De Luc (1727-1817) moved to England in 1773 and resided at Windsor.[9] Unlike Mary Anne, Elizabeth is remembered mainly for the diary she kept during her five years in Canada. Otherwise her life was very much that of a wealthy woman whose intellectual endeavours were mainly for her own amusement.

Chapter 3

HEMBURY FORT HOUSE

Admiral Graves' house, in the parish of Buckerell, Devon, still stands. Built by the admiral, it was named for Hembury Fort, the ancient stronghold near it. Elizabeth became a great favourite of the admiral during her many visits. In her he had the daughter neither of his wives had given him. Pleased that she could ride well, he bestirred himself to join her. Elizabeth was happy at Hembury Fort House, but for the first few years she did not regard it as a permanent home. After the death of her grandmother Spinckes in 1776, her visits to Aldwinkle were less frequent, but she still spent considerable time with her aunts at Whitchurch.

Lacking children of his own, Admiral Graves also took a keen interest in at least two of his nephews, Thomas and Richard. They were the third and fourth sons of his brother, the Reverend John Graves, of Castle Dawson, Ireland. At the time of the admiral's marriage to Margaret Spinckes, Thomas Graves was about twenty-two years of age and a lieutenant in the Royal Navy. Richard had been born in 1758, and was thus four years older than Elizabeth.[1] Thomas was kind to her, but Elizabeth found Richard a tease and a bully. She avoided his company when their stays at Hembury Fort House coincided. When their paths did cross, she soon found that she could get the better of him in any verbal confrontation. Elizabeth thought that he was rather spoiled because he was the youngest son. Mary Anne Burges admired the way Elizabeth could intimidate Richard when he became of a nuisance.

Conscious that Elizabeth had to be protected from fortune hunters, her aunt and uncle made certain that she met only the right sort of young man. Admiral Graves may have thought that Elizabeth and Richard would make a suitable match. Perhaps after seeing that they conflicted, he turned his thoughts to a more appropriate partner for his bright yet formidable, dark-haired niece. Years before, one of his fellow-captains had been John Simcoe, of Cotterstock, Northamptonshire. Back in 1756 and 1757, the court martial of the unfortunate Admiral Byng took place on Captain Simcoe's ship of the time, the *St. George*. The captain was one of the officers of the court that condemned the admiral to death before Byng was shot on the quarterdeck of the ship *Monarque*. Captain Simcoe had died aboard his ship *Pembroke* off Anticosti Island in 1759, during Wolfe's campaign against Quebec at which Elizabeth's father was present. Simcoe had left a widow, Katherine Stamford, and two lively boys, John Graves, who was the admiral's godson, and Percy William. Two older sons, Pawlett William and John, had died young.[2] John Simcoe Esquire was married to Katherine Stamford on 8 August 1747 in Bath Abbey. The Abbey records show him at that time as the commander of His Majesty's ship *Prince Edward*, and his bride as a spinster of Walcot parish, Bath. Katherine also had relations in or near Northamptonshire.

19

Soon after the death of her husband, Mrs. Simcoe had moved from Cotterstock with John Graves, aged seven, and Percy William, then four, to Exeter. There she was close enough to Hembury Fort House to receive the guidance and patronage of Admiral Graves. In 1764, Percy William Simcoe was drowned in the River Exe that ran through the city. At that time the twelve-year-old John Graves was studying at the Exeter Grammar School. Two years later he went to Eton, where his natural talent for leadership, his liveliness and capacity for original thought sometimes landed him in trouble. In later years, Simcoe's friend and contemporary at Eton, William Boscawen, wrote a poem hinting that they had acquaintance with the school's birching block and Dr. John Foster, an unpopular headmaster:

> With you rebellions chance I tried
> Old Foster's threats, his arm defied
> And dar'd his empire mock
> But oh, how short our glory's fate
> How few escaped *The Block*.[3]

At the time of Admiral Graves' marriage to Margaret Spinckes in 1769, Simcoe was at Merton College, Oxford.[4] He stayed only one year; he had decided on a military career. He spent the next year at home in Exeter, studying history with a tutor. His interest in the past was stimulated by reading reports his late father had compiled while at sea; some of Captain Simcoe's journals described coastlines of the Gulf of St. Lawrence and Cape Breton Island. In 1770, through the influence of his mother's relatives, John Graves Simcoe obtained a commission as an ensign in the 35th Regiment of Foot.[5] Between 1769 and 1774, he may have met Elizabeth Gwillim at Hembury Fort House. On 12 March 1774, he was commissioned a lieutenant in the same regiment.

At that time, Admiral Graves was away, in command of the Royal Navy's North American squadron. He was soon ordered to implement the Boston Port Act amidst the growing threat of rebellion in the Thirteen Colonies. The admiral was expected to close the port of Boston, following the Tea Party of 16 December 1773. His nephew, Lieutenant Thomas Graves, had accompanied him.[6] Lieutenant Simcoe's regiment was among those dispatched to Boston because of the famous Tea Party. When he arrived the British garrison was under siege from an army of rebels who controlled the landward approaches to the port. Early in 1776 Admiral Graves was recalled under a cloud. He retired angrily to Hembury Fort House to nurse his grievances. The squadron assigned to him had been too small to blockade Boston effectively, and his failure resulted from parsimony, not through his inadequacies. After his return to Devon he applied repeatedly for active duty, but the Admiralty ignored his pleas. By 1778, Britain's own shores were menaced, because France declared war and formed an alliance with the American rebels. Regiments of Fencible Men — soldiers raised to serve only in Britain — were called out locally, and every other able-bodied

20

man was in the militia for part time duty along the Devonshire coasts. Amidst considerable tension at home, Elizabeth helped her aunt to prepare bandages and other dressings for the use of the army, doing the war work that fell to women before and since. Meanwhile, young John Graves Simcoe was faring better than his godfather the admiral. He sold his lieutenant's commission in the 35th Foot and purchased a captaincy in the 40th Regiment. In 1776 his mother died.[7] For Simcoe, as well as for Elizabeth, Admiral Graves now became a substitute father. Undoubtedly the admiral spoke of the young man with enthusiasm, describing his godson's exploits and rapid rise in the army. Simcoe was severely wounded at the Battle of Brandywine, near Philadelphia, on 11 September 1777. Then in October, when barely recovered, he received a field promotion to the local rank of major, though he remained a captain in the British army. He was displaying the kind of zeal that was characteristic of him, a quality that would show itself repeatedly and with which Elizabeth would become so familiar.

Simcoe advocated the creation of mobile light corps, convinced that such troops would be more effective against the guerrilla tactics of the American rebels. He was refused permission , and instead, he was placed in command of the Queen's Rangers, a Provincial Corps of the British Army that had been raised in the colonies. This was the second corps named the Queen's Rangers; the first had served during the Seven Years' War and had been disbanded afterwards.

As the commander of this second regiment of Queen's Rangers, Simcoe became a legend in his own time, and Elizabeth must have been aware of the reports circulating about him. His corps never amounted to more than 400 men, yet it was one of the finest fighting forces that operated in the rebelling colonies. At his insistence the corps retained the green jackets with which provincial troops had been issued early in the war. As the war dragged on, the War Office authorised red coats for provincials, but Simcoe thought that green was a safer colour for men engaged in irregular warfare. He was captured in an ambush in 1779, and spent six months as a prisoner of war before he was exchanged and returned to duty. Through his journal he left a record of his time as the commander of the Queen's Rangers. On 2 May 1779, in recognition of valuable service, five Provincial Corps of the British Army were given special status, as an American establishment. Simcoe's corps was known as the Queen's Rangers 1st American Regiment.[8]

In October 1781, he was with the British army under Lord Cornwallis that General Washington and his French allies had surrounded at Yorktown, Virginia. Because Simcoe's health was very poor, Cornwallis agreed that he should be invalided back to New York City, which was still securely in British hands. Fearful that his men might be treated as traitors if they were captured, Simcoe arranged to have some of the rangers smuggled aboard the *Bonita*, which carried him away — the only ship permitted to pass the rebels' blockade because it was taking Cornwallis' dispatches. From New York, Simcoe was sent home to England. When Cornwallis surrendered, Simcoe's fears were confirmed. By order of General Washington, some twenty-five Queen's Rangers taken prisoner at Yorktown were shot in cold blood.[9]

Despite this atrocity, Simcoe retained a naïve faith in the goodness of American colonials; he thought the rebels were misguided men who would soon return to their true allegiance. The colonists were not to blame for the revolution; at fault was the prevalence of non-conformist religious sects. The greatest dangers humanity faced were republicanism and the rejection of an established church that could control its members and curb the spread of radical democracy. The Americans would soon admit their folly, and ask to rejoin the British Empire. Since Elizabeth shared the same beliefs in the role of crown and church, later on she would read the situation exactly as Simcoe did.

While her future husband was making a name for himself in the colonies, Elizabeth was growing up at Hembury Fort House and her other residences, and continuing her studies and enhancing her sketches with her watercolour brush. (In later years her Aunt Elizabeth, and others of Elizabeth's acquaintance, were referred to as "Mrs." although they never married. Older women, especially those who ran their own estates, were often called Mrs. regardless of marital status.) Elizabeth visited London with her Aunt Margaret and the admiral, and she sometimes accompanied them to Bath. Her friendship with Mary Anne Burges deepened as both approached womanhood. Neither intended to marry, but the admiral often broached the matter of a suitable husband for his niece. The right man must be found, for her wealth had to be preserved and used wisely. A suitor need not be a man of great means, as long as he sincerely loved Elizabeth and was the sort who would be a good manager of her inheritance. Margaret Graves, possessive of her niece, disagreed. Elizabeth was very young, and there was no hurry over finding a husband. They were still discussing the matter in the autumn of 1781, just about the time that John Graves Simcoe was leaving Yorktown. Elizabeth, Admiral Graves insisted, was now nineteen years old and no longer a child.

The Whitchurch aunts sided with the admiral, especially Aunt Elizabeth. If Elizabeth was to have the pick of the available young men, they should not delay. Otherwise she might make a childless marriage, like her Aunt Margaret's, or be left a maiden lady like the two Gwillims. In letters, and while all were at Bath, the aunts argued the matter. Aunt Margaret reminded her sisters-in-law and first cousins that Elizabeth's mother had died in childbirth. Women who married early might have child after child, which wore them out prematurely, or worse, whereas a woman who took her time about marriage might avoid the hazards of childbirth altogether, as Margaret herself had done.

Thus in late December 1781, when John Graves Simcoe arrived at Hembury Fort House, a highly eligible young woman was there to keep him company. Simcoe had come at the invitation of Admiral Graves to convalesce after the rigours of the campaign which had not allowed his wounds to heal completely. For Britain, the struggle had been in vain, as she had decided to give the colonies their independence. For Simcoe, however, the war had meant the opportunity for promotions in the field that had advanced his military career without having to purchase higher ranks. On 19 December, just a few days before he came to Hembury Fort House, he had been made the full colonel of the Queen's Rangers, although he did not as yet hold that rank in the British army. He was addressed as Colonel Simcoe by everyone who met him, old friend and new alike. No matter how intimate they would become, Elizabeth probably never addressed him as John, apart from their marriage vows. On the December day when Simcoe arrived at Hembury Fort House, he was Elizabeth's senior by just over a decade; he would turn thirty on 25 February 1782.

At first, the colonel spent most of his time in the library, relaxing with the admiral before a crackling fire. Then as he grew stronger he started going for long walks, accompanied by Aunt Margaret and Elizabeth. As his health improved, Aunt Margaret could no longer keep up with his long strides of this tall man, and Elizabeth stayed abreast by running every few steps. Finally, and not without reservations, Aunt Margaret allowed them to go off by themselves. They speedily found a mutual interest in sketching, and took books and pencils with them when they left the house; on their return they completed their work with watercolours. A favourite objective was the ruins of Dunkeswell Abbey, which the Cistercian order founded in 1201.

From walks the couple graduated to long rides each morning before breakfast. To Mrs. Graves' chagrin, she found herself looking on, helpless, as the two were obviously falling in love. Admiral Graves was delighted with the train of events, and sought to give the couple every encouragement. John Graves Simcoe was the perfect choice for his strong-minded niece. His godson was clearly infatuated, and the age difference would help him exert some influence over her. And Elizabeth's inheritance could be put to good use by Simcoe, who lacked private means. With access to Elizabeth's wealth, he could establish himself as a country squire. Furthermore, a man of such decided opinions on Britain's destiny ought to be in politics; the young man should have a seat in Parliament. The marriage would give Simcoe the resources he needed to finance an election. Before Simcoe was ready to leave Hembury Fort House in late February, the admiral was willing to give his consent and work out a marriage settlement. Aunt Margaret was still demurring. This time, she maintained that Simcoe loved Elizabeth more than she loved him. The admiral thought that was as matters should be; his godson would always be kind to their niece. Furthermore, since a soldier might be taken from her early, she had enough independence of spirit to take care of herself.

When Simcoe left Hembury Fort House, he was bound for London to resume his military duties. The war would not end until September 1783, and in the meantime he would be on full pay. With the coming of summer 1782, he and Elizabeth became formally engaged, despite Mrs. Graves' opinion. Another who had reservations about the coming marriage was

Mary Anne Burges, who was certain she was losing her best friend forever. Both parties strove to reassure Mary Anne. Simcoe declared that he would never come between Elizabeth and her dearest friend. When Mary Anne worried that Simcoe might be sent to some distant part of the empire, he assured her that they intended to make their home in Devonshire. The marriage need not make any difference to Mary Anne, and she would always be welcome to stay with them wherever they lived, or at Hembury Fort House. At that Mary Anne protested that she was too terrified to stay there without Elizabeth to protect her. Mary Anne, Elizabeth thought, was a wonderful person, so clever, but too shy.

In London, Simcoe cultivated men of influence, for he wanted the Queen's Rangers put on the British establishment as a numbered regular regiment. The corps was then in New York City, waiting resettlement in the part of Nova Scotia that would be separated to form New Brunswick in 1784. On 25 December 1782, Simcoe was granted his wish. Henceforth the Queen's Rangers would be a regular regiment (although never numbered) and the officers' names would appear on the next Army List. However, Simcoe was not yet a full colonel in the army, only in the regiment.

Five days later, on 30 December, 1782, John Graves Simcoe and Elizabeth Posthuma Gwillim were married, by licence, the fashionable way. Reading of the banns was only for the lower orders. The service, in the Church of St. Mary and St. Giles, Buckerell, the Graves' own parish, was conducted by the curate, Thomas Rosskilly. The witnesses were Admiral and Mrs. Graves.

The Simcoes began their married life in a rented house near Honiton while they looked for a suitable property to purchase. Before long they learned that the manor known as Wolford Church was for sale. With Elizabeth's money, they bought 5,000 scenic acres on the River Wolf, in the parish of Dunkeswell, an area they had learned to love during their long walks and rides of the winter before. Part of the land they bought had belonged to Dunkeswell Abbey before Henry VIII dissolved the monasteries. The onetime abbey church now served as the parish church. The ruins of the rest of the monastery had long been used as a quarry for stone, from which people erected buildings and cottages .[10]

Soon after they acquired the Wolford property, they went to inspect Aldwinkle. The Gwillim aunts managed the Whitchurch properties well, but since the death of Elizabeth's grandmother Spinckes the Aldwinkle property had been somewhat neglected. They visited Simcoe's friend and contemporary, William Walcot, at his town house in Oundle, and arranged for him to keep a supervisory eye on Elizabeth's birthplace. Between the two men was a friendly rivalry, for Walcot's "alma mater" was Cambridge.[11] Walcot was also a second cousin of Elizabeth's mother, and she had a special regard for him that lasted all his life.

Feeling fully recovered from his wounds and the wear and tear of the campaign, Simcoe attacked the improvement of Wolford with the vigour that Elizabeth had come to expect of him. He was often away from home, but she used the time to do the things she liked best, to sketch and paint, to read classics and whatever was current, and to have Mary Anne Burges stay with her.

At the beginning of their marriage the Simcoes began the habit of family prayers, attended by all members of their household. Servants, master and mistress would meet in the parlour, where the colonel, if he was at home, would read from the scriptures and lead the prayer. In his absence Elizabeth filled this role. They followed the widespread custom of their time, where family prayers were the rule, rather than the exception.

The calm of the Simcoe household was shattered early in 1783 by disturbing news from New York City. The British military governor there was Sir Guy Carleton, who was arranging the evacuate the city, because a preliminary peace treaty would be signed shortly. He had made insulting remarks about the Queen's Rangers, and had accused them of looting while they were in action. Colonel Simcoe was outraged when word of Carleton's criticisms reached him.[12] As soon as he had time, he decided, he would edit the journals he had kept while he commanded the Rangers, and see that they were published, to set the record straight.

Carleton, Simcoe learned upon making enquiries, had a reputation as an impetuous man, one who spoke his mind before he weighed the consequences. Had she been forewarned, Elizabeth would have prayed that her husband would never have to serve under him.

Chapter 4

WOLFORD LODGE

By the early summer of 1783, Elizabeth knew that she was expecting a child, and she wondered how best to break the news to her husband. She suspected he would be delighted, but she decided to wait a while. If she should miscarry, he might be extremely disappointed. When her clothes would no longer fit, she chose a quiet time when they were by themselves. Immediately Simcoe looked alarmed.[1]

Unspoken between them was the fate of Elizabeth's mother. Of the two, the colonel remained the more anxious. Elizabeth assumed that just because her mother had died giving birth was no reason to think she was doomed. She had as good a chance as any woman of bearing healthy children at no detriment to herself. When Mrs. Graves was told, she pursed her lips in disapproval. It would most likely be a nasty boy, and she would not want to raise one. Unperturbed, Elizabeth ignored the insinuation. A boy would be nice, an heir to Wolford.

As usual, Elizabeth's ally was her Aunt Elizabeth Gwillim, who came from Whitchurch at the end of December to be on hand when the time of "lying in" would begin. In January when Elizabeth's labour pains started, she found the long hours a tiring ordeal, but according to Aunt Elizabeth, the birth was a fairly easy one for a first baby; this boded well, Elizabeth decided, for other young Simcoes. The infant was a girl, whom the colonel promptly named Elizabeth after her mother, but to avoid confusion they would call her Eliza. Towering over them, the new father stared in awe at the minute person beside his wife. How could anything so tiny be a human being? And how grateful he was to see the mother looking fatigued but otherwise fit.

Now that they had a child, Simcoe was more eager than ever to move his family onto the Wolford property. Since he knew little about farming, he looked around for an experienced manager to help him learn to run the estate and deal fairly with the many tenants. He chose John Scadding, a man of considerable knowledge in farm management. Little is known of Scadding beyond that he was deemed a man of impeccable honesty, and was the father of Henry, one of Toronto's favourite sons, and remembered for his book *Toronto of Old*. The Scaddings were an old Devon family who had in the past owned the manor of Windsor, north of Wolford. John's brother, Thomas, was a tenant on the Wolford manor, and the man Mary Anne Burges referred to as "Scadding" during the Simcoes' sojourn in Canada.[2]

The original Wolford house was small, with only one storey. Yet it was admirably sited, on a knoll with a view all the way to Sidmouth and the sea beyond. The Simcoes decided to tear down the house and replace it with a two storied stone dwelling of some forty rooms. It would be known as

Wolford Lodge. With the colonel so fully occupied on the estate, Elizabeth invited Mary Anne Burges to come for a long visit. They watched in delight as little Eliza grew and became daily more interesting. She was baptised on 1 September 1784 in the Dunkeswell parish church.[3]

Life moved on serenely, and in August 1785, a second daughter was born to the Simcoes. Again the colonel had been terrified that Elizabeth might not survive, but again she flourished, and so did the new baby. They named her Charlotte, probably in honour of the Queen, Charlotte of Mecklenburg-Streleitz, the wife of George III. Elizabeth was a little disappointed that she had not produced a son this time, but the colonel was unperturbed. He thought girls were very nice. He assured his wife that he would not be sorry if he never had a son, but he wanted to have enough children so that they could be company for one another. He had been happy while his brother Percy was alive, but truly lonely after he died. Elizabeth, who had never minded being an only child, was surprised. She had relished the way every adult in her life had made her feel important.

A few weeks later, Elizabeth's Aunt Henrietta Maria Gwillim died at Whitchurch. Elizabeth regretted that she had not named her second daughter after her, rather than Charlotte, because she was fond of this aunt, about whom so little was recorded.

The work on the new Wolford Lodge was progressing, but the Simcoes decided to lease a house in London. Admiral Graves was urging his godson to establish a presence in the capital as a first step to being seen by the right people. Military and other appointments were not awarded to men who hibernated in the country. Any man of ambition needed to be speaking frequently to politicians and other men of influence.

In the summer of 1786, Mary Anne Burges fulfilled her old dream of living in Devonshire. Her father died in March, and the family sold the house in Bath. Using part of her inheritance she leased Tracey House, in the parish of Awliscombe, which adjoined Dunkeswell.[4] Tracey House was scarcely three miles from Wolford Lodge, which had not yet been finished. Elizabeth was delighted that her dearest friend would soon be a close neighbour. Mary Anne settled into Tracey House with a few servants and a miscellany of pets, and spent her days sketching and painting, collecting plant specimens and butterflies, studying geology and foreign languages, and visiting friends and her Somerville relatives at Fitzhead Court. With plenty of help to care for the two children, and with Colonel Simcoe so busy on the estate and in London, Elizabeth joined Mary Anne on many of her excursions, and at improving her own skills in Spanish, French, and also Italian.

At Hembury Fort House, meanwhile, Admiral Graves' health was deteriorating; one cause, perhaps, was the snubs he had received from the Admiralty. The end came on 8 March 1787, and he was buried on the 12th in Buckerell churchyard. His heir was his nephew, Richard Graves, now a captain in the Royal Navy. The Simcoes invited Mrs. Graves to live with them once Wolford Lodge was ready for occupancy. In the meantime, Aunt

Margaret would stay on at Hembury Fort House. Elizabeth was becoming anxious to move into Wolford Lodge, since she was expecting her third child. In April she gave birth to another daughter, whom they named Henrietta Maria, in honour of the aunt who had died soon after Charlotte's birth. The name was at once contracted to Harriet, the sobriquet in vogue at that time. Elizabeth could not conceal her chagrin at having a third girl, but the colonel was delighted. They would have heiresses, and he, of all men, had cause to appreciate heiresses.

Simcoe was the more demonstrative parent. Elizabeth loved the children, but was more reserved. Yet as each girl learned to talk and to express her own personality, Elizabeth found her good company. She had little difficulty over discipline for that was the responsibility of their nurse, a woman she referred to as "Williams" using only her surname as was customary. At the same time, Elizabeth had definite ideas about how her daughters should be raised, and she was exacting in the demands she made upon the nurse. Women of her class did not breast feed their babies, and for each newborn Elizabeth followed the practice of hiring a wet nurse. Then as each girl was weaned, she was handed over to Williams, who ruled the nursery. What was presented to Elizabeth to take for a walk or to read to was a well-scrubbed child, attired in clothing that met with her approval. As Aunt Margaret had done, Elizabeth concentrated on educating her daughters' minds; servants under Williams performed the menial tasks.

Elizabeth passed part of her time in visiting at friends' houses, as often accompanied by Mary Anne Burges as by Colonel Simcoe. The latter rose at 6.00 a.m. each morning, and whatever the weather rode for the next two hours, inspecting various parts of the estate, often accompanied by John Scadding. After breakfast at 9.00 a.m. he would retire to his study to write. He was editing his notes that pertained to the Queen's Rangers. Late in 1787 an Exeter printer published the book, which was titled *A Journal of the Operations of the Queen's Rangers from the ending of the Year 1777 to the Conclusion of the Late American War*.

Simcoe was also penning recommendations on the future government of Britain's remaining North American colonies, those that had stayed loyal to the mother country. He was furious that so many people in Britain regarded the American rebel cause as just, and dismayed over the way Britain had used the Indian tribes as allies during the war, and then abandoned them to the mercies of the United States afterwards. He also wanted better compensation for the American Loyalists who had fought for the King, and who had been largely overlooked in the peace treaty of 1783. He recalled George Washington's remark that the best thing those Loyalists could do would be to commit suicide. So incensed was he over the Marquis de Chastellux's unfairly biased version of the American revolution that he wrote a rebuttal to it. The French officer's work was appallingly biased in favour of the rebels, and yet it was being accepted as truth in Britain. Simcoe stated that the rebels had hanged more Loyalists in public than had been executed by both sides in Cromwell's wars. The rebuttal to Chastellux's account was published later in 1787, in London.[5]

Wolford Lodge was now habitable, and the family moved in. Elizabeth furnished it comfortably, with Axminster carpets, and with many pieces she had brought from Aldwinkle. Mrs. Graves contributed other items, effects she had purchased for Hembury Fort House on which the admiral's nephew had no claim. Soon after Elizabeth's aunt joined the Simcoes at Wolford Lodge, Captain Richard Graves married Louisa Caroline, a daughter of Sir John Colleton, Bart., of South Carolina and Hertfordshire, on 22 September at St. George's Hanover Square, London.[6] At first, Mrs. Graves remained the official owner, and she leased the house to one Richard Fry after she joined the Simcoes at Wolford Lodge.[7] Richard Graves and his wife lived in London for a while, but they had moved to Hembury Fort House by 1791.

A near-contemporary description of Wolford Lodge and its surroundings was left by the Reverend John Swete, who toured Devonshire between 1792 and 1801:

> In the front rose some fine oaks which for some way bordered the base of a steepish hill within whose under-wood and plantations a walk, running parallel with the road was conducted to the House [of which] the eastern front with a bow to the south were seen to great advantage. It consisted of two stories and was covered with a stucco of yellowish tint. The trees which appeared beyond the House gave it a fine relief, and the Hill at some little distance, making a quick turn to the south descended far into the valley in front, whilst on the opposite side a similar ridge pursued the same direction — both richly clad with indigenous wood or flourishing plantation and forming a theatre open only to the south and whose area was altogether comprised in the lawn which from the front sloped gradually into the distant valley. [8]

The Simcoes were philanthropic, but sensible about what they donated to help the poor. They were willing to give money to worthy causes, but when they did they kept a close watch to ensure that their gifts were properly used. Swete reveals the rural poverty in the parish in the 1790s. This was caused, in part, by the agricultural revolution that was taking place. Fewer labourers were required on the land, which led to unemployment. Swete described his arrival at Dunkeswell:

> I was in an instant encircled by a little host of children and females whose tattered garments and meagre looks betrayed a variety of wretchedness. The sight brought forth to my recollection the objects of penury that I had some years ago beheld at Tintern Abbey.[9]

Thus the kind of social work which Elizabeth, and later her daughters, performed was much needed.

By the spring of 1788, Colonel Simcoe was worrying himself sick because Elizabeth was expecting their fourth child. The baby was born in November, and to her dismay it was another girl. They called her Caroline, not after anyone in particular, but because they liked the name. Simcoe joked that they had honoured the wife of George II, who had been Caroline of Anspach. He delighted in his children. Whenever he had a spare moment, he took Eliza, now nearly five years old, and Charlotte, more than three, for walks. Eliza, small-boned like her mother, was a quiet, sensitive child, shy with strangers and anxious to please. Charlotte, sturdier and promising to be statuesque, was boisterous — more like himself, he thought with a chuckle. Harriet, now twenty months and toddling, seemed to be a pleasing balance between the two older ones, more sure of herself than Eliza and gentler than Charlotte. Thus far Caroline seemed a placid, happy infant who cried less than any of the others at the same age.

As 1789 opened, Simcoe was becoming discontented with life as a country squire, and he was even more anxious for a public appointment. Eager to assist him was Mary Anne Burges' brother, James Bland, who since 1787 was the Member of Parliament for Helston, Cornwall, and an under-secretary in the foreign department.[10] He was a frequent visitor at Tracey House, usually accompanied by his second wife, Anne, and some of his ten children. Other visitors to Tracey were Mary Anne's sister, Frances Anne, the latter accompanied by her children, but not her husband, the eccentric James Roper Head. Both Elizabeth and Mary Anne were fond of Frances Head, but they found her mate a trial. Nor was Mr. Head popular with the men in their circle of friends.[11]

Elizabeth, expecting her fifth child, was resigned to another girl. Again Simcoe assured her that his only worry was for her health. Her premonition was correct. The child born that October was named Sophia Jemima. Sophia was Aunt Elizabeth Gwillim's second name, while Jemima had been the name of the baby's great grandmother Jemima Steward Spinckes. Eliza and Harriet decided that Sophia would be their baby, and Charlotte said that the next one would be a boy, who would be hers. Simcoe laughed and retorted that he was destined to be ruled by petticoats.

Once her strength returned after Sophia's birth, Elizabeth concentrated more on being the accomplished hostess. Since Simcoe wanted a public appointment, she had to cultivate the right people. Wolford Lodge provided the perfect setting, and it became a place of lavish parties. Guests included James Bland Burges and his political acquaintances. Sir George Yonge, the Member of Parliament for Honiton and owner of Escot (also spelled Escott) an estate not far from Wolford Lodge, was a frequent guest.[12] A potential patron was Henry Addington (the future Lord Sidmouth). A good friend at a greater distance was George Grenville, the 1st Marquis of Buckingham, whose country homes were Stowe (now Stowe School) and Wooton, both in Buckinghamshire.

When Colonel Simcoe went to the London house, Elizabeth and Aunt Margaret sometimes accompanied him. Mary Anne Burges was always invited to join them, but she rarely accepted because of London's proximity to Hermitage, at Higham, Kent, the home of the James Roper Heads. She could hardly go to London without visiting the Heads, but every time she was near her brother-in-law they had fierce arguments.[13]

In 1790, Simcoe was elected the Member of Parliament for St. Mawes, Cornwall. He was not particularly interested in serving his constituents, who were few for St. Mawes was a pocket borough and he did not even need to go there. He really aspired to a public appointment. The old Province of Canada was to be divided in two, to accommodate the wishes of the American Loyalists who had been resettled west of the Ottawa River after the revolution, without interfering with the religious and language rights of the French-speaking residents of the Lower St. Lawrence area. The new Provinces of Upper Canada (now Ontario) and Lower Canada (Quebec) would each require a governor. At present, Sir Guy Carleton, recently created First Baron Dorchester for his services during the revolution, was the governor of Canada. He might continue as governor of the lower province, since he was known to be devoted to the French Canadians. Simcoe longed to govern the upper one, which the government intended to establish in 1791. He envisaged Upper Canada, that fine heartland of the continent, becoming the hub of a second British Empire in North America, and he campaigned for the appointment. He also had another notion, another plum in mind. After governing Upper Canada, he might be appointed British ambassador to the United States. A tour of duty in the new province might serve as a stepping stone to the more important posting.

Elizabeth supported him loyally, until they discussed the realities of spending at least five years on the other side of the Atlantic, and in a primitive place. Simcoe assumed that Elizabeth would be by his side. She expected that wherever they went the family would accompany them — until the colonel described the conditions they would face.

Upper Canada was a howling wilderness. The entire population was scarcely 8,000 souls. Apart from the few native Indians, the people were all pioneers, and few had more than a one-roomed cabin for shelter. There were no roads to speak of, and except for a few vessels on the Great Lakes only open boats, mostly bateaux and canoes. They might not even have a house until they built one. And they would not be able to find tutors to instruct the girls. There were few people of any education, and even fewer schools. He did not see how they could educate the older ones if they took them along. Elizabeth felt, in that case she should remain behind. Much as she longed to travel, to see new places, and much as she disliked the prospect of a long separation, her place was at home. Simcoe argued that he could not do without her. There would be important people to entertain. His Royal Highness, Prince Edward the Duke of Kent, was being posted to Quebec, and he would want to inspect Upper Canada. Elizabeth was torn. His Royal Highness was the commander of her father's old regiment, the 7th Royal

Fusiliers and he was taking the regiment with him. The thought of seeing Quebec, a place her father had known, filled her with longing. Finally they agreed that if they could find reliable people to fill her shoes at Wolford Lodge for so long a time, she would accompany her colonel.

On 18 November, possibly in preparation for his new appointment, Simcoe was promoted to full colonel in the British army. By then no one doubted that he would be sent to Upper Canada. Friends such as James Bland Burges, while helping him secure the appointment, thought his desire to go to the back of beyond bordered on insanity.[14] Devastated at the prospect of the long separation, Mary Anne Burges passed their opinions on to Elizabeth, in the hope of persuading her not to leave Wolford Lodge. Elizabeth did not comment for her thoughts were elsewhere. Her sixth child would be born early in June, and she wondered how that would fit in with the colonel's travel plans.

Simcoe himself was off in London, so full of enthusiasm that he was blind to any problems he might face as governor of Upper Canada. Sir Guy Carleton—or Lord Dorchester—would probably remain in Lower Canada as governor-in-chief, and he might have some authority over Upper Canada, a possibility Simcoe hoped to forestall. Meanwhile he was consumed by thoughts of the fine work he would perform on behalf of the British Empire.

Back at Wolford Lodge, Elizabeth was working out arrangements for the girls during her absence. She turned first to Mary Anne Burges, who promised to write almost every day. Though Elizabeth would receive letters only occasionally, Mary Anne would put them in the form of a journal, so that her friend could picture what was happening at home. Elizabeth wanted reports on how the girls' education was progressing. As long as they were forging ahead in their studies, her conscience would be clear. She begged Mary Anne to tell her everything, the bad as well as the good, and to spare her nothing that would cause her to worry. A mother had the right to worry about her own children.

Mrs. Graves had offered to mother the girls, but Elizabeth was apprehensive over giving her so much responsibility. Her aunt was not young, and even more erratic now than when she had helped to raise her niece. If she felt too burdened, Elizabeth suspected, Aunt Margaret might decide to leave Wolford Lodge. No, she must find a dependable person to take her place.

Despite Elizabeth's mistrust of her aunt, Mrs. Graves solved the problem of who should be in charge at Wolford Lodge. She recommended Mrs. Ann Hunt, the widow of one of Admiral Graves' captains, an old friend from Northamptonshire then living in Exeter. Her three grown up children were Edward, a curate at Benefield, Northamptonshire, not far from Oundle where William Walcot lived, Caroline and Mary. Mrs. Hunt agreed to take the position at an annual salary of £450. Simcoe thought her somewhat old, but her daughter, Mary, was looking for work as a governess or tutor. After interviewing her, Elizabeth decided to hire both the Hunts, who were fine gentlewomen although the daughter was better educated than the mother.[15]

Throughout the spring, Simcoe was speaking in Parliament on the potential Upper Canada offered, stressing that it should be a separate colony from Lower Canada, and its governor should answer only to the King and Parliament. His motive for these speeches was to ensure that he would not be Dorchester's subordinate.

June brought satisfaction and defeat for John Graves Simcoe. On 6 June, a triumphant Elizabeth presented him with their first son, whom they named Francis Gwillim. On the tenth, the Canada Bill was passed by Parliament. Lord Dorchester would be the governor-in-chief, responsible for the defence of both provinces. Simcoe would be subordinate to Dorchester in the event of threats from the United States on isolated, vulnerable Upper Canada. Most men with his credentials would have resigned at once. Now that France was in the throes of a revolution and there was tension between that republic and Britain, a full colonel in the army could expect a command of significance in any coming war. Simcoe might eventually be a lieutenant-general with at least a knighthood. Yet he turned his back on all that to spend five years in the backwoods of Canada, obliging his wife to travel and to live in ways she could not have foreseen. He who so loved his children was willing to be parted from them for much of their formative years because he felt himself a true patriot. As Elizabeth pointed out, if a child died, they might not hear of it for six months or more.

When the time of departure approached, Elizabeth decided she could not do without all her children. Sophia, who would not need much education for a while, and Francis, would come with them. They would take a nurse, and the wet nurse who was feeding Francis. Only the four eldest would be cared for by the Hunts and Williams the nurse. In leaving them the Simcoes followed the custom of many English parents serving the empire. But the ones who needed them most were Eliza, Charlotte, Harriet and Caroline; being left behind caused much heartache.

Chapter 5
DEPARTURE FOR UPPER CANADA

At the time of John Graves Simcoe's appointment as the lieutenant governor of Upper Canada, British North America consisted of the territory of the Hudson's Bay Company, Newfoundland, Nova Scotia, New Brunswick, the Island of Saint John (Prince Edward Island), Cape Breton Island and the Canadas. Two provinces were separated from older ones to accommodate the needs of the American Loyalists who had been given new living space because they could not return to their homes following the American Revolution. New Brunswick had been separated from Nova Scotia in 1784. Upper Canada was being established so that the Loyalists who had been placed west of the Ottawa River could have English civil law and freehold land tenure, both of which they believed to be their right as British-born subjects.

Under the terms of the Quebec Act of 1774, French civil law and the seigneurial system of land tenure were confirmed for the Province of Canada. Neither provision suited the loyal American settlers. The Canada Act of 1791, often called the Constitutional Act, which divided the old province, made provision for English civil law in Upper Canada. The Act also abolished a form of the seigneurial system, whereby the settlers were to exist as tenants of the King, paying quit rents for the lands they had been granted as compensation for having remained loyal to the Crown. The Canada Act replaced this feudal system with outright land ownership. The settlers welcomed the establishment of the new province, and were predisposed to like Simcoe. The colonel had commanded a Loyalist corps, which stood him in good stead in their eyes. Elizabeth resolved to support him in every way. She intended to be pleasant to everyone they met, and to be punctilious, when she and her husband hosted social gatherings, about having a word with each guest.

Both the Simcoes were predisposed to like Canada, since both had had fathers who had served there, men neither actually knew. John Graves Simcoe cherished the journals his father had written, before his death, of his experiences in Canadian waters. Elizabeth already had potential friends in Quebec in Henry Caldwell and his wife, the former Ann Hamilton. Caldwell was a militia colonel and a half-pay regular officer who had known Thomas Gwillim during Wolfe's campaign. Afterwards Caldwell settled in Quebec, leased several seigneuries and built mills. He was a successful businessman, whose house, Belmont, on the Ste. Foy Road, would become a favourite home away from home for Elizabeth.[1]

By that summer of 1791, both the Simcoes were deeply involved in preparations for their journey and the strange new life that awaited them. Elizabeth travelled to London to shop for many items they required that could not be purchased in Upper Canada, and probably not even in Quebec City or Montreal. She found that several pairs of shoes which she ordered from a maker in Exeter would not be ready, and Mary Anne Burges promised to send them.

Time was now running out. Simcoe insisted that they must sail no later than mid-September, to ensure that they would be able to enter the St. Lawrence before it was blocked by ice. With Mary Anne, Elizabeth discussed the best way of making certain that letters and parcels would reach her. James Bland Burges agreed to send parcels, postage free, in his "bag" which would prevent pilfering. Letters could go by ordinary post, but that would be more expensive.[2] Mary Anne again promised to give Elizabeth bad news as well as good, and to send plenty of gossip. She would find much to report on Richard Graves' wife, whom Aunt Margaret Graves considered rather odd. Elizabeth tried to be impartial when the Richard Graveses were subjects of conversation. Under the admiral's will her aunt had to pay Richard an annuity, and she resented parting with the money.[3]

Elizabeth organised the collection of household goods and clothing, and decided which servants, and items of furniture they would take with them. Among the more valuable furnishings she chose were a tapestry, and a spinning wheel which Queen Charlotte had had made for the Marchioness of Buckingham. The tapestry had been given to the Simcoes during a visit to Stowe.[4] The marchioness had sent the spinning wheel as a gift for Elizabeth.

Meanwhile, the colonel was making his own arrangements for the comfort of the family and the development of Upper Canada. At a sale of the effects of the late Captain James Cook (the navigator on the *Pembroke* under Captain John Simcoe at the time of the latter's death) he purchased two "canvas houses" that had wooden frames and floor boards. The glorified tents could be erected or taken down and packed away. They were clumsy, but more portable than any other sort of temporary house. He also bought several conventional tents which he suspected would be useful. He was choosing men to serve on his executive council, appointees that required the approval of the King.

He received permission to raise a new regiment to be known as the Queen's Rangers (the third so named; the first was raised in 1756, the second in 1776). Full strength should be 1,000 men — potential settlers who would have learned the skills needed in the new province once their terms of enlistment were over. Upper Canada desperately needed people, especially those trained both as artificers and as soldiers. The province, in the western wilderness, protected only by small British garrisons at forts widely separated along the border, could easily be annexed to the United States. Simcoe asked for a reinforcement of other regular soldiers for the border outposts. To his dismay, he was allowed just 400 men for the Queen's Rangers, organised into two companies, each with a captain, captain-lieutenant, two lieutenants, two ensigns, six sergeants, six corporals, and a drummer, as well as staff officers. Simcoe himself would serve as the colonel-commandant without pay.[5] The War Office also refused to authorize any further increase in the number of regular troops in Upper Canada. The province had been established as a concession to the Loyalists, but the home government was not prepared to invest heavily to retain it.

The Queen's Rangers, although classed as regulars, were not intended primarily as a fighting force. They would serve as workmen to cut roads and erect public buildings. The temporary headquarters of the regiment were in Honiton, and many of the officers and recruits were Devonshire men. Simcoe was also offering commissions to officers who had served in the earlier regiment who were in New Brunswick. Recruiting was going well in Devonshire, for Simcoe was popular around Wolford Lodge. Elizabeth was delighted with the regiment. Having so many men from the county would be like having a bit of home in the wilds of Upper Canada. The rangers were to be uniformed in short green coatees and tall hats of leather, like those the men had worn during the revolutionary war.

Simcoe was already plagued by frustrations, an ill omen for the future. The Queen's Rangers' reduced size was only one of his stumbling blocks. Ugly rumours were afoot that Lord Dorchester was anything but pleased with Simcoe's appointment to Upper Canada. For the lieutenant governor of the new province, Dorchester had recommended a Loyalist of stature, Sir John Johnson, the heir to the famous Mohawk Valley Superintendent of Indian Affairs, Sir William Johnson (who had died in 1774). Sir John had led a Provincial Corps of the British Army known as the King's Royal Regiment of New York. It amounted to two battalions, and now nearly all these disbanded troops had been settled in Upper Canada. They would constitute Simcoe's largest single body of settlers, and they might well resent the slight to their former commanding officer. Sir John lived in Montreal, but he had been awarded substantial land grants in Upper Canada, which implied that he would have dealings with the lieutenant governor.

Simcoe, the incurable optimist, was not unduly worried about Sir John, nor about his former soldiers. As he told Elizabeth, they were settled along the upper St. Lawrence, and only as far west as the Bay of Quinte, on Lake Ontario. That territory did not interest him. The heart of the new province would be the along the River La Tranche, which he planned to rename the Thames. At the forks of the river, inland where the Americans would have difficulty attacking it, he would build his capital. It would be called London, or perhaps Georgina, in honour of the king.

He envisaged the vast peninsula bounded by Lakes Ontario and Erie, Lake Huron and Georgian Bay as his heartland, a kingdom to be filled with subjects who were both loyal to the Crown and adherents of the Church of England. This would be his paradise, the bulwark against republicanism and non-conformist religious sects.

Elizabeth shared his vision entirely. Monarchy and the established church lay at the heart of a well-ordered society and were bastions against democracy and radicalism. Agreeing with everything he wanted to do came naturally to her, and later she would sympathize with him when his superiors blocked many of his requests or refused to let him carry out his favourite projects. If Colonel Simcoe had a dream of a vast new empire in the heart of North America, the home government did not, nor for the most part did Lord Dorchester, who had never wanted Simcoe in the first place. Elizabeth would survive the frustrations because she had a great capacity to be detached when he was fuming, and to keep herself busy when Simcoe had little time for her. In fact, despite the altered setting, she would carry on in much the same way as she was accustomed to doing at Wolford Lodge.

As the day of departure drew near, Elizabeth was once again of two minds about the venture. She was looking forward to seeing new places and making new friends, but her mother instinct cast a shadow over the preparations. Leaving the four eldest girls behind would be a wrench. Colonel Simcoe, so devoted and affectionate, could leave the children without strong feelings of remorse because he placed patriotism and duty to King and empire above all else.

Amidst Elizabeth's reservations, all was bustle and cheer at Wolford Lodge as the packing proceeded. The others, whether leaving or staying, were in high spirits. The four girls did not envisage what life would be like with the two formidable people at the centre of their universe no longer to be seen or heard. One who was acutely aware was Mary Anne Burges. In her drawing room at Tracey House stood a miniature which she had painted of Elizabeth.[6] At least she would have a picture if she were never to see her friend again. The Simcoes were to sail from Weymouth, Dorset, aboard the 28-gun frigate *Triton*, which would be waiting for them by the beginning of September. An Atlantic crossing was a very hazardous undertaking, as Mary Anne knew. Besides, if war were declared against France, a French privateer or war vessel might overhaul the *Triton* and the Simcoes might find themselves captives.

The carriage left Wolford Lodge on 15 September. During the farewells, everyone was smiling, although Elizabeth had to force herself. The only one who did not look festive was Miss Burges, who stayed in the background hoping no one would notice her. As soon as the departing loved ones, with the two nurses, Sophia and Francis, Elizabeth's maid, a French chef and other servants, were out of sight, Miss Burges and Miss Hunt took the four girls for a walk. When Caroline complained of weariness one of the women carried her. The other girls capered happily around them, stopping often to pick flowers. The blow did not fall until they returned home for tea, and the girls faced a table no longer presided over by their parents, but by Mrs. Graves. To add to their sorrow, their great aunt had turned against the Simcoes for leaving. She was hard enough on Elizabeth, but she reserved the fullness of her wrath for the colonel. He had insisted on the overseas venture that left Mrs. Graves in the lurch.

Beside Miss Burges, seven-year-old Eliza began to weep softly, but Mrs. Graves continued her diatribe, and glared at Elizabeth's best friend. Then noticing Eliza's tears she demanded, "Why are you crying so, child?"

"I can't help crying when you are so cross with my dear Mama and Papa," the child said through her sobs. "Oh, if only they would turn back and stay with us."

Mary Anne Burges walked home to Tracey in the early evening, to begin the first of nearly 900 pages she would write to Elizabeth over the next five years. Elizabeth's diaries after her departure for Weymouth were published. From the outset she wrote them with the intention that they would be public property, although she probably never contemplated publication, only that they would be read to many listeners. Miss Burges' letters were meant mainly for Elizabeth's eyes. As she promised, she described Mrs. Graves' pique and Eliza's tears. Farther on in the letter she wrote that Eliza's sobs would have a "happy effect", for Mrs. Graves would be more careful in future over what she said in front of the children.[7]

The Simcoes reached Weymouth on 17 September, and found that they had to rent rooms temporarily. The *Triton* was ready to sail, but the colonel's commission as lieutenant governor, which had been signed on the 12th, had not arrived from London. Simcoe was annoyed, but Elizabeth found that the society was all she could wish for. King George and Queen Charlotte were staying at Gloucester House, their Weymouth residence. Simcoe met several times with Prime Minister William Pitt (the younger) who was there in order to have access to the King. After each such meeting, Elizabeth more than half expected to learn that Pitt was recommending Colonel Simcoe for a baronetcy or at least a knighthood, but no such honour seemed forthcoming. This nagging doubt suppressed, she found that she was caught up in a social whirl typical of a place where the monarch or any of his offspring were staying. Every night there was a ball. Usually someone gave a tea party in the afternoon, where she met all sorts of people of importance. Most mornings she rode before breakfast, sometimes with her husband, more often with an officer delegated to accompany her because the colonel was busy. On most afternoons she walked with other ladies on the esplanade.

As time passed, Simcoe grew increasingly agitated. With each day's delay, the possibility that they might not reach Quebec that season increased. Elizabeth was perturbed on only one account. Once they had set out bag and baggage, she felt she could not return to Wolford Lodge to wait until navigation on the St. Lawrence opened in the spring. She could not brave those heartrending farewells again.

At more than one gathering, the Simcoes met the King and Queen. Stolid Farmer George took a fancy to the pert, petite Mrs. Simcoe, and he often held her in conversation for quite some time. He sent a message to the *Triton's* commanding officer, Captain George Murray, bidding him to see that the lieutenant governor's lady was made as comfortable as possible during the long voyage.

Simcoe had selected several men, who were in England, for his executive council, most of whom were arranging to sail for Canada in the spring. On the council was William Osgoode, a London lawyer who worked only as a solicitor because a stammer prevented him being effective in court. Osgoode would also be the chief justice. Peter Russell, who had served in America during the Seven Years' War and the revolution, and who had returned to England in 1782, would be both a councillor and the receiver general. William Robertson, with a home and mercantile interests in Detroit, and Alexander Grant, who had served as commodore on Lakes Erie and Huron during the revolution, would also be councillors. Of the four, only Grant was in Canada; Osgoode had never been across the Atlantic, while Robertson was temporarily in Britain. Other members of the government would be John White and William Jarvis. White, a lawyer recommended to William Osgoode, would be the attorney general. Jarvis was a Loyalist from Connecticut who had served under Simcoe during the revolution, had married a fellow-Loyalist in England afterwards and taken up residence there. He would be the provincial secretary. Accompanying Jarvis would be his wife, Hannah Peters, while Peter Russell's unmarried sister, Elizabeth, would travel with her brother. Both women would be mentioned in Elizabeth Simcoe's diary, but not Marianne, the wife of John White, who did not join her husband in Upper Canada until 1797. William Osgoode, the chief justice, was a bachelor. Simcoe hoped to receive approval for one more executive councillor, and he recommended James (Jacques) Baby of Detroit, a gentleman of unswerving loyalty who would have a good influence over the French-speaking residents of his neighbourhood.[8] The Queen's Rangers, still gathering at Honiton, would also be sailing for Canada in the spring. One officer who joined the Simcoes at Weymouth was Captain Charles Stevenson, who had served in the old Queen's Rangers, and who was going to Upper Canada as the lieutenant governor's deputy quartermaster-general.

Meanwhile, Elizabeth still hoped to hear that Simcoe had received an honour from the King, at the very least a knighthood. She was convinced that his service in America during the revolution had earned him that much. A title gave a colonial governor the proper authority over other officials he had to deal with. She began to suspect that the prime minister had not recommended Simcoe to the King, as was necessary. Perhaps Simcoe's persistence in asking for what he thought he required had annoyed Mr. Pitt. Perhaps, too, the prime minister did not regard Upper Canada as a vital part of the Empire.

She sent letters home to Wolford Lodge, and to Tracey, and replies came from Mrs. Hunt and Miss Burges before they sailed. Mary Anne reported that she was still finding Mrs. Graves a trial. That lady remained angry with Colonel Simcoe for leaving, and Mary Anne admitted that she had no idea how much Elizabeth had suffered from "caprices of such a Temper". Mrs. Graves was being very hard on the servants, too, and she seemed to want the whole neighbourhood to know "of her worth in the house."[9]

Elizabeth put down the letter with a sigh of resignation. She had been wise to hire Mrs. Hunt and her daughter, and she hoped that her aunt's behaviour would not cause them to leave Wolford Lodge. If anyone were to leave, Elizabeth hoped it would be Mrs. Graves. Since she was being hard on the servants, she was probably not being pleasant to the Hunts. Thank goodness Miss Burges was close at hand; Elizabeth could count that she would make other arrangements if need be, and see that the children were not neglected.

Finally, Simcoe's commission reached Weymouth and the family boarded the *Triton*. Elizabeth found the ship small but clean, and they expected to be quite comfortable. They actually sailed on 26 September, by which time the equinoxial gales of autumn had already begun.

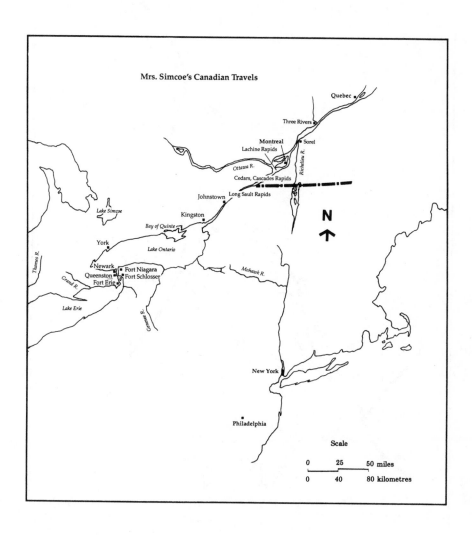

Mrs. Simcoe's Canadian Travels

Quebec

Three Rivers

Montreal
Lachine Rapids
Sorel

Ottawa R.

Richelieu R.

Cedars, Cascades Rapids

Johnstown   Long Sault Rapids

Lake Simcoe

Kingston

Bay of Quinte

York

Lake Ontario

Mohawk R.

Newark   Fort Niagara
Queenston   Fort Schlosser
Fort Erie

Thames R.

Grand R.

Lake Erie

Genesee R.

N

New York

Philadelphia

Scale

0   25   50 miles

0   40   80 kilometres

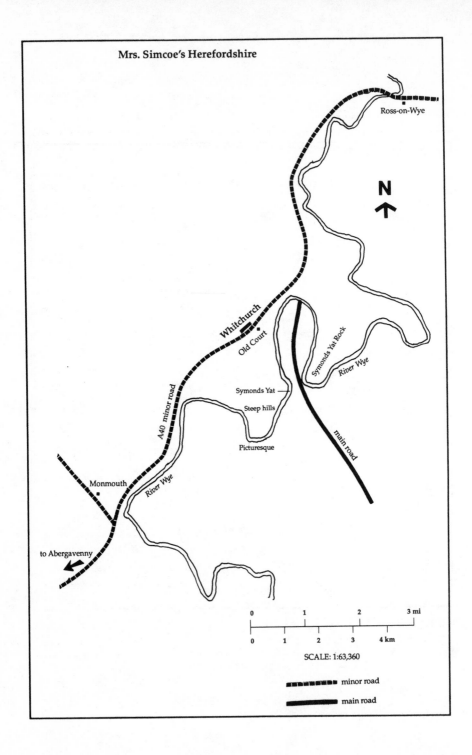

Mrs. Simcoe's Herefordshire

Ross-on-Wye

N

Whitchurch
Old Court

Symonds Yat Rock

River Wye

Symonds Yat

Steep hills

A40 minor road

main road

Picturesque

Monmouth

River Wye

to Abergavenny

| 0 | | 1 | | 2 | | 3 mi |

| 0 | 1 | 2 | 3 | 4 km |

SCALE: 1:63,360

minor road

main road

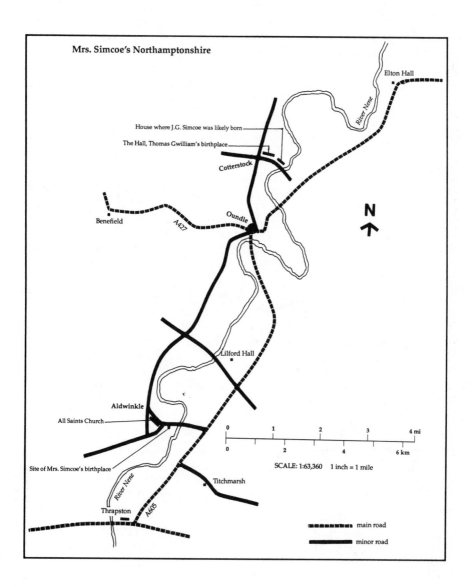

Mrs. Simcoe's Northamptonshire

Elton Hall

River Nene

House where J.G. Simcoe was likely born

The Hall, Thomas Gwilliam's birthplace

Cotterstock

N

Benefield

A427

Oundle

Lilford Hall

Aldwinkle

All Saints Church

Site of Mrs. Simcoe's birthplace

River Nene

Titchmarsh

Thrapston

A605

0   1   2   3   4 mi

0   2   4   6 km

SCALE: 1:63,360   1 inch = 1 mile

main road

minor road

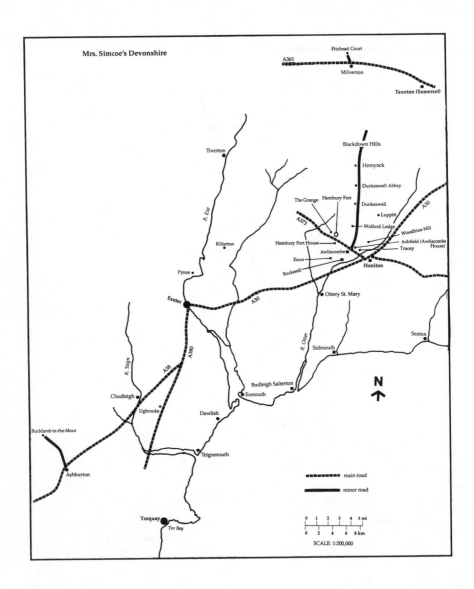

Mrs. Simcoe's Devonshire

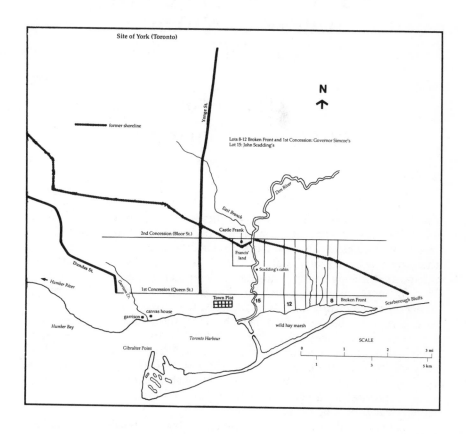

Site of York (Toronto)

N

Yonge St.

former shoreline

Lots 8-12 Broken Front and 1st Concession: Governor Simcoe's
Lot 15: John Scadding's

Don River

East Branch

2nd Concession (Bloor St.)   Castle Frank

Francis'
land

Dundas St.

Scadding's cabin

Humber River

Garrison Cr.

1st Concession (Queen St.)

Town Plot   15   12   8   Broken Front

canvas house   Scarborough Bluffs

Humber Bay   garrison

wild hay marsh

Toronto Harbour   SCALE

Gibralter Point

0   1   2   3 mi

1   3   5 km

PART II

"SOVEREIGN LADY OF UPPER CANADA" 1791-1796

Chapter 6

WINTER AT QUEBEC
1791~1792

The *Triton* rolled badly, even on gentle seas. The six weeks that followed embarkation were, for the most part, a nightmare, as storms tossed the frigate about. During the first week Elizabeth was dreadfully seasick, but then, on the advice of the ship's cook, she ate salt beef smeared with mustard. Strangely enough, this helped keep her sickness under control. Finding her sea legs took longer, but she resolved not to miss a day writing in her diary, recording her adventures. She felt most comfortable wedged in a corner of the deck, from which perch she could not be washed overboard. In the fresh air, where she felt less queasy, she wrote and sketched. Sophia's nurse was even sicker than Elizabeth, who felt that the only safe place for the little girl during the worst weather was her bed. The confinement was hard on a lively child, who celebrated her second birthday at sea. Fortunately, a young midshipman asked for permission to keep watch over Sophia on deck.

That young man was truly a godsend. Sophia was restless if she had to stay below all day. The Simcoe's were fortunate that Francis was so small and unable to run about. Elizabeth was dismayed when Simcoe informed her that Captain Murray was thinking of sailing for the Barbados as he feared they were too late to enter the St. Lawrence. If they could not reach Quebec that season, they might as well have delayed setting out until the spring. The four little girls at Wolford Lodge would not have had to do without their parents for quite so long.

One officer regaled Elizabeth with tales of shipwrecks, and of lizards and scorpions that plagued Barbados. Shuddering over such lurid details, she prayed that the ship would be able to stay on course. Her cabin was continually wet because the deck of the *Triton* was badly caulked. Water dripped down between the boards, except during the gentlest of swells. At times her hammock swung so wildly that she was bruised when it hit the walls. Simcoe arranged for padding to be stuck close to the hammock, which softened the blows but did not eliminate them. Though badly frightened most of the time, Elizabeth put on a brave front and appeared to take the experience in good part. The sight of plates and other items flying off their dining table was amusing.

On 28 October they were off Sable Island, and the following day the coast of Nova Scotia was visible. At Sydney were Captain McCormick and his wife, who were friends of the Simcoes. Elizabeth identified the captain as the governor of Cape Breton Island, but he was Robert McCormick, a naval surgeon and the senior officer there. Elizabeth wanted to land at Sydney and see the McCormicks, but they did not have the time. Simcoe had hoped to go through the Strait of Canso, which his father described in his journals, but Captain Murray warned him it was dangerous and they could be detained. Murray decided to take the longer route around Cape Breton, where the winds were steadier and the passage wider. Elizabeth thought how much more pleasant a voyage in these waters would be in summer. The closer they drew to Quebec, the colder it became.

The Simcoes were disappointed not to glimpse the remains of the old fortress of Louisbourg because a sea fog had closed in. After it cleared and they were proceeding through the Gulf of St. Lawrence, several outward bound ships passed them. Off the Magdalen Islands, the *Liberty* hove to, and a ship's boat brought newspapers and took mail for England. Elizabeth sent the next installments of her diary; the first ones had gone before they sailed. Eagerly they went below out of the wind to read the newspapers. They had scarcely begun before the colonel threw down the piece he was reading, his face a study of anger and dismay.

Lord Dorchester would not be at Quebec to receive him. His Lordship had sailed for home, on leave of absence, at the end of August. He had waited until he had greeted Prince Edward, who arrived with his regiment on the eleventh. Major-General Alured Clarke, the lieutenant governor, was in command of Lower Canada, which meant that no important decisions could be made until the governor-in-chief returned. Simcoe fumed over the inconvenience, while Elizabeth suspected Lord Dorchester's departure was a deliberate snub to her husband. She may have wondered again if Mr. Pitt and the governor-in-chief considered Upper Canada important.

On 11 November the *Triton* sailed into the harbour of Quebec and dropped anchor. A gloomy panorama met Elizabeth's gaze. Grey snow covered the land and steep roofs, and driving wind was sending sleet sifting through the bitter air. The sight of carriages on runners passing uphill to the Upper Town depressed her, but dogs of all sizes pulling sleighs caught her attention.

Otherwise the scene was so bleak that she did not want to go ashore. Simcoe, who was anxious to see Major-General Clarke, hurried off in a ship's boat, assuming that his family could remain on board until he returned. Not long after he left the ship, Captain Murray came to request Mrs. Simcoe to disembark as soon as convenient. The *Triton* had to be under way by the 13th in order to regain the Gulf of St. Lawrence ahead of the ice. Outward bound passengers were waiting for her cabins. Elizabeth sent

Captain Stevenson, who had not gone ashore with Simcoe, to look for some place to stay. He returned shortly, having reserved rooms at an inn close to the wharves. He helped Elizabeth, the nurses and servants, assisted by some of the ship's crew, to move their trunks to the inn and their other possessions to a warehouse near the docks. Then he walked up the hill to the Upper Town, where stood the Château St. Louis, the residence of the governor, to inform Colonel Simcoe where he would find his family.

When Simcoe rejoined Elizabeth he looked glummer than ever. They must find a house to rent, since they would not be able to leave for Upper Canada until some time after 26 December when the Canada Act took effect. And that might not be the end of the delay. He could not be sworn in as governor until a majority of the executive council had arrived here. Thus far, only Commodore Grant, whose home was at Detroit, was in the country.

Elizabeth tried to sound sincere as she murmured appropriate words of comfort, but she was looking forward to enjoying the small society Quebec offered. It would resemble the social life in Devon, where the aristocracy and landed gentry constituted an extremely limited class. Colonel Henry Caldwell, who had known her father in 1759 at Quebec, invited the Simcoes to his home, Belmont, four miles to the west along the Ste. Foy road. Oddly enough, nothing was said about Colonel Gwillim at the time. Nearly three years were to pass before Colonel Caldwell would discover that Elizabeth was the daughter of his onetime colleague; in the beginning she had no reason to mention her maiden name.[1]

A week after disembarking the Simcoes found a house, but it was barely adequate and they looked for something better. They found a three storied one in the Rue Saint-Jean, and began renovating it to their taste. They planned a supper room on the ground floor. Partitions were removed on the floor above to make a ball room, with tea room and card room adjoining. The top floor would serve as a nursery and servants' quarters.

They soon found they had more invitations than they could accept. Elizabeth danced with Prince Edward, but she made no mention of Mme. St. Laurent, his constant companion, who was certainly present on the many occasions when the Prince accepted invitations. His Royal Highness' mistress was hardly a topic of discussion for the Simcoe girls, though she may have commented in a letter to Miss Burges that has been lost. She dined with Mme. Delle Marie-Anne Baby, whose husband, François, was an executive councillor and the adjutant-general of militia for Lower Canada. Mme. Baby also took her to see the Ursuline Convent, which Elizabeth found spotlessly clean. Of the Mother Superior, Elizabeth wrote, "The Superieure is a very pleasing conversible woman of good address. Her face & manner reminded me of Mrs. Gwillim."

She probably regarded Roman Catholicism as the established religion of Lower Canada — on the same basis as the Church of England at home, —and felt tolerant of Roman practices, although she did not want to see that church proliferate in England. In Quebec, she was pleased to see how the Roman Catholics were accommodating the Protestant minority amongst them. Protestant services were held in the Recollect Church, when the regular Catholic congregation did not require it. Elizabeth never missed a service, even though the building was unheated. She formed a firm friendship with the Babys. Marie-Anne was scarcely twenty years old when they met, while her husband François was fifty eight. They had been married in 1786 when she was fifteen and he fifty-two, and would ultimately have twelve children.[2]

When offered strange and exotic foods, Elizabeth was game to try them all. She took roasted moose lip in her stride, and chicken pie decorated with coxcombs, since she was quick to appreciate how people had to live off the country in winter when the St. Lawrence was closed to shipping. She found that her ability to speak French was an asset; many people complimented her that she spoke it like a Parisian.

Elizabeth delighted in being driven out in a sleigh or carriole, and she made many sketches of the vehicles she saw. The bold scenery around the city enchanted her — which was so picturesque, much more so than the flat farmlands of parts of the river shore. Her pencil and sketchbooks were usually with her, and she would complete her pictures at home with water colour. The Simcoes often walked over the hills, looking for ever better views of the St. Lawrence. They slid about on the icy surfaces, and noticing the cloth shoes which others wore to prevent slithering, they copied them by putting socks over their footwear. The extra traction gained made walking much safer than on slippery leather soles.

Simcoe's new regiment of Queen's Rangers was put on the British regular establishment officially on 20 December. From that date on, all the officers were entitled to half-pay when the corps was reduced.[3] Simcoe's good friend, the Marquis of Buckingham, donated the instruments for the regimental band.[4] The two company commanders were Captains David Shank and Samuel Smith. The captain-lieutenants were George Spencer and Aeneas Shaw, the latter a resident of New Brunswick who had served as a captain in the old Queen's Rangers. Captain Stevenson was soon confirmed as Simcoe's Quartermaster-General.

On Christmas morning, Elizabeth accompanied Mme. Baby to the Cathedral Church in the centre of the city, to see the brightly lit alter and listen to the service. The following day, as promised, the Canada Act came into effect, with appropriate rejoicing, which was cold comfort for Colonel Simcoe. He was desperate to escape from Quebec and take up his duties inland, and winter was a good time to travel. Despite the searing cold, driving over snow-covered trails or on frozen rivers was much more comfortable than through forests hazy with stinging insects, or boating along rivers choked with rapids.

On New Years' Eve, the Simcoe's attended another celebration. This occasion was the anniversary of the defence of Quebec in 1775, when an army of American rebels led by Benedict Arnold and Richard Montgomery had been put to flight. Colonel Henry Caldwell had commanded the British militia, and he took great pleasure in recounting the events of the battle. Arnold, wounded, had escaped, and Montgomery's body had been found under the snow the following day and buried with full military honours.

Early in January the ice of the St. Lawrence was firm and thick, and people were walking across to the town of Lévis on the south shore. The Simcoes decided to join them, to watch people fishing through holes in the ice. They set forth, but near midstream they found a gap, with a board across it. Simcoe stepped out, offering a hand to Elizabeth, but the ice gave way, and he slipped into the frigid water up to his shoulders. A shocked Elizabeth shouted for help. Some men who were not far off rushed to the rescue, pulled the colonel from the water, and carried him to the Baby house, close by on Rue Sous-le-Fort. While the Babys' servants wrapped Simcoe in blankets warmed before the fire and gave him hot rum, Elizabeth ran home and gave a servant some dry clothes. The colonel was none the worse for the accident and, Elizabeth noted with satisfaction, he did not develop any infection.

They also drove to Montmorency Falls, even then a tourist attraction, and Elizabeth bought three pairs of moccasins to send home to the eldest girls. She already had a pair that Sophia had worn, which she thought would fit Caroline. With the parcel for home went a letter to Mrs. Hunt. She thought Caroline would not notice that her moccasins were not new, for her mother had brushed them well. Mrs. Hunt was not to let any of the girls wear them long or their feet would grow too fast.[5] Elizabeth admitted that she did not feel the cold, even though the thermometer had registered minus thirty degrees, but she did complain of the oppressive heat inside the houses she visited. She was among the earliest, but far from the last, Englishwoman to complain that Canadians kept their homes far too warm in winter. Her complaints were confined to her first winter. After the heat of a Canadian summer she felt the cold as much as anyone.

Frustrated with the inactivity when he was so anxious to begin administering Upper Canada, Simcoe was becoming ever more peevish. And he was plagued with ailments, many of which might have gone away if he had had something important to occupy him. Elizabeth tolerated his black moods, without feeling guilty that for her life was so agreeable. She went alone to a performance of a play by officers of the 7th Fusiliers, and found it a "lark". Simcoe felt it was most undignified for officers to be play-acting, and was surprised that Prince Edward allowed it.

Late in January, accompanied by Captain Stevenson, he drove, muffled in bearskins, to Montreal, the carriole or sleigh warmed by hot bricks. In his absence the surveyor general, Samuel Holland (who had known Captain John Simcoe during Wolfe's campaign) lent Elizabeth some Italian landscapes, which she copied for her collection. She particularly admired one of Mount Vesuvius. At Prince Edward's invitation she attended a winter picnic near Lorette, where they stood about in the freezing air eating the cold food they had brought with them. When, eight days later, the colonel returned, he was in better spirits. With him came Lieutenant Thomas Talbot of the 24th Regiment, who had been stationed in Montreal. Talbot was Irish and a relative of the Marquis of Buckingham. The twenty-year-old officer had agreed to take leave from his regiment to serve as Simcoe's private secretary. Of a charming and happy disposition, Elizabeth found Talbot a good companion.

The social whirl continued as February passed. The Simcoes entertained often in their renovated house on the Rue Saint-Jean. Elizabeth found the chore much simplified by Lieutenant Talbot, who showed a facility for arranging the dinner parties and dances. On 4 March, to Elizabeth's astonishment, a rather startled servant announced some unusual-looking visitors. Elizabeth put down her needlework and followed Simcoe into the hallway, where a dozen unkempt men stood about. Simcoe recognised their leader at once, greeted him warmly and introduced him as Mr. Shaw, who had served in the old Queen's Rangers. He had come all the way from New Brunswick to be a captain-lieutenant in the new regiment.

Elizabeth was bursting with questions and thrilled by Aeneas Shaw's responses. Had they just arrived? Did they travel on snowshoes? How many miles was their journey? Did they mind the cold? They had come from Parrtown, he explained, a distance of 240 miles, and they had walked on snowshoes through intense cold, but they were accustomed to it. Their only casualty had been Mr. John McGill, also from the old Queen's Rangers, who had injured his leg along the way, and had had to stay behind until he would be fit to travel. Simcoe was sorry to hear of McGill's misfortune. Elizabeth, too, was sympathetic, but almost overwhelmed by the devotion all the newcomers had shown her husband.

By early April the milder weather brought chaos to Quebec. The ice and snow were melting, and the streets were slippery. Rivulets of water ran down everywhere. People stopped visiting one another, for getting about was too much of a trial. Elizabeth was bored, and missed the society of the winter when travel had been easy. She began to look forward to the end of the spring breakup, when they would be setting out for Kingston, the largest settlement in Upper Canada. Later in the month the first contingent of Queen's Rangers arrived, and Captains Shank and Smith were expected with the rest. Simcoe soon arranged for the rangers to be sent up the river to begin erecting huts that would serve as barracks at Kingston. The first detachment left under Captain-Lieutenant Shaw, and Captains Smith and Shank soon followed with the rest. The other captain-lieutenant, George Spencer, was delayed in England by illness.

On 1 June the ship *Henneken* arrived bringing Provincial Secretary William Jarvis, another former officer in the old Queen's Rangers. With him were his wife Hannah and their children. The following day another ship brought the chief justice, William Osgoode, as well as the attorney general, John White, and the receiver general, Peter Russell, and his sister, Elizabeth, who would keep house for him and also be company for Mrs. Simcoe. With Alexander Grant, four members of Simcoe's executive council were on the scene, which gave him the quorum he needed to govern Upper Canada. He promptly hired three bateaux to take his own party up the St. Lawrence River as far as Kingston. A bateau was a flat-bottomed, oared boat with an awning to shelter passengers from the sun, and a lateen sail. It was about twenty-four feet long rowed by a crew of eight. Supervising the bateaumen was the pilot, making in all twenty-five in the crew.

51

One bateau was for Elizabeth and the colonel, with his two aides, Lieutenant Talbot, and Lieutenant Thomas Grey of the 7th Fusiliers, who, like Talbot, had left his regiment to serve Simcoe. In the second bateau rode the two children, their nurses and other servants. Now that Francis was weaned, his wet nurse had returned home, and Elizabeth had hired a new nurse for him in Quebec, an American girl named Collins. The third bateau carried the baggage, including some substantial pieces of furniture, but not the legendary canvas houses, which would be sent after them. Captain-Lieutenant Shaw's party of rangers was well ahead of the Simcoes. The Richelieu Rapids that impeded the St. Lawrence near the mouth of the Richelieu River delayed Captains Shank and Smith, but both expected to be in Kingston with their men before the lieutenant governor's party arrived there.

The Simcoes left Quebec City on 8 June. Each night the men slept in the boats, but Simcoe tried to make arrangements for the women and children to sleep under cover. They stayed in houses or inns, and on one occasion with the wife of a local seigneur. At Trois Rivières Elizabeth was annoyed when a landlord overcharged them for their breakfast. They reached Pointe aux Trembles, on the Island of Montreal on the thirteenth.

Waiting for them was a carriage belonging to Mr. Joseph Frobisher, the wealthy fur trader, which took them to the government-owned Château de Ramezay (now a museum). Elizabeth found the château spacious, but infested with bedbugs. Also the heat and the high humidity of summer in the St. Lawrence Valley were debilitating. Long before she reached Montreal she had discovered that bane of travellers in the Canadas, the blood-thirsty female mosquito. The crew of the bateau warned her to keep well away from a three-leaved plant which they called poison ivy, which could cause painful skin eruptions. The plant looked distinctive, and avoiding it, she decided, would not be difficult. The swarms of thirsty mosquitos were a vastly different matter. Their vicious bites were so itchy and so given to swelling; the little pests, impossible to eschew, were so trying of patience. By the time they left for the new province, she also knew she was pregnant. Colonel Simcoe would be alarmed. And yet, Elizabeth admitted, though he often said they had enough children, they would not be having more if he did not play his part.

Chapter 7

NEWS FROM HOME

September 1791~June 1792

Mary Anne Burges wrote almost daily to Elizabeth, and she numbered her pages in order to know exactly how much she had sent before the Simcoes' return. Often she began with *"Mi mas querida Amiga"*, and added some phrases in Spanish. She admitted that she was missing Elizabeth more than she had ever missed anyone who had died. Every time a fierce storm had shaken Devon, she fully expected to hear that all the Simcoes had been drowned at sea. Contradictory accounts on the progress of their voyage had been published in the newspapers, reports which disturbed her. She had made regular visits to Wolford Lodge since that first sad teatime after the children's parents had left in their carriage for Weymouth.[1] She had been delighted with the drawings and letters Elizabeth had sent before the *Triton* sailed.

Mrs. Graves was still being difficult, resenting the colonel more than her niece. Miss Burges was concerned that Elizabeth would receive differing versions of the situation at Wolford Lodge, and she was meticulous at giving details in her reports. Mrs. Graves was threatening to leave the house and find somewhere else to live the moment she heard that the Simcoes were back in England. Captain Richard Graves was the source of much of her discontent, He, too, was very critical of Colonel Simcoe, and he was keeping his aunt constantly stirred up. She had once ordered him out of the house for denigrating her relations. She asserted that she kept two carriages, and was under no obligation to keep *him*. She was now so angry with him that she was thinking of withholding the annuity money she was to pay him under the terms of the admiral's will.

Whenever Miss Burges went to Wolford Lodge, the children were delighted to see her, because, she thought, they connected her with their mother. Eliza, in particular, liked accompanying her to Tracey House, so that she could gaze on Elizabeth's miniature. The child was dreadfully worried that she would not remember what her mother looked like, and she was mourning her parents' absence more than the younger ones appeared to be. She sought to sit close to Miss Burges, but when she looked up her eyes were usually full of tears. Mary Anne suggested she write to Mama and Papa, but Eliza did not reply. When other people spoke of the Simcoes, Eliza would leave the room. Nonetheless, all the girls were "much improved", a phrase Miss Burges frequently put in her letters. Elizabeth would be gratified, because the fact that they were improving, both in manners and at their lessons, would justify having left them at home. Yet there were other hints, not just Mary Anne's reports on Eliza, that suggested the girls were not blissfully happy. For instance, she admitted that there was not so much crying over their lessons, a suggestion that they were being pushed rather hard by the Hunts, in their efforts to carry out their instructions to the full.

Eliza delighted in reading, and was proficient in astronomy. Miss Hunt needed to purchase "deeper Books" in order to keep ahead of her. When Miss Hunt needed to go to Exeter, Miss Burges and Eliza went with her in a hired chaise. They visited the cathedral and did some shopping. "I never knew a child", wrote Mary Anne, "who takes such delight in learning". Eliza was in good spirits while they were in Exeter, and she seemed less fearful of strangers since. Charlotte was now reading to herself. Miss Burges was spending two hours each morning listening to the girls' piano practice. While practicing on their own they had acquired too many bad habits. Afterwards, they would all set out for a walk, accompanied by Miss Burges' dog, Ranger, and by other children from the neighbourhood. She found herself so surrounded by small people that she had difficulty preventing some from straying.[2]

A few days later she wrote that Eliza was playing Miss Hunt's "game of questions" and was liking history. Mrs. Graves was still vexed with Captain Richard Graves, and she had withheld his annuity payment of £100 for eight days. He wrote asking her to send the money, which offended her. At that he wrote an apology for his impertinence. Mrs. Richard Graves wanted to move to Bath, for she was afraid to remain at Hembury Fort House. The sight of all those green fields terrified her, and she thought she would have to keep the curtains drawn and live by candlelight.

Eliza and Charlotte were much improved by their collars, which neither considered a "misfortune". Eliza's French was progressing, and she was finding in Miss Hunt a real friend. All the girls were learning multiplication tables. Mrs. Hunt was very attentive to them, and Miss Burges had only one small negative criticism. Mrs. Hunt had made them jackets, garments which Elizabeth did not like for she thought they made girls look clumsy. However, "Eliza's little figure does look nice in them". Charlotte danced well, and Harriet's reading was progressing nicely. Caroline, now talking, was the most changed. She joined in everything and was the merriest of all. Mrs. Graves approved of Mrs. Hunt, but she felt that the girls were not getting enough exercise because Mrs. Hunt did not like going outside. Miss Burges suggested Elizabeth write and insist on more time outdoors.

Mary Anne was to have the four girls at Tracey on a Saturday, when Mrs. Graves would be entertaining friends. Elizabeth's aunt had included her, but she did not like one of the guests who had been invited, and was using the girls as an excuse to decline. After their day at Tracey, she would not be seeing them for the next fortnight. She had to go to Fitzhead Court, to see her aunt and uncle. Hugh Somerville and his second wife, Mary Digby, now had seven children, in addition to John Southby, the son of his first marriage.[3]

In a letter dated 14 December 1791, Miss Burges enclosed Eliza's first attempt using water colours. Eliza had worked in secret and she only showed the sketch to Miss Burges when it was finished. Now all three eldest girls loved going to Tracey to view the miniature Miss Burges had painted of Elizabeth. Visits brought them closer to Mama. After dinner they asked to have their parents' health drunk, to which Mary Anne agreed.

"That's just the same as we do," said Eliza.

Now the Christmas festivities were under way. Mrs. Montagu had arrived from London to stay at Wolford Lodge as Mrs. Graves' guest. Mary Anne was distracted because she was having to make frequent journeys to Fitzhead Court. Her Aunt Mary was in the early stages of her eighth and last pregnancy, and far from well. The weather was beastly. After much rain, heavy snow had fallen on Devonshire. The snow buried two women of Dunkeswell, who were not found until they had died of exposure.

To Mary Anne's delight, early in the holiday season a packet of letters arrived from Elizabeth, one which she had posted soon after she reached Quebec. Miss Burges' next letters fairly bubbled over with joy that her friend was safe. She admired Elizabeth's heroism during the storms at sea. The drawings she had enclosed gave an excellent impression of the countryside. Mary Anne had never been much interested in geography, but now she wanted to learn all she could about where her friend had been. After hunting carefully among her own books, she found good maps and was able to follow the Simcoes' journey. Mrs. Graves had had some journals Colonel Simcoe had sent bound. The book was handsome, except that the emblems the bookbinder had selected were two turtle doves, which Miss Burges did not think quite appropriate.

While dining at Wolford Lodge on 14 December, she was startled to see an officer in the uniform of the Queen's Rangers. He was Ensign William Mayne, who would be taking some rangers to Canada in the spring. Miss Burges was preparing a package for Canada, and Eliza and Charlotte were bringing items to go in it. Eliza was pale, not having been outside because of the rain and snow. When they were unable to go into the fresh air for exercise, the girls danced each evening to the tunes of a fiddle played by the gardener. When Harriet had had to have a tooth drawn, she was brave. Also, when a cut on her finger required stitching she did not cry, and was "indifferent, as tho it was the finger of a glove". One evening, when Miss Burges had ridden over on her horse, Placid, the children's dancing was postponed because of a "furious argument" between Mrs. Graves and Mrs. Montagu. Miss Burges left before it was settled. She found the lanes icy, but Placid was sure-footed and she reached home safely.

The girls spent 24 December at Tracey House, walking, writing letters and drawing. Harriet was so eager to send Elizabeth a letter that Mary Anne guided her hand. She told dear Mama that she could read a psalm, and about having the tooth drawn, and ended her letter, "Tell Papa I would like to take a walk with him. I am your dutiful daughter Harriet Simcoe."[4] In the course of their walk, they were delighted to meet a party of Queen's Rangers, looking splendid in their neat green jackets.

Mrs. Graves was now in better humour. She had not written to Elizabeth, nor could she bring herself to do so as yet, but she was being kind to the children. Among the visitors to Wolford Lodge that holiday season were the Captain Thomas Graveses and Mary, their only child. Their home, Woodbine Hill, was three miles southeast of Wolford Lodge. Thomas tried to persuade Mrs. Graves to send his brother Richard his annuity payment, but in vain. Miss Mary stayed on after her parents left.

Eliza was now reading aloud in Spanish extremely well. Miss Burges was pleased, but not with the child's choice. She picked a chapter Mary Anne fondly remembered Elizabeth reading, which she would rather not have heard. The little girl was trying hard to remember exactly how her mother looked, and still mourning her departure. The weather continued to be miserable. The children's only exercise was their dancing.

Writing early in January 1792, Miss Burges relayed a conversation between Eliza and Mrs. Graves. Eliza asked her great aunt how many letters she had received from her mother.

"Three," replied Mrs. Graves.

"And how many have you written Mama, Aunt?"

"None."

"But you will," the child insisted.

"No," said Mrs. Graves.

"But that is rude!"

"I don't believe I shall."

"O naughty, naughty Aunt!" Eliza exclaimed. "I shall write Mama that you have not written because you have hurt your hand, then."

Mrs. Graves was also pressing Eliza to eat more, but left to herself Eliza instinctively chose the foods of which her mother would approve, and she could be "trusted in the management of herself". She was still not reconciled to her parents' absence. When a guest had enquired whether she was happy that they had reached Quebec safely, she asked him not to talk about it.[5]

Miss Hunt was creating a happy atmosphere at Wolford Lodge. Mrs. Graves approved of the growing friendship between Miss Hunt and Miss Burges — so much better than a friendship between a married woman and an unmarried one because she was jealous of Mary Anne's closeness to Elizabeth.

"An unmarried woman's conversation might be passed on by a married woman, to a man," Mrs. Graves said primly. "Or a single woman might consult a married one about her lovers."

"That can easily be overcome by not having any lovers," Miss Burges retorted.

For Elizabeth's amusement she added some bits of gossip. The Duchess of York had such tiny feet that people were saying she must be Chinese. Mrs. Fitzherbert, longtime mistress of the Prince of Wales, was out of favour. The Duchess of York was upset over the Duke's gaming at Brookes.[6] Mary Anne was arranging for John Scadding to take the next packet of letters. He was going to Canada shortly as an assistant to Colonel Simcoe.

At Wolford Lodge, Mrs. Graves was cross with Miss Burges for listening too attentively to Miss Hunt, who spoke too softly for the old lady to hear. Mary Anne was feeling quite "independent" after having been terrified of Mrs. Graves when she was young. She admitted that she would never have had the courage to stand up to Mrs. Graves if Elizabeth had been at home.

Among other matters of interest to Elizabeth was the death of a man in Buckerell after he had been bitten by a mad dog. While walking to Wolford Lodge, Mary Anne had longed for Elizabeth's "mask" for she had to hold her muff up to shield her face from the bitter wind. Mrs. Graves was amused because Mr. Charles James Fox, an opponent of Prime Minister Pitt, recommended that instead of sending Colonel Simcoe any troops, he should be asked to raise a militia in Upper Canada. (This had in fact had been done, commencing in 1788.) In view of the paucity of people in the province, Mrs. Graves wondered whether Simcoe should arm some rattlesnakes.

Mary Anne admitted that Elizabeth had been wise in not leaving Mrs. Graves in charge of the children. At first she had approved of the Simcoes' wish to have the girls learn as much as they could absorb, and as early as possible. Now she had decided that girls would only forget what they had learned if they were taught too young. They should be kept ignorant until at least twelve years of age, and better still, fifteen. Miss Hunt was paying no attention to Mrs. Graves, and the children's progress was truly remarkable. Eliza was an impressive grammarian; Charlotte was taking well to French; Harriet was good at arithmetic; Caroline was quick, but had more "odd fancies than any child I ever knew". Caroline was everyone's favourite, but Mrs. Hunt was being careful not to spoil her. Mrs. Graves favoured Eliza, but she too was not being spoiled because she was too sensible and amiable. Eliza would not accept any gift or favour unless it was also offered to her sisters. Mrs. Hunt and Mrs. Graves were enjoying each other's company, for two people with such different ideas.

On 25 January 1792, Miss Burges described an adventure Captain Thomas Graves had had in Exeter. He had taken his daughter Mary to a play, and a drunken man had entered their box. After a sharp verbal exchange the fellow had challenged Thomas to a duel. The two met at dawn, but the other "gentleman", by that time sober, apologized, and there the matter had ended. Both Richard and Thomas Graves were justices of the peace, which made a duel all the more improper.[7]

The Simcoes seemed much closer to Mary Anne in February when a midshipman came to Honiton after being shipwrecked off the Devon coast. He reported having seen the colonel and his lady in Quebec before his ill-fated ship had sailed. By early March, Miss Burges reported that Eliza was looking more cheerful than at any time since her parents' departure, although she was still unable to talk about them. Charlotte loved drawing pictures of Mama and Papa, and making up stories about them to amuse Caroline. One time they were talking about fairies, pretending Mrs. Hunt was one, and deciding on what gifts they would ask of her. Eliza wished for wings so that she and Miss Burges could fly to America.

"I would expect to be paid for the wings," Miss Hunt said, teasing.

"I have no money," Eliza said quickly. After some reflection she added, "I could give two frocks, a petticoat and my green sash." Then her face saddened, since this was all make-believe.

Mrs. Graves was still being awkward. She decided that the bedroom she occupied was too cold, and had taken over the great parlour. She was affronted if Mary Anne wanted to work at anything while she was at Wolford Lodge because she expected her to sit and entertain her. The only acceptable occupation was needlework, but Miss Burges preferred painting and sketching. Her other interests were her butterfly collection and her botanical and rock specimens.

When she received her next packet of letters from Canada, Mary Anne saw them as proof that her friendship with Elizabeth was as strong as ever. She could not think of anyone whose conversation was worth a paragraph of one of Elizabeth's letters. Second hand reports hinted that Colonel Simcoe and Francis were unwell, and she hoped they had recovered by now. On 20 May 1792, Mary Anne had just returned from a visit to Teignmouth and Plymouth. She gave a detailed description of the construction of a destroyer which she was sure would be of interest to both the Simcoes.

On 8 June she wrote from Exeter that she had met a couple named Martin. Mrs. Martin had heard of a silkworm native to North America that might be as valuable as the Asian worm, and she wondered whether Elizabeth could find out anything about it. Mary Anne wished that Elizabeth would give her a field in Canada, where she would build a shed to live in. She could not afford anything better, but she longed to be near her friend. Her brother-in-law, James Roper Head, was talking of going to Canada, and her sister Frances was alarmed that he might divide or uproot the family.

The tensions at Wolford Lodge had not abated. Mrs. Graves had remarked that Elizabeth had been much more civil to the Hunts than to her own aunt. She was discoursing on who was the more learned, Miss Burges or Miss Hunt, which both women found odious. Sixteen new books by the Roman historian Livy had been discovered in the Church of St. Sophia in Constantinople. The manuscripts, in Arabic, had been translated into Italian, and would soon be published in Italy. Mary Anne hoped to obtain a copy. She was about to plant some seeds that Elizabeth had sent, which a friend, Mr. Miller, assured her would do well in the open air in Devon.

The conduct of the Prince of Wales, the future George IV, was disgraceful. Mrs. Graves had long detested Mr. Pitt, but now she was one of his converts — because he had made the King pay the Prince's gambling debts. By the time Miss Burges was sending off her latest packet, the Simcoe family had left Quebec in the three bateaux, bound for Upper Canada.[8]

Chapter 8

NATURE UNTAMED

While they were on their way to Upper Canada the Simcoes spent ten days in Montreal, and Elizabeth was busy with her sketchbook. The strange-looking hills that rose so unexpectedly from the flat river plain intrigued her. The Frobishers entertained them and made their carriage available to take Elizabeth on drives. The visit would have been most agreeable had it not been for the appalling heat. She felt constantly damp and sticky, her clothes clinging to her. Simcoe, in his heavy regimentals, was even more uncomfortable. Yet Elizabeth braved the high temperature in order to be driven round the mountain from which the city took its name. She enjoyed a visit to the home of the Baronne de Longueuil and her husband, William Grant, on St. Helen's Island, before they set out again.

When they left Montreal they were accompanied by Edward Littlehales, a former lieutenant in the 58th Regiment and now a captain in the garrison. He had been appointed major of brigade for Upper Canada, and Simcoe's military secretary. The family travelled in the Frobisher carriage as far as Lachine, where they joined the bateaux that had been pulled through the rapids. At the Cascades Rapids everyone evacuated the boats, and the crews pushed them upstream using long poles with special iron tips. At Coteau du Lac, instead of having to worry about the Cedars Rapids, they found a small canal, barely deep enough to float the bateaux, and locks through which they passed. Still the heat was exhausting, and the children were fretful. Elizabeth found one of the rooms where they were to stay so dirty that she covered a table with a blanket and slept upon it, rather than use the disgusting bed. At Pointe au Baudet, Simcoe informed his wife and staff that they were now in Upper Canada.

Soon a boat arrived from John Macdonell, a half-pay captain whose home was Glengarry House, farther along. Aboard were kilted Highlanders, come to escort the governor and his three aides to the Macdonell house. Pipes skirled as Simcoe left the bateau. Elizabeth would follow with the others and meet him at Glengarry House. Soon afterwards the sky blackened, billowing clouds of a threatening grey-blue filled the heavens. Great flashes of lightning, the like of which Elizabeth had never before beheld, bombarded her senses. When the wooden awning on the bateau tore, and the boat rocked fiercely, she demanded that the crew land. She passed the night in a farmhouse. At Glengarry House early the next morning Elizabeth breakfasted with the governor and Macdonell, who had met Simcoe during the revolutionary war.

Farther on they spent a night with James Gray a half-pay major from Sir John Johnson's regiment. From there Simcoe went to St. Regis, a Mohawk Indian village on an island, to greet those loyal friends of Great Britain. On their way again, they reached the Long Sault Rapids, which were among the most spectacular Elizabeth could imagine. There, John Munro, another of Sir John Johnson's half-pay captains, met them with horses to take them along the rough track that bypassed the dangerous stretch of water. Elizabeth found the ride alarming. The track was so bad that she feared for the horse's legs. The several bridges they had to cross were nothing but large logs laid side by side where a horse could easily catch a foot and break a bone. Fortunately, her mount — the property of Richard Duncan, a half-pay captain who lived at Rapide Plat — was experienced and sure-footed, and they arrived beyond the rapids without incident. She recorded a delicious meal of fresh-caught black bass, so delicate a flavour, and wild strawberries tastier than those grown in the garden at Wolford Lodge.

Off Johnstown, a tiny hamlet in the forest, a group of half-pay officers in their old uniforms met them in a boat, and took Simcoe to inspect Chimney Island, where the French had built Fort Lévis. The officers fired an old cannon, and on their return, as Simcoe was climbing back into the bateau, they saluted him with shouted military slogans. Elizabeth thought they were behaving like silly schoolboys, but Simcoe seemed delighted with the camaraderie.[1]

She suggested that Simcoe would enjoy governing such men, but he looked grave. He had heard disturbing facts that boded ill for an established church. Very few of the settlers were adherents of the Church of England. The Loyalists had been awarded townships according to their denominations. The Highlanders closest to the last seigneury were Catholics. Next came Lutherans to the west of the Catholics, while in the upper townships were entirely too many New England sectaries. Simcoe thought there were at least as many followers of John Wesley in Upper Canada as in the West Country at home. Even more disturbing were Moravian missionaries on the River La Tranche, who had come with some refugee Delaware Indians after the revolution. Now they might be spreading their non-conformist notions in what he hoped would be the heart of the province. They must, Elizabeth decided, ask the Society for the Propagation of the Gospel to send out Anglican missionaries without delay.

At Gananoque, they were to stay in a house, but Elizabeth said it was much too dirty. Instead, Simcoe had the crews pitch some of the tents on an island now called Grenadier. While the men moved on to the island, Elizabeth took time to sketch a mill on the Gananoque River that belonged to Joel Stone, a Loyalist from Connecticut and militia colonel. Simcoe added a dog in the water below the mill, and some notes that amused her. They were now in the midst of what the French had called *Les Milles Iles*, the Thousand Islands, which the Indians, more poetic, had named the Garden of the Great Spirit. The little convoy followed the bateau channel, close to the north shore of the St. Lawrence. Elizabeth caught only a glimpse now and then of the south channel, which was wider and used by sailing vessels. The islands, many of them small, rounded lumps of granite, were fine subjects for Elizabeth's pencil, and she sat happily recording them, too busy with her sketching to do needlework that had occupied her hands lower down the wide blue river. By the morning of 1 July, they were off Kingston harbour, before which were a number of large, flatter islands. As the bateaux moved towards the mouth of the Cataraqui River, Elizabeth felt the strong wind, and noted the whitecaps whipping high on the crests of the waves on Lake Ontario.

Simcoe resolved to move the naval base from Kingston. With the prevailing wind blowing straight into it, the harbour offered little shelter. Carleton Island had a superior harbour, but the international boundary might run north of it, and he hoped to find a more suitable harbour farther up the lake.

They went ashore to a warm welcome. Some of the half-pay officers were in their old uniforms as others had been near Chimney Island in the river. Cannon boomed, joined by musket volleys as Mohawks from their village at Deseronto discharged their weapons. Best of all, drawn up in neat ranks were the Queen's Rangers, whose rows of small white tents were visible in the background. Elizabeth found the spectacle daunting. Having been told that this was the military, naval and commercial heartland of the province, she was surprised that Kingston seemed to consist of some fifty wooden homes, interspersed with stumps and muddy tracks, and some merchants' storehouses along the waterfront. Yet she was delighted with the house assigned to the family. It was not very big, but it stood on a knole where it caught every breeze, and it was cool, clean and airy.

The honeymoon, as far as the Kingstonians were concerned, was short-lived. As the foremost community in Upper Canada, they assumed that Simcoe would choose Kingston as his capital, especially as Lord Dorchester had more or less promised it would be. They were dismayed when, at the outset, Simcoe made it clear that he would be moving on to Niagara, which was more central, although in the long term no safer from attack. For the present, Niagara suited Simcoe best, and it was defensible as long as Fort Niagara, across the narrow Niagara river, was in British hands. Since 1787, although legally in New York State, it had been garrisoned by the 5th or the Northumberland Regiment of Foot, and Simcoe assumed Britain had no intention of withdrawing the troops as long as the Loyalists and Indians needed protection.

Especially indignant with Simcoe was Kingston's leading merchant, Richard Cartwright, a Loyalist who had served at Fort Niagara during the revolution. (Cartwright's grandson was Sir Richard Cartwright, the most prominent cabinet minister under Prime Minister Sir Wilfrid Laurier.) His house, visible from the water, was the only one of stone in the settlement. The logical place for the capital was here, where, incidently, Cartwright owned many of the mills and had almost a monopoly over the carrying trade. Elizabeth was perturbed at the hostility she encountered, but as Simcoe remained adamant she agreed with him. Besides, she may have suspected that Lord Dorchester had suggested Kingston for the capital as a way of embarrassing her husband.

She accompanied him on some of his tours of inspection of the defences and the mills, and she also went on her own, escorted by Lieutenant Talbot.

They walked into the woods, but were often stopped by the stinging insects or impassable underbrush. She had always loved nature, she complained to Talbot when they had to abandon a walk because the trail was too overgrown, but here it was so untidy.

A mosquito had bitten her so severely through a leather glove that she felt faint. That "Musquito" was more likely a hornet or ground wasp. Going about by boat was much more pleasant than on land, and she soon resorted to travelling on the water for her explorations. An exception was an evening when some woods had caught fire. Elizabeth noticed that the mosquitos were not biting, the smoke having driven them away. Besides, the woods were so "picturesque" as flames illuminated the dark trees. "Perhaps you have no idea of the pleasure of walking in a burning wood, but I found it so great that I think I shall have some woods set on fire for my Evening walks," she wrote Mary Anne Burges.[2]

On Sunday 8 July 1792, Simcoe and his officers set off in solemn procession for St. George's Church where he would take his oath of office. The members of his executive council had arrived in Kingston, and he was ready to begin governing in earnest. A gowned and wigged Chief Justice William Osgoode administered the oath. Witnesses were Receiver-General Peter Russell, and James Baby of Detroit, the fifth member of the executive council. Resplendent in knee breeches and silk stockings were Richard Cartwright of Kingston, and Robert Hamilton, who had come from Niagara. Simcoe himself was in the scarlet and gold of a colonel in the army, rather than the green and silver of the Queen's Rangers. A stickler for form, Simcoe insisted on every ounce of pomp that could be wrung from the situation. Elizabeth attended the swearing in, where the Reverend John Stuart gave the blessing afterwards. She was much impressed by Stuart, who had been missionary to the Mohawks before the revolution. He was the first clergyman in Upper Canada, after serving as a chaplain to the 2nd Battalion King's Royal Regiment of New York. Elizabeth was so pleased with his preaching that she went to St. George's Church twice the following Sunday.

While Simcoe was meeting with his executive council, and appointing the members of the legislative council, the other portion of his upper house, Elizabeth was making friends with Elizabeth, the young wife of the surgeon to the garrison, James Macaulay. Their son, who had just been born, was christened John Simcoe Macaulay, to please the governor. James Macaulay had been the surgeon in the Queen's Rangers during the revolution. To Elizabeth's delight, the Macaulays would be coming on to Niagara, the new capital. The government vessel, H.M.S. *Onondaga*, an armed 80-ton topsail schooner, would carry the Simcoes and their entourage across Lake Ontario. Simcoe wanted to go around the lake shore in a small boat, to evaluate harbours and townsites, but after listening to the advice of local men, he agreed to postpone his explorations until everyone was settled at Niagara. He had decided to rename it Newark, to dispose of the ugly Indian word. They sailed on the *Onondaga* on 23 July, in a fair wind that soon dropped for a time. Two days later, Lieutenant Talbot pointed out the spray rising from the great Falls of Niagara while they were still forty miles off. Elizabeth could hardly wait to sketch them.

If she was surprised with Kingston, the sight of Newark must have astonished Elizabeth. It was a tiny settlement of scarcely half a dozen houses — if they merited the name, for they were really only cabins. The zone along the Niagara River had been settled by Butler's Rangers, an active Provincial Corps that had operated from Fort Niagara during the American Revolution. The commanding officer, Colonel John Butler, was one of the leading settlers and a deputy superintendent of the Indian Department.[3]

No house awaited the Simcoes such as they had found at Kingston; they would have to make do with four rundown wooden government buildings called Navy Hall, once a headquarters for the navy on the lake. These were being prepared for their occupancy, although they would not make a proper dwelling. Simcoe had three tents erected on the hillside overlooking the Niagara River. One would be for themselves, one for the children and their nurses, and the other for the servants. Elizabeth appreciated the magnificent view, and was not dismayed by their accommodation. She had fewer complaints than Elizabeth Russell, who could find only a cabin of two rooms as a home for her brother Peter, the receiver general, and herself. Simcoe, however, was unperturbed. His councillors and civil servants would have to build houses, and a lovely new town would spring up almost overnight.

Nevertheless Simcoe was not at all enchanted by Navy Hall. He wrote to James Bland Burges:

> I am fitting up an old hovel, that will look exactly like a carrier's ale-house in England when properly decorated and ornamented; but I please myself with the hopes that some future 'Gentleman's Magasine' will obtain drawings of the first Government House, the first House of Assembly, etc., and decorate it with the "Aude, Hospes, Contemnere opes" of old Evander.[4]

To Elizabeth he talked enthusiastically of making a journey to Detroit without delay, and he wanted her to accompany him. She looked forward to seeing the countryside and sketching it, while he was anxious to inspect that post's defences. Afterwards they would follow the La Tranche River to its forks, where he thought he would find a site for the future capital of Upper Canada. On their return he would establish the provincial government. Thus far the only form of government in Upper Canada was the district court where appointed magistrates presided. There were four such districts: Luneburg, the settlement on the St. Lawrence River; Mecklenburg, that on the Bay of Quinte; Nassau, centred on Niagara and including the Toronto Carrying Place; and Hesse, opposite Detroit — given German names by Lord Dorchester to please George III. Simcoe resolved to substitute English ones, in keeping with his intent to make Upper Canada a copy of the mother country. Luneburg would become the Eastern District; Mecklenburg, the Midland; Nassau, the Home; and Hesse, the Western, names both the Simcoes thought more appropriate.

As yet tiny Newark did not have a church building, but an Anglican congregation had recently been organised; a Church of England missionary, the Reverend Robert Addison, was its leader. The members met at Navy Hall, unsuitable though it was. Mr. Addison was the only clergyman at Niagara. Simcoe had arranged for the Reverend Edward Drewe, of Broadhembury, close to Wolford Lodge, to be appointed the chaplain to the garrison. Now the governor was wondering whether Drewe, thirty-six years old, would ever be coming. Apparently Drewe regarded the appointment as a sinecure since he was fully occupied with his parish at Broadhembury.[5]

Four days after the Simcoes had disembarked, they set out very early in the morning, in caleches, to see the great Falls of Niagara. They stopped for breakfast at the fine stone house of Robert Hamilton, a legislative councillor and merchant. Hamilton was a former partner of Richard Cartwright, who had remained in the Niagara area after the Revolution. The Hamilton house stood at what was called The Landing, or Queenston, below the Falls, where goods had to be removed from boats and carried by land around the cascade to an upper landing. The Queen's Rangers were building huts at Queenston because most would be stationed at that strategic place. The height of the river bank above Queenston reminded Elizabeth of the Wye River near Whitchurch.

She was enchanted by Mrs. Hamilton, the former Catharine Askin, a daughter of the Detroit fur trader, John Askin. Elizabeth admired the stone house greatly, with its enclosed gallery where one could walk in all kinds of weather. The Falls were everything for which Elizabeth could have hoped. Above the huge cascade they continued on to Chippawa Fort, close to the upper landing, fascinated by the long stretch of rapids they beheld. Elizabeth was disappointed not to see any rattlesnakes, after all she had heard about them, and she suffered a severe insect sting. When they returned for the night at the Hamilton's, the sleeve had to be cut from her dress because her arm was so badly swollen.[6] Back at Navy Hall, a message was waiting for Simcoe. Prince Edward was about to set out to inspect the garrison and defences of Upper Canada, and he expected to be at Niagara in three weeks' time.

A dismayed Elizabeth wondered where they could put such an exalted guest. Simcoe spared some of the Queen's Rangers from other tasks and set them to completing the alterations to Navy Hall. The Prince was coming at an inconvenient time, and they would also have to make their journey to Detroit at a later date. Elizabeth referred to the swarms of winged grasshoppers in the field around Navy Hall. They were "hard & ugly as Rhinoceros, & the color of dead leaves." On 1 August the Simcoes dined at Fort Niagara, the guests of the garrison commander and his wife, Major and Mrs. John Smith. Elizabeth was less impressed with the buildings at the fort than by

Mrs. Smith's two tame racoons, which she thought resembled foxes. The flying squirrel Elizabeth did not admire; the ground squirrel was much prettier, while the black squirrel tasted like young rabbit.

At Navy Hall, because of the intense heat, the Simcoes dined beneath an oak tree, which they found cooler than inside their tents. On the evening of 16 August, Elizabeth insisted in being taken for a drive, although she was warned that a thunderstorm was blowing up. She regretted her persistence, for she was terrified that the horse would bolt as the streaks of lightning flashed across the sky making everything as bright as day. A pretty set of blue and white Nankeen china, from England, had been almost all broken when an oak bow above their temporary kitchen caught fire and servants tried hurriedly to remove the delicate pieces.

Meanwhile, the Queen's Rangers had been endeavouring to finish the work on Navy Hall. Even with the extra help, by 19 August, the place was hardly habitable. It smelled atrociously of fresh paint and damp plaster. The Simcoes admitted that they had no choice but to give their comfortable tent to His Royal Highness and make do with Navy Hall.

The Prince and his entourage arrived the following day, and Elizabeth recorded from Navy Hall "we came here on a cold and blowing night. I sat by myself in a miserable, unfinished, damp room, looking on the lake, where it blew a gale, the Bear, a gunboat, tossing about terribly, and not a cheerful thought passing through my mind[.]"[7] Happily, a letter from home eased her depression.

Despite his busy schedule entertaining royalty, Simcoe stole some time to write to his two eldest daughters so that the letters could be sent on the ship that would be carrying the Prince down the lake. He advised Eliza to stay outdoors as much as possible, and he stressed the importance of reading. He hoped she would pass on the benefit of her instruction to Francis. She should study the Good Book, especially Genesis and Exodus, and the classics. A particular hero was Alexander the Great, and he hoped Francis would follow a military career. He never saw an unusual flower without wishing he could show it to his daughters.[8]

His letter to Charlotte was on a lighter vein, as though he regarded her as less serious-minded: "here I am & Mamma sitting in a very large Bower, fronting upon a fine river, & as high above it, as the sand cliff above the Shrubbery, with Sophia sitting upon the Table, little Francis with his bald Pole [sic] laughing & eating Bilberries."

He told them he would be completely happy if only the four girls were with them. He was delighted that Charlotte loved to dance. Perhaps he should learn to play the fiddle in order to accompany her. He was pleased she was growing fond of reading, and hoped she would make Francis fond of it, too, and would teach him not to destroy too many birds, sail his little boats and fire his cannon "as Boys are apt to do". He was looking ahead since Francis was only fourteen months old.[9] (The letters would reach Wolford Lodge in November 1792. Miss Burges reported on the twentieth that Eliza and Charlotte were delighted with their letters, but Harriet was perturbed that there was none for her. Mary Anne explained to the now five and a half-year-old Harriet that when Papa wrote his letter, he was not aware that she could read.)[10]

On 23 November, Simcoe accompanied the Prince to Fort Niagara to inspect the garrison. He stood close to one of the guns when a royal salute was fired, which deafened him temporarily, and left him with a searing headache which sent him to his bed for the remainder of the royal visit. The commandant of the fort, Major John Smith, was the Prince's host until his departure, to Simcoe's everlasting chagrin. Elizabeth often referred to Simcoe as being in bad health. Describing the headache, she wrote:

> [He] kept to his room a fortnight. He had a gouty pain in his hand before & it is supposed the Shock of the Cannon firing so immediately above him fixed the disorder in his head. He is now recovered & has a pain in his foot, which perhaps would more effectually relieve his head if it was more violent.[11]

During the summer, a general election had chosen Upper Canada's first Parliament, which convened at Newark on 16 September. For the opening, Simcoe resolved on all the pomp he had been denied in the later part of the Prince's visit. He rode forth in his full scarlet regimentals, escorted by Major Littlehales and Lieutenants Talbot and Grey. A guard of honour of the Queen's Rangers, and some of Colonel John Butler's disbanded rangers, in their green coats, lined the route from Navy Hall to the Masonic Lodge building, where the legislature would meet. Elizabeth, arrayed in a gown made for the purpose in London, watched proudly, the band of the gown cutting into her swelling waist. She was fatigued by evening, when everyone was invited to a grand ball, but she attended. She was meticulous in seeing that she spoke to each and every guest — members of the councils or of the legislature and their wives, and Simcoe's staff of civil servants. Once all the guests had left, the colonel hurried her off to the tent, looking anxious.

He begged her to get more rest because she meant everything to him. She promised to be quiet for the next few days, proud that she had been such a good hostess to so many strangers. Simcoe thought so too; his tiny wife had managed to create an hospitable atmosphere much like that at Wolford Lodge.

Chapter 9

WINTER IN THE WILDS

While the legislature was still in session the canvas houses arrived at Newark. One house, which became Elizabeth's own quarters, was thirty feet long. She had the space divided by a partition to make a sittingroom and a bedroom. She never explained in her writings where the rest of the family and the servants were housed, or whether Simcoe shared her bedroom or had his own somewhere else in Navy Hall. Nor did she specify who lived in the second canvas house, though it probably accommodated the children, their nurses and other servants. Simcoe also had a hut built above the Niagara River at Queenston, the spot that reminded Elizabeth of the view of Whitchurch from the high bank of the Wye River. There, in future summers, the family could catch all the breeze there was, and be more comfortable than during the heat of the past one. In the hut he hung the tapestry that was the gift of the Marquis of Buckingham. On 17 February, Elizabeth wrote that Simcoe had built the hut "for himself". Perhaps he lived there part of the time.

Some kind person gave the Simcoes a dog, which Elizabeth named Trojan. He was for the children but he quickly attached himself to her and slept in her bedroom. Another canine, named Jack Sharp, adopted the Simcoes. Elizabeth said he was a Newfoundland dog who belonged to a Mr. Shane at Niagara. Their other pet was a grey and white cat.[1]

Elizabeth's days now began to resemble those in Devon, except that instead of having Mary Anne Burges as a frequent companion, she was writing to her and hoping each ship that arrived would bring a packet of her replies. Elizabeth sketched many wonderful new scenes, and walked often to the Hamilton house, where Catharine Hamilton always made her welcome. Other good friends were Elizabeth Macaulay and Elizabeth Russell, whose cabins were near Navy Hall. Late afternoons were spent with the two children. Francis was biddable, but she was surprised to find that she could not manage Sophia. The truth was that in tents, canvas houses, or the cramped rooms of Navy Hall, nothing could be kept from her. The two nurses were inhibited in how they corrected the children, and Elizabeth was experiencing what parents whose children were usually under foot know all too well — that three-year-olds are not reasonable, sensible human beings. Since what was not sensible and rational offended her, Elizabeth was often displeased with the child.[2]

If Colonel Simcoe was working in his study at Navy Hall, Elizabeth sometimes sat with him, listening to his problems, which were legion. He was distressed that the government would not allow him any more troops. To the south the Americans were at war with the native peoples, attempting to push them farther west to make way for white settlers. Destitute Indians arrived often at Newark and at the other British-held posts along the frontier, in need of provisions and clothing. Simcoe felt hard-pressed to find supplies to hand out. Newark was close to the end of the long line of supply that stretched back to Montreal, and nearly everything people needed, except what they could grow and make in their homes, had to be transported from that city. As yet Upper Canada did not produce a large surplus of food that could be purchased by the government, and the Indians had no means of paying for the things they needed. The once-proud natives who had brought their furs to exchange for the white man's trade goods, found that their hunting grounds had been stripped of beaver through overtrapping and the encroachment of settlers.

Their plight was partly England's fault, Simcoe maintained. Having used them as allies during the American Revolution, afterwards she abandoned them to the mercy of their enemies. Now all he could do was succour them when they came to his forts. The Americans were accusing the British of arming them, an outright falsehood. He was feeding and clothing them, but the only weapons and ammunition the Indians were receiving were for hunting game. Simcoe felt an obligation to keep them from starving and freezing to death.

Elizabeth agreed that the natives must be helped in the name of humanity, but she had doubts she did not voice. She knew how much Simcoe admired them. The Indians she had encountered thus far — Mississaugas at Kingston and around Newark — seemed a dirty, idle lot. She did not yet realise that their condition was a consequence of the presence of the white settlements, sedentary agricultural communities foreign to them. Mississaugas were hunters and gatherers of the forests whose way of life had been disrupted, and they were further demoralised by liquor.

To Elizabeth's delight, the horse she had ridden around the Long Sault Rapids on the journey inland arrived at Newark. Captain Richard Duncan had lent it for her to use. She sent seeds to Miss Burges to experiment with, and she mentioned May apples, and cotonier — wild asparagus. She thought the silky cotton from the latter plant would be fine for stuffing pillows, and hoped that Mary Anne could collect enough to fill a muff. Elizabeth listed other foods available — cherries, peaches that were small but delicious, plums and apples. Beef was scarce but there was no shortage of deer, bears, small mammals, birds, salmon, whitefish, trout and sturgeon. She longed for a bake oven like Catharine Hamilton's. At Navy Hall bread was baked on the hearth, in an iron kettle with hot ashes on the lid.

Lieutenant Talbot accompanied Colonel Butler to Buffalo Creek to distribute presents to the natives. When he returned he presented Elizabeth with a faun skin, which he had purchased from the Indians. It smelled wondrously of wood smoke, and Talbot explained that the Indians smoked the skin to cure it. She set to work at once and made herself a tippet, or shoulder cape, from the soft skin, which she had finished on 4 November. By that time Captain Stevenson had left for England, with orders to procure artillery for Upper Canada. Major Littlehales left about the same time for Philadelphia, to consult with George Hammond, the British minister.

Simcoe hoped that Hammond could arrange a peace between the Indians and the Americans. The major crossed the Niagara River and set out on the 600 mile journey.

The autumn had been lovely and mild, and by the end of November Elizabeth still did not need to heat the canvas house. They had brought dainty grates from England, suitable for coal, but not for the large wood logs that were their only fuel. Simcoe procured a stove but it had yet to be lit. She was finding whist a pleasant pastime, a game she had deplored as time-wasting when she was at Wolford Lodge. On 3 December she visited Fort Niagara to see Captain Henry Darling's collection of stuffed birds and animals, of particular interest because they were local. The meadow lark, red-winged blackbird and cardinal were all new to her. The skunk resembled a pole cat but with black and white marks. On the ninth, Captain Joseph Brant, the Mohawk war chief, dined with the Simcoes. Elizabeth thought he might be cunning:

> He wore an English Coat with a handsome Crimson Silk blanket lined with black & trimmed with gold fringe & wore a Fur Cap, round his neck he had a string of plaited sweet hay. It is a kind of grass which never loses its pleasant scent.

On the tenth, Simcoe set out with a party to walk to Burlington Bay, at the head of Lake Ontario, a distance of fifty miles. He did not return until the 17th. In the interval, Elizabeth enjoyed being on her own. Every fortnight there was a ball, but she did not attend because her baby was expected in less than two months. Elizabeth Macaulay dropped in to see her and described the latest ball. Fourteen couples attended, the room was well lit with candles, and both supper and tea were served. On 16 December, Elizabeth stayed up all night reading "Don Guevara ". (Don Antonio de Guevara, ca. 1480-1545, was a Spanish priest and courtier who created the much-copied literary style known as guevarism.) The book was likely *The Diall of Princes* (1529) in the original Spanish, or in one of its many translations. She also read the history of Prince Ctesiphon, and some pages of *Don Quixote*. Then she slept in her clothes.[3] She tried to pretend that Mary Anne Burges was there, sharing the vigil, as they had done back at Wolford Lodge.

After Simcoe returned, Elizabeth drew maps from the rough sketches of his explorations. He was competent at drawing himself, but with so many other duties demanding his attention he was happy to hand over this task to his wife. She was especially proud of a large-scale map of most of North America, but on 23 December:

> I left Trojan my Hound in my Room while I went to dinner & he tore to pieces my best Map of Canada & the United States which I had taken great pains to draw. I must paste it together again but its appearance is spoiled. The Gov. made some pretty verses on the occasion.

Once the cold weather set in, Elizabeth was taking her dinner in the mess since her chef had no proper kitchen. Simcoe's "pretty verses" have been preserved, entitled "Upon the Dog Trojan tearing the Map of N. America".[4] They run to forty-one wide-ranging lines in five stanzas. Numbers four and five will suffice; the first three have even less to do with the dog:

> Awful Omen, prodigy unknown,
> In mystic manner Provinces devours,
> Shakes to the center Pondiaus throne,
> Scatters the Mississippi in its course,
> And o'er Alleganny plays with unresisted force.

> Prototype of Albion's power,
> Trojan, born from ancient Brute
> I hail the omen of the hour
> Of bold emprize & high pursuit;
> Britons crush the frail design
> Of mean Pretenders poor in Art
> Freedom & Fame to you impart,
> The delegated Power by Heav'n designed
> To bless th' obedient World, & elevate mankind.

Having touched on Trojan, Simcoe returns to his usual theme, that the British system is the best. His sense of the patriotic, expressed in elaborate phrases, is typical of his other poems, and they are not memorable. Writing verses and passing them among themselves was a popular pastime. It was even more useful at Newark by Christmas time. The sailing vessels that brought news of the outside world were laid up in the ice at Kingston. All news was brought by runners through the woods, who, once winter truly set in, moved on snowshoes. "The Gov. will now have less to write & I hope fewer headaches," Elizabeth observed. Now that Newark was so isolated, the few men and women of the best society were probably getting on each other's nerves. The whist parties went on, and the fortnightly balls. One who was critical of Mrs. Simcoe was Hannah, the wife of the provincial secretary, William Jarvis. Hannah found Elizabeth patronising, and suggested that the governor had married her for her money, and now he suffered from petticoat rule.[5] What Elizabeth thought of Mrs. Jarvis is not known; Elizabeth tended to omit anything unpleasant from her diary.

She probably felt less stultified than other women by the smallness of her circle, for she had been confined within a select coterie of friends in Devon. A restricted number of the "best" people stuck together, attending the same parties week after week, and seeing the same faces at the Honiton assemblies. Hannah Jarvis was the daughter of a Connecticut Church of England clergyman, the Reverend Samuel Peters. Although Connecticut had its own upper crust, society was less inflexible than in Devonshire where the landed gentry were the apex. In Connecticut, wealth counted as much as land and pedigree. Hannah had belonged to the best in that society, and she was perhaps more accustomed to offending than to tolerating condescension in others.

For a time after their arrival in Newark, the chief justice, William Osgoode, lived with the Simcoes. On 31 December, Elizabeth noted that Mr. Osgoode now had his own house, but it was so close to Navy Hall that he frequently came to join them. "Coll. Simcoe finds him a very agreeable companion."

The Simcoes' seventh child was born in the canvas house at Newark on 16 January 1793, an event Elizabeth did not mention in her diary, but she informed Miss Burges and Mrs. Hunt in letters home. The child was another girl, named Katherine, after Simcoe's mother, Katherine Stamford. Elizabeth asked Mrs. Hunt to register the birth at Dunkeswell, and invited both Mrs. Hunt and Mrs. Montagu to be the baby's godmothers. Elizabeth decried the want of a wet nurse; feeding little Katherine herself never occurred to her. The canvas house had proved to be quite comfortable at the time of the birth. It had been boarded over to keep snow from lying on it, and was quieter than the rest of their home:

> Pray give my love to Miss Hunt; tell her there are as many feathers, flowers and gauze dresses at our balls (which are every fortnight) as at a Honiton Assembly, & seldom less than eighteen couples. I have not attended them because I was, the greatest part of the winter, in daily expectation of being confined.[6]

Elizabeth's sole entry for January was a lengthy account of Major Littlehales' journeys to and from Philadelphia. At that time the capital of the United States, Philadelphia was 600 miles by travelled routes from Niagara, but by the route Littlehales took, fording the Tioga River seven times and crossing a steep part of the Allegheny Mountains to the Genesee River, the distance was only 400 miles.

On 4 February, Simcoe went off on a much longer journey than the mere stroll to Burlington Bay. This time his objective was Detroit, travelling by the La Tranche River, "no European having gone that track & the Indians are to carry Provisions." Elizabeth was disappointed not to be accompanying him, but she had not recovered her strength sufficiently to attempt a winter journey. Simcoe's first stop would be the Mohawk village on the Grand River, where Captain Joseph Brant and a party of braves were to join him, serving as helpers and guides. The "Gov. wore a fur Cap tippet & Gloves & maucassins but no Great Coat. His servant carried two Blankets & linen. The other Gentlemen carried their Blankets in a pack on their Back." The other gentlemen were Major Littlehales, Lieutenant Talbot, and Lieutenant David William Smith of the 5th Regiment (a son of Major and Mrs. John Smith who had entertained the Simcoes at Fort Niagara). They were escorted by a dozen Queen's Rangers. Governor Simcoe also took with him a brace of pistols, a gift from Hugh Percy the 2nd Duke of Northumberland for Joseph Brant. His Grace, a full general in the British army, had served in North America during the Revolution, and he had also met Brant on one of the war chief's visits to England.[7]

From the Mohawk village, Simcoe sent Elizabeth a letter describing Brant's fine house. Brant's wife was tall and gracious, and their children handsome. Tea was served as if they were in England, but by two Black slaves. Brant's stature was thus diminished in Simcoe's eyes, since the governor detested slavery. What delighted Elizabeth the most was his description of the Mohawks' church, the first Protestant one built in Upper Canada. It was also an Anglican one, of the establishment. The Mohawks were much more to the governor's taste, and to his wife's, than the majority of the white settlers, who were so exasperatingly non-conformist. Simcoe was impressed at how well the Indian women sang psalms, their voices remarkably sweet.

During the governor's absence, Elizabeth found plenty to do. She drew maps, wrote, read, and did needlework. On 17 February, a Sunday, she went to dine with "some Ladies of the Queen's Rangers" at Queenston. She spent the night in the hut which Simcoe had had built, and the Marquis of Buckingham's tapestry made the room very comfortable. The next day she had tea with Mrs. Hamilton, and in the evening she gave a dance which ten couples attended. Now more recovered from the birth of Katherine, she was eager to do her share of the entertaining. On the twentieth she dined with Chief Justice Osgoode and played seven rubbers of whist. A letter from the governor the next day told her that the LaTranche River, 150 miles from its mouth, was as wide as the Thames at Reading, and he had renamed the river the Thames, in honour of the English river.

The coldest day Elizabeth had ever known was 27 February 1793. The thermometer registered fifty-five degrees inside Mr. Osgoode's house, yet the stove was red hot. The snow still fell as March arrived, and the ice in the Niagara River was piling up in a great jam. On Saturday the ninth, in the afternoon, it began to break apart and float downstream. A boat came across from Fort Niagara, and the crew placed oars over the ice close to the water's edge, and stepped on the oars. Thus they were in less danger of falling through than if they stepped directly on the soft ice. Only one did fall, and he was soon rescued. As in Quebec, early spring was a time of boredom. Getting about was again difficult when the snow was melting.

Simcoe, accompanied by Lieutenant David William Smith, arrived at Newark on Sunday 10 March. He looked remarkably fit, better than at any time since the family had reached Quebec. His party had travelled 600 miles. Part of the way had been by sleigh, but more often the men were on foot or snowshoes. Life in the woods truly agreed with Simcoe. If he had not been missing Elizabeth, he believed, everything would have been perfect. The next time he was determined to take her with him. He had sketched many maps which she was eager to redraw for him.

She was startled when he said he would arrange for tools and seeds to be sent to the Moravian village in time for planting. Hitherto he had disapproved of those non-conformist missionaries, but he now thought them fine men, doing good work among the Delaware Indians who had sought refuge during the revolution. The Indians had fed Simcoe's party and let them sleep in their houses. They were squatters, and they merited a grant of 5,000 acres. He also wanted to encourage as many settlers as he could to come to Upper Canada, no matter what their religion or country of origin, to fill up the empty lands. Simcoe thought this was the only way of ensuring that the province would not be absorbed into the United States. Elizabeth found his thinking inconsistent, pondering how Americans could be trusted to be loyal, but the governor was complacent. Those who came would speedily recognise the superiority of the Upper Canadian constitution. He would have preferred English men and women, but he could not wait until emigration schemes had been worked out. In time, he hoped that most of the settlers would be from England, but until that time he had to trust the good will of the Americans.

In her diary to Mrs. Hunt, Elizabeth put down what she thought would interest the four girls. She told them the governor had been absent exactly five weeks. He had spent only four days at Detroit, and when he was leaving, the government ships in the harbour fired a salute. Simcoe had ordered prayers to be read in the woods on the Sunday of his visit, and forty people attended. The garrison at Detroit was the 24th Foot, and the commandant of the fort was Lieutenant-Colonel Richard G. England, of that regiment. The prayers Simcoe ordered were for civilians since the troops had their own chaplain. The turnout was small because most people were French-speaking and Roman Catholic.

His Excellency had eaten racoons, which he found rather like pork and quite tasty. However, Jack Sharp, their Newfoundland dog, had a nasty brush with a porcupine. The long, barbed quills which adhered to his neck when he attacked the slow-moving creature proved difficult to remove, and the dog was ill for some days afterwards. A party of Indians who preceded Simcoe and his officers had built shelters of bark and boughs each day, and when the governor's party stopped at five o'clock each evening, a meal was cooked and ready. After supper the officers sang "God Save the King" before settling down to sleep, their feet close to a roaring fire. Best of all, Simcoe's expectations for the site of his capital were confirmed. The forks of the Thames River would make the perfect spot.

The land along the banks of the Thames was excellent. There was a fine plain at the forks, dry and without underbrush, which abounded in oak trees. He would call the capital New London. Not far off was a spring of petroleum which they found because of its offensive odour. Elizabeth had heard of petroleum from Mary Anne Burges, who thought it might be useful some day. Altogether this was a wonderfully rich land that had everything. Even if man did not find a use for petroleum, the many waterfalls would provide power for mills of all sorts. Caught up in his enthusiasm, Elizabeth longed to stay. If they could have had a fine house and tutors for the girls, she would have wanted to see all the marvellous changes taking place. Within three days of his return the pressures on Simcoe were again affecting his health, and he had gout in one of his hands. He was anxious to begin work on the new capital, because Niagara might soon be handed over to the Americans. In that event Newark would be directly under the fort's guns and a tempting target. Britain and France were on the verge of war. If the Americans should ally themselves with the French, or simply declare war on their own account, they could destroy Newark within hours.

Simcoe sent John Scadding and the deputy surveyor, Augustus Jones, to the forks of the Thames, to explore the site for the capital more thoroughly. He longed to see a city growing there, but of greater importance was a safe naval base on Lake Ontario. He planned to take a party himself to explore the Toronto Carrying Place, which, he had heard, had a fine harbour. If he did not take Elizabeth on the first journey there, he promised she would accompany him the on the next one. He was also frustrated because he had asked that a surveyor general be appointed for Upper Canada, but the Colonial Office decided that Surveyor General Samuel Holland would serve for both provinces without extra pay. Elizabeth sympathised, for Major Holland was old, hardly fit to keep abreast of Lower Canada alone. Early April was hot, and Elizabeth moved with the nurses and children to the hut above Queenston. The Queen's Rangers' mess supplied the meals. After dinner, an officer escorted everyone back to the hut, and the band played until six o'clock. "Music adds chearfulness to this retired spot & we feel much indebted to the Marquis of Buckingham," she wrote on 3 April.[8] Two days later she recorded the demise of Trojan, the hound who had chewed up her map. With the thermometer registering 78 degrees in the shade and 112 in the sun, the dog became ill. One of the soldiers mistook his condition for rabies and shot him. The children were distraught and Elizabeth was angry. Trojan was not mad, for he had the good sense to run into the water to cool himself off shortly before he was killed.

On 10 April it snowed and they returned to Navy Hall. On the eighteenth, Captain Aeneas Shaw, who had marched from New Brunswick on snow shoes to Quebec City in the spring of 1792, came to Newark with his wife and seven children. The family had travelled through the United States by boat to Oswego, where the captain joined them for the winter. An Indian had accompanied Mrs. Shaw and the children, and had helped them build huts and shoot partridges and ducks. Shaw gave Elizabeth a tea chest of bird's eye maple from New Brunswick that was the colour of satinwood.

She was enjoying daily rides now that the country had dried out after the spring thaws. A favourite was to the whirlpool below Niagara Falls. On 2 May, Simcoe left in a bateau with seven officers for Toronto and was absent until the thirteenth. Elizabeth borrowed Sir J. Reynold's *Discourses*, which she found amusing, and she wrote replies to the letters she received and took note of the news. To Mary Anne Burges, who had enquired, she explained that the correct pronunciation for Niagara was Niágara.

On 19 April, Elizabeth had replied to a letter from Miss Hunt, expressing concern over a report on Eliza's French. She had written the child giving her advice on how to improve her vocabulary, surprised that she disliked speaking the language. Elizabeth was also surprised to learn that the girls sang well, for she had no notion that they could, or that Eliza could be persuaded to try — a hint that Elizabeth was not particularly musical herself.[9]

She soon learned of other developments at Wolford Lodge. Mary Anne reported that Mrs. Graves planned to move out and take away her furniture and an Axminster carpet. Elizabeth's aunt was having a house built for herself on Lansdown Crescent in Bath. Miss Burges wondered whether the Simcoes might feel that keeping Wolford Lodge open without Mrs. Graves' support was too costly. If they wanted to put a tenant in it, the girls, the Hunts and a servant could stay at Tracey until the Simcoes returned from Canada.[10]

Chapter 10

MISS BURGES REPORTS

1792~1793

Mrs. Graves actually moved out of Wolford Lodge in November 1792, news contained in a letter by Mrs. Hunt that did not reach Elizabeth Simcoe until early in March. Elizabeth admitted she was not surprised. She asked the Hunts to remain at Wolford Lodge, for neither she nor Colonel Simcoe wanted the girls moved. The colonel had requested Mr. C. Flood, his bookkeeper, to purchase a second-hand carriage for the use of the Hunts and the children, so that they would be less isolated. The Hunts were not to skimp with fires, but to keep everyone in comfort. She wanted the girls to see Miss Burges often, but not to move to Tracey, although the offer had been kind. The Simcoes did not need to economise by renting out Wolford Lodge.[1]

By July 1792, Mary Anne was becoming interested in the teachings of the late John Wesley, while she continued attending Awliscombe parish church regularly. Although still part of the Church of England, the Methodists had a chapel in Honiton, and she had become friendly with the preacher, a Mr. Haynes, and his wife. The Wesleyans had a strong following in the West Country, but unlike Mary Anne, Elizabeth never joined them. After her return to England, she was suspicious that the Methodists might cause a schism in the established church.

Mary Anne reported on the antics of Richard Graves, who had been named a second for a duel, but fortunately it was called off. Richard, the agitator, had called a meeting of farmers to petition Parliament to abolish tithes, but less than 100 signed. He was spreading word that Colonel Simcoe's measures in Upper Canada were being "overthrown". Mary Anne added, "the idea of a rebellion in a Country before it is inhabited is certainly extremely brilliant & worthy of Capt. Graves."[2]

She was delighted with a box that arrived from Canada, containing a book of drawings belonging to Colonel Simcoe and some of Elizabeth's maps. The girls were at Tracey reading their letters. Eliza was wondering what part of her letter Elizabeth had touched so she could kiss it. Harriet was found sitting quietly in a corner, learning Mama's letter by heart. Eliza and Charlotte were upset because they had not thought of it first. All were happy to hear that Francis had recovered from his smallpox inoculation. Mrs. Graves was as disapproving over it as over Caroline's. Inoculation at that time carried considerable risk. Scrapings from smallpox victims were used, in the hope that a mild case would result. Too often the patient developed a severe case and died. (Edward Jenner did not inoculate his first patient with puss taken from a lesion on a milkmaid with cowpox until 1796.)

The girls, Mary Anne reported, had all "left off crying over lessons unless they have done them badly." Eliza's only affliction was Mrs. Graves' attitude towards Elizabeth. Mrs. Hunt felt that too much bending over the girls' desks was bad for their posture. Miss Burges had listened to many arguments over how long the girls should draw, and at what time of day. She asked Elizabeth to decide.

Of the marriage of Miss Peggy Putt, Eliza said, "it was wrong of her to marry before her two elder sisters."

"It's like Harriet marrying before you and me," Charlotte added. "And that would not look well at all."

Mrs. Montagu was still at Wolford, and Miss Burges hoped she would stay much longer as she was a peace maker. Mrs. Graves was furious that there was no letter for her in the box, though she had not written at all. Elizabeth's shoes had arrived from Exeter, and would be sent on whenever someone was going to Canada. Her reports on mosquitoes suggested that they were no worse than "Harvest Bugs" in Devon that were tormenting Miss Burges as September began. She went to Fitzhead to visit her aunt, Mrs. Somerville. When she returned she stopped at Wolford Lodge but could not stay since the place was full of guests. Elizabeth's distant cousin, William Walcot, from Oundle, in Northamptonshire, was among them, to the delight of the children. He loved playing with them.

On 26 September 1792, Mary Anne noted that it was the first anniversary of the departure of the Simcoes for Canada. She went to Wolford Lodge, without an invitation, which put Mrs. Graves in a temper. By now Mary Anne was used to her "caprices" and admitted she rather enjoyed the fuss. Mrs. Graves planned to take to Bath every piece of furniture she owned, except a clock Colonel Simcoe had given her, and she hoped to "get Eliza to herself". She had taken a dislike to Charlotte and Harriet. She had told Mr. Walcot that the children's health was neglected, which was not true. She claimed that she was only taking the furniture away to preserve it from being spoiled, and after her death Elizabeth could have it back. The only expense would be for a cart.

"What!" Caroline exclaimed on seeing so many of Mrs. Graves' packages. "All these things to go to Bath? I suppose they will cut down the house next and carry that away."[3]

Mrs. Graves had destroyed her will after the Simcoes left for Canada, and made a new one leaving everything to Eliza. Then in the summer she became ill and Mrs. Montagu and Miss Burges urged her to make another in favour of the Simcoes before it was too late. Now she had done so, and Mrs. Hunt had witnessed it. She was leaving her books to Colonel Simcoe, some trinkets to Eliza, and everything else to Elizabeth except £100 for the servants. Miss Burges wondered whether Richard or Thomas Graves could lay claim to any of Mrs. Graves' estate.[4]

By 1 October Miss Burges was again at Fitzhead, resolved to stay until Mrs. Graves had left Wolford Lodge. Her aunt had given birth to a daughter on 28 August and was feeling much better. On the fifteenth Mary Anne attended the christening of Julia Valenza Somerville, her first cousin. (Julia would become the wife of Sir Francis Bond Head, Upper Canada's sixth lieutenant governor. He was the son of James Roper Head and Mary Anne's sister.)

Early in November she was back at Tracey. Letters arrived from Upper Canada on the ninth and twentieth. Eliza was much affected by hers, reading the end first, then the middle, and lastly the beginning, after which she went off by herself. Charlotte "jumped for joy at every word".

Mary Anne was delighted with the installment of the diary that made Upper Canada seem so real. Reading it was almost like having a conversation with her friend. Elizabeth's travels in Canada were more "gratifying" than anything in England or Europe. Miss Burges was impressed that her friend found satisfaction in accustoming herself to hardships. She was trying to identify a flower and a butterfly which Elizabeth had sketched for her.

After she left Fitzhead, a Miss Digby came to stay at Tracey. She was a sister of Mary Anne's aunt by marriage, Mary Digby Somerville. The Digby family home was at Meriden, Warwickshire, on the main road that led from Birmingham to Coventry, where Miss Digby lived with her two brothers. Mary Anne referred to them as Mr. Digby and Mr. Kenelm Digby. Miss Digby went with Miss Burges to inspect a school in Honiton that was kept by the Wesleyan preacher, Mr. Haynes, because Mrs. Somerville was thinking of sending one of her boys there. When they arrived, Miss Burges was "seized by an unreasonable panic" and could not speak. They had to leave without obtaining the information they sought. Later they went to see the monument erected to Admiral Graves at Buckerell Church. Considering what it cost, Miss Burges was not impressed by it.[5]

The offer to have the children and the Hunts at Tracey still stood, and Miss Burges was waiting for a reply from Elizabeth, or if the Simcoes wanted the girls to move to Canada, she would be glad to escort them, but she would not expect to stay with them once they arrived. She was pleased that the stream of letters showed no sign of slowing down. When a dear friend moved away, letters tended to be frequent at first, but to be less so as one made new friends. Elizabeth, however, was not like that. Mary Anne wondered if there were any females in Upper Canada "with marks of civility". Men were found there, but women? At least neither Elizabeth nor Colonel Simcoe had been swallowed by serpents as yet. She was delighted with the sketch of Niagara — "Should I write Niàgara or Niagàra?"

She was sorry Elizabeth was finding Sophia so "tiresome", and was surprised that any child of her friend's could be so disagreeable: "but that is her age when all children are so self-willed & unpleasant....Most children make a struggle for independence but when they find they must submit do so with a good grace & the trouble is over". The day would come when Mary Anne could use her own advice.

She was intrigued to find that Elizabeth was often having similar experiences. We "are as scorched in England at the same time as at Niagara". Thus far, most of her news concerned doings at home, but she was expecting to spend part of the winter in London, and would write a packet on politics at that time. She was about to sell some stories, which would earn her the extra money she needed. Mrs. Hunt was enjoying herself much more now that Mrs. Graves had left Wolford. That lady was affronted with Mrs. Hunt for refusing to send one of the Simcoes' beds to Bath. One friend claimed that Mrs. Graves would like no one but the Empress of Russia, and if she died, Mrs. Graves would succeed her and no one would notice the difference. The girls were well, but Charlotte was high spirited and in disgrace more often than the others. Yet she was never depressed for long when corrected.[6] Mary Anne had received Elizabeth's map, and was pleased that Simcoe had named a lake after the family. So many of the place names in Upper Canada were hard to pronounce and sounded uncouth.

Miss Burges journeyed to London between 9 and 28 January, accompanied part of the way by their mutual friends Misses Frances Anne and Mary Elliot, whose father was an admiral in the Royal Navy, and whose home was in Colchester. Along the way she passed on bits of gossip. At a party an intoxicated Prince of Wales was given a "good reproof" by a French lady. *"Prince ce sont vos manières que font les Democrats."* At a meeting of the Je ne sais quoi Club, the Prince of Wales voted to remove Philip Duc d'Orleans' name from the list of members. Mary Anne reached London and was at Drury Lane when she heard of the execution, on 21 January, of the King of France. At all fashionable entertainments, the "central monument" was a guillotine with a "cut off head of a paste figure below it, and the head filled with sugar plums etc." On 1 February 1793, threat became reality. France declared war on the Dutch Republic and on Britain. Suddenly republican ideas were extremely unpopular, and Thomas and Richard Graves had been very quiet of late.

After pondering over an invitation to visit the Heads at Hermitage, which was near Rochester, Mary Anne decided to accept it. James Roper Head was indignant over the conduct of the French, but otherwise tried to be polite. Her sister's children she found not overly handsome, but they were almost as well-behaved as the Simcoe girls. These children were George (born in 1782), Mary (1787), Frances (1788), Hugh (1789), and James (1790). (The Heads had lost three children in infancy. Francis Bond was born later in 1793, followed by Henry in 1794 and Sophia in 1796.)[7] Miss Burges thought that George showed promise, but all the children had "those frightful brown teeth" which disfigured them. They had been taking French two years longer than Eliza and Charlotte, who were far ahead of them. The Simcoe girls were lucky, Mary Anne noted, to have such white, strong teeth.

She recounted a visit to Chatham, nearby, where she saw the 74-gun *Thunderer*. False reports circulated that the French had landed in Romney Marsh and were stealing sheep. One French general boasted that he would be in Amsterdam by 17 March, and would plant trees of liberty in London on 4 June (the King's birthday) and send Pitt to the Tower. He would stand a better chance of lodging there himself, Mary Anne wrote.

In London, she rented the second floor of a house in Brook Street, at one guinea per week, rather than stay with her brother, James Bland Burges. She was not certain that her sister-in-law liked her. She passed on Miss Hunt's explanation for the French being called *Sans Culottes*, because they wore nothing but shirts on which they pinned cockades. Many refugees were flocking to England, and her brother was giving what succour he could. Now that she had lost weight and was as slim as Elizabeth, Mary Anne was dismayed by the latest fashions — gowns so high-waisted that every woman looked as though she was within a week of "lying in". In fact, petticoats hung so badly that Lady Charlotte Campbell wore a cushion to make her look sufficiently big. She enclosed a sketch of a woman in what would later be known as the Regency style, topped by a turban that was *de rigeur*. Although Mary Anne promised plenty of local prattle, she also reported that Mrs. Graves was said to have gone to Bath to find a husband. Elizabeth's aunt was also the butt of much gossip in London. Mrs. Montagu was being blamed for setting Mrs. Graves against her niece and causing the quarrel with the Hunts. Miss Burges denied that Mrs. Montagu had had anything to do with Mrs. Graves' conduct.

On 25 February 1793, Mary Anne went to the office of the secretary of state to view the departure of troops for the Netherlands. She breakfasted with her brother and other public officials at 7.00 a.m. Soon the King rode by, followed by his sons. The Prince of Wales looked "knightly" on a white horse, the gift of the King of Prussia. His Light Horse regimentals were blue with yellow accoutrements, and he wore a high cap with a white feather. The Duke of York was on a grey horse; the Duke of Gloucester's son Prince William rode astride his father's saddle bow — a pretty little figure in blue regimentals with a white feather. The Duke of Clarence, who had recently broken his arm, rode in a coach and six. The parade set out for Greenwich, where the Duke of York would embark with the troops. Prince Ernest left to take command of a Hanoverian regiment. The Queen and princesses also went to Greenwich, where Princess Elizabeth cried violently.

When Mary Anne shopped for books she was drawn to Simcoe's bookshop by the name. How pleasant it was to talk with Mr. Simcoe, although he was not closely related. He kindly agreed to deliver the books she purchased in person. She suspected a lady in the shop was Mrs. Simcoe but was too shy to ask. Mary Anne was enjoying London, but the friendliest people she met were from Devon. She was glad she had decided to make her home there.

She wondered what Elizabeth needed which she could obtain while in town. Caps were all ugly, but Elizabeth would not be obliged to wear one in Canada as she would be here. Mary Anne made two copies of a hat she admired at the Duchess of York's milliner's, one for each of them. She chose "black mode" for Elizabeth's hat, knowing that Colonel Simcoe liked black bonnets. She remembered how she and Elizabeth always liked having the same bonnets. She also bought a length of blue and white calico for a gown, and a length of the same for Elizabeth. If her friend did not like the pattern, she could make something for Sophia. Mary Anne made her a handkerchief cap, on which Elizabeth's paradise feather would look right. She would soon send a box, but was vexed that the children's drawings were stained.

They had been washed with milk so that they would not rub off, but the result was unsatisfactory. She was adding a sketch she had made of the new road to Honiton.

On 12 March, Mary Anne plucked up her courage and had a tooth drawn. It was not aching, but she thought it would give her trouble soon. She went alone to the dentist, and behaved, she hoped, as she would if she were going to have her head cut off. She could not banish the image of French aristocrat ladies mounting the steps to *Madame la Guillotine*.

Lord Somerville was being kinder to her than ever before, and had even lent her his carriage. (This was James, the 13th Lord Somerville, a bachelor and the elder brother of Hugh Somerville of Fitzhead; both were Miss Burges' uncles.) His Lordship accompanied her to her brother's, where the talk was of 10,000 French being killed by the Prince of Saxe-Cobourg's army. When she went to Billingsgate to buy a fish for herself, ladies were filling baskets to donate to impoverished priests from France. After a month she was ready to return to Devon, but because she had given Lord Somerville £12 for indigent old ladies, she was short of money. With much embarrassment she went to see her brother, who lent her a few pounds for her journey.[8]

By 23 March Mary Anne was home at Tracey House. After church the following Sunday she went to Wolford Lodge, remaining until the twenty-seventh because of cold and snow, the worst weather of the winter. The Simcoe girls seemed wonderful after the other children Miss Burges had seen. Harriet had had three teeth drawn, to make way for permanent teeth that were growing in above them. Eliza was copying Elizabeth's map, so that she would be helpful to Papa when he returned.[9] The girls enjoyed acting out various characters. Eliza's favourite was Minerva; Caroline's was Jupiter. Miss Hunt was planning a holiday in Bath. The waist of her gown was about a yard lower than that worn in London. Captain Richard Graves was upset because the Admiralty would not give him command of a ship. Nor was he successful in arranging to emigrate to the Carolinas, where his father-in-law was one of the Lords Proprietor. To add to his irritation, Mrs. Margaret Graves was refusing to pay for the education of Richard's son Samuel, who had been named in honour of the admiral.

Mrs. Graves had invited Eliza to stay with her in Bath. In a letter dated 13 March 1793, Elizabeth informed Mrs. Hunt that the Simcoes did not want Eliza staying more than six weeks, or her education would be neglected, but the family did not yet know of her orders.[10] At Wolford Lodge, Miss Hunt agreed to escort Eliza, and Mrs. Graves was suggesting they come by public coach. Miss Burges was horrified at such an unsuitable arrangement. In the end they left in a hired chaise on 16 April.

She had sown some seed which Elizabeth had sent her, but she was not sending to Canada any of the seeds she had received from Botany Bay, since they did not look healthy. A drawing of Gananoque (on the St. Lawrence River) she thought very good, although Elizabeth had written that she was not satisfied with it. Mary Anne especially liked the notes and illustrations

Colonel Simcoe had added. Now that Eliza was away, Charlotte was "putting herself forward". She relayed other conversations the girls had had, showing their efforts not to forget Mama. They "talk about you & quote your expressions." Mrs. Hunt said, "Pooh," to some scheme they were devising.

"I daresay," said Harriet, "if it had been Mama, she would have said, 'Pooh, pooh, a pack of nonsense' for I remember that was what she used to say."

Caroline pretended she remembered her parents, although she was so young when they left. To test her, Miss Burges asked her if Colonel Simcoe was a little, short man. She replied, "No, a great, a very great man indeed."

"And what was Mama?" Miss Burges asked her.

"Oh, Mama was a little man."

At that Mary Anne could not suppress a laugh, and Caroline was affronted. Later she said that Mama wore a coat just like Miss Burges'. After much discussion, Charlotte and Harriet allotted the new baby in Canada to Caroline, "who is more vain on the occasion than you can imagine." Charlotte chose some of her possessions to give the baby, and when Harriet said she would give the new sister things from her garden, Caroline curtseyed to her.

"Thank you, Harriet, for making presents to my child Katherine."[11]

The war with France was causing inflation, and Miss Burges was worried over how she would meet her expenses. She had visited the Thomas Graveses, at their home, Woodbine Hill, where the captain quizzed her on the London political scene. The scandalous stories about the Royal family horrified both the Graveses. Gossips in Honiton were saying Mrs. Margaret Graves kept a Mr. Lathy hidden in her house at Bath, where, incidently, Eliza was still staying. Miss Hunt wrote early in June that the child had grown fat, a proof that she was well, but she was also "learning to be idle". Mrs. Graves was attending card parties every night, though she had deplored them as a waste of time when she was at Wolford Lodge.

Mary Anne had been embroidering some "trimming" to send Elizabeth in her next box, "for your royal habiliments as Sovereign Lady of Upper Canada".[12] She was sending a sonnet to a goldfinch, which she had composed in Spanish, and some translations of Cicero. Edward Drewe, who was going to London to be married shortly, would take the box and find someone to carry it to Canada, to avoid heavy postal charges.

Mrs. Mary Drewe, the widow of Francis Drewe of Grange, near Wolford Lodge, was a close friend of the Simcoes. Colonel Simcoe had arranged for her son Edward, to be appointed the chaplain to the garrison of Upper Canada. Edward never went to Upper Canada, and he apparently regarded the modest salary of £115. 5. 0 per annum as a sinecure. Miss Burges also mentioned the Herman Drewes, who lived in the neighbourhood, and Mr. Richard Drewe. Herman and Richard were Edward's older half-brothers, stepsons of Mrs. Mary Drewe. (Edward married Caroline Cresseley on 1 June 1793, at St. Anne's, Soho.)[13]

By 2 June Mary Anne was at Fitzhead with the Somervilles. On the fifth she received more of Elizabeth's letters, and learned of her all-night vigil in the canvas house. She would hold her own vigil when she returned to Tracey. At Fitzhead, her room was uncomfortable, with a "superabundance of fleas".

She trusted that little Katherine would thrive, and she recalled how "despairing" Colonel Simcoe was during each of Elizabeth's confinements. "Tell me what she is like & how she gets on because I consider her a dear future friend." She congratulated Elizabeth on her new accomplishment of whist playing, and hoped that this did not imply a "changed character". Things were going well at Wolford Lodge. When Mrs. Graves first announced that she was leaving, she caused much confusion, but now everything had settled down. When she wrote this letter, on 5 June, she still had not heard whether Elizabeth would accept her offer to have the girls at Tracey. Elizabeth's reply arrived on 13 June, explaining that Mrs. Hunt was now reconciled to staying at Wolford Lodge. Mary Anne assured Elizabeth that should anything happen to Mrs. Hunt, she would care for the girls as though they were her own nearest relations. She hoped that Elizabeth's message would hasten Eliza's return from Bath, where she had now been two months.

Mrs. Graves' attitude towards the Simcoes had softened, and under pressure from Mrs. Gwillim, she had replied to one of Elizabeth's letters. Mr. Walcot had upset Aunt Margaret by telling her of a report, in cypher, of a plot against Colonel Simcoe's life. Mary Anne was translating passages of Cicero, which she would send, since Elizabeth would not bother to read Cicero in the original. By 15 July, she had fulfilled the promise she made herself while at Fitzhead, for she had had stayed up all night reading German and Don Antonio de Guevara's works.

When out on a walk, the now nearly five-year-old Caroline stopped before a pond on the estate. "I wonder how Papa and Mama could get over all this water!"

Mary Anne was puzzled, until she realised that this was the largest body of water Caroline could remember seeing. By 26 July, Eliza had returned home, escorted by Miss Hunt. Mary Anne thought Eliza less shy, which was beneficial. Miss Hunt was feeling cool towards Mrs. Graves, because although she had given Eliza regular French lessons, Elizabeth's aunt had wanted to place her in a day school to improve her French. Eliza said most of Mrs. Graves' guests were Irish, not the most fashionable people in Bath. Eliza was still very sensitive. When Mrs. Hunt ordered Charlotte to apologise to her elder sister for some offence, Eliza wept, although she no longer cried on all occasions as she used to.

In August, Mary Anne took care of four of the Somerville children while her aunt and uncle were away, and was glad to see the last of them. They had used her books roughly, and pulled paper off the wall of the best bedchamber. If only all children were as well-behaved as the Simcoe girls![4] By November, Mary Anne was reporting on how well the four of them danced.

Astonishingly, Eliza was not afraid of performing before strangers, and she did not mind being watched. Mary Anne thought Charlotte the most like Colonel Simcoe, while Eliza and Caroline resembled Elizabeth. She reported on the girls' progress in reading and arithmetic, but she disliked the way Mrs. Hunt insisted on their reading poetry—pausing after every word.

The record of events preserved in the Devon Record Office stops with Mary Anne Burges' letter of 15 November 1793 and does not resume until 2 September 1795 . The originals for the missing pages are in the Ontario Archives. The Ontario collection may have been left in Canada when the Simcoes went home, and acquired by the Archives at a later date.[15]

Chapter 11

THE MOVE TO YORK
1793~1794

On 13 May 1793, Elizabeth wrote to Mary Anne Burges:

> Coll. Simcoe returned from Toronto & speaks in praise of
> the harbour & a fine spot near it covered with large Oak
> which he intends to fix upon as a site for a Town. I am going
> to send you some beautiful Butterflies.

At that time the situation at Newark was tense as the possibility of war with
the United States loomed large. A quick conquest of Canada, many Americans believed, could bring Indian resistance in the northwest to a halt.
Elizabeth was fearful, and Simcoe felt helpless because of his lack of
weapons and troops. He was eager to start work on a fortified naval
dockyard at Toronto, but could not leave until the next session of the
legislature was over. A further interruption was caused by negotiations
between the Indians and the United States government that were to begin
at Newark. Simcoe was appalled to discover that the Americans harboured
such hatred of the British and would never accept them as mediators with
the Indians. For security, he wanted an Indian buffer state between his
domain and the United States.

The day following Simcoe's return from Toronto, three Americans
arrived at Newark, commissioners to treat with the Indians of the interior.
They were General Benjamin Lincoln of the United States Army, John
Randolph, a gentleman from Virginia, and the Postmaster General Thomas
Pickering. "Coll. Simcoe calls the latter my cousin, his ancestors left England
in Charles the Ist's Reign & this Gentleman really bears great resemblance
to the picture Mrs. Gwillim has of Sir Gilbert Pickering".[1]

Sir Gilbert was Elizabeth's great great great grandfather, from whom
both her parents descended.[2] At the time the commissioners arrived,
Elizabeth was suffering from a severe cold and the "ague" that was the
cause of many complaints. The fever was a form of malaria contracted from
local mosquitoes, thought to have been infected initially by British troops
who had served in India and had carried the disease to North America. To
make room for the commissioners at Navy Hall, Elizabeth gratefully
accepted an offer from Anne, the wife of Lieutenant David William Smith,
to stay with her at Fort Niagara until she was well. The children and their
nurses would also be welcome.

Thus Simcoe's family was absent when the members of the legislature
assembled in late May for the 1793 session, which began with due pomp. On

4 June, the King's birthday, Simcoe held a levee at eleven o'clock in the morning, and General Lincoln left a lengthy account of the ceremony. In the evening the governor staged a splendid ball with "two of his family" in attendance, presumably Sophia and Francis. Lincoln remarked on the presence of several daughters of Sir William Johnson and Molly Brant, Chief Joseph Brant's sister. While "from the aborigines of the country" they "appeared as well dressed as the company in general". Their dignity impressed Lincoln.[3]

Of the same occasion, Hannah Jarvis wrote, "Mrs. Simcoe being ill Mrs. Hamilton was Lady President — Mrs. Secretary [Jarvis] second in command". She noted caustically that this was the first assembly she had attended in "this country" that was opened with a minuet. As Mrs. Hamilton did not want to dance it, Hannah led off, but no one else joined in until country dances began. Some twenty couples were present.[4]

To Elizabeth's annoyance, the American commissioners were still at Navy Hall when she returned, much recovered, with the children on 14 June. Both the Simcoes resented having to accommodate the Americans, who were waiting for instructions from President Washington in Philadelphia. Nor could they leave until the various tribes had assembled at Sandusky, in the Ohio country. Meanwhile, they held talks with Joseph Brant at Newark. Not until 26 June did the commissioners take their leave. Lieutenant Talbot went ahead of them to carry papers to Colonel Alexander McKee of the Indian Department, whose quarters were at Detroit. Before he left, Thomas Pickering gave Elizabeth a recipe she appreciated, for a chowder of salmon, sea biscuit and pork.

On 26 June, the family dined alone for the first time since leaving Quebec. They crossed the river to drink tea at a spot with a fine view of Navy Hall, and enjoyed the "half holiday amazingly."[5]

"How glad I am to be rid of them," Simcoe said. "General Lincoln was civil enough, but Mr. Randolph is a Virginia rake, and Mr. Pickering is a low, violent, cunning New Englander."

Elizabeth pretended horror, at Simcoe's suggestion that he resembled Sir Gilbert. Mr. Pickering argued that the colonies had a right to become independent, just as children grow up. Simcoe said "I countered, what if General Mad Anthony Wayne set up an independent nation on the banks of the Ohio? To that he retorted, 'Oh, no, Wayne is too unpopular.'"

The heat descended again, and Elizabeth decided to make camp on the mountain, which would be cooler than Navy Hall or even the hut overlooking Queenston. In the sticky heat, Francis was ill and she was anxious about him. On 5 July, with Francis and Sophia, she left in a gunboat up the Niagara River. She did not say where Baby Katherine was at that time. Their escort was Ensign William Mayne of the Rangers, in the absence of Lieutenant Talbot. They made poor headway against the strong current which still had much momentum from the Falls. The gunboat lacked topsails, which might have caught the breeze above the sides of the gorge, and some soldiers rowed them the last three miles in a small boat. Everyone was exhausted after climbing the mountain, where the governor joined them for supper. Not having remembered a mosquito net, Elizabeth spent a miserable night.

The session of the legislature ended on 9 July. Both legislators and governor were exultant. Simcoe wanted to abolish slavery in Upper Canada, to which many of the elected representatives objected. Some were slave owners, while the others were sympathetic because of the severe shortage of labour. With nearly every settler a Loyalist, entitled to a free grant of land, hiring anyone was nearly impossible. All the legislators wanted town meetings. Simcoe disapproved, because these smacked of democracy. As a compromise, he permitted a limited form of town meeting, in return for phasing out slavery.

The district magistrates to were empowered to call meetings, despite his fear that he had given in to Yankees who wanted to elect all officials, but the legislators also passed a law forbidding any more slaves being brought into the province. All children born to slaves from then on would be free at age twenty-five, and their children free from birth. In a generation Upper Canada would no longer be besmirched by this barbaric system. Elizabeth was as pleased as he, for she agreed with the opinions of William Wilberforce and other abolitionists. Now that the session of the legislature was over, she was eager to leave for the Toronto Carrying Place without delay. Simcoe promised they would go as soon as the councils at Sandusky were over.

That evening, Mrs. Catharine Hamilton and her sister, Madeleine Richardson, came to visit the camp. Madeleine's husband was Dr. Robert Richardson, a surgeon's mate in the Queen's Rangers. A violent thunderstorm arose, and the women ran to the tent. An oak tree close to the "Arbour was much blasted by the lightning". Mrs. Hamilton took Francis home for the night, lest he catch cold in the damp tent. Later Elizabeth joined them, but she did not say whether Sophia or any nurses and servants slept at the Hamilton house. When Elizabeth returned to the camp, Francis remained at the Hamiltons' for he did develop a cold.

Seven of the nations of Canadian Indians set out from Newark to the conference at Sandusky, accompanied by Lieutenant Talbot. They were going to show solidarity with their brethren in the United States, whose lands were threatened. During Talbot's absence, Ensign Mayne continued helping Elizabeth. On 16 July, Mayne drove her to Navy Hall in a new conveyance — a gig the Simcoes had had made, to which the two horses were hitched tandem so that it did not need a wide road. It was so light that they covered the seven miles from the spot below the camp in three quarters of an hour. Two days later they returned again to the camp, and that evening rode to an inn kept by Mrs. Gilbert Tice, whose husband, until his death in 1791, had been a captain in the Indian Department. Mrs. Tice was of a New York Dutch family, the former Christian Van Slyke. The Tice house was three miles from the camp, "a pleasant situation like some in Epping Forest".[6]

They remained at the camp, the governor coming when he could spare the time. On 20 July, the first contingent of Queen's Rangers — 100 men commanded by Captain Shaw — left Newark to begin work on the new naval base at Toronto. On 22 July, the Simcoes crossed the river "to the Ferry House opposite Queenston" where an arbour was pleasantly cool. Simcoe sent for his writing box and they spent the whole day there. Meanwhile, Francis remained at the Hamiltons', and was much better but still weak. Elizabeth visited him each day, though she did not stay there since she did not want to impose. On the twenty-fifth she received word that the ship *Onondaga*, under Captain Joseph Bouchette, was at Newark waiting to take the Simcoes to Toronto. After claiming Francis from the Hamiltons she returned to Newark to prepare. They were to sail at first light on the twenty-ninth, but the wind shifted. Instead, they accepted an invitation to dine with Chief Justice Osgoode. Afterwards, as they were out walking at nine o'clock, the wind changed again, and they embarked as the band of the Queen's Rangers played on board.

Elizabeth was exhausted, especially by the heat, which was still overwhelming. On the lake the air was cool and she slept until eight o'clock on the morning of the 30 July, and woke to find herself in Toronto harbour. The ship had arrived during darkness, and Captain Bouchette had waited for the principal local resident, Jean Baptiste Rousseau, to come aboard as the pilot. A long, low curving sandspit protected the harbour, and access was by way of a narrow gap at the western end. Even there the water was shallow. Rousseau, a fur trader, had guided the *Onondaga* carefully along the deepest part of the entrance. Elizabeth could see the tents of the Queen's Rangers in a clearing. (The sandspit of 1793 is now the Toronto Islands. A severe storm in 1858 broke through the eastern end, creating a gap and turning the spit and its lagoons into a little archipelago.)

The site for the naval base was the dry bed of a post-glacial lake, flat and somewhat swampy, punctuated by low knolls. It was bounded by two substantial streams, now the Don River on the east and the Humber River on the west. Both flowed through steep-sided, flat-floored ravines which drained the higher lands to the north beyond the shoreline of the lake bed. As she explored further, Elizabeth would find very picturesque the many steep slopes between the lake bed and the upper surface above the shoreline. To the east of the camp of the Queen's Rangers was a small stream (later Garrison Creek), and east again was some rising ground. Here the Simcoes decided to erect the canvas houses, where they would catch the breezes, and the Rangers began clearing away trees. Meanwhile, they lived aboard the *Onondaga* and explored during the day. By Sunday, 4 August, another armed government ship, the *Mississauga*, arrived, bringing horses. The governor and Elizabeth rode on the sandspit, which she named the Peninsula, dined aboard the *Onondaga*, and returned to spend the night in the canvas house. The next morning the children, nurses and servants came ashore.

Elizabeth walked to the ruins of old French Fort Rouillé, that had been abandoned in 1760 because the British were about to capture it. The Peninsula became a favourite spot for her; it was fairly open and a fine place to gallop. The air was clear, and she admired loons who swam and dived in the bay. Someone sent her a dead one so that she could study it. She rode with Simcoe to the cliffs east of the Don River, which they named the Scarborough Bluffs in honour of the long-popular Yorkshire spa, and thought the top would make a fine spot for a summer home. They explored the shoreline, inspecting it and the Peninsula for defensive sites. There should be a fort on the shore, close to the west end of the sandspit, to protect the entrance to the harbour, and a blockhouse on the sandspit itself. Simcoe called it Gibraltar Point. The land was low and it bore no resemblance to the rocky promontory, but he chose the name because of the spot's importance. He ordered some cannon brought by ship from Carleton Island and Fort Oswegatchie because the government refused to send any guns from England. Elizabeth thought the setting of the new naval base a very healthy place, where she longed to spend the winter, away from the hated fever and ague that so plagued Newark. Simcoe approved, as he wanted to be on hand to inspect the work soon to be in progress.

The following Sunday, 11 August, Lieutenant David William Smith read prayers to the Queen's Rangers, who were drawn up under trees near their parade ground. Simcoe had appointed Smith acting deputy surveyor general, hoping that the appointment would be confirmed in time. Elizabeth wrote that the white cat with grey spots who had adopted her at Niagara had fared well on the voyage, and seemed to like its new home, news that would delight the girls at Wolford Lodge.

Once the governor's presence became known, Ojibway Indians from the north and the shore of Lake Huron began coming to Toronto to satisfy their curiosity. Elizabeth thought them "extremely handsome & have a superior air to any I have seen, they have been little among Europeans therefore less accustomed to drink Rum." They presented Simcoe with a blanket of beaver pelts and invited him to visit their country.

On 24 August, an official report arrived on the Duke of York's distinguished service at Famars, when he drove the French out of Holland. Simcoe ordered a Royal salute, and named "this station" York. The salute was fired by his few 12- and 18-pounder guns, joined by the guns on the *Onondaga* and *Mississauga* and the muskets of the Queen's Rangers. Beforehand an Ojibway named Canise picked up Francis in his arms, thinking that the noise might frighten the two-year-old boy. Canise was pleased when Francis not only showed no fear but seemed delighted by the sound.[7]

Four days later, a gunboat arrived from Newark bringing a report from Detroit. The American commissioners had returned to the United States from Sandusky without making peace with the Indians. The western tribes wanted the Ohio River as the boundary, and all white settlements beyond it removed, but the Americans refused. Simcoe was bitterly disappointed that all hope was lost of a neutral Indian nation south of Lake Erie to protect Upper Canada from the Americans, and worried that the war with France might extend into North America. President Washington had declared the United States neutral, but he was allowing French privateers in American ports. The new French ambassador, Citizen Edmond Charles Genet, had sent agents into Lower Canada to stir up the French Canadians. These activities alarmed Washington, who did not want war with Britain while his army was heavily committed against the Indians. Had Simcoe been aware, he might have been less alarmed about the many vocal threats to the safety of Upper Canada. What he did learn was that Paris agreed to recall Genet, who instead married a daughter of Governor George Clinton of New York and retired.

Early in September a packet arrived from James Bland Burges, containing a work called Alfred's *Letters*. Elizabeth was surprised to find that she enjoyed this decidedly political book. It was passed around, and Chief Justice Osgoode thought that Burges himself was the author. In a letter to Simcoe, Burges warned him that a far greater threat than France was Catherine of Russia, who had territorial ambitions. On 23 September, Simcoe replied, "I ... from my Cradle have looked with dread on the aspiring Politicks of Russia; France may threaten the Invasion but Russia can perform it —". He referred to the dreadful partition of Poland of September 1793 by Russia and Prussia, adding, "I equally deprecate the darkness of Despotism, as the Lunacy of Liberty!" Elizabeth's contribution to a packet for Burges was a map of the colony.[8] The same day that Simcoe wrote, Lord Dorchester arrived in Quebec after his leave of absence, and Simcoe was less than ever his own man. A few days later, Bishop Jacob Mountain reached Quebec as the first prelate of the Canadas; earlier the provinces had been a dependency of the see of Nova Scotia. Both the Simcoes were pleased with the appointment for it might strengthen the Church of England in Upper Canada.

Captain Samuel Smith left with 100 Rangers to open a road from the head of Lake Ontario to the Thames River. "I hear they kill Rattlesnakes every day yet not a man has been bit tho they have been among them for 6 weeks". Smith sent two snakes in a barrel so that Elizabeth could see them. She thought them "dark & ugly & made a whizzing sound in shaking their Rattles when I touched them with a stick." Meanwhile, a second party of Rangers was working on a road that ran north, which Simcoe named Yonge Street, in honour of his Devon friend, Sir George Yonge, Member of Parliament for Honiton and Secretary at War.[9] The second canvas house would soon be erected. The first would serve as a bedroom, and the other as a dining room. They ate under a marquee once it was too cold outside in the "Arbour".

On 25 September, Simcoe left for Lac aux Claies with a party of Rangers, Deputy Provincial Surveyor, Alexander Aitken, Captain Henry Darling of the 5th Regiment, Alexander Macdonnell, Sheriff of the Home District, Lieutenant James Givins of the Queen's Rangers, and the Newfoundland dog Jack Sharp. From that lake they hoped to find a water link to Lake Huron. They reached Lake aux Claies on the twenty-ninth, and renamed it Lake Simcoe, in honour of the governor's late father. On the same date, Francis Simcoe's name was placed on a grant of 200 acres on the Don River, where his parents would build Castle Frank as a summer home. Young Francis' was one of many grants the governor was awarding in the neighbourhood of York. John Scadding received 235 acres on the east side of the Don River and had begun building a cabin for himself.[10] Many officers in the Queen's Rangers had received grants, and some families from Newark joined the Simcoes. Others were reluctant to make the move. Hannah Jarvis wrote that with the governor at York, the chief justice, attorney general, receiver general and secretary at Newark, and the acting surveyor general (David William Smith) at Fort Niagara, "thus our government is to spend the Winter at respectable distances." Elizabeth Russell was disturbed, because her brother had paid for the building of a comfortable house at Newark, and now he would face the expense of building another.[11]

By 25 October, the governor's party had returned from Lake Simcoe, after dividing into sections and becoming lost. They visited the village of the Ojibway Canise, but found that he and his eldest son had died and their widows and children were lamenting them. Young Canise, heir to the older man, gave the governor a blanket of beaver pelts. Simcoe had enjoyed meeting another Ojibway named Great Sail. Because of losing their way, Simcoe's men had been short of provisions. They had decided to eat Jack Sharp. The Newfoundland dog's life was spared when they sighted Lake Ontario and knew they were nearly home. Jack Sharp, Simcoe admitted, was ungainly in a canoe.

Soon after Simcoe's return to York, a freight canoe arrived, the gift of the North West Company of Montreal. "It required 12 men to paddle":

> An Indian Woman came today with Pitch which is made ... from Fir Trees, to gum the Canoe ... Her figure was perfectly wild & witchlike & a little fire with her kettle on it by her side in a stormy dark day ... formed a scene very wildly Picturesque.

Elizabeth had her first ride in the canoe on 9 November:

> A Beaver Blanket & a carpet were put in to sit upon. We carried a small table to be used in embarking & disembarking for the Canoe cannot be brought very near the Shore lest the gravel or pebbles injure her, so the table was set in the water & a long Plank laid from it to the Shore to enable me to get in or out the Men carrying the Canoe empty into the water & out of it upon their shoulders.

They had less than "board between us & eternity" for the birch bark cracked and punctured easily. The Indians always carried "Gum or Pitch" to mend breaks in the bark.[12]

At night the Indians speared salmon in the bay, using torchlight to attract them. Flights of wild pigeons darkened the sky and soldiers over at Fort Niagara killed many by throwing sticks at them. Some pigeons that had been shot along the Mohawk River, not far to the south in New York State, had rice in their craws. Since rice did not grow closer than North Carolina, Elizabeth assumed they must have flown a great distance. At that time she did not know about the wild rice that grew in the province, especially around Rice Lake.

They made several trips to admire the tract of land which Simcoe had chosen for Francis. The boundary began at the top edge of the ravine through which the Don River flowed. From this bluff they had a fine view of the harbour, and the lake beyond the Peninsula. Here they would build their summer home, and work began before the end of November. The name "Castle Frank" was rather grand for what would be a rustic log structure; the Grecian columns Elizabeth mentioned were trunks of white pines.

On 2 December Great Sail arrived at York, with his wife and ten children, and they grouped themselves in the manner of a Van Dyke family painting. Francis handed around apples. "He shakes hands with the Indians in a very friendly manner, tho he is very shy & ungracious to all his own Countrymen."[13] She made a sketch of Great Sail, resolving to improve it later. She was impressed at the way Indians spoke, which to her resembled the great orators of Greece and Rome. On the twelfth, Simcoe, Talbot and Lieutenant Grey left York. Grey was going to join his father, the 1st Lord Grey, in the West Indies, and the other two were accompanying him as far as Niagara. On the twenty-second, they were back and Talbot was skating on the bay.

Meanwhile, work parties of Queen's Rangers were north of the town plot of York, cutting a road towards Lake Simcoe. Such a road would make possible a bypass to the upper lakes beyond Detroit. Since Detroit was on the United States side of the boundary, the governor was afraid that it would soon be evacuated. With the Americans in possession of Detroit, they would control Lake Erie and could block the passage of British vessels attempting to supply Michilimackinac and interfere with the valuable fur trade of the northwest. The new road was Yonge Street, while Simcoe named the road to the Thames Dundas Street after Sir Henry Dundas, the Home Secretary.

Elizabeth wrote nothing about Christmas celebrations, but on 27 December it was so cold that water froze in a pail next to the stove. On 11 January 1794, the Queen's birthday, Simcoe ordered a twenty-one gun salute fired, loading the cannon with pebbles , possibly to conserve ammunition. The day was mild. At a dance held in the evening the ladies were "much dressed". On the nineteenth, they rode seven miles north to the log houses of some German settlers. On the twenty-sixth, Captain Shaw's children set fire to long grass of a marsh close to the bay, which Elizabeth thought picturesque. The next night she set her own fire to amuse herself. They went out on the bay to watch the Indians spear fish through holes in the ice, while sheltering under blankets for warmth. The last day of the month was mildly disastrous, for a horse drawing hay across the bay fell through the ice and drowned, and John Scadding's cabin burned down. Nevertheless Elizabeth was in high spirits. In March she would be going to Detroit.

March brought news of the execution of the Queen Marie Antionette of France, and Simcoe ordered a dance postponed. The weather was bitterly cold, and Elizabeth could hardly hold her cards though she wore three fur tippets. They divided the dining room by hanging a carpet, which helped a bit, but the canvas ceiling had not been boarded over and most of the cold air came through it. Deer were scarce that winter, and starving Indians came often to York. Elizabeth spared what she could, which was "inconvenient", cut off as they were from supplies, and having to conserve food.

On the 14 March, riding across the bay, she felt her horse sink and threw herself off. The horse apparently wanted to roll in the snow, and she thought she prevented it crushing her because she struck it with her whip.

The following day, Simcoe received an order from Lord Dorchester to proceed to the Maumee River as soon as navigation opened, to build a fort below Detroit in country claimed by the Americans. Simcoe did not fancy Dorchester's order. It was provocative and could be more of a danger to Detroit than a protection. Yet he had to obey because Dorchester was his superior. He again had to disappoint Elizabeth, because he could not take her into country where his party might be attacked. She did not mind, since she found much to interest her in her new surroundings. She watched the settlers making maple sugar, boiling the sap in great kettles, and observed the ice as it floated through the gap at the foot of the peninsula. John Scadding brought whitefish from Niagara, and on 18 April pork came on the sloop *Caldwell* from the settlements on the Bay of Quinte.

The next entry was dated 2 May, when Simcoe returned from the Maumee River. On 19 April Elizabeth had suffered a grievous blow. She wrote to Mrs. Hunt in May:

> It is with pain I take up my pen to inform you of the loss we have sustained & the melancholy event of our losing poor little Katherine, one of the strongest healthiest children you ever saw... She had been feverish one or two days cutting teeth, which not being an unusual case with children I was not much alarmed. On good Friday she was playing in my room in the morning, in the afternoon was seized with fits. I sat up the whole night the greatest part of which she continued to have spasms & before seven in the morning she was no more... She was the sweetest tempered pretty child imaginable, just beginning to talk & walk & the suddenness of the event you may be sure shocked me inexpressibly.[14]

Katherine was buried in the military cemetery near the huts of the Queen's Rangers, which Simcoe had named Fort York, on Easter Monday, 21 April 1794. A few days later Francis seemed unwell, and Elizabeth was panic-stricken. When Katherine died, Surgeon Macaulay was at Newark. Elizabeth wondered whether he might have saved the child, and appalled that she might lose Francis, too, she sent for him. By the time Macaulay arrived Francis was better. Of Katherine's death, Elizabeth wrote, "The loss of so promising a Child must long be a painful thing."

Simcoe learned of his daughter's passing when his ship reached Fort Erie. Elizabeth was also reported to be ill, and he galloped the eighteen miles to Newark in scarcely two hours, over a road that was a quagmire from spring rains. He learned that Elizabeth was well, but "from that melancholy event in the family, which affected him in a less degree than it would otherwise have done if he had not been so frightened on my account."

When Elizabeth's letter reached Wolford Lodge, Mrs. Hunt had the unwelcome task of informing the four children, who had so long looked forward to becoming acquainted with Katherine. The following year a grave marker arrived from England, ordered by Mrs. Hunt, and inscribed "Katherine Simcoe, January 16, 1793 - April 19, 1794. Happy in the Lord." How the Simcoe girls took the news, and what Mary Anne Burges wrote to comfort Elizabeth, can only be imagined. Miss Burges' letters for July 1794 have been lost, and Elizabeth probably never received them. Preserved, however, were two letters that illuminate the sorrow felt by family and friends. On 12 August 1794, Mary Anne Burges wrote to her brother of her "great concern" at the sudden death of Katherine. Eliza received a letter from her great aunt Elizabeth Gwillim, undated and written from Whitchurch. She reminded her great niece that all who die in infancy go to heaven. After this note of sympathy she continued, "Your brother wears Indian dress that is more becoming than English on the young." Their Mama had sent her two sermons, which she, in turn, would send to Wolford Lodge.[15]

Chapter 12

MISS BURGES AND MRS. GRAVES

May 1794~January 1795

In August 1793, Mary Anne Burges was responding to the part of Elizabeth's diary that had been written in April: "Your account of Capt. Shaw made me very desirous to be acquainted with him. I could not help liking a person who deserved such a description from you."[1] The Reverend Mr. Coplestone had reported that Elizabeth was utterly miserable in America, in ill health and dying with anxiety to return to England. Mary Anne corrected him.

"Mrs. Simcoe regrets nothing in England but the society of her children."

Though a sensible man, Coplestone was a little gullible, inclined to believe all the "absurd reports that originate with the Republicans of this country." At the time the family of Mary Anne's aunt and uncle, Colonel Hugh and Mary Digby Somerville, were imposing on her. Hugh's son, John Southby, was from his first marriage, and by his second he had Hugh, Mary, Frances, Mark, Harriet, Kenelm, William and Julia.[2] The Somerviles had gone to Kittery, near Dartmouth, leaving seven-year-old Harriet, who was hopelessly homesick. "If Mark comports himself in her style on going to school, the Lord have mercy on Mr. Hayne!"

Of the flowers Elizabeth had sent she loved the trilium, which Miller described exactly. She thought the blooms on the plants grown from the seeds must be smaller in Devon than in Canada, or Elizabeth would never have fancied them. Mary Anne promised to send her a short account of the different plant classes. Elizabeth might not read a book on the subject, but would read what her friend wrote. The arrival of a packet from Elizabeth "equals a shock of electricity", and she confessed to feeling ill if one was delayed too long. She felt fortunate not to have passed on any bad news about the children to their mother.

Meanwhile, Harriet Somerville continued to be troublesome, and she hated calling her Harriet, the name of Elizabeth's "good-tempered little creature .... If this child had been carried away by Indians like the Boy you mention, neither Coll. Simcoe's intercession, nor a sum of money, would have been requisite to induce them to dismiss her."[3]

On 21 August, Mrs. Hunt and the girls came to dine at Tracey. Their behaviour was a complete contrast with Mary Anne's little cousin's, and they were "uncommonly good natured to her, & and she was delighted with them." After that, Harriet calmed down and was easier to manage. Meanwhile a letter came from Mrs. Graves, who wanted to make arrangements for Eliza to visit Bath. Mary Anne enclosed it so that Elizabeth could see exactly how the letter was phrased, to avoid any misunderstandings.

She was concerned about a Mr. Haskins, who was about to move into a cottage near Tracey since he was a Democrat. "Shall I dig a mine under the foundation and blow him up?" After a dream, she felt relieved that she had not been guillotined for the murder of some Jacobin chief, and if she was so charged for disposing of Haskins, could she seek shelter in Canada?[4]

Near the end of August, Mrs. Herman Drewe was nearly killed while returning from Sidmouth. The horses refused to draw the chaise up Sidbury Hill and began kicking. A servant tried to pull her from the chaise, but instead she fell into a bramble bush. The chaise then overturned, and Mary Anne was certain that had she remained with it, she would have been crushed. The Somervilles returned on the thirtieth with three more of their children to stay a few days. The "riots of the children" wore Mary Anne's patience thin and prevented her enjoying her aunt's company. Once the Somervilles left, she would go to Wolford Lodge, where all the girls were well.

On 1 September she wrote that seven years had passed since her move to Tracey. She felt indebted for such a friend as Elizabeth, and she valued her society above all others. Another packet would soon be on its way to Canada, with a drawing for Elizabeth, and a shirt for Colonel Simcoe, both made by Charlotte. Eliza's sketch of a cowslip was not quite ready and would come in a later packet. Colonel and Mrs. Somerville would take the packet on the first stage of its long journey. With her aunt she went to Honiton to make arrangements for Mark to attend Mr. Hayne's school. Her aunt and uncle left on the third with the two youngest, but one boy and one girl were still at Tracey. The next day the young Somervilles broke down the ceiling of the housekeeper's room, and a garden roller nearly killed one of them. Next they spoiled a table. Miss Hunt was with Mary Anne for a change of scene, and the two women had been having "learned disputes". Miss Hunt argued more scientifically, but she had read less Locke than Mary Anne. After watching the antics of the cousins, Miss Hunt remarked that she had no idea such children existed in England.

Mary Anne received a curious letter from Mrs. Graves, taking issue with her for suggesting she might leave the country after blowing up the Democrat Haskins. Who would look after Elizabeth's "poor helpless deserted children"? She begged her to stay at Tracey. Miss Burges deplored such "epithets from the only person who has disconcerted them". Elizabeth was truly lucky in having Mrs. Hunt care for the girls, who were looking so well. If that good lady should die, as Mrs. Graves loved to predict, Mary Anne would take care of the children at Tracey, assisted by Miss Hunt. Yet Elizabeth need have no worries. Mrs. Hunt was a healthy woman though she often imagined things.[5]

The senior Somervilles returned to Tracey on Friday 6 September, and left the next morning for Fitzhead Court, to Mary Anne's relief. At church that Sunday Reverend Neale preached on the duties of women. Mary Anne would be sorry if he could produce any good authority, for he "totally excluded me from every good prospect in either World."

When Harriet Simcoe learned that Miss Burges had accepted an invitation from Mrs. Graves to visit Bath, she begged her to say how much a pair of white gloves cost. Her face saddened when Mary Anne said twenty pence; she had only fifteen. After some teasing, Harriet admitted to the others that she had seen the gloves in a shop window in Honiton, and thought Miss Burges would need some in Bath. Eliza agreed to make up the difference, and Charlotte, hurt at being left out, offered one penny. Mary Anne felt embarrassed but agreed to receive the money for the gloves "with as good a grace as Mr. Fox himself". Afterwards Charlotte asked Harriet if she had as much as a halfpenny left.

"No," Harriet replied.

"Then Madame I am extremely happy to hear it." At Harriet's look of surprise, Charlotte continued," Because I have got a great deal of money and I am going to give some of it to you."

She offered Harriet a shilling and a penny which she refused to accept at first, insisting she only needed money for the gloves. Mary Anne liked to give the girls opportunities to show their generosity. Elizabeth need have no fear that her daughters would forget people soon. Before she left Wolford, Eliza gave her many messages to her acquaintances in Bath, and Charlotte added more. She did not know anyone but she did not want to to be left out. Eliza had informed the family that Captain-Lieutenant George Spencer of the Queen's Rangers was in Bath to recover from a severe malady. Harriet, who had never met Spencer, asked Miss Burges to see him, tell him she was sorry he was ill, wish him better and send him her love.[6]

Mary Anne arrived in Bath on 12 September by coach from Taunton, and was met at an inn by Mrs. Graves' carriage. That lady received her generously, but Bath had too many memories of Mary Anne's late parents and the sight of the furniture taken from Wolford Lodge depressed her. The poor Axminster carpet had been cut down to fit a small back room.

Captain-Lieutenant George Spencer called on Mrs. Graves on the 14th, and Mary Anne was horrified at how altered he was, and unable to speak. Mrs. Graves was disappointed that Mary Anne took Spencer's condition in stride. Eliza had burst into tears at the sight of him, and Mrs. Graves expected the same reaction from Miss Burges. Her hostess maintained that Colonel Simcoe would deprive Spencer of his commission if he did not recover enough to serve with the Rangers, which made Mary Anne impatient. Simcoe would never "starve someone in such a situation". She was glad when her hostess went off to an evening card party.[7]

The next day was a Sunday. After church she called on Miss Harriet Bowdler, well known for intelligent conversation, a bluestocking friend of Miss Hunt. When she got back to Lansdown Crescent Mary Anne found that Mrs. Graves had sprained an ankle falling from her carriage.

> I think if I had committed any great crime, & wished to do penance for it, I could hardly have devined one more effectual, than coming to this place ... La dama Duende as

you used to call her, is sinking into violent disgraces ... Mrs. Graves thinks she is going mad, fancies she may break into her room at night & murder her, she has procured stronger night bolts.[8]

The sixteenth marked two years since Elizabeth had left. By then Mrs. Graves' company was becoming wearing. She talked all day every day, and her main topic of conversation was Captain-Lieutenant Spencer. She invented shocking things to say about him; in fact, she was so absorbed that she had left off anticipating a calamity befalling the Simcoes.

Mrs. Graves' friends criticised her for buying silver plates and books instead of furnishings she needed for her house, especially since she did not give dinner parties. She had set apart some of her income to buy the plates because Colonel Simcoe liked them, and she planned to purchase some more each year until she had three dozen. In fact, Simcoe was now in such favour that Mary Anne was taken to task for not praising him enough. Nor was Mrs. Graves critical of Elizabeth. Mrs. Graves had the welfare of little Francis so much at heart that she relayed everything she heard of him to her friends. After church on Sunday, she allowed Mary Anne to invite eleven-year-old George Head, her eldest nephew, to dine. George, at school in Bath, was a charming boy who so pleased Mrs. Graves that he became a frequent guest.

On 26 September, Mary Anne reported a disaster at the Bath races. Many people were injured, though no one was killed, when a stand erected for the crowd gave way. Among the 500 on it were her maid Jenny and some of Mrs. Graves' servants. Several people landed on Jenny, bruising her badly, while Betty Hayes hung by her hands on some scaffolding until rescued. One man whose leg was broken refused treatment until he saw which horse won the heat being run. George Head did not sit on that stand because he thought it looked insecure.[9]

Daily Mary Anne grew more irked with Mrs. Graves, and she regretted promising to remain in Bath another fortnight. That lady decided both Hunts might die, leaving Elizabeth's children with no one to protect them. An angry Mary Anne told her that the children would never suffer while she lived. If any of her nieces needed protection and she did not choose to give it, she would at least be silent! The dissent continued:

> You would be diverted to see how I give myself airs in all
> the disputes I have with her, now that she has no hold over
> me & that I know she wishes me to stay longer at Bath, I
> never give up the least point, very particularly if you are
> mentioned[.][10]

By the end of October she was back home at Tracey and very anxious for a packet from Canada. It finally came in late December. Colonel Simcoe was well off not to have received a more violent letter from Mrs. Graves than Elizabeth described. Of late, that lady's letters to Tracey had been "so full of bleeding hearts ... that any person ... would certainly suppose them to be violent love-letters." In the next parcel Mary Anne was sending an ear Harriet had drawn. Elizabeth's drawing of a caterpillar resembled one found in England, but the colouring was different.[11]

By Christmas, she was delighted that her maid Jenny had recovered completely after the terrible accident at the Bath races. Jenny had suggested, if she could not work, she would go to live with a sister in Scotland. Captain Hudson Lowe of the 50th Regiment arrived from Canada bringing another box of Elizabeth's letters. "You can not think what a fancy I have to see Francis. I am uncommonly glad that he deserves such an account as you give of him. Is Katherine like the rest?" The Simcoes were most fortunate to be in Canada. Otherwise the colonel would "be employed against these villainous Frenchmen" while Elizabeth would have to endure Mrs. Graves' temper and her particular art of tormenting people who were anxious for the safety of others. One might dismiss all as merely her way of talking, but her gloom and doom predictions disturbed people.

> I know not what enemies who may attack you in Canada, but if I was to live in the house with a green Perroquet who repeated from morning till night, that everything which would vex me was about to happen, I should at last believe him inspired, & abandon myself to despair . . . Eliza has been drawing today with so much more freedom than I ever saw her before, that I am quite pleased with it.[12]

On 2 January, Mary Anne left to visit the Somervilles at Clifton, outside Bristol, where they had a house overlooking the Avon River estuary. Colonel and Mrs. Hamilton dropped in, a most entertaining Scottish couple who had fled the French Reign of Terror. They had lived in Savoy and had had to pose as civilians when the French took over and set up a guillotine. He came perilously close to being denounced as an aristocrat when he tried to prosecute a girl who robbed his cherry orchard. Mrs. Hamilton harangued a mob saying they were good citizens and acquainted with Thomas Paine's *Rights of Man* until the rabble dispersed. The Hamiltons sold their estate, left "disguised in National Cockade" and reached England safely. "At one place the Municipal Officers measured the length of Mrs. Hamilton's Nose, which happens to be a pretty considerable one, & entered it in their Books."[13]

Miss Digby, who was Mrs. Mary Somervile's sister, had been informing Mary Anne of the latest London fashions. Lady Charlotte Campbell, last seen with a cushion so placed as to appear with child, was the "inventress of the high waist". She had scored again for she had been seen last winter in Kensington Gardens with only one thin petticoat. It was short enough to "discover a part of very fine Muslin Drawers, trimmed with lace". Ladies about to be married now presented their husbands not with pictures of their faces, but of limbs. "Many ladies give an arm but Lady Susan Gordon gave the Duke of Manchester a leg".[14]

Mary Anne would sow the seeds Elizabeth sent. The drawing of the two ships was very pretty, the effect of smoke gave them a singular appearance. The caterpillars were the oddest she ever saw. Elizabeth mentioned that their fine hairs stung, and she found that touching them injured a finger and her eyes grew inflamed when she put some near her face. Of the twenty-one gun salute fired on 7 June for Francis' third birthday, Mary Anne responded to Elizabeth's description, "Francis displayed great intrepidity in standing by the cannon, an incident which may be related in a history of his life if he proves as great a man as I chuse he should."[15]

James Bland Burges surprised Mary Anne by sending her a copy of a book entitled *Cavern of Death* . She was the author, but her brother had it published anonymously. Mary Anne was "diverted" by seeing it in print, but fearful lest strangers discover that she was responsible for it. She would send a copy to Colonel Simcoe. The story took place in Germany, and the Cavern was "Die Hole des Todes", a death hole feared by peasants "who entertain many wicked superstitions ... Now if he had but retained me in the office of his Secretary, I should not have been mis-spending my time in writing all this nonsense." She thanked Elizabeth for the pretty little map, "which I intend shall be my travelling companion that I may always be able to ascertain the spot of any of your future adventures." Elizabeth's new accomplishments seemed endless. She made her own garden while Mary Anne was only a "spectatress":

> I can well imagine that the whole forest may fall beneath the strokes of your Tomahawk. I do not think the danger of being starved, & of eating Jack Sharp [Simcoe's Newfound-land Dog] was included even in Mrs. Graves's list of those which awaited Coll. Simcoe. There is something so wild & odd in your description of his journey [to Lake Simcoe]; & of the Indians with whom you have intercourse that it is some time before my ideas return into any sublumary road.[16]

In March 1794, Mary Anne paid another visit to Mrs. Graves in Bath. Her hostess was civil to her guest at first, though her frown had become habitual, and her headdress was

> increased by a considerable losenge of frizzed hair in front, of which one point comes a considerable way down on her forehead, which gives an uncommon fierceness to her countenance, like some foreign Bird I have seen.

Mrs. Graves sent Mrs. Gwillim a report of a peculiar letter she had written Colonel Simcoe. Mrs. Gwillim replied, if she would not write him in a style more conciliatory, she should not write at all. "Since Mrs. Graves had a Bible as well as himself & could read of the duty of forgiveness more than she could tell her."[17]

Mary Anne accepted an invitation to Miss Bowdler's to meet a Mr. Smith who had a large family and wanted to emigrate to Upper Canada. Since his wife felt as enthusiastic as her sister Head, when Mr. Head talked of emigrating, Miss Bowdler wanted Mary Anne to present the province "in the most uninviting light possible". She talked of rattlesnakes, and of Indians starving on their marches, and felt certain Mrs. Smith would win. A few days later she learned she had succeeded:

> Mr. Smith has given up all hope of going to Canada at present. ... If you want more Settlers, you had better employ me to enlist them for you; for if I have proved so successful an Orator when speaking against my conscience I might hope to effect anything by an Oration on the contrary side.[18]

Mary Anne liked Miss Bowdler quite well. Her conversation was sensible, but on occasion it lacked substance. "I believe I am very selfish in friendship; or at least I do not like to be the common place." She had occasion to read aloud the letters of some of her friends which contained expressions of the strongest affection ."Such would make a figure in a book of sentiment; & yet they did not convey to me a quarter so much meaning as I often find in a single line of your letters, which would not do to be printed at all."[19] Miss Burges was correct. Miss Bowdler's letters of later years, mainly to Eliza, are beautifully penned but say very little.[20]

After church of Sunday 30 March, Mrs. Graves lectured her "on the propriety of assuming the name Mrs. Burges", which she ought to have done five years ago.

> I replied that such a dignified appellation had long been the object of my particular ambition that if she would be pleased to give it to me, I would forthwith demand it as my due from everybody else. She immediately commenced & has actually called me so at every other word throughout the day. . . I hope you will not be disgusted from this new dignity of mine, but will henseforward give me my title of Mrs. or rather Mrs. Mary while you continue to enclose your letters to my Brother.[21]

That was almost the last cordial exchange between Mrs. Graves and Mary Anne. The new Mrs. Burges arrived at Tracey from Bath on 12 April, never expecting to return. The final insult followed a quarrel that began with Mary Anne's offer to have Mrs. Graves stay at Tracey if she wanted to visit her great nieces. Wolford Lodge was so "compleatly disfurnished" that there not enough beds for herself and servants.[22] Worse, after she had been home for a while, the Hunts admitted that Mrs. Graves said Mary Anne only pretended to be interested in Elizabeth "because of Colonel Simcoe", mischievous talk implying she coveted her friend's husband.[23]

In her absence a packet had come from Canada. Mary Anne enthused over a drawing of a bird and one of a bat Elizabeth had sent to "add to my collection of curiosities". While she was in Bath, Reverend Edward Drewe had had a paraletic attack while preaching but was recovering. There seemed more Democrats in Honiton than ever and she wished to avoid them. If the French landed, Mary Anne feared, most people would join them. However, William, her servant, was so "well disposed" that he longed to leave her and raise a regiment of dragoons. He loved to go to Honiton on market day, when the Democrats harangued farmers, and answer them. If a corps of volunteers were raised in Honiton, William would join it, since she could not "deprive the country of such a hero for the sake of a few cabbages". If this crop failed they could eat thistles. William liked "the prospect of dying a field marshal" but he could not have Placid for his charger.[24]

James Bland Burges forwarded £20 from the sale of *Cavern of Death*, but Mary Anne was still worried he might betray her. She hoped people would assume he was the anonymous author. She was also looking for oranges for Jenny to make into the marmalade Elizabeth liked, to send in the next box.[25]

In June, Mrs. Hunt informed Mary Anne that Mrs. Graves had invited all four Simcoe girls to spend a fortnight in Bath. Here was a welcome surprise, for the three youngest thought their great aunt cared only for Eliza.

A packet from Elizabeth reached Tracey a few days later. Mary Anne thought her friend's plan to go to Quebec if Niagara was theatened seemed wise. Elizabeth admitted having no fortitude when her loved ones were in danger, to which Mary Anne replied, "fortitude is no virtue", but she had more success in controlling her fears when she was at a distance from Mrs. Graves.[26] Thomas Graves called and gave Mary Anne an excellent reason for Howe's victory over the French; he could not help it. "Captain Thomas Graves continues to hold a high opinion of Robespierre as an amiable man."

Responding to another packet, Mary Anne praised Elizabeth for her beautiful drawing on bark (several of her watercolour sketches are done on birch bark).

> You are grown so gay in Upper Canada; that I shall hardly know you when you return to England. I used to think you secluded yourself too much at Wolford Lodge, & that going oftener from home than you did, would have done you a great deal of good, indeed, when you had things to vex you, I wished you very much to change the scene a little.[27]

When Mary Anne called on Mrs. Richard Graves she found that Margaret Graves' invitation to the Simcoe girls "raised great speculation . . as her former conduct had been much talked of." At the time this letter was written, Mary Anne had not yet heard of the loss, at York, of little Katherine Simcoe.

Chapter 13

WAR CLOUDS

May 1794~January 1795

For weeks Elizabeth was in the doldrums over the loss of Katherine. Her blue mood was not helped by plans to return to Newark for the second session of the legislature. Francis had been healthier at York and she longed to stay here in the wilderness community that Lord Dorchester was ordering Simcoe to regard as his capital. Two Home Secretaries, Henry Dundas until 1794 (in 1802 the 1st Viscount Melville), and now William Bentinck, the 3rd Duke of Portland, were not enthusiastic about the site on the River Thames. Simcoe's frustrations, both with Lord Dorchester and the home government, did nothing to help Elizabeth recover her equilibrium. Aware of her depression, he took heart, and suggested returning to Niagara along the shoreline in open boats. Elizabeth brightened at once. The anticipation of travelling helped more than anything else to restore her spirits.

They set out on 9 May, a Friday, with the children and their nurses and other servants. Here Elizabeth identified each nurse, by surname only, as Collins and Junk. The trip proved disappointing for the weather was poor. They picnicked under umbrellas in the rain, and while the children and nurses bedded down in a tent, Elizabeth and the governor slept in their boat. Near Forty Mile Creek (now Grimsby) they received very good bread, milk and butter from a family from Pennsylvania, whom the Governor had helped choose land the summer before. Elizabeth expected to go part of the way by canoe, but the wind was too strong, and she remained in the boat. Her description of the shoreline was apt—the valleys along the streams that descend the face of the Niagara Escarpment and empty into Lake Ontario are steep-sided, and they often had ponds in them on the flat surface of the former lake bed. They reached Newark at noon on the eleventh; the heat was so oppressive that Elizabeth longed to return to York.[1]

Soon after she settled into Navy Hall, she went to inspect Samuel Smith's new house. (Smith was now the major of the Queen's Rangers.) Lieutenant Pilkington, then supervising work at Fort Miamis, near Detroit, sent Elizabeth some sketches of Lake Erie which she copied. She was soon caught up in the panic frame of mind of the residents of Newark. War with the United States seemed imminent. Here, at least, she reckoned, a campaign would not last long; the "result must be speedily decisive".[2] The governor might well find himself a prisoner of war, but he was safer than if they had stayed in England, in which case he would be on the Continent, where one campaign followed another endlessly. If Newark was menaced, as she had written Mary Anne Burges, she would take the children to Quebec. Simcoe felt he could carry out his duties best if he knew his family was safe.

To keep her mind off the danger, Elizabeth entertained at a frantic pace. She recorded the arrival of a new merchant vessel called the *Gov. Simcoe*, a ship that would later be armed and serve during the War of 1812. To amuse "Mrs." Burges she recalled driving in a gig along the road with Talbot, now a captain in his regiment. It was passing over a prone cow before either of them noticed. The gig did not overturn, and the cow suffered no ill effects. On 25 May, out riding with Simcoe and Talbot, they encountered a sharp rainstorm and were soaked through, the "pleasantest mode of taking a shower bath". All were less likely to catch cold because of the violence of it.

On the twenty-ninth the *Mississauga*, *Caldwell* and two gunboats brought members of the legislature to Newark. The speaker, John Macdonell, member for the second Glengarry riding and the owner of Glengarry House, dined with the Simcoes. The conversation was on the possibility of war, despite Elizabeth's desire to put it out of her mind. The governor told Macdonell of Mrs. Simcoe's plan to take the children to Quebec for safety. Macdonnell thought that Quebec was more likely to be besieged than Niagara, because of its importance.

"There the siege would be carried on regularly," Elizabeth explained. "And my friend Mrs. Caldwell, who was there through the siege of 1775, will be a comfort to me."

"Here," the governor continued. "We could fall with one blow." He thought the Americans would try to seize Upper Canada, rather than attack such a well-fortified stronghold as Quebec.

On 3 June, Elizabeth and Francis accompanied Simcoe to Fort Niagara. Mother and son walked on the high ground of the military reserve where the air seemed more healthy. Francis lay down and fell asleep on the grass before the governor was ready to return to Newark. The next day, the King's birthday, a ball was held in the council chamber. The arrangements were made by Captain Talbot, who would soon be returning to Britain, his tour of duty over. Elizabeth was among the watchers, but, still in mourning, she did not dance. The sixth was Francis' third birthday, but they delayed a celebration because Simcoe had to go to Fort Chippawa.

The party was on the seventh, a Saturday. Rangers fired a tiny cannon which Mr. Speaker Macdonell had given Francis. The shots were barely two inches long, but they "made a loud Report & pleased him much".[3] For the occasion Francis wore a rifle shirt and a sash. The clothes, his black hair, dark eyes like hers, and skin browned by the sun "gave him somewhat the air of an Indian." The lad offered a dead snake to one of the gentlemen who was visiting at that time. A few days later some Senecas came to Newark, who danced and sang. When they left Francis imitated them very well.

They bid farewell to Captain Talbot on 22 June, who sailed for Kingston on the *Gov. Simcoe* en route to England. (He would resign from the army on Christmas Day 1800 and return in 1801 to promote land settlement.) Elizabeth was soon troubled over seeing rattlesnakes near the wharf, barely 100 yards from Navy Hall. She suspected there was a nest, which was too close for peace of mind. By 7 July, when the assembly was dissolved, everyone was worried about the activities of General Anthony Wayne beyond Detroit. The American general was spreading a rumour that a chief of the Six Nations who had attended the conference at Sandusky the year before had been poisoned by members of other tribes. Wayne was trying to divide the Indians to make conquest simpler.

On 13 July the Simcoe's said goodbye to another dear friend, Chief Justice Osgoode, who sailed for Quebec. The chief justice of Lower Canada, Sir William Smith, had died, and Osgoode was to replace him. As yet no new chief justice had been chosen for Upper Canada, to Simcoe's dismay. Three days later, some fifty Seneca adults and children camped close to Navy Hall. Elizabeth was amazed at how quiet they were, compared to the same number of Europeans.[4] On the seventeenth, Simcoe returned to Navy Hall with a wounded finger, and after sending for Surgeon Macaulay, Elizabeth asked how it happened

"I was walking near the guard's tent at Queenston with a gentleman", he explained, "when a soldier aimed at an Indian's dog that had stolen some pork. The musket was loaded with pellets, and the gentleman, the dog, another Indian, and myself, were all wounded. I gave the gun to the wounded Indian to appease him and I reprimanded the soldier."

When Dr. Macaulay arrived he probed the wound carefully while Simcoe clamped his lips together and tried to hold steady. The surgeon could feel something rather large for a pellet, and wanted to remove it. The governor refused. The wound might heal itself, or the pellet might move closer to the surface and be easier to extract; let nature do its work if possible. Besides, he wanted to set out shortly for Forty Mile Creek, taking Elizabeth and the two children with him. Neither the surgeon nor Elizabeth could sway him, though both were concerned that the wound might become septic.

They left in boats on 26 July, escorted by Ensign Mayne, on what turned out to be a three-day disaster. Simcoe's injured finger was the least of their troubles. The first night they pitched the tent in a spot that was swarming with mosquitoes, and for relief they rose and breakfasted at half past three in the morning. Then Francis caught cold, and by the time they reached the Twenty Mile Creek, halfway along, he was so ill that they left him, with a servant to care for him, at a house belonging to Colonel Butler. The weather was unkind, with rain and high winds. At Forty Mile Creek a settler, Mrs. Green, recommended boiling a plant called crow's foot in milk till it was red and thick and giving it to Francis.[5] They went some distance up the creek, and Elizabeth saw wild rice growing and gathered some crow's foot. By that time Ensign Mayne was ill with ague and they started back. After collecting Francis, they reached Newark at nine o'clock on the night of the twenty-ninth Immediately the weather cleared.

On 1 August, Elizabeth visited Mrs. David William Smith, who was staying at a house on the Newark side of the Niagara River, in the hope that the different air there would help her sick child. On the eighth, Bishop Jacob

Mountain and his brother, Jehosophat, a clergyman at Trois Rivières, arrived for a visit. They were attended by the brother's son, who was the bishop's chaplain. On Sunday the tenth, the bishop preached an excellent sermon, by which time all hope of peace had faded. Two days later they decided that Elizabeth should soon take the children to Quebec. The governor escorted the bishop to see the Falls on the fourteenth, and their guest left for Kingston the next day, taking a letter which Elizabeth had written to Mrs. Ann Caldwell, asking her to find a house for her to rent.

Simcoe had not been complaining about his wounded finger, but when Surgeon Macaulay examined it on 19 August, both agreed that the shot had to be removed. The governor endured the agonizing probing with gritted teeth, beads of perspiration standing out on his forehead. The shot Macaulay removed was indeed large, and the surgeon feared that Simcoe would always have a stiff finger. Elizabeth was glad that the shot was out and the finger beginning to heal before she had to leave.

They decided she would sail early in September, since the governor expected to set out for Detroit where he would remain some weeks. Elizabeth was again disappointed not to be able to accompany him to Detroit, although she had no desire to be any closer to the enemy; any thought of musket fire made her shudder.

On 25 August, by order of Lord Dorchester, Captain Shank arrived from York with a detachment of Queen's Rangers, bound for the Maumee as reinforcements. Four days later an express arrived with a report on the battle at Fallen Timbers when General Mad Anthony Wayne defeated the Indians. He ordered the British garrison at Fort Miamis to surrender, but the commander, Major William Campbell of the 24th Regiment, refused. The garrison and fort were stronger than Wayne expected. The fort was saved, Elizabeth maintained, because of Simcoe's foresight:

> If the Gov. had waited til the opening of the navigation of the Lakes to have gone to the Miamis as Ld. Dorchester proposed, the Fort would not have been rendered defensible by this time to have intimidated Mr. Wayne, & War would have commenced with the U. States.[6]

"The Gov.", however, was furious that any Queen's Rangers had been dispatched to reinforce the troops at the new fort. He had intended from the outset to use the regiment to develop the country, not as a fighting force. Short of Queen's Rangers, Simcoe commissioned Mr. William Berczy and some German settlers he had brought from New York State to settle north of York, to continue the work on Yonge Street. Simcoe was fuming, and he prayed the Germans could work as quickly as his soldiers. He had no authority to pay wages, and had offered them extra grants of land in return for their labours.

At about the same time, news reached Newark that Admiral Richard Lord Howe had captured "7 sail of French ships" on 1 June (because he could not avoid it, as Thomas Graves told Mrs. Burges). This called for a celebration, and the merchants arranged a fine dinner that was attended by the governor and his officers. Elizabeth invited some ladies to dine with her. September arrived, and the eighth was a momentous day. The renowned explorer, Alexander Mackenzie, reached Newark after his journey of many months to the Pacific coast. To Mary Anne, who hungered for details on the geography and wild life, Elizabeth wrote:

> Mr. McKenzie went down the River of Peace near 2 degrees north of L. Superior & came to the Rocky Mountains on which rise some Rivers that fall into the Atlantic & others which empty into the Pacific Ocean. He went down a River which falls into the latter, & rises not 700 yards from the River of Peace. He afterwards travelled 17 days by land.

Mackenzie did not descend a river all the way to the Pacific; he touched the Fraser River, but then struck overland. Eagerly Elizabeth listened to the wonders he described, of sheep on the Rocky Mountains that had horns the size of a cow's, of how natives on the coast speared salmon and cured it for winter storage. He presented a sea otter skin to Simcoe as proof that he had reached the Pacific. Elizabeth longed to see the Rockies, but she was not interested in the long stretch of unpicturesque grassland that separated the mountain chain from the eastern part of North America.

On 11 September the governor left with a party for Detroit, and Elizabeth was ready to set out for Quebec. The next night with the children and Collins, Elizabeth boarded the *Mississauga*, escorted by Captain John McGill, to be ready to sail at dawn on the thirteenth for Kingston. McGill was shown as an ensign in the Queen's Rangers on The Army List, and as a commissary of stores for the garrison, with a captain's rank and pay. The leg injury he had suffered, which prevented him continuing the march from New Brunswick with Captain Shaw, still bothered him. Simcoe had appointed him commissary because he was not fit for more rigorous duty with the regiment.[7]

On board, they received a request from Molly Brant, the Mohawk wife of the late Sir William Johnson and a sister of Joseph the war chief. She had been visiting one of her daughters at Newark, but was ill and anxious to return to her own home in Kingston. The governor had reserved the entire vessel for his family, but Elizabeth allowed "Brant's sister" to join them. Molly was in reality Lady Johnson, but she did not use her husband's name because she was a Mohawk matron. Unlike the white society, in the matriarchical society of the Iroquois, a man joined a woman's tribe. "She speaks English well & is a civil & very sensible old woman", Elizabeth wrote, scarcely hinting that Molly was well educated. Elizabeth admired what her contemporaries called the noble savage but she may have felt ill at ease with a brown-skinned woman who behaved like a well-bred white lady.

The passage over the lake was stormy. Elizabeth stayed most of the time on deck to avoid seasickness. They reached Kingston at 8.00 a.m. on the morning of 15 September. Captain Richard Porter of the 60th Regiment, the garrison commandant, came aboard to offer his help, followed by some ladies. Then Captain Porter and Captain McGill went to find bateaux. Only one government bateau was to be had, and they hired a second one from a merchant to carry the baggage. Along with clothing and some furniture, Elizabeth had brought a "boudet" to sleep on if she did not fancy any of the beds, and a supply of non-perishable food. They left Kingston at noon for Gananoque, where they were to sleep at the home of one of the Fairfield brothers. The family had pioneered at Amherstview, west of Kingston, and this brother was building a new mill for the principal settler, Colonel Joel Stone. The awning on the bateau was low and of twisted "osiers" (willow shoots), which offered more shelter than the high wooden awnings used in the summer. She appreciated the lower awning for it rained all the way to Gananoque.

As the baggage bateau with her boudet did not arrive when she was ready to sleep, she took planks and small boxes from the boat, supported the planks on the boxes, covered them with a carpet and slept well. The children and Collins "had a small Room within mine". Captain McGill slept in the boat. In the morning Colonel Stone sent over some fresh cream and butter. Again the weather was showery. They had good accommodation below Prescott, at a potash-maker's home. Elizabeth was pleased with the spacious room that had six large windows in it.

She was frightened when the bateau descended the Galop Rapids, but she did not mind the longer and rougher rapids at Long Sault. At Glengarry House they stopped to deliver a letter. Passing along Lake St. Francis, a storm was brewing and Captain McGill suggested they find a place to spend the night.

"No," she said. "It's only four o'clock, too early to stop."

She quickly regretted her rashness. They were well out in the lake when the storm struck. Amidst claps of thunder and a nearly pitch dark sky, the boat tossed, the children cried out and Collins showed her alarm by sighing. Worst of all was the thought that the bateau might be captured by an American boat and they would be taken upstream to New York State as prisoners.

"An extra tot of rum for each of you when you reach shore!" McGill shouted above the storm.

At that Elizabeth realised he was as frightened as she was. They landed, but not near any house. As the storm had passed, she agreed to proceed to Pointe au Baudet, where there was a post house, as long as they hugged the north shore all the way. At the post house they found Hugh Macdonell, the adjutant-general of militia, who gave up his rooms to them. There was already a roaring blaze in the fireplace. Farther on, rather than ride down the Cascades Rapids, Elizabeth hired a caleche for herself and the children, leaving Collins and the other servants to go in the bateaux. The road was so rough that she had to stop and ask Collins to come with them to hold Francis:

I determined never to go in a Post Calash [sic] again. The Carriage was driven tandem the first horse tied to the other by a rope which did not in the least confine him. The horses generally went different ways & at a great rate.[8]

At Montreal, where they arrived on 18 September, Elizabeth expected to stay at the home of William Henry Gray, the postmaster and district sheriff, but his house was undergoing renovations. A message was waiting, inviting her to come to Beaver Hall, the town house of the Joseph Frobishers, whose carriage soon arrived to convey them. Mrs. Frobisher came from their country home to welcome her. An officer of the 7th Fusiliers brought her letters from England, and Major George Duke of the 26th Foot offered to send men of his regiment to row the bateaux. She thanked him, but she was quite happy with her Canadian crew, who were much more picturesque, in their sashes and capots, than the soldiers.

They left Montreal on Sunday 21 September, warmly covered in buffalo robes against the windy, unpleasant weather. Elizabeth walked the last half mile to a post house to warm herself. Kept by some English-speaking people, it was clean and the room had a good fire, but the proprietors overcharged her. She was better pleased by the post house at Trois Rivières, where a French-speaking couple charged her much less. She was surprised that the children minded the cold so little. Francis would not keep his gloves on:

> After drinking tea & the Children are gone to bed I dress my hair (which I have not had time to do in the morning) change my Habit & lay down on a boudet before the fire, covered with a fur Blanket. I do not undress when I have not my own bed, which is the case at present.

At Cap Santé they went to a house where they had stopped by chance on the way to Upper Canada and been kindly received. The woman recognised Elizabeth, and welcomed her with "with her usual French politeness". She told her that the Simcoes' visit there had given her the idea of "saving her Money to make the miserable Cottage it had formerly been fit for the reception of travellers". Elizabeth was very pleased to think that she had been the inspiration for an improvement in the life of this good woman. Her husband was "quite uncivilized but she had been educated at a Convent." Before Elizabeth left, a letter arrived from Mrs. Caldwell, inviting her stay at Belmont House until a house at Quebec could be made ready for her.

On 24 September the bateaux reached Cap Rouge "3 leagues from Quebec". Elizabeth walked to the next post house, dressed herself and hired a caleche for the four-mile ride to the Caldwell house, where she "met with the most friendly reception". The social whirl started at once. Many people came to call, and on 26 September Lady Dorchester invited her to the Château St. Louis, the governor-in-chief's official residence in the Upper Town. Elizabeth had to decline because her "cloathes" had not yet arrived. She was flattered by this attention, even though she knew full well that Dorchester was a thorn in Simcoe's flesh. She appreciated the kindness, especially as the Dorchesters were in mourning. Their second eldest son, the Honourable Thomas Carleton, just twenty years old and a lieutenant in the 1st Regiment of Dragoons, had died recently while on duty.[9]

By 29 September, Elizabeth's clothes had come, and she was welcomed by Bishop Mountain, Lieutenant-Colonel John Despard of the 7th Fusiliers and Mrs. Despard, Mme. Baby, and the wives of many senior civil servants and army officers. The next day, Captain McGill was ready to leave for Newark amidst rumours of peace. Elizabeth considered going with him but she decided not to, because no confirmation of peace had reached Quebec. Instead she went to inspect a house of Colonel Caldwell's at Sans Bruit which he had offered her. She refused his kindness since the house stood in an extremely cold place, and instead she rented a house in Palace Street.

At a party at Belmont House on 12 October, Elizabeth met Colonel George Beckwith, the adjutant of British forces in North America. Casually he mentioned that Mrs. Simcoe's father was Colonel Thomas Gwillim. At that Colonel Caldwell broke into a smile. The information was a revelation. He remembered Colonel Gwillim well, and while visiting England after General Wolfe's death he had stayed with him at his London house. He had known Mrs. Simcoe all this time, and had only now learned that she was his old friend's daughter.

Afterwards he was even more attentive to Elizabeth's needs. She took possession of the house in Palace Street two days later. Thinking that a school would benefit Sophia, she chose one, but she gave no details about it. Only in the notes she used to prepare the diary for Mrs. Hunt did she mention the school.[10] She bought a closed carriole so that she could get about, but she could not use it until there was enough snow. In the meantime, the Caldwells lent her a caleche. To her Quebec household she added a horse, cow, cat and a picturesque Canadian driver.

Simcoe, now back at Newark, wrote to his "Dear Girls" on 25 October. Mama, Sophia and Francis were in Quebec, but he expected that peace would come soon. He planned to set out for Kingston to meet them. He closed with, "Fear God & honour Mrs. Hunt & all who care for you."[11] On the thirteenth he had already written of his return to Elizabeth on the eighteenth, but his letters did not reach her until 4 November. On the sixth, Elizabeth saw the 7th Fusiliers sail for Halifax, their tour of duty in Canada at an end.

To Charlotte, on 8 November, Simcoe asked her to have "Mr. Scadding" cut down trees "without mercy" to improve the views around Wolford Lodge. ("Mr. Scadding" was Thomas, a brother of John Scadding who had come out to Upper Canada to assist the governor.) Simcoe would soon be leaving Newark for York, and all round the lake to Kingston, to meet

Mama and Sophia and "the little dog Francis. . . He thought himself so fine in his red stockings or leggings & Indian cloak that he acts as if he was twenty years old" but, the loving father added, he was good natured.[12]

When Elizabeth saw Sophia on the morning of 17 November, she was appalled to find her covered with a rash. She kept her home from school and sent Francis to Belmont to prevent him catching whatever his sister had. By the twenty-first the rash was gone, and Francis returned home.[13] Early in December Elizabeth received letters from the governor, forwarded by Mr. Gray from Montreal. Simcoe proposed meeting her at Pointe au Baudet sometime in January or February, whenever the ice was sound. Ensign Mayne would meet her in Montreal.

Yet the war news from Europe was bad. The French had sunk the ship *Briget* and captured the *August*, which had many British officers and their families aboard. They threw overboard the collection of drawings by an officer's wife, an action which Elizabeth considered disgraceful vandalism. The poor woman had lost the records of her travels and the memories they could have evoked. On 20 December, Francis fell ill and Elizabeth sent for Dr. Merwyn Nooth, who could not find a cause. By Christmas day, Elizabeth felt able to leave the boy, and she attended a service at the French church, followed by one Bishop Mountain conducted.[14] On the twenty-sixth Francis was much better and she attended a ball, but was too fatigued to enjoy it after sleepless nights watching over her son.

The Dorchesters hosted a "rout" on 1 January 1795, to which Elizabeth was invited. A rout was often held to introduce strangers, but there had been few of late because of the death of young Thomas Carleton. A further worry was the illness of one of the Dorchesters' daughters. Yet the governor general and his lady were both being solicitous of Elizabeth. She was particularly impressed, for they had not waited to invite her until after she had been formally introduced, as was usually required. Afterwards Elizabeth was invited to the Château frequently, and to ride in Lady Dorchester's carriole, an open one with seats in front for the children. Again, Elizabeth remarked that the Canadian driver was so picturesque.

Colonel Beckwith called on 11 January, and congratulated her on Simcoe's being promoted to major-general in the army as of 3 October last. The promotion was long overdue, and Beckwith thought an honour should not be long in coming. Elizabeth resolved not to be too optimistic. She knew Simcoe deserved a title, but whether he received one depended on which way the political wind was blowing.

Elizabeth had admired Lord Dorchester's enclosed "Dormeuse", a sleigh which he used for winter journeys, and she ordered one built for her journey to meet Simcoe:

> It is like an open Carriole with a head made of Seal Skin & lined with Baize, a large Bear or Buffalo skin fixes in front which perfectly secures you from wind & weather, & may be unhooked if the weather is fine or mild, a low seat & feather bed to keep one's feet warm.[15]

She arranged, with the help of Hugh Finlay, the postmaster general, for a courier to precede her, and to pay in advance for accommodation and fresh horses, to avoid delays.

On 20 January the Dorchesters gave a ball at which Miss Carleton, somewhat recovered, made a short appearance. Elizabeth now counted among her friends Miss Ann Johnson, the eldest daughter of Sir John and Lady Johnson. They lived in Montreal but the Johnson children were often in Quebec. Sir John, who had once seemed a threat to Simcoe, was proving to be a compatible colleague. Elizabeth also visited William Osgoode. On the thirty-first, she sent a load of baggage to Montreal where Ensign Mayne had arrived. Then she closed the house on Palace Street and moved to Belmont. They left there on 6 February; Elizabeth and the children, Collins and some of the baggage rode in the Dormeuse. Francis had a cold and was feverish, but his mother trusted that the fresh air would do him good, especially since they were comfortably warm on their feather bed, smug under fur robes.

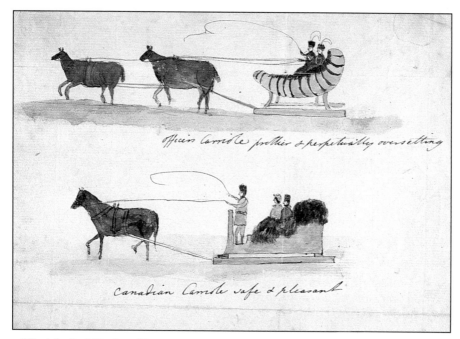

"Carioles" at Quebec City.

Montmorency Falls, a short distance east of Quebec City, was a favoured spot for tourists before Mrs. Simcoe sketched them.

Mrs. Tice's House, probably drawn while Mrs. Simcoe was staying with the Tices in the summer and autumn of 1795.

St. George's Church, Sibbald Point, Georgina. The Simcoe daughters painted a window for this original wooden church. The sketch was made from one the Sibbald family sent Mrs. Simcoe, since it was not opened until 1839.

Looking over the St. Lawrence River at Pointe aux Trembles, between Montreal and Quebec City.

Cascade in Wolfe's Cove. The waterfall was west of Quebec City, close to the Plains of Abraham.

Belmont on the Ste Foy Road, was the home of Colonel Henry Caldwell, who had known Mrs. Simcoe's father in 1759.

Bateaux Running the Long Sault Rapids. Watercolour sketch on birch bark.

from Richmond hill August 19ᵗʰ 1797

Richmond Hill, near London. The name is commemorated in Richmond Hill, north of Toronto, which the Simcoes named.

Castle Frank, the rustic summer home named for Francis Simcoe, overlooked the Don Valley. Its Greek columns were white pine logs.

A view of the Queen's Rangers' barracks at Queenston.

Mrs. Simcoe made many watercolour sketches of the "picturesque" Niagara Gorge that reminded her of Whitchurch, Herefordshire.

Queenston, where cargoes had to be brought ashore and carried around the Falls, was also called the lower landing.

Camp at Niagara. This watercolour sketch shows the tents which the Simcoes pitched at Newark before Navy Hall had been renovated.

Mrs. Hamilton's House at Queenston. No wonder Mrs. Simcoe envied the Hamiltons their fine home while she had to make do with the canvas house and Navy Hall.

Drawing of a Miami Chief.　　　　*Mrs. Simcoe's sketch of Great Sail.*

Mohawk Village on the Grand River. St. Paul's, also known as Her Majesty's Chapel to the Mohawks, is to the right. It was built in 1785 with the aid of a grant from George III.

View of Burlington Bay.

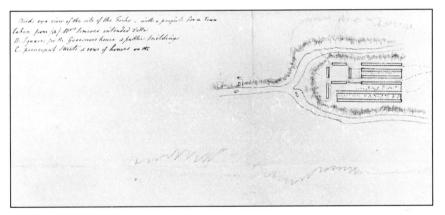

Plan for the capital in the Thames valley (the site of London).The caption on the drawing reads, "Bird's eye view of the site of the Forks — with a prospect for a Town taken from (a) Mrs. Simcoe's intended Villa. B. Square for the Governors house & public buildings. C. principal Streets & rows of houses on the . . ."

Playter's Bridge over the Don River.

John Scadding's Cabin. It stood close to the Don River south of Francis Simcoe's land and Castle Frank.

Thousand Islands. Mrs. Simcoe made many sketches of this picturesque stretch of the Upper St. Lawrence River. The awning on the bateau in the foreground, and the boatman with his setting pole illuminate conditions of travel.

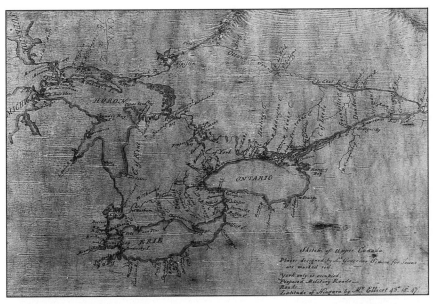

The famous map that Trojan chewed up. Mrs. Simcoe patched it, and "the Gov."
wrote his "amusing verses."

Joel Stone's Mill at Gananoque. Simcoe added the swimming dog in the foreground.

Bend in the St. Lawrence River. The hills on the horizon suggest that this spot was not far west of Quebec City.

Wolford Chapel was dedicated in 1802. Who might the three women on the left be?

Mrs. Simcoe's watercolour sketch of a church in England. This may be Mr. Guernsey's church in the Forest of Deane.

Inchbrooke House. Many of Mrs. Simcoe's Canadian watercolours and sketches have been preserved, but her English ones are more rare.

Harbour Boat Scene. The exact place was not identified, but it was likely one of the ports along the south coast of Devon.

Left: *Rock Bass. Mrs. Simcoe did not comment on how bony this fish was, nor did she record eating one.*

Right: *Sketch of a Whitefish. Many of these drawings were for Miss Burges, who shared Mrs. Simcoe's interest in biology.*

This sketch of a butterfly could have been the one Mrs. Simcoe sent her friend Miss Burges in May 1793.

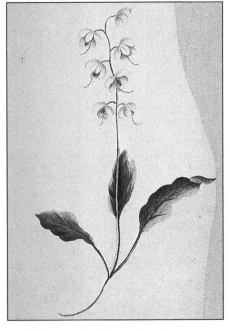

Wildflower. The Simcoe daughters probably enjoyed the sketches of plants and fish as much as Miss Burges did.

Window designed by Mrs Simcoe for Holy Trinity Church, Parish of Dunkeswell Abbey, Devonshire, England. This and other windows were prepared in the Simcoe workshop in Wolford Lodge.

The Simcoe Window, St. George's Church, Sibbald Point, Ontario. This window was designed by Mrs Simcoe's daughters for their friend Susan Sibbald.

Chapter 14

MRS. BURGES' "COMMISSIONS"

Back in Devonshire, Mary Anne, now Mrs. Burges, except to the Simcoe children who still called her Miss, continued her round of visits, entertaining, drawing, studying languages, botany and geology. By 11 August she was very worried about her Aunt Somerville, who was ill with jaundice. Mark Somerville had been joined at Mr. Haynes' school by his younger brother Kenelm. Both boys were "stupid mortals" who paid scant attention to Mary Anne when she breakfasted with the Haynes.

According to the newspapers, dispatches from Quebec indicated that peace would continue in Upper Canada:

> It is a circumstance particularly gratifying in the high rank you bear in the country where you are that no mischief could happen either to Col. Simcoe or yourself, which would not be transmitted to England in the accounts which come from any part of America & inserted in all the papers; so that tho' I have not gratification of hearing immediately from yourself yet on the arrival of every packet [boat] which brings no ill news of you, I may assure myself you are safe, & that assurance is almost equivalent of good news.[1]

At Wolford Lodge, a trifling dispute arose between Charlotte and Harriet. Eliza touched Charlotte's elbow and changed the subject. "I thought this little transaction much to the credit of both the two eldest, as it shewed ...that strict union, which at present subsists among them all." Miss Hunt was arranging for an emigrant Viscount, whom Mr. Haynes had brought to Honiton to teach in his school, to tutor the girls in French. He was miserable that an application he made for a commission in the Emigrant Legion had been declined.[2]

On 7 September, Mary Anne's Aunt Somerville died. She offered to care for Julia, the youngest, although the Digbys might decide they wanted her. When Mary Anne told Mark and Kenelm Somerville, they "took little notice". The Simcoe girls showed more concern, and only because they saw how grieved Mary Anne was.[3]

By 23 September, a letter from Canada raised Mary Anne's spirits, and she was looking forward to the arrival of Captain Thomas Talbot, bringing a large packet to England. She was attending to the "commissions" the Simcoes sent her, preferably before the last ships sailed for Quebec. She wrote Mr. Alexander Davison in London to enquire when to send the items, since Simcoe had arranged with him to forward them. Simcoe wanted a major-general's regimentals from Mr. Cannon, a tailor, and Elizabeth a muslin gown from Miss Rush, a seamstress, and a corset from M. LeJeune, shoes, and a selection from Mr. Thomas Payne, Mrs. Graves' bookseller in Bath, the last a surprise for the girls. If Captain Lowe could take the items to Canada, either in the late autumn or spring, the regimentals need not be insured.[4]

By the end of September the French viscount was tutoring the girls, and teaching them to speak with a Parisian accent. Thomas Talbot had forwarded Elizabeth's packet when he reached London. Mary Anne had collected Elizabeth's drawings from the engraver and they looked "wonderfully spirited", but the books ordered for the children had not come. Then Eliza received a letter from a Mr. Russell in Exeter, apologising that she had not received the pair of boots Thomas Payne had sent, which she could collect from the Swam Inn. "If Mr. Payne had sent her [Thomas Paine's] *The Rights of Man*, or of a Guillotine, well & good; but a pair of Boots!" Mary Anne then explained that the parcel held books for the girls, that she had ordered for General Simcoe.[5]

In reply to an installment of Elizabeth's diary dated 9 September at Newark, she congratulated her on discovering

> a nation of Icthyophagi [fish-eaters, the natives on the Pacific coast described by Alexander Mackenzie]. If peace is secured, I expect to hear that you have set out for the Pacific Ocean to visit them & to render your name as famous among travellers ... . Your voyage down the St. Lawrence must have been sublime, but I hope you may have better weather for your return.[6]

In November, Mary Anne went to Clifton to see her bereaved Uncle Hugh Somerville. Mary and Fanny Somerville were fine girls, but were not being well educated. Julia, the youngest, took fright at the sight of Mary Anne, and screamed, refusing to allow her to come near. She called on Mrs. Gwillim, who was in Bristol for a change of scene, and was looking well. In her mild way she regretted any estrangement between Elizabeth and Mrs. Graves. Mary Anne assured her that Mrs. Graves' stories that the Simcoe children were neglected were untrue.[7]

By Friday 5 December she was home. Sunday was her thirty-first birthday, celebrated with a "superb festival" at which the four Simcoe girls were among the principal guests. She had resisted the fashion of short waisted gowns, until Miss Digby presented her with one. She had to admit "I have seen few people whom the fashion so little misbecomes as myself." She drew a sketch, adding that Miss Hunt would look well in one, if she could "persuade her not to sit so".

Letters from Elizabeth were coming after only two months now that she was in Quebec, instead of the usual three. She had sent Elizabeth's stays to Miss Rush the seamstress so that she would know what size to make the gown. Mary Anne forwarded the following account, in pounds, to the Simcoes:

Books from Mr. Payne	3. 15. -
"Corsett" from M. Le Jeune	2. 2. -
Shoes	2. 6. 6
Coloured Cottons	7. 6
Muslin Gown & making	3. 1. 6
Great Coat	4. 15. -
Total	16. 7. 6

Miss Rush required eleven yards of muslin for the gown, which made it so expensive. Eliza, who never looked better, would be exactly Elizabeth's height. Charlotte and Harriet were taller, but Caroline promised to be small like Eliza.[8]

By Christmas day she had received Elizabeth's box containing a quill pen and a charming fur tippet. "I never saw one so soft & so warm & the colour of the fur is just what I have always liked the best" and she would never catch cold while wearing it:

walked to church in my tippit & despised the north East Wind. As for the Indian Chief, I consider him as the most illustrious Guest I had ever the honour to entertain ... I am sure, if ever I write anything sufficiently sublime to employ my Eagle's quill, it must be when I am inspired by so heroic a tete tete ... You never told me of your discovery that Coll. Caldwell had been a friend of your father's but Mrs. Gwillim did, when I saw her at Bristol[.][9]

The weather had turned frosty, with icicles as thick as her arm hanging by the door. Her brother, James Bland Burges, had sent another £20 from the sale of *Cavern of Death*, which she would use to travel to Copford, near Colchester, to visit Admiral Elliott. En route, she arrived in London, 31 December, the roads very deep with snow, the horses' manes and tails so hung with icicles "I could imagine myself at Quebec."[10]

Mary Anne reached the Elliotts' on 8 January, 1795, and was received most hospitably. She went with some of the family to Colchester, to see "the Stadholder & family who arrived on the twenty-first". This was William V, the Prince of Orange, whose government had been overthrown by French troops and Dutch exiles. The Princesses had huddled together below in a small boat where fishermen threw their catch "more dirty than a Pigsty & full of every ill smell".[11]

She then went to Hermitage to stay with the Heads. The weather was so cold that the Thames was frozen over below Westminster Bridge. The Heads were glad to see her, but the hours they kept were not to her liking. Breakfast was not until noon, and dinner so late that little of the evening remained. By the time dinner was served she had developed a headache:

> the Heads are, as usual, but on indifferent terms just now
> with most of their neighbours; so that we neither visit nor
> are visited .... I believe my sister feels a degree of obligation
> to me for the interest I take in the children, & the pains I am
> very willingly at in hearing their lessons & teaching them
> anything I can. I really think the Girls extremely pleasant
> children.

Fanny was her aunt's favourite, partly for the interest she showed in
Elizabeth's drawing of a butterfly. Mary was the least well disposed, while
Sophy's lively imagination would frighten Elizabeth if any of her daughters
possessed it. Their mother sent her compliments:

> I really believe she considers Genl. Simcoe as her greatest
> benefactor on account of his having refused to take Mr.
> Head with him to America; for she has often spoken to me
> of it as a personal obligation conferred on herself.[12]

She was still looking for oranges so that Jenny could make the marmalade
to send to Canada. The present embargo was preventing any fruit being
landed in England.

On 11 March she was relying to Elizabeth's letter of 6 December. By
now, Elizabeth would be back in Upper Canada. If the Simcoes should
remain abroad for seven years, half that time had now expired, and this
page, number 750, completed half of what she expected to write.

> I know not what to think of Sophia's temper; so unlike the
> rest of your children, unless that there must have been
> something in the Corinthian system of education, which
> Mrs. Graves read the whole evening to you & me ... &
> which was compleatly reversed with regard to her ... I have
> no doubt but that the future events of Sophia's life will be
> such as to require all that pertenacity of opinion, which you
> now may call stubbornness; but which will then acquire
> the name of very heroic firmness.[13]

On her way home she stopped with friends at Woolwich. Now everyone was talking of the forthcoming marriage of the Prince of Wales to
Princess Caroline of Brunswick. Among the people Mary Anne saw at
Woolwich was Captain John Fisher, of the Royal Artillery, who had recently
come from Niagara. He showed her his drawing of the Falls of Niagara
"which fully answered my expectations, high as they had been raised. I was
the more gratified with them because you had seen them".[14]

From Hermitage she went to London, and found that Reverend Edward Hunt was going to Exeter in the same coach. She was happy that she would not meet with anything disagreeable on the journey. At Salisbury, Lord Arundell's carriage was waiting:

> with the most venerable looking man I ever saw, who was to go to Exeter, where I learnt from their conversation with the Coach man, he was to be met by Lord Clifford's carriage, & conveyed to Ugbrooke. He was a French Emigrant Priest, I suppose a man of eminence since so much attention was paid to him ... I soon found he could not speak a word of English, & that was just such a sort of opportunity as I liked for speaking French ... so I took the first opportunity that came of explaining to him some demand made on him at breakfast; he seemed obliged to me .... I wish I could draw his picture. And his manners are as venerable as his appearance.[15]

The Arundells and the Cliffords were prominent Roman Catholic landed gentry. Lord Clifford was 6th Baron Clifford of Chudleigh. His wife was Eleanor Mary Arundell, younger daughter of the late 8th Baron Arundell of Wardour Castle, Wiltshire. The present Lady Arundell was Eleanor Mary Lady Clifford's elder sister, Mary Christine. Her husband, the 9th Baron, was James Everard, who had taken his wife's name because the 8th Baron had had no son. The Clifford family seat is still Ugbrooke House, near Exeter. Wardour Castle, a beautiful Palladian house near Salisbury, Wiltshire, was built close to the ruins of Old Wardour Castle that had been destroyed in Lord Protector Oliver Cromwell's time.

A letter addressed to M.A. Burges Esq. had arrived at Tracey soon after Mary Anne reached home. It was a bill for £91 from Mr. Cannon, Simcoe's tailor, the cost of his new regimentals. As the tailor offered a five percent discount for "ready money", she directed Cannon to draw on her funds. "I have not disclaimed the title of Squire, which I obtain from most of my correspondents on your account."

The dog Ranger, "transported" to see her when she returned, was a genius. He would follow William to the stable to see which saddle was put on Placid. If the saddle was hers, he ran back to the house and exerted "all his rhetoric till I tell him I will take him with me; but if it is a man's saddle he never thinks of advocating his petitions to me." By 8 April, she had acquired two dozen oranges in spite of the embargo, and Jenny was making the marmalade at last. Now she was trying to persuade Mr. Flood to reimburse her for Simcoe's regimentals, who as usual was taking his time about paying. He thought the bill excessive, but he was hardly in a position to know what a general's regimentals cost. Captain-Lieutenant George Spencer, although still hoping to join the Queen's Rangers, was now going to Spain in the hope of a cure from the "native air".[16]

She was delighted to receive a letter from General Simcoe, outlining plans for his library. She was much interested and she intended to be an inhabitant if he would "readmit me to my post of Under Secretary on his return."

> General Wolfe's bust did arrive soon after you went away,
> & has ever since remained in the box in which it came, so
> that probably it is in better plight than Ld. Moira's, which
> stands on the top of the Bookshelves, & is very dusty but I
> suppose it may easily be cleaned.[17]

When she went to Wolford Lodge, Harriet, dancing about joyfully, asked her to guess who had written. In turn Mary Anne asked Harriet to guess who had written her.

"I am sure nobody half so good as the person that has written to me," said Harriet.

"Your are mistaken," Mary Anne replied. "My correspondent is fully equal to that of yours."

At that all the girls were affronted; "there was nobody in all the World that was a quarter as good as the person who had written to Harriet". Mary Anne stood her ground for a quarter of an hour, until Eliza said. "Since it is Miss Burges that says her correspondent is as good as Harriet's, I do believe he must be the same person, for she would not tell us of anybody else."[18]

By 23 April, Mary Anne had received Elizabeth's letter of 2 January. Charlotte was upset because General Simcoe had not acknowledged the shirt she had sent him — a year and a half ago. If he never received it, Mary Anne thought that was a pity, for it was well made. Mrs. Graves had invited Mary Anne to Bath, but she would only drop in if she had to see her uncle at Clifton.

> I am vastly glad that you have met with a person whom you
> like so much as Lady Dorchester, which must have contrib-
> uted more than any other circumstance could towards
> making you comfortable at Quebec. If she is such as you
> describe her, I am not at all surprised that she likes you.

Next she returned to the subject of Sophia:

> I think a little more stay at School may be just the thing for
> such an intractable temper as Sophia's. I wish she could be
> transported to Wolford Lodge, for a rebellious subject is
> really a great amusement to Mrs. Hunt; & she has had that
> relaxation for these two years past; Caroline being not
> quite as good as her Sisters; only that she has so perfect a
> consciousness of her own accomplishments that I seldom
> express any admiration of them ... she is extremely fond of

reading her little books aloud to her sisters, & of her own accord she adapts her voice to the different speakers in the dialogues[.][19]

At last, on 7 May, Mary Anne learned that Captain Lowe was leaving, and taking the Simcoes' things, including the two jars of marmalade Jenny had made. As a special treat she had invited the four girls to a play in Honiton. To keep it a surprise, Mrs. Hunt did not tell them until they reached the playhouse door, and "you never saw four people in such transports". They laughed so much that they "afforded entertainment to all who were present."

Mary Anne intended spending the summer in Honiton, but a message that arrived on 10 May 1795 signalled an vast change in her life. Her uncle, Colonel Hugh Somerville, had died suddenly at Clifton on the seventh. His nine children ranged in age from John Southby, thirty, to Julia, who would be three on 28 August.

She informed Mark and Kenelm that they were now orphans, and again was surprised at how little emotion either displayed. Her own grief was alleviated at the arrival of an installment of of Elizabeth journal, describing the frozen journey from Quebec to Upper Canada. She replied on 15 May:

> I am to have little Julia Somerville to live with me. It was my own offer last Autumn on the death of her Mother; & on my having now written in general terms to offer my services to the whole family, Miss Digby answered me in a very handsome manner, & informs me that the eldest girl [Mary] is going to leave school, & live with her & her brother & they likewise mean to take charge of the two next [Frances and Harriet] & all the boys; that about Julia alone they are at any loss, & that in short they shall be very glad to dispose of her to me.

She had a reservation about becoming Julia's guardian, because of the way the child behaved at Clifton:

> her having taken such an aversion to me, that she always screamed when she saw me; & I thought would have thrown herself into fits once or twice when I attempted to touch her. But I think there cannot be a decided bad temper in the Somerville family, & when she is once used to me, I do not doubt but that she will take me as other children do ... I had certainly rather have her than any of her sisters, .. because of her age[.]

Since Julia was so young, Mary Anne hoped to "form her character to please my own fancy." Her apprehensions would fade if she thought she could make Julia like the four Simcoe girls. She hoped that having Julia would not mean seeing less of Elizabeth once she had returned home, but she was confident her friend would not object to her bringing the little girl whenever she visited Wolford Lodge. Also, if Julia turned out to be disagreeable, she had plenty of other relations to cope with her. With the Simcoe girls to set a good example, she ought not to fear that Julia would turn out a disaster. She was determined to teach Julia Spanish, since she had a Spanish name. (Her father had served as an officer in the Dragoon Guards at the capture of Valenza d'Alcantara in 1763.)[20]

Since Mary Anne was not wealthy, she required some financial assistance, and while arrangements were worked out, she was full of plans for Julia. If the child was a genius, she would try experiments on her. "I shall educate her as much as possible as I have done my dog Ranger, since I have made him very obedient & companionable". The Digbys asked for advice on the size of allowance she would require to care for Julia, and she consulted Mrs. Hunt, who recommended not less than £50 a year. Mary Anne felt awkward at asking for so much

> lest it should exceed their ideas & look as if I wanted to make a property of the child. If you were here, I should follow your advice in everything. . . I take the more pains to perfect myself in Moral Philosophy, that I may set a proper example to Miss Julia, & then if I cannot benefit her, I hope at least to improve myself.[21]

The Digbys agreed to an allowance of £25 a year for board and wages of Julia's maid, Betty, and £50 a year for Julia's maintenance, to be paid from the interest of her inheritance. Since Julia's estate would be about £2,000, Mary Anne was reluctant to accept, "to deprive an orphan of money which might accumulate for her use." Yet she had to take it, for she did not have enough means herself. She resolved to make Julia the heir to her estate as a way of increasing her fortune.[22]

John Southby Somerville would be bringing Julia to her early in June, and Mary Anne decided to spend a few days in Exeter with her friend Miss Jordan before taking on the responsibilities of parenthood. When she returned to Tracey, John had already arrived, with Julia and his youngest half-brother, five-year-old William. She was delighted that Julia's disposition seemed completely altered since she had last seen the child at Clifton:

> I think I never saw so perfectly good humoured a creature. I cannot as yet have contracted any great partiality to her, having set out with a private prepossession against her, tho' for the sake of her parents, & of her own unhappy situation, I had resolved to render her every service in my power, it can therefore be as more than the truth to say that

she is exactly the sort of child which I should have
chosen from amongst a thousand others.

Mary Anne had seen more beautiful children, but never one so suited
to her own fancy. Julia was small, but fat and healthy, with a tolerable clear
complexion and light hair. She had no particularly good feature except her
eyes, which were light hazel and rather large. Betty the maid said she was
very weary as their carriage crossed the Blackdown Hills, but when she saw
the valley she called out in delight, "Oh pretty pretty garden!"[23]
While Mary Anne was preoccupied with Julia, James Bland Burges was
awarded a baronetcy and a pension of £1,200 a year, as well as a sinecure as
Knight Marshal of the Royal Household that gave him an additional income
of £600 a year. He retired to devote himself to literary pursuits, and Mary
Anne was pleased that she would now hear more often from her brother.[24]

Chapter 15

THE SEASON OF 1795

Elizabeth's return journey to Upper Canada was notable for her descriptions of the uncertainties of driving on frozen rivers. After a night at a "tolerable post house" six leagues west of Belmont, they drove a league inland to find safe ice to cross a stream that flowed into the St. Lawrence. At Champlain, where they crossed another river, the sound of the ice so terrified her that they stopped beyond it at a "wretched House", although she was warned that travellers avoided it. The children slept, but people talked all night; the owners "looked as if they belonged to a souteraine." At Cap Madeleine, she was so impatient to have the next crossing behind her that she would not wait for breakfast. They had to go two leagues above the usual crossing place and "even there saw water on each side of the carriage."[1]

The driver was so old that Postmaster Finlay dispatched a younger man to take over on the most dangerous part of the road. Elizabeth wanted him to stay, but he would not offend the old man, who had been driving for more than sixty years. The latter nearly overturned the dormeuse before they came to Trois Rivières. It was Sunday 8 February. They found the streets of the town so full of people that Elizabeth felt intimidated and ordered the driver to keep going. They did not stop until they reached Maskinonge at 5.00 in the evening, where the post house was good. Collins "(who never liked losing a meal)" was not at all happy.

From there on the ice was safe. They left Maskinonge at 5.00 a.m. on the next day, changed horses, still hitched tandem rather than side by side, every three leagues, and reached Mr. Edward William Gray's house in Montreal twelve hours later. Ensign Mayne was waiting, and they left on Tuesday the tenth, in three sleighs. Elizabeth and the children rode in the dormeuse. Mayne followed in a carriole with the baggage, while the servants brought up the rear in the other. When the driver informed her they would have to make do with the same horses all the way to Pointe au Baudet, Elizabeth was downcast at the prospect of such slow progress. But they made good time because the ice was excellent. The drive across the wide part of the St. Lawrence below the confluence of the Ottawa River was "delightful". After stopping at the Cedars two hours to rest the horses, they reached Pointe au Baudet. Of late the track had been better, for the horses were hitched side by side, which made a wide packed-down pathway. Along Lake St. Francis, Elizabeth was perplexed when her driver left the carriage and walked behind it with the other drivers:

> Every mile he came & whipped the Horses violently & I
> saw no more of him till we had gone another half mile the

Horses steadily pursuing a slight track on the Snow, but had there been air holes in the track they pursued as sometimes happens on the Ice, what would have become of us? It put me in mind of the Rein Deer who travel self-conducted.

At 11.00 a.m. on Wednesday 11 February, the sleighs reached the home of Major James Gray, in Williamsburgh Township. There, Governor Simcoe, who had been staying at a house farther west, in Johnstown, had come to wait for them. At the sight of his tall figure exiting from the square-timbered house, the children broke into cries of delight, leapt from the sleigh, and ran to him.

Simcoe had been so anxious to see them that he had gone to Pointe au Baudet the day before, and he had been most disappointed when they did not arrive. Elizabeth explained that their journey would have taken much longer if Postmaster Finlay had not made the arrangements, for which the governor was grateful.

They remained with the Grays until Friday the thirteenth. Ensign Mayne returned to Montreal to attend to some business of the regiment, and the Simcoes left in sleighs for Kingston. The first night, in a house at Rapide Plat, Elizabeth found the room assigned to them miserably damp. They came to the tiny hamlet of Johnstown, the administrative seat of the Eastern District the next day. Everyone was accommodated in St. John's Hall, where the governor and Major Littlehales had been staying for the past fortnight, then being converted into an inn. Simcoe had been consulting with local half-pay officers and other public servants on the needs of the St. Lawrence settlements. Here the Simcoes had two fine rooms with good stoves. Outside the cold was intense, the sky bright blue, but the stoves kept them comfortable. They played whist that evening, and Elizabeth was happy at the prospect of waiting the next ten days in so pleasant a place, until the governor finished his business.

She was growing to love the bright sun of a Canadian winter, which was so much more cheerful than the grey skies of an English one. Yet the sun was deceptive. It suggested warmth, but instead people had to watch one another to ensure that noses and cheeks did not freeze. Francis was now fully recovered from his fever because of the healthful journey. By 16 February, Elizabeth had caught a severe cold and an eye infection, both of which she blamed on the damp room at Rapide Plat. On the nineteenth she wrote:

> I was obliged tonight to throw off most of the wrappings I had bound about my eyes & head & go to a Ball given by the Inhabitants of the province to the Gov., people came forty miles to it in Carrioles. I was really so ill I could scarcely hear or see & possibly neglected the very persons I meant to be most civil to.[2]

They continued towards Kingston on the twentieth, stopping each night with half-pay officers. On the morning of 23 February, when they were leaving Captain William Fraser's in Edwardsburgh Township, it began to snow heavily. Local men advised them against setting out until the storm had abated, but another guest who was desperate to reach Kingston assured the governor they would have little difficulty in proceeding. They were scarcely on their way when two gentlemen, both named Jones, came to advise them not to continue (They were probably sons of the former commissary, Ephraim Jones, who lived in the next westerly township.) When Simcoe was determined, they went ahead to "beat the way & hasten our Journey".

They struggled on as far as the home of the community's only physician, Dr. Solomon Jones (no relation to Ephraim) where they remained until the twenty-sixth Then changing to lighter "carriages" they reached "another Jones's", who was probably Ephraim's son, Charles Jones, in what is now Brockville. There Elizabeth found the largest wood fire she had ever beheld. With Mr. Fraser's son driving Elizabeth's carriole, they reached the rustic home of Captain Joseph Jessup, in the woods. The people who had helped them had to return to their homes with their horses as there was no place for them to sleep. Leaving Jessup's on the next day, they reached the Gananoque River. The ice was extremely bad,

> so we drove as fast as possible as that is thought the safest way on rotten Ice. I was very much frightened for it was dark & I knew that if they did not keep exactly the right track (which could scarcely be seen) we were in the greatest danger.

At Cary's, where they stopped for the night, they heard that a Mr. Forsyth had lost his team three days ago when he kept too far out near the mouth of the Gananoque River. His men saved the carriole by cutting the traces, but the horses drowned:

> The people of the States are particularly expert in saving Horses from drowning, they travel with Ropes which they fasten round the Horses' neck if they fall into the Water, pulling it stops their breath & then they float & can be pulled out; then they take off the rope as quickly as possible & the horse travels on as well as before. When Gov. Simcoe was driven ... to Detroit, he carried these Choke Ropes & had occasion to use them.

Cary's was "an indifferent House but warm." Elizabeth had amused herself as they drove by trying to identify the leafless trees from their bark. They reached Kingston on Sunday, 1 March, and were lodged in part of the barracks.

> As there are few Officers here, we have the mess Room to
> dine in & a Room over it for the Gov.'s office, & these as well
> as the Kitchen are detached from our other Three Rooms
> which is very comfortable. The drawing Room has not a
> stove in it which is a misfortune, but it is too late in the
> winter to be of much consequence & we have excellent
> wood fires.[3]

Elizabeth attended church that day and was pleased with the Reverend John Stuart's sermon. The governor was anxious to have a better look at the Bay of Quinte, and he and Elizabeth left Kingston in sleighs with a small escort on the ninth. Elizabeth was still coughing from the infection that had afflicted her at Johnstown, and she hoped the journey might help. At the Napanee River they inspected mills built by Richard Cartwright, the Kingston merchant, and slept in a house he owned. A sudden thaw cut short their tour; if they went any farther the ice might not be safe for their return. Instead of going to the portage at the west end of the bay, they turned back just west of Tyendinaga, the Mohawk Indian village half way along the bay from the lake. When they reached Kingston on the twelfth, Elizabeth felt much better.

A story someone related touched a tender nerve. A party of men crossing Lake Champlain saw a large hole in the ice and an infant lying beside it. Tracks suggested that a heavily loaded sleigh had been lost. An occupant of the sleigh:

> probably the Mother threw the Child out as the Sleigh went
> down. The Gentlemen carried the Infant to Montreal where
> a subscription was raised for her Maintenance — a good
> circumstance this for the commencement of a Heroine's life
> in a Novel.[4]

By 21 March Simcoe was ill with what seemed to be the same infection that had stricken Elizabeth. On 24 April, she wrote that she had scarcely left his room for more than a month. He had such a cough that he sat in a chair all night in order to breathe, and such headaches "that he could not bear any person but me to walk across the Room or speak loud." She could find only a horse doctor to attend the governor, and he "pretended to be an apothecary." Elizabeth regretted that Simcoe had allowed James Macaulay to remain in Newark. When Molly Brant learned of Simcoe's distress, she sent Elizabeth a root. She thought it was "calamus — which really relieved his Cough in a very short time."

Simcoe had hardly recovered when Elizabeth was afflicted by another cold followed by ague, which she attributed to getting wet while walking home from church on Sunday in heavy rain. Because they would soon be leaving for York, she felt obliged to invite some Kingston ladies to dinner on 4 May. She no appetite to join them, and she remained in the drawing room while they ate their meal. Still feeling wretched, she entertained more ladies on the sixth and eighth. By the twelfth, with the children, Collins and the servants and baggage, Elizabeth was aboard the *Onondaga* awaiting a favourable wind for York. Delayed until the fifteenth by contrary wind and wet, she watched the launching of the new government ship *Mohawk*, which was the same size as the *Mississauga*. "She came down with such rapidity that it appeared as if she would have run over the Ship we were in which was at anchor ahead of her." Even on the fifteenth, the sailing was held up by a stiff gale that sent the *Onondaga* back into the harbour. At 2.00 p.m. the wind changed, and they left, rain still pelting down.

Entering the harbour at York proved to be an alarming experience. When Simcoe decided that the captain was not sober, he singled out a lieutenant from one of the regular regiments who knew something about handling a vessel, and ordered him to pilot the ship. The young man brought them safely inside the sandspit — Elizabeth's beloved peninsula:

> I was unusually frightened having *dreamt twice* following the other night that I was lost in the Onondaga. My servant came several times to tell me we were going to the bottom. I told her to shut the door & leave me quiet, for the motion of the vessel made me sick.

By 21 May, Elizabeth was in her canvas house, the Marquis of Buckingham's tapestry in place, where a moor hen was brought to her. It "repeatedly pecked at the reeds represented in the Tapestry not touching any other part."

On 1 June, she went by boat up the Don River to "Francis's Estate", Castle Frank, where work was proceeding on the house. The fourth, as usual, was celebrated with a ball to mark the King's birthday, while on the sixth "Francis gave a dinner on his birthday to the Soldiers' Children. The Shaws dined with him at an Upper Table". On the ninth, the children and servants went aboard the *Onondaga* for the sail to Newark, where Simcoe would oversee the next session of the legislature. The governor and Elizabeth, with a small escort, would follow the shoreline in the bark canoe, the gift of the North West Company. They were delayed by bad weather until 15 June.

Then good weather held, and they reached the home of Surveyor Augustus Jones, three miles beyond Burlington Bay, by evening:

> I was delighted with the Canoe, the motion so easy, so pleasant, so quiet, like what I should suppose being in a Palanquin [a covered litter used in India]. We sat on Cushions in the bottom of the Canoe. The Indians brought us Strawberries not quite ripe. Jones's sister put them in a saucepan with water & sugar & boiled them & I thought them very good with my Tea.[5]

142

Her disclosure on Jones' sister is interesting. Jones' wife was a Mississauga, but Elizabeth did not mention her. Possibly she felt ill at ease, as she did with Molly Brant. They left the Joneses early on the morning of 16 June and reached Navy Hall at 8.00 p.m. Before they were properly settled in the Simcoes played host to some not overly welcome guests.

The Duke de Liancourt-Rochefoucault was a French emigrant who had been living in England and was on a visit to North America. He arrived at Fort Erie from Philadelphia, then the United States capital, on 20 June, accompanied by an Englishman named Guillebard, a French naval officer Elizabeth called Petit-Thouars, and the Marquis de Blacon. The duke had letters of introduction from the Duke of Portland, the colonial secretary, and George Hammond, the British ambassador. Simcoe received them politely, his duty as he saw it, and offered them accommodation at Navy Hall. Liancourt-Rochefoucault wrote a memoir on the visit. His description of Mrs. Simcoe is partly in character, but he makes her four years older than she actually was:

> Mrs. Simcoe, a lady of thirty-six, is bashful, has wit, is obliging and kind-hearted, speaks little, is occupied with her duties as mother and wife which she carries so far as to be her husband's confidential secretary; her talent for drawing, which she applies to tracing maps, gives her also the ability to be useful to him.[6]

Elizabeth spoke little because she felt she had nothing in common with the duke and his companions. Her comment, on 22 June, the day they reached Newark, was blunt, "Their appearance is perfectly democratic & dirty." On the twenty-ninth she added, "The Gov. took the Duke of Liancourt to see the 40 Mile Creek. I dislike them all." More to her taste was a visit from Mrs. McGill, the wife of Commissary John McGill of the Queen's Rangers. The McGills had moved to York, in accordance with Simcoe's wishes.

In the autumn of 1794, the chief justice of the United States, John Jay, had visited London and negotiated a treaty whereby the British would hand over to the Americans the forts on their side of the boundary. The treaty had aroused controversy in the United States, but Simcoe expected it would be ratified. He was determined to bring the session of the legislature to an end quickly, and to finish moving the government to York with all possible speed, in anticipation of the British garrison being removed from Fort Niagara. (Jay's Treaty was ratified on 24 June 1795, but the evacuation would be delayed some months.)

The Duke of Liancourt-Rochefoucault asked Simcoe for a pass to travel to Lower Canada, and the governor wrote Lord Dorchester to enquire whether he should issue one. Replying on 6 July, Dorchester apologised for the inconvenience, but he had orders to restrict the entry of French subjects to Lower Canada, where they might stir up discontent among French-speaking Canadians.[7] The duke left Newark on 22 July for New York State; now Elizabeth could enjoy her friends.

She entertained William Campbell, now the lieutenant-colonel of the 24th Regiment, and Mrs. Campbell, who had arrived from Detroit. With Mrs. Macaulay, Elizabeth went to Queenston, and dined "by the Rock which Hennepin mentions".[8] She was referring to Louis Hennepin, a French monk who viewed the Falls in 1678, and published his travel books in the 1680s and 1690s.

She was becoming friendly with Anne, Mrs. William Dummer Powell, whose husband was a Judge of the Court of King's Bench. They had recently moved from Detroit to Queenston, and built a house he called Mount Dorchester, probably to annoy Simcoe. Judge Powell was a friend of Lord Dorchester, who had recommended him for the first chief justice of Upper Canada, an appointment that had gone to William Osgoode. Powell was acting chief justice, but Simcoe had applied for "an English lawyer" to replace Osgoode.[9] Regardless of how the husbands felt about each other, Mrs. Powell made Elizabeth welcome, whatever her private reservations. No lady of Upper Canada would offend the governor's wife. Elizabeth also renewed her friendships with Mrs. Hamilton, Mrs. Richardson and Mrs. Tice.

The legislature was dissolved on 10 August, and the next day the Simcoes rode to Judge Powell's and dined at Mrs. Tice's. The air was so cool and fresh here on the mountain, five miles south of the Falls, that Elizabeth thought of a way of escaping the muggy heat of Newark more effectively than the hut at Queenston or tents on the heights above. Mrs. Tice's inn was large, with a gallery along the front, and oak trees that always gave shade — altogether an inviting place. She asked if she could rent two rooms for a fortnight; the servants could stay in a tent nearby. Mrs. Tice agreed, and His Excellency would be most welcome whenever he could spare the time away from Newark.

The very next day, all the Simcoes went by boat to Queenston and by carriage the rest of the way to the Tice house, arriving in time for dinner. The fortnight at the Tice house stretched to two months, until October, because Elizabeth was so happy, amidst scenery that she loved. The family enjoyed many excursions to explore the neighbourhood. On 15 August, with a tent and provisions the governor drove the children to see the whirlpool below the Falls, and Elizabeth rode part of the way.

> [They] dined on a Pt. from whence the Whirl Pool & the opposite Bank of the River on which is a Mill form altogether a very fine scene, the Mill appears like a part of the Perpendicular flat Rock on which it stands. In the Bay [whirlpool] formed by two immensely high Pts of land are now a number of Logs from a sawmill above the Falls ... the dam which confined them having given way in a flood ...[10]

She loved the view of the "Fort Schlosser Fall" (the American Falls). The best spot to see these Falls, she wrote on 17 August, was near the farm of people named Painter, "just above what is called the Indian Ladder". This was a notched tree which the natives used to descend into the gorge. Fearful of using it herself, she had Lieutenant Pilkington build some short ladders to enable her to climb down to the rocks below the Falls. By the twenty-fourth the ladders were in place, and partway down Elizabeth sat and sketched until her paper was damp from the spray of the American Falls. "The Gov. walked with a guide nearly underneath [Table Rock], but as the path over the Rocks was bad & not one picturesque scene to be gained by it I did not attempt going ..."

Afterwards Elizabeth rested at the Painters', who prepared

> besides Tea those Cakes baked in a few minutes on an Iron before the fire which the people of the States make so well, eggs & sweetmeats & bacon or salt fish they usually offer with Tea. I believe it is a more substantial Meal with them than their dinner which is slight."

A letter dated 15 October (the year is missing) shows how well Elizabeth's letters were received by friends and relatives in England. It is not in Elizabeth's hand, but it has extensive quotations and refers, in part, to a letter she wrote in August 1795 "near the Falls of Niagara" while she was staying with Mrs. Tice. Francis "has come through the heat better this summer & is stronger". She had been dipping him in the river for ten minutes at a time, which kept him comfortable. The boy had a passion for ships, boats, cannons, paddling and roving, "we may respect his will to become a sailor, you would laugh at his dancing & singing like the Indians".

Francis attended the Indians' councils in blanket and silver armbands with great solemnity. "This will amuse Mrs. Graves," the writer added, before quoting Elizabeth again. As Francis had a "great deal of sense" and learned quickly he ought to be in school. Being the only boy, Elizabeth admitted he might be a bit spoiled. He was more afraid of his father than of her, and she sometimes called on the governor for help. The last part of the letter is missing.[11] Letters were often copied and circulated, so that many people could have the pleasure of savouring their contents.

On 25 August, Elizabeth and Francis went with the governor by carriage to Fort Chippawa, the first leg of a journey he was making to Long Point to choose the site for a naval base on Lake Erie. The garrison commandant at Fort Chippawa, Captain James Hamilton of the 5th Regiment, gave them a room in the blockhouse. Simcoe was ill and the heat was oppressive. The room would have been unbearable but for the loopholes which let in some air. Elizabeth felt cooler lying on the floor rather than on the bed. In the morning the governor set off on horseback, while Elizabeth and Francis went by boat, bound for Fort Erie. The boat soon put in and took the governor aboard, for he was too ill to ride. They stopped at substantial-looking building:

> he stay'd the whole of the day till 6 in the Evening when we proceeded in the barge to Fort Erie. We ordered dinner & made ourselves quite at home here supposing it an Inn, & afterwards found we were mistaken. It was not an Inn but the House of a very hospitable Farmer.

Elizabeth found the shore of Lake Erie flat and "uninteresting", and there was more green than in most parts of Canada "without being enriched by warm brown tints". The green so much suggested dampness that she put on a fur tippet and felt more comfortable although the heat and humidity were the same. They pitched a tent near the beach, where she amused herself catching crayfish in shallow pools. The heat did not abate. On 28 August:

> One of the servants went to the Lake to wash his cloathes. Francis followed him up to his knees in water & sat on a Rock by him, presently an Indian went to wash his cloaths & the group looked very picturesque. Francis came back completely wet to fetch a loaf of bread he desired to give to the Indian.

The governor had to attend an Indian council the next day, and Elizabeth and Francis went by boat to Chippawa. She planned to ride, with Francis in front, to Mrs. Tice's, but in such heat she preferred the carriage:

> having no Gentleman with me I was obliged to drive the Carriage myself which I had never done & the Roads are excessively rough till passing by the Falls. I tied Francis into the Carriage & drove him very safely tho he complained of being much bruised & shook. A violent Rain began just as I arrived at Mrs. Tyce's.[12]

The autumn harvest foods were delicious. Mrs. Tice grew fine water melons, and Elizabeth ate two or three every day (they were much smaller at the time). Indian corn was at its best, and she and Francis ate it roasted for dinner. All the vegetables were so fine that people ate little else except small amounts of salt pork. "The Asiatics eat no meat in the summer & I dare say they are right". Wild pigeons were abundant, and people were preserving the wings in salt for the coming winter. Mrs. Tice had "a number of Standard Peach trees, some produce small fruit, others large quite green but very well flavoured tho they look unpromising."

She was again enjoying her friends. Mrs. Powell was "a very sensible pleasant Woman. "Sweet briar" with boiling water poured over it, purified jars and milk pans. Mrs. Tice used the liquid to keep her dairy pans clean.

That good lady gave no hint that she wished her visitors would return to Navy Hall, and Elizabeth stayed on. Word of an outbreak of ague at Queenston convinced her she was better off where she was. When she learned of a school someone was keeping nearby, she enrolled Francis, now four and a half years old. On 12 September, Simcoe returned from Long Point, which he had renamed Charlotteville. He was very pleased that the site would make a fine naval base for Lake Erie, but desperately ill. By the fifteenth Simcoe was much worse, for he was bilious and feverish, but Elizabeth had been fortunate; she had fallen through a trap door in her room, but was only bruised. On 22 September, she wrote: "We walked with Francis to the School where he goes every day a mile from this house. He carries some bread & butter or Cheese for dinner with him & returns in the Evening."

The weather soon turned autumnlike, and the time came to return to Newark, before going to York for the winter. They left Mrs. Tice's on 2 October, the night very cold when they reached Navy Hall. On the thirteenth they sailed for York aboard the *Gov. Simcoe*, arriving at 5.00 p.m. They were accompanied by John Brown Lawrence, an American friend of the governor's who had been a prisoner of war with him during the revolution. Lawrence had come to Upper Canada, at Simcoe's invitation, to take up land.

Elizabeth settled happily into the canvas houses, her main worry Simcoe's continued ill health. At the root of the governor's afflictions was frustration. From the start, the Duke of Portland had vetoed many of his plans. His only consolation was the establishment of an Agricultural Society at Newark. (It is now described on a plaque at the site.) He appointed county lieutenants to foster an aristocracy, but Portland disapproved; county lieutenants, mayors and aldermen would decrease the powers of the lieutenant governor, and encourage a spirit of insubordination. For the same reason, when Simcoe proposed incorporating Newark and Kingston as cities, His Grace refused permission. Simcoe disagreed, for both he and Elizabeth felt that there was more danger of independence if he did not create an aristocracy to control the lower orders and set an example, as had happened in England. In denying Simcoe permission to build fortifications, and in refusing his requests for more soldiers, both Home Secretary Dundas, and now his successor, Portland, seemed to be preparing the province for its eventual annexation to the United States rather than as a focus for a new empire. While the governor fretted, Elizabeth kept calm by concentrating on her friends and on domestic matters.

Finding Francis eager to be helpful, Elizabeth had him bring in wood for her stove. "He has a little sledge to draw it upon." She was happy to visit with Mrs. McGill and Mrs. Shaw again, and Francis was delighted to be reunited with the Shaw children. Meanwhile, work was proceeding on Castle Frank on the site overlooking the Don River. On 28 December, she referred to the Berczy settlers, who were cutting a road through to Lake Simcoe. By 1 January Simcoe was better, and able to walk four or five miles without fatigue. Mrs. Macaulay came to call, and they arranged a dance attended by ten ladies. There were not enough men to go round, but as they danced reels even numbers did not matter. As 1796 opened, Elizabeth was in high spirits, cheered by the hope that they might be going soon to Wolford Lodge. Because of ill health her beloved general had applied for a leave of absence. Even if they had to return to the province afterwards, she would at least be able to see for herself how the four eldest girls, never far from her thoughts, were faring.

On 6 January she wrote Mrs. Hunt, replying to a packet from Wolford Lodge that was dated 31 July 1795. She was concerned that Charlotte had been ill when the packet was sent, and amazed at how much all the girls were learning. How astonished she was to learn that Eliza had the patience to read "Withering" or Latin grammar, "she certainly has a very peculiar turn of mind for her age". Elizabeth added that she would brush up her own knowledge so the girls would not think her illiterate.

She admitted that Francis had reached an assertive age. "Francis will be a charming boy when he gets to Mr. Copplestones where we have always intended to send him on our return, but he wants a little of the discipline of a school." His many illnesses, tender age and cleverness, "prevent me being as strict with him as I should & he is almost beyond my control." Mr. Coplestone, who kept a school in Honiton, was probably the Reverend John Coplestone, a son of the Reverend Edward Coplestone of Tedbourne St. Mary. He attended Merton College, and received his Bachelor of Arts degree from Oxford in 1771.[13] Mary Anne Burges made many references to him in her letters.

Chapter 16
JULIA
1795~1796

By 5 June 1795, the Hon. Julia Somerville was making herself at home at Tracey, and testing Mary Anne Burges:

> My trouble with my little girl has commenced. She has not been contradicted from her birth, but has been accustomed to carrying every point by crying .... Of this I had the first instance yesterday at dinner; I happened to affront her by offering her a spoon, & she instantly left the table, would eat nothing, & continued as cross as possible, tho' her Maid tried for half an hour to please her .... I thought if I suffered this to go on, I should only make more work for myself in future ... .

She picked the child up and put her in a different room, to stay until she was ready to come and give Mary Anne a kiss. Julia cried for ten minutes, while Mary Anne pretended not to notice although she was trembling all over and conscience-smitten at treating an orphan in such a manner. When Julia complied all was peace for the rest of that day.[1] However, the testing continued. Amidst the struggle to dominate the three-year-old, Mary Anne received a proposal of marriage. She wrote the "particulars" to Elizabeth:

> but I am sure you must be more of a Witch than I, & you can guess from what quarter it came, for I never imagined that the man liked me, even so well as I did him ... so I wrote him word that I had more a determination to continue single all my life ... . I wish my Suitor would take her [Julia] instead me. I am quite discouraged at the prospect I have with her ... . I think myself the most unfortunate of any Monarch on earth, that Julia, my only subject, should prove a Jacobin.[2]

As her own house had become odious because of Julia's behaviour, she dined at Wolford Lodge on 12 June. Mrs. Hunt was very kind, and offered to have Julia for a while. "I know she has as great a satisfaction in taming children, as great Jockeys have in breaking Colts", and she hoped Elizabeth would not object to having Mrs. Hunt help her. For the present, Mary Anne had to struggle on alone, for Mrs. Hunt was taking the Simcoe girls to the seaside at Seaton, to bathe and strengthen them.[3]

Her suitor came to visit, but luckily he did not repeat his proposal of marriage. Later he sent her a moth. "I know not what I ought to have done with that, according to Mrs. Graves's rules; but not having the advantages of her counsels, I opened the window, & let it fly away."[4]

She complained of a Mr. Barnard, who was buying tracts from the Enclosure Commissioners who were selling off common land. (The enclosure movement was an integral part of the agricultural revolution then under way.) Barnard was also enclosing Combe Raleigh Hill "in a way that will not meet with the approbation of General Simcoe". She was afraid Barnard would block the road, which Simcoe would resist when he returned; "all the Drewes of course take part with Mr. Barnard; & there is therefore nobody great enough to rebel."[5]

The poor were restless, because the price of corn was so high, and often the farmers would not bring it to market. There had been riots in Honiton. She was at the Herman Drewes when Dr. Honywood, a magistrate, attempted to disperse a crowd and had his coat torn to pieces. Rather than pass through Honiton, Mary Anne had to stay with the Drewes until a troop of light dragoons arrived from Exeter and restored order. At the Assizes in Exeter, three ringleaders of the riots were condemned to death. General Simcoe would be diverted that Sir John de la Pole had chosen as the motto for his volunteers "Pro Aris & focis" (for our alters and our hearths). Farmers in his troop thought this meant "for the Hares & the Foxes".[6]

She spent a night at Seaton, where the girls were enjoying their holiday. Eliza and Charlotte showed her their mother's letter in which she laughed at the preparations for their stay at Tracey. Yet that was nothing compared to the next packing. Mrs. Hunt had brought four Bibles to Tracey, and everything in like proportion to Seaton.

Julia's behaviour was improving, but Mary Anne still had not taken her to Wolford Lodge. Mrs. Graves issued another invitation for the girls to come to Bath. They passed the month of August there, although Eliza was disappointed to miss seeing how the seeds she had planted would grow, and Charlotte admitted she would rather stay home with Mrs. Hunt. When they returned from Bath, all had had a good time. Mrs. Graves had been kind to them, but she was brooding that she would die before the Simcoes returned from Canada, and was again pretending there was no one to protect the girls. During August, Admiral Elliott died at Copford, near Colchester. His daughters, Frances and Mary, thought they would like to settle in Honiton, to be close to their friends in the neighbourhood. Mrs. Richard Graves was crying constantly, because she did not want to leave her children and go to America. Richard told Mary Anne that "nothing would induce him to have the plague of children on a voyage." Julia was improving daily, but Mary Anne wished she were nearer in age to the Simcoe girls. They were a little too grown up to be her close friends, but they could at least set her a good example.[7]

On 2 September, Mary Anne took Julia to Wolford Lodge. "I introduced my little Julia to them. She was delighted to see them & they were good to her". Eliza was now nearly twelve; Charlotte had turned ten in August; Harriet had had her eighth birthday in April; Caroline would be seven in

November. Eliza, Mary Anne added, was quite grown up, and her companion on walks, while the three younger girls took care of Julia. Eliza's questions showed that she was concerned about current events. She wanted to know the causes of the French Revolution and of the present war, and she listened attentively to Mrs. Burges' account, showed "political sagacity" and questioned the morality of raising money through lotteries. Mary Anne felt out of her depth, and could not find satisfactory answers.

The Richard Graveses still talked of emigrating to South Carolina, but claimed they could not find a ship. Mary Anne suspected the real reason was the serious illness of Mrs. Mary Graves, the wife of Richard's elder brother, Captain Thomas Graves, whose death was expected almost daily. The Richard Graveses were planning to spend the winter at the Golden Lion, an inn in Honiton. Having them living in such close proximity would greatly annoy the Haynes. Among Mr. Haynes' pupils was Master Samuel Graves, the only son of Richard Graves. The Haynes had told Mary Anne that they wished they could emigrate themselves, to avoid having such disagreeable neighbours. Mrs. Richard Graves had gone to the Haynes' house during their absence, had taken the liberty of scolding their maid, and had accused the whole Haynes family of neglecting Master Samuel.[8] That young man's mother had formulated some odd notions about education. Since teaching children to read was cruel, only Samuel should learn. The other children, all girls, were attending school, but only to learn to dance. Mrs. Herman Drewe, Mary Anne added, approved of her "cruelty" in teaching Julia to read.[9]

She had taken many of Elizabeth's sketches to have them made into etchings. Some had come back from the engraver, and she was very pleased at how well they had reproduced.[10] The process involved having a tracing made, which could be reversed and the lines cut into a copper plate. The lines were inked and damp paper pressed against the plate so that the drawing was transferred to the paper.

On 17 October she received a long-anticipated letter, dated 22 August from Elizabeth, who was then at Mrs. Tice's. Mary Anne was certain her ghost would haunt the Canadian forests, so much did she long to be there. She reported on much excitement at Tracey a few days before, when her dog Ranger ran off, an event that plunged the "whole family in confusion". William went to look first, followed by Dinah, who went to find William. Then Jenny set out and brought everyone back, with Ranger.

Julia was turning out to be a source of joy and interest, as well as a challenge for Mary Anne. On 23 October she had a party for the little girl, attended by many children, among them the four Simcoes. The children's party was much more enjoyable than the Honiton Assembly that followed. The Richard Graveses had quarrelled openly. Mary Anne "went & sat in the worst possible place looking proud .... You never saw such a lot of people as this neighbourhood is now composed of". She felt she had had enough of assemblies.

Many times Mary Anne had mentioned her poor health, particularly blinding headaches for which a London physician had prescribed bark. Again she admitted to the headaches, and to being under the care of Mr. Teed of Honiton. He was treating her for chilblains on her fingers, a common ailment in houses that were impossible to heat in cold weather. She recalled that Elizabeth had eaten boiled mutton when convalescing from an illness, and she had done the same. The mutton, she thought, was helping her.

Mr. Flood had now reimbursed her for the clothes sent to Canada with Captain Lowe. On 7 December a letter arrived from Elizabeth, enclosing the governor's draft for £100 that more than covered the cost of them. Much embarrassed, Mary Anne enquired whether to turn the draft over to Flood, or to await instructions from the Simcoes. In the meantime she wrote to her brother asking what he thought she should do.

The Austrians were having success against the French, which was good news. On the home front, the radicals had been active. The right people in Honiton were scandalized when certain "low persons" sent a petition to London asking that Sedition Bills, then before the House of Commons, be withdrawn. As might be expected, Richard Graves' radicalism had surfaced again. At Weymouth, with two other naval officers, he had presented a petition to the King. His Majesty turned away, saying only, "Three post captains!"[11]

Julia had been quick to absorb the Burges political stamp. After listening to conversation on the fate of the executed Louis XVI, she told Mary Anne, "the naughty Democrats wanted to cut the King's head off; but the King said No, thank you, Ma'am". When she had misbehaved and was scolded, she called herself a democrat. Elizabeth had often complained of Sophia's obstinacy, but Julia could match her, and Mary Anne wondered how to "reform" her. On 16 December Julia was particularly perverse, and refused to repeat some words after Mary Anne. No matter how she was punished she kept saying she liked it. This was hard on Mary Anne's nerves, and she could not paint because her hands shook so. The next day, "My little subject returned to her allegiance". How stupid she was, writing such trivialities, but in the gloom of the Devon winter she had little else to interest her.

As she hoped, Mary Anne heard more often from her brother, now that he had retired. He advised her to keep General Simcoe's draft until the latter could send instructions on its disposal. Sir James had written poetry and had given a "performance" before Princess Elizabeth, whose drawing had invoked the muse. If the Royal family so wished, the poem might someday be printed.[12]

Mrs. Thomas Graves had more seizures, and she died at Woodbine Hill on Christmas Day 1795. She was buried on 31 December. Thomas' brothers, John and Richard, attended the funeral, and Richard was not in mourning dress. With Miss Hunt, Mary Anne went to Woodbine Hill a few days later to express their condolences. To her relief, Mr. Herman Drewe arrived, and he carried the conversation for everyone.

A new personage had entered the small circle of Devon's best people. Sir John Kennaway had now taken up residence at Escot, the estate close to Wolford Lodge he had purchased from Simcoe's friend, Sir George Yonge. Sir John had had an impressive, and lucrative, career in the service of the East India Company. By 1794 his health had suffered, and he had retired. As he was a bachelor in his late thirties, speculation was rich on who might be a future Lady Kennaway.

Replying to some of Elizabeth's letters on 2 January, she was happy that her friend liked the clothes that had reached her. Mary Anne was certain they would suit Elizabeth's figure, because they suited her own. Now that she had slimmed, the styles looked well on her, but she thought that large, stout women looked ungainly. "Think of Miss Betty Putt, for example, with a waist up to her arms." She enquired whether Elizabeth had read Locke on education. Mary Anne was finding it satisfying and felt the need of it now that she was raising Julia. She did not want to be too severe with a child who was not her own. Julia was now the plaything of the Simcoe girls. Whenever Mary Anne had to spend a few days in Exeter, Julia was welcome at Wolford Lodge and never lonely.

On 7 January Mary Anne replied to Elizabeth's letter of 8 October, by which time her friend knew that Julia had come to live at Tracey. Mary Anne was gratified that Elizabeth approved of her new "pursuit" since her other interests no longer satisfied her. Julia was becoming better behaved. Her displays of temper were less frequent because she was learning how little she gained by them. Mary Anne was happy to have the seeds Elizabeth sent, and she would plant some in the spring. She planned to give some to the girls, although she wondered if they would be wasted as they were allowed so little time to tend their gardens. Mr. Tuck, a gardener at Wolford Lodge, sometimes did it for them, but was careless and inclined to pull up plants as well as weeds.

Returning to the subject of Julia, she wrote something obscure, agreeing to observe the governor's "caution for her and Francis". Possibly Simcoe hinted that Julia would one day make a suitable bride for Francis; "a lady with such a name must build such a castle as in fairy tales & seclude her from view of all the world:" while she [Mary Anne] "impersonated a dragon". Perhaps she meant guardianship of Julia.[13]

January was the party season. Eliza was to have been the "principal personage" at a festival on the eighteenth but she developed what Mrs. Hunt insisted was whooping cough, although she had had it once before. Mary Anne was certain Eliza had just an ordinary cough, but Mrs. Hunt was adamant and the festival had to be postponed. The next day Mary Anne gave a party for the local children and some adults, which the three youngest Simcoes attended. It was a delayed celebration of Twelfth-Night. The children assembled in the drawing room, and she led them into the parlour where they drew sketches of "twelfth cakes", and she drew a set such as Elizabeth used to like. Everyone wore the picture he or she had drawn for the rest of the party. After skits there was dancing to the Luppit fiddler. Master Charles Drewe flirted with Miss Charlotte Simcoe, whose dancing everyone admired. Charles was a son of John Rose Drewe, brother of Herman and half-brother of Reverend Edward. At the time Charles (who died at age twenty-three) was eighteen and Charlotte not quite eleven.[14]

Mrs. Margaret Graves wrote that she had had no letter from General Simcoe since one dated 21 December 1794, which she had answered. She was not well and thinking of selling her carriage and making do with a sedan chair. Major Charles Domville of the 7th Fusiliers, had breakfasted with the Haynes, where three of his brothers were at school. Domville had recalled meeting the Simcoes in Quebec. As he was to be posted to Halifax on his return to duty, he would take letters and send them from there. Many people were talking of the Simcoes' return, but Mary Anne refused to be optimistic. She set the summer of 1797 as the earliest time she could expect to see her friend, to ensure that she would not be disappointed by delays. Mrs. Graves wrote from Bath that Lord Dorchester was expected to take a leave of absence, and General Simcoe would go to Quebec to govern in his stead. She declared that the Simcoes might never come home at all.[15]

Two packets from Elizabeth reached Tracey on 9 February. Mary Anne thought her descriptions of the forests were "sublime", and she hoped the sight of the fish pond at Wolford Lodge would not be offensive to her after all the grand scenes she had sketched and painted. A lady had asked Mary Anne if the tippet Elizabeth sent was of a sphinx's skin. While Mary Anne was aware of Elizabeth's aversion to tall people, neither Charlotte nor Harriet would be "improved by stopping their growth". Charlotte had the face, and Harriet the figure, that "demand height", but "Eliza's small face & prettily formed person would be very well if she never grows from this moment." Next, she described the recent French lessons at Wolford Lodge.

The French viscount had ceased tutoring the girls, and a M. Degenaux had replaced him. Now Monsieur had left Honiton, possibly out of despair. He had been a good teacher who had improved Miss Hunt's pronunciation, and that of the children, especially Eliza. Charlotte had not done quite as well as she did not have as good an ear. Yet the girls spoke but little during the lessons, because Mrs. Hunt intimidated them. All were in a formal circle, with that well-meaning but awesome woman "sitting ready to scold when he found the slightest fault". Mary Anne admitted that she could never have uttered a word under such circumstances.[16]

She had received a letter from a George Davison, who would take Elizabeth's straw hat and silk stockings to Canada, but not until mid-April when he would stop to collect them. Mary Anne expected to have a box ready for him in good time. She wondered whether Mr. Davison was a friend of Simcoe's or a merchant. Sir James Bland Burges' poem had now been printed, and she would send a copy for General Simcoe in the next box.

Thomas Graves and his daughter Mary had gone to Bath, and had advertised Woodbine Hill for rent, on a five-year lease while they decided where they wanted to live. Master Samuel Graves hated school because the boys called him "Miss Molly". The Richard Graveses had threatened to withdraw him from school if Mr. Hayne did not stop the teasing. That gentleman felt their demand was beyond his power to implement. Boys would be boys, and much of the problem arose because Samuel was so spoiled.[17]

The Reverend Mr. Coplestone, the proprietor of the school in Honiton which the Simcoes favoured, had had a "vexacious" time with two boys, one of whom told lies about him, and their father removed them from the school. Worse, he persuaded Sir John de la Pole to remove his son. Coplestone said he might have to close his school as he had only three pupils left. Mrs. Burges disagreed since he had a waiting list. Later, the three boys who remained, two of them sons of Mr. Edward Bastard of Buckland in the Moor, had run away. They got nearly halfway to Exeter before Coplestone caught up with them. All had returned home, and now the clergyman had no pupils, although two other boys would be sent to him soon. At least, he would have room to take Francis when the Simcoes came home. Elizabeth could judge for herself whether there was any truth to the stories about Coplestone.[18]

By Easter time the Thomas Graveses had returned from Bath, having decided not to let Woodbine Hill. They were as happy there as anywhere, for only time would heal the void left by the death of wife and mother. When they called at Tracey, Julia took a fancy to Thomas. Noticing dust on his boot, she took off her pinafore, knelt and wiped it away. That day the bells of Honiton rang to announce that the government had ordered the price of bread reduced. Mary Anne was pleased, for inflation had cut into her income, making it difficult for her to cover her expenses. When the local bakers did not respond at once, the justices of the peace ordered the bread seized and distributed to the poor.[19]

On 3 April she reported a "curious happening". Some hospital surgeons went to steal from its grave the body of a man who had been hanged. They were interrupted and attacked by surgeons of a fencible regiment quartered in Honiton, who had come to the cemetery with the same purpose in mind. Now the hospital people were talking of going to the law, yet, Mary Anne observed, such a lawsuit would be founded on an act "illegal to both sides". This would certainly be "a new thing". The best part was that no one got the body. The keeper, who was responsible for the cemetery was forewarned, and moved it to a safe place.[20]

As Mary Anne had feared, her access to Wolford Lodge had been blocked. Mr. Barnard fenced the land on the hill between the Simcoes' and Tracey and closed the road. Upon discovering a locked gate, Mary Anne "walked straight over the fence". Mr. Barnard would never have dared block that road if General Simcoe had been at home! She complained to Herman Drewe since Barnard was his proxy. On 28 April, Mr. Barnard arrived and presented her with a key to the gate. Placated, Mary Anne paid a courtesy call on Mrs. Barnard.[21]

Meanwhile, Lord Somerville had died in London, unmarried and intestate. Sir James Bland Burges had written asking Mary Anne to contribute, from what she would inherit, to the upkeep of His Lordship's natural children. Lord Somerville's estate was valued at £40,000, and would be divided among the legitimate heirs. After much discussion, arrangements were made for some of the estate to be used to support the children. Mary Anne's share would be £100 a year, money she badly needed. The black silk gown she used for mornings had been new in 1782. Yet if Lord Somerville had left a will in favour of his natural children, she might not be inheriting anything at all. The title passed to John Southby, the son of Mary Anne's Uncle Hugh by his first wife and Julia's half-brother, who became the 14th Lord Somerville.[22]

On 27 May, aware that Elizabeth would be coming home soon, Mary Anne was "transported" with happiness, and confident that the air at Wolford would do wonders to restore General Simcoe's health. The country was in the throes of a national election, a matter of great interest to the Simcoes. If the packet should not be delivered to them, she hoped it would not fall into the wrong hands, though gossip about Honiton politics would not be construed as a danger to the state. She had attended a tea party of "Democrats" where Thomas and Miss Graves and the Unitarian minister of Honiton and his wife were among the guests. She was "diverted to know my presence kept them in order". Not a word of politics or elections had been spoken "in my hearing".[23]

Elizabeth had sent her a drawing of the Indian Great Sail to have an etching made of it, as a gift for General Simcoe's friend, "Mr. Abbott". (This was probably Charles Abbot, in 1796 clerk of rules in the Court of King's Bench, Member of Parliament for Helston, Cornwall.) Mary Anne had taken the drawing to the engraver. Before sending the "impression" to Abbott in Elizabeth's name, she had "added a few strokes" as Elizabeth would have done. On election day she would go to Major and Mrs. Williams at Rhode Hill, to be out of the way until the voting was over. She would send a "most valuable collection " of state papers to use as an appendix to "my history of the Election".[24]

Chapter 17

END OF THE TOUR OF DUTY
1796

York now seemed a substantial settlement. Most of the civil servants and officers in the Queen's Rangers had each been awarded 200 acre lots in the vicinity, and nearly all had town lots as well. The town plot for York had been laid out under the supervision of Surveyor Alexander Aitkin, a neat grid plan that echoed those of the Romans, and which suited Simcoe's military mind. January 18 was the Queen's birthday, and marked by the firing of a salute and a ball. Elizabeth went visiting — to Skinner's mill, to the Ashbridges, who were a new family, to the McGills, where she met Miss Rachel Crookshank, Mrs. McGill's sister, to Captain David Shank's lot, and to the Macaulays. There they found four-year-old John Simcoe Macaulay cutting through large chunks of wood with an axe. Francis was envious, and banishing reservations at the sight of the sharp blade, she agreed to let him learn to handle an axe since that would be useful.

If her son was content, her husband's complaints were legion. Lord Dorchester would not permit him a separate quartermaster-general for Upper Canada, and disapproved of any fortifications for York because he thought that reinforcing the province would be too costly. Most of the lake vessels came under Dorchester's command, on the excuse that he had to be able to move troops, military stores, and provisions at will. Both the Indian and Commissariat Departments were subordinate to Dorchester, while Simcoe wanted to have separate ones for Upper Canada. Requests for more troops were met by Dorchester with the assertion that Upper Canada was "too far away "in time of war. Dorchester considered Upper Canada too difficult and costly to defend, and the province could be abandoned in the interest of retaining only Lower Canada. Dorchester disapproved when Simcoe allowed William Berczy's workers government rations. Provisions were only for troops. Simcoe had ordered the men to return to their clearings, and had sent some Queen's Rangers under Lieutenant David William Smith to complete Yonge Street to Lake Simcoe.[1]

The governor dreamed of founding a university, and in each district a grammar school to prepare boys to enter it. He had not been permitted enough funds to open even one grammar school. Some parents had banded together, hired teachers of indifferent education and opened schools, but the state, he believed, should be giving leadership. Teachers ought to be Church of England clergymen, to ensure proper instruction.

While Elizabeth was a sympathetic listener, she busied herself with matters at hand. Many were complaining that the fishing was poor through holes in the ice of the Don River and the bay, but they had better luck in the Humber River. Elizabeth concluded that the noise of carrioles being driven on the ice was frightening the fish away. Fish were biting in the Humber because no sleighs were there. The dormeuse, which they had had to leave near Johnstown during their journey back, was now in York, and Simcoe found it comfortable when the weather was bitterly cold. Meanwhile, Elizabeth was eager to see Castle Frank finished and habitable. She made many trips to the site, usually accompanied by friends and with a picnic. They would build a fire, and roast strips of venison skewered on sharpened sticks.

A packet of letters from Wolford Lodge come by sleigh from Kingston, and a parcel contained the long-missing shirt Charlotte had made for her father finally arrived. Eliza and Harriet had written, but to Simcoe's chagrin there was no letter from Charlotte for him. She may have been irked that the governor had not acknowledged her gift. On 12 February he thanked her. "Mama, a better judge, says it is well worked and shows industry". He continued, "Francis will be a fine plaything for you all." He hoped Charlotte would help him become fond of reading. Sophia did not "love her books" and he was looking to Charlotte "to mend her taste". He expected to teach Sophia himself when he had time during the winter.[2]

On 18 February the work party of Queen's Rangers, who had gone to finish cutting the road to Lake Simcoe, returned. David William Smith, acting deputy surveyor, reported the road, hardly more than a rough track among the stumps, measured 33 miles and 56 chains. The men brought two trout, each weighing about twelve pounds, from Lake Simcoe, where black bass seemed "torpid" in the cold water. When they lifted a hollow log from the lake, they found thirty bass inside it. Mr. Lawrence, who had gone with the party to see the country, gave Elizabeth two spoons and small wooden bowls which the Indians had made. She planned to have the children use them for breakfast when travelling.

The next day they attended festivities at Captain Shank's lot, dining in an arbour on perch and venison, the band playing. Jacob, a Mohawk, danced "Scotch Reels" better than anyone Elizabeth had ever seen. He was resplendent in a black blanket that resembled a Spanish cloak, leggings of scarlet, silver bands on his head and arms, altogether a handsome figure. The winter passed with more card parties and dances. By 13 March, geese and blackbirds denoted the approach of spring. On Easter Day, a strong east wind blew the ice out of the bay, but then a west wind blew it back, making a fine sound. Wild pigeons filled the sky, and the Indians were making maple sugar. Early in April Elizabeth bought from them, for three dollars, thirty pounds of the sugar in birch bark baskets. Other Indians brought wild geese and ducks from Lake Simcoe. Elizabeth thought them tastier than wild ducks in England, for they had fed on wild rice.

On 18 April they moved to the yet unfinished Castle Frank. Francis was not well, and Elizabeth thought the "change of air" would improve him. They divided the large room with sail cloth, and pitched a tent in the inner part where they slept on wooden beds. Irritated, she watched the launching of a large wooden canoe, made by the men who were supposedly completing Castle Frank. By the twentieth, Francis was better and planting current bushes and peach trees. At night Elizabeth could hear strange sounds, and she found insects like large maggots eating into the timbers. Then the time came to return to the garrison: they had to move to Newark before the session of the legislature opened. They sailed on the *Mohawk* on the twenty-ninth, a rough passage.

The tiny community was soon plunged into mourning the death of John Butler, the founder of the Niagara settlement and onetime colonel of his famous rangers during the revolution. He was buried in the family plot on 15 May, Whitsunday.[3] Fort Niagara would soon be handed over to the Americans, for Jay's Treaty had been ratified. As the British garrison would leave during the summer, Simcoe warned the legislators that this was the last time the legislature could meet at Newark. All civil servants must move to York without further delay. The house was prorogued on 3 June, and Elizabeth attended, to hear the governor's speech. Already they were packing to return to York.

Francis celebrated his fifth birthday on 6 June, and Simcoe drove Elizabeth to bid farewell to Mrs. Hamilton at Queenston and to see other friends briefly. They left Newark by canoe, a boat following, on the seventh — their final journey of exploration of the margins of Lake Ontario and the Niagara Escarpment. During a shower, they sought shelter in a vacant house beyond Twelve Mile Creek, where they dried their clothes and slept. Farther on they stopped at the home of the Greens, who had given them hospitality on their earlier journey to Forty Mile Creek. Elizabeth admired their pumpkins, which they told her made fine food for milch cows. To combat the heat, she was again dipping Francis in the lake. This time she was having a closer look at the face of the escarpment, and the many fine waterfalls that descended it.

On 10 June they sent the children and servants to the head of the lake in the canoe and boat. Mrs. Green had offered to guide them overland, up and down the mountain, to the King's Head Inn, which the governor had had built at government expense to serve travellers.[4] The trio set off on horseback through the woods, skirting swamps, and mounting steadily the steep face of the escarpment. For the first time Elizabeth mentioned the striking red colouring of the Niagara area, where a thick layer of red shale underlies hard limestone. The shale gives a reddish colour to the soil, the sides of the gorge and the scarp face.

"We should have a road up here," Simcoe observed. "The land is dry, and without swamps. A road above the mountain could be used all year round."

Elizabeth found the view of Flamborough Head breath-taking, and they could see the canoe passing near the shore below them. They found the descent towards the head of the lake difficult. Mrs. Green's memory of the exact route was faulty, and much time passed before they found the path down. At the bottom they floundered again amidst swamp and undergrowth, their horses' feet endangered by partially submerged logs. The moon was out before they reached the inn, and the setting was all the more picturesque. Elizabeth, who had been dreading the ride in broad daylight, enjoyed it more when she could not see the dangers below her horse's feet. Outside the King's Head Inn, they found:

> Walbekanine & a number of his tribe (who were encamped a mile distant) were assembled to compliment the Gov. & fired Musquets in our Horses' faces their usual mark of respect which frightened me & my Horse very much, he started & I shrieked, but the sound was lost in the Whoops of the Indians. They gave us the largest land tortoise I ever saw.[5]

Of the inn, she wrote:

> There are 8 rooms in this House besides two low wings behind it joined by a Colonade, where are Offices. It is a pretty plan. I breakfasted in a Room to the S.E. which commands the view of the Lake on the S. shore of which we discern the Pt. of the 40 Mile Creek. . . From the Rooms to the N.W. we see Flamborough Head & Burlington Bay. The Sand Cliffs on the N. Shore of Burlington Bay look like Red Rocks. The Beach is like a park covered with large spreading Oaks.

They again saw the Augustus Joneses, and continued on to the farm of Adam Green. He showed them a spring of salt water, and with his daughter guided them to see "the fall of Stoney Creek from the bottom":

> We went through pathless Woods over Rocks, Logs & in fact the most difficult walk I ever took & if the girl had not preceded me I should have given it up. We came too near the fall to see it in a picturesque view. I crossed the River on stones. A man climbed a considerable height up part of the Red Amphitheatre to get me a piece of the Stones. He had no apparent footing it was so perpendicular.[6]

She was describing the plunge pool near Stoney Creek, a basin-like hole carved out more than a million years ago by the waterfall of an ancient river. This river was obliterated during the last ice age, when the glacier scooped out the great lakes. After the ice melted, the lakes were drained by the Niagara River, that plunged over the escarpment some forty miles further east. On the way back Elizabeth gathered many plants, and Adam Green told her what the medicinal properties of each were. Green, a widower with ten children, gave them refreshments before they returned to the King's Head Inn — cakes baked on coals, eggs, a boiled black squirrel, tea and coffee made of peas, and sugar made from the sap of black walnut trees, which she found sweeter than that from the maples. After dining at the King's Head, they made camp past that of the Indians near a house that was only partly finished.. The winds were contrary, and they were forced to remain in this beautiful setting until 16 June.

In the meantime she admired the Indian camp, so picturesque with its huts and dogs. On the fifteenth, Joseph Brant arrived on horseback, accompanied by two of his sons and an escort of Mohawks. They were on their way to Niagara, where the two boys, both aged about ten years, were to be put in school. They gave Francis a boat, and his parents had him give the Mohawks a sheep for their dinner. Afterwards the boys danced and played ball, and they slept in the house while the other Indians sheltered under planks that belonged to the owners of the unfinished house.

The Simcoes left on the afternoon of 16 June, and reached the Credit River after an unpleasant canoe ride on heavy swells. The governor wanted to explore the Credit in the canoe. With him went Elizabeth, Sophia and Francis, and two Indians, which made a full load. Three miles on they reached some rapids, noted the abundance of salmon, and turned back. They arrived at York at 9.00 p.m. After ten days at the canvas house, Francis was ill. Elizabeth cancelled a plan to go up the Humber River in the canoe "attended by music", and sent both children to Castle Frank by boat. A large party from the garrison came to dinner on 1 July, attended by a boatload of musicians. Elizabeth left soon afterwards for Castle Frank. Even high above the Don Valley the mosquitoes were "troublesome". Castle Frank had an "underground room", with windows overlooking the Don Valley, that had been cut into the side of the hill. It was delightfully cool, but the unglazed windows let in the mosquitos, and she sat under a mosquito net to read. The heat was still oppressive, made worse by a rainstorm so heavy that water poured in through the windows and they had to abandon the underground room.

She crossed a "quaint" bridge built by George Playter, a farmer near Castle Frank who managed John Scadding's pioneer farm in the same area. The bridge was a butternut tree that lay across the Don, its branches still in full leaf; a pole made a railing, but even holding it she was frightened as she edged her way over. On 12 July she rode to town, by a new road that had been opened to reach the government farm that produced food for the soldiers. On the fourteenth they learned that Simcoe's leave of absence had been granted, and they were to sail on the armed frigate *Pearl*, Captain Samuel James Ballard in command.[7] The *Pearl* was at Quebec, and due to leave on 4 August, which would not allow much time for farewells. In Simcoe's absence Receiver General Peter Russell was to administer the government of Upper Canada. Lord Dorchester had resigned, and was returning home on the ship *Active*. His successor, General Robert Prescott, was already in Quebec. For the Simcoes the remaining days were taken up in packing and seeing friends for the last time.

On 21 July, Elizabeth bid farewell to Mrs. McGill and Miss Crookshank, so much "out of spirits" that she was unable to dine with them. Mrs. McGill sent her dinner but she could not eat, and cried all day. The governor dined with Captain McGill, and at 3.00 p.m. they set out on the *Onondaga* for Kingston, while other vessels in the harbour saluted. With them went mountains of baggage and furniture, and many souvenirs of their five years in the Canadas. They took a sleigh to use on those rare occasions when there was sufficient snow at Wolford Lodge, a stove to help heat their home, and the canoe given by the North West Company. The breeze was light, and they did not anchor in Kingston harbour until 11.30 p.m. on the twenty-fifth. While the men were unloading the baggage, they accidentally dropped Elizabeth's trunk into the water. They fished it out quickly, but her clothes were dampened.[8] They slept aboard the *Onondaga*, and left in bateaux at 11.00 a.m. on the twenty-sixth for the journey down the St. Lawrence.

This time they usually slept in their bateaux, which they found cooler than houses and which the governor, feeling unwell, preferred. They placed beds on their trunks, and found that the breeze kept the mosquitoes away. Making stops at many of the friends whom they had visited on earlier travels, they sailed downstream, Elizabeth sketching as they went. She found the Long Sault Rapids, which they descended in an hour "without sailing & seldom rowing" more alarming than in 1794 on the way to Quebec:

> These Rapids appeared little formidable to me last year. I suppose my mind was then more engaged by the cause of my Voyage & the Governor's situation at the Miami, then I thought not of myself, now I had nothing to think of but the present danger & was terrified.[9]

The Cedars Rapids seemed worse than the Long Sault. Despite the intense heat, the crew "insisted on taking off the awning":

> The preparation seemed formidable but the ensuing trajet more so. People usually go from hence in Calashes [as she had done while going to Quebec] four miles to the Cascades, but the Gov. wished to see all the Rapids & would not go on shore.

They slept the night of 29 July at Ile aux Soeurs, where some nuns from Montreal kept a house for the care of the insane. "We pitched a tent at the foot of the Hill & near the House." At Lachine they found a pilot to guide the bateaux through the last intimidating set of rapids. On this journey she was more aware of scenery, and the timber rafts so important to the Canadian economy:

> We stopped a little while that we might not overtake or run foul of an immense Cajeux or Raft that was going down, however she struck on a Rock & we passed her. It was a fine wild accompaniment to the Scene we were in, the distant view was fine ... the Gov. wished me to sketch, I believe he wished to take off my attention from the Rapids.[10]

"Reason" told her she was in no danger. Canadians rowed the rapids every day. The pilot did not help; he bragged that only his skill could save them from perdition. They reached Gray's house in Montreal on the thirtieth. The thirty-first was a Sunday, and Lieutenant-General Gabriel Christie, in command of the garrison, loaned them his coach to ride to church.

"Why, it's a room on Wheels," said Francis.

He had ridden only in open carriages as long as he could remember. Elizabeth liked Gray's Venetian blinds, which threw such a "sombre light" that all the women who called looked handsome "tho they were not so in broad daylight".[11] They visited the Frobishers at their country house. Seeing the Frobishers' dogs, Francis wondered if people here kept them as "Centinels", so accustomed was he to seeing sentries on guard at Newark and York.

Elizabeth was proud that she had not caught cold, despite her damp clothes. She had had no opportunity to dry them on the way because men were always cooking at their only fire. When they were ready to continue, the commissary supplied them with a fresh crew, men who were clumsy and so inexperienced that they often asked her which way to go. The only one who knew anything was "dying of Ague & of no use." On the night of 3 August, the men had not fastened the awning securely on the bateau, and when they came aboard they found that rain had soaked their beds. Elizabeth sat by a fire and dried what she was wearing, and again bragged that she slept in the damp without catching cold. She admired the high banks of the river and the distant blue hills. At Grondines, they slept in a room belonging to Mr. John McCord, a Quebec merchant and member of the legislature for the village. They could not sleep in the bateaux because the St. Lawrence was now tidal. The crew had to draw the boats up on shore to ensure that they would not float away when the tide rose.

At Trois Rivières they stopped briefly to greet the Reverend Jehoshaphat Mountain, the bishop's brother, and reached Belmont, the home of the Caldwells', on 5 August, and found the *Pearl* waiting for them, though they were a day late. The next day General and Mrs. Prescott called at Belmont. Prescott was elderly, and Simcoe wondered if he should give up his leave and stay to help out. Elizabeth was appalled at the very idea for he needed the leave to recover his own health. If he did not take it, the government would think he did not really need it, which would call his integrity into dispute. Her husband was too patriotic for his own good.

They received a message from Bishop Mountain, offering to loan the Simcoes his house and carriage, since accommodation was almost impossible to find in Quebec that season. The Mountains' youngest child had died the night before and they were going to Trois Rivières to stay with his brother Jehoshaphat. Gratefully the Simcoes accepted the offer. Mrs. Prescott had described to Elizabeth the dismal lodgings she rented while waiting for the Dorchesters to vacate the Château St. Louis.

On 16 August, at the Mountain home, the Simcoes learned that the *Active* had been wrecked off the Isle of Anticosti, but with no loss of lives.

163

The Dorchesters had been taken, by schooner, to Gaspé Bay and were awaiting transport to Halifax. The *Pearl* left to take them, and the Simcoes would have to wait until the ship returned to Quebec. On the 18th:

> The ship Adriatic arrived from Hallifax [sic]. Dined at the
> Chateau, Ther[mometer]. 88. We are under great anxiety
> least Lord Dorchester should take the Pearl to carry him to
> England from Hallifax.[12]

She was still minding the heat. The only comfortable time was from eight to ten at night, when they walked on the ramparts. Nevertheless the social round went on unrelenting, as they were entertained by Chief Justice William Osgoode, Postmaster Hugh Finlay, Paymaster General Joshua Winslow and the Babys. On 29 August, two ships that had been waiting for the *Pearl* to convoy them left Quebec, their commanders tired of the delay. The *Pearl* finally returned from Halifax on 3 September.

On 6 September, a few days before they were to sail, fire broke out in the Upper Town. In the afternoon, as Elizabeth was stepping into a carriage to go to the château, she found the street full of smoke. The blaze, which had started in a barn not far from the Mountains' house and spread rapidly from roof to roof because all were shingled in wood. By that time the Mountains had returned. Once Simcoe was warned of the danger, he sprang into action and took command of the defence of the houses. He organized the crew of the *Pearl* to carry water. Thus he saved the Mountain house and several adjoining it, although all caught fire several times. Sparks ignited the Recollect church as Elizabeth arrived at the château, and fearful that the fire would reach the Mountains' house she sent orders to her servants to have their trunks sent to Chief Justice Osgoode's house for safety. She was terrified as she returned to the Mountain house, to change for a ball at the château that night. The château itself was in danger, with hoses trained on it to keep it damp. Elizabeth abandoned her plan to return to the château and instead took the children into Palace Street, where they sat watching the destruction. At eight o'clock

> Gen'l Simcoe came to fetch us to the Chief Justice's where
> we slept for tho the danger was at an end, the sight of
> everything still burning around the Bishop's House, made
> me wish not to sleep there.[13]

On the seventh, their baggage was put aboard the *Pearl*. The ruins of the Recollect church were bright inside, and presented "an awful grand appearance as we walked home in a dark night, the effect of color was very rich." She enquired whether the Ursuline nuns were safe. The roof of their convent had been endangered, and the nuns had carried water to the top floor to keep it damp. Pleased with this attentive concern, The Mother Superior sent Elizabeth a polite note and a basket of plums from the convent garden.

They boarded the *Pearl* on Saturday 10 September at 11.00 a.m. Elizabeth's cabin was larger than on the *Triton*, "but the Guns are very incommodious." The cabin contained bulkheads which had to be opened in order to fire some of the ship's guns. If they met any French ships, she had orders to clear out the cabin. She kept as few items as possible lest in their haste the crew throw her belongings below "in confusion". She found one trunk of Bishop Mountain's clothes, accidently included with their belongings, and sent it to Quebec on a passing boat. She accounted for all her things, except a pretty Indian basket with shoes in it.

Their fellow passengers were the officers of the *Active*, returning home having lost their ship. Progress was slow, because the *Pearl* was convoying ten merchant ships. The *Brook Watson* and the *Earl of Marchmont*, sailing badly, detained everyone. On 18 September they sighted a sail, and in case it belonged to a French ship Elizabeth hurried to tidy up her cabin. It proved to be a brigantine out of Quebec, but Captain Ballard admitted that a more serious threat had been a row of breakers indicating a shoal. The *Pearl* had drifted towards them in the night, but was saved when the breeze freshened and they were able to sail away. Elizabeth sketched "Portreau Bay", gazing at it through a telescope, finding the rocky shore and scrub pine so bleak.

A fishing boat came to warn Ballard of two French frigates and a brigantine that had been sighted two days earlier and were about forty miles distant. The French ships had already captured six of the merchantmen the *Pearl* was escorting since they sailed too far ahead to be protected. Elizabeth sent all their belongings below, and Captain Leveson Gower, the commander of the doomed *Active*, led Elizabeth, the children and a servant down two flights of stairs to the bread room, which was barely big enough for everyone. There they spent six hours in "perfect misery", and unable to eat. (The captain was probably John, the only son of late Admiral John Leveson Gore.)

A sailor who brought food advised her, "You had better take it now, for there's no knowing when you may be able to get any more."

Rumour told that the *Progress*, carrying General and Mrs. Richard England home, had been captured. Then "Captain" Malcolm (First Lieutenant James Malcolm of the Royal Marines) offered Elizabeth his room, which was one flight up from the bread room and cooler though it was only six feet long and four feet wide. Being below decks, she could hear talking all night.

The next noon that cabin was cleared "& the bulk heads thrown down", but Elizabeth found a better place to stay, in the gun room. There she could hardly feel the motion of the ship and her appetite returned. She passed the time pleasantly, playing backgammon and cards with the officers of the *Active*. The French ships were following three leagues behind. The *Ephon*, one of the merchantmen, escaped after the French captured her, but she did not rejoin the convoy. The *Pearl* took the *Brook Watson* in tow twice, but when her master let the cable go, Elizabeth was glad to be rid of the merchantman. The *Adriatic* was safe, but the *London* was rumoured to have run aground. By 23 September the French were no longer pursuing, and Elizabeth returned to her cabin.

On board was a Mr. Hill, who had sailed the North Sea, and who told of eating salt pork raw for if boiled it became a "cake of ice". He told so many terrifying tales that Elizabeth felt unsafe being on the same ship. On 26 September she made nine copies of a drawing depicting the action on 1 June 1794 when Admiral Richard Howe had captured the seven French "sail".

They encountered very rough weather. On the twenty-eighth they had no breakfast until noon. The forestay sail split in the gale, but she resolved to continue her drawing as long as "they left a Table in the Room." Nearby ships were "India Men", a sign that they were nearing home waters. Then they met a ship from Jamaica that had been separated from her convoy by the gale four days before, her topsails split "We ran 9 knotts an hour under bare poles."[14] For a few days she neglected her diary. The next entry was made on 9 October, when the *Pearl* took the West Indian vessel *Lioness* under convoy. She had lost sight of her own convoy of 130 ships during the late gale. Elizabeth went on deck to watch as the *Pearl's* "lead heav'd & the Ship lay to" which was a "terrific sight". The waves seemed likely to overwhelm the ship, and the noise was frightful. By the eleventh they were near Berry Head, hoping to land at Tor Bay, Devon, but the breeze was too stiff.

Elizabeth was echoed by Sophia in her desire to get off the ship after such a long voyage. Francis felt differently. He had not been sick a day, and declared, when he was old enough, he would be a sailor like his grandfather Captain Simcoe.

By 12 October they were off Dover, but until the seas subsided landing was too hazardous. They anchored near a large Indiaman, and other vessels "in the Downs", all waiting for better weather to disgorge their passengers and cargo. The *Ville de Paris* passed close, a clumsy looking vessel. Elizabeth preferred the clean, sleek lines of the frigates. On the next day, a wet morning but calm, they left the *Pearl* accompanied by Captains Ballard and Leveson Gower and other officers, and dined at an inn in Deal, on the road to Canterbury. Francis descended the stairs backwards, as he had done aboard the *Pearl*. The officers offered to help if Francis wanted to enter Royal Navy as a midshipman.

Elizabeth could hardly wait to see the girls at Wolford Lodge after five long years. And what a pleasure it was, she reflected, to have dined in a room that had not been heaving up and down!

PART III

PARTINGS: HUSBAND, SON, DEAREST FRIEND 1796-1813

Chapter 18

RETURN TO WOLFORD LODGE

At Wolford Lodge Mrs. Hunt was still in command, but her daughter Mary had left to take a post as a tutor to a family near Exeter. On 3 June 1796 Miss Hunt wrote to Harriet that she was glad "Mrs. Bell has left off her headdress & is again Miss Caroline Simcoe". The girls would all be pleased that a parcel had arrived from Canada. "Would you like to ride in the sleigh?" They would need four sleighs with great dogs to draw them, like Juno and her "peacocks" or Bacchus and his tigers. She asked Harriet to warn Miss Burges that she would transfer her affections to a cat with only three legs who sat on her gown, if she did not hear from her soon.[1]

By October everyone knew that the five-year separation was nearly over. From on board the *Pearl* while awaiting calm seas so that they could land, Elizabeth dispatched letters announcing that they would be arriving home within the next fortnight. At Whitchurch, Mrs. Gwillim was most relieved to have a letter from her niece. Elizabeth was "quite the heroine". Mrs. Gwillim had worried that the Simcoes might fall into French hands — disastrous since all the French were devoted followers of Thomas Paine, whose two volumes entitled *The Rights of Man* were a vindication of the French Revolution. There was enough unrest in England because the war was making people "turbulent". No doubt the revolutionists in France would soon be overthrown, and religion and monarchy restored.[2] She commented on the content of Elizabeth's letter, which matched the information about their landing and travels in the diary.

From Deal the Simcoes backtracked to Dover, to accept an invitation to dine from General William Grinfield, the commander of the local garrison whose home was in Sidmouth. Then they walked around the castle and other fortifications high on the white cliffs:

> The bold Cliffs, the Town & Beach beneath, form a charming Picture, & the horizon of the Sea was terminated by the fleet which sailed yesterday the Ville de Paris towering

above the rest, we sailed round her before we came on shore but a large Frigate such as the Diamond is a finer sight to my taste.[3]

They found Captain Ralph Henry Bruyere of the Royal Engineers, whom they had known in Canada, and he accompanied them on a walk around new construction to enlarge the fortifications at the castle. From one of the tower ruins, where they could see Roman bricks, the coast of France was visible, and she could make out the entrance to the harbour at Boulogne and a church at Calais. They saw cannon given to Queen Elizabeth by the Dutch, and passed through a tunnel from the castle heights to the town:

> it is a handsome stone staircase of twelve hundred steps, at the bottom of every 2 or 300 feet it is lighted by a passage & window at the extremity of the Rock, we descended with a Lanthorn, it cost 700. I was much pleased with Capt. Bruyere, for he talked with delight of Canada. He married a sister of Mrs. Selby's of Montreal.

They left for Canterbury on the night of 14 October. Before setting out in the morning they went to the cathedral, which impressed Elizabeth more than Salisbury for it had not been "modernized". The tomb of Thomas à Becket was "plain", but she approved of the Black Prince's tomb: "There is a monument of Edward the black Prince in Brass in great preservation. The Armour, helmet & Gloves he wore at Cressy are hung over it."

On 22 October, Mrs. Gwillim wrote to thank Elizabeth for a long, entertaining account of all the perils and dangers, but "you are not faint hearted". Her aunt had a print of the monument to the Black Prince, and she recalled how much she loved to hear her mother tell the prince's history on a winter night. The Black Prince had been the scourge of France, but men were not half so bad as they were now. She could not have coped with all those steps in Dover, because heights made her giddy. She was happy that Elizabeth reported the general in better health as a consequence of the long voyage. Simcoe would be needed at home if the French invaded, but no doubt he longed to join the "Iron Duke". (Whom she meant is a mystery; Wellington did not earn the nickname until after 1809.) As for Thomas Paine, his book was "blasphemous"! She hoped that war with Spain could be avoided, but the French were turning every power against Britain. Elizabeth would probably find her friends in London much altered since the dissipation of life there aged them. She had a petition to give to General Simcoe from some worthy people who expected to be sent to Canada, and who hoped for assistance.[4]

As they drove towards London, Elizabeth was seeing her homeland through fresh eyes. The country from Canterbury to Dartford was "woody & beautiful" but the weather was damp and unpleasant. They passed many fine homes, but people had little inducement to go outside. Everything seemed "so cheerless from the want of our bright Canadian Sun that the effect was striking & the contrast very unfavourable to the English climate."[5]

They slept at Dartford on 15 October, and stopped at a hotel in Cork Street when they reached London the next evening. Simcoe conferred with the Duke of Portland, and they leased a house at 53 Wellbeck Street before setting out again for Devonshire and the reunion. At Bath they stayed a might with Mrs. Graves, who welcomed them warmly, as though she had never felt any animosity towards them. Elizabeth found her thin and aged. She declared, though she had no appetite and was wasting away, she was much better than last winter when she daily expected to die. She was now sixty-nine, just one year short of the three score and ten that she should expect to live.

The Simcoes' carriage drew up at Wolford Lodge on the afternoon of 22 October. Letters had warned Mrs. Hunt when to expect them, and within seconds the entire household was assembled in front — the four girls with Mrs. Hunt in the foreground, and the servants in a neat line behind them. Off to the side was the person Elizabeth recognized first. Mrs. Burges was keeping in the background, a small girl by her side, until the parents had greeted their daughters. Elizabeth stared at the four girls as they came forward and dropped perfect curtseys. Twelve-year-old Eliza was a trifle shorter than she was, but Elizabeth almost recoiled from Charlotte and Harriet, who, aged eleven and nine, were actually taller than their mother. Sophia was watching the others with a glint in her eyes. Five-year-old Francis was as shy as Eliza, Elizabeth noted, turning to study the four eldest more carefully. Meanwhile, Sophia, not the least bit awestruck, was dancing up and down, and laughing aloud.

Elizabeth took note of the expressions of shock on the faces of the four who had been separated from them, and she hesitated, uncertain how to greet them after five years. The general had no such qualms or inhibitions, and he gathered the four to him, bestowing the hugs and kisses withheld for so long. That broke the ice and soon everyone was laughing.

Then Simcoe greeted Mrs. Hunt warmly, and thanked her for taking such good care of the girls. Meanwhile, surrounded by children, Elizabeth hurried towards Mary Anne Burges, and they embraced, as girls capered around them. Upon hearing a soft, "Mama" behind her, Elizabeth turned to find Eliza leading the smallest girl in the group by the hand. Elizabeth knelt, put her arms around Julia and raised her eyes to look into those of Mary Anne, her gratitude shining. After all the letters her friend had written, she did not feel that she was coming home to complete strangers; if ever they were in danger of forgetting, Eliza piped up, they would gaze at Miss Burges' miniature.

The next few days were like a dream to Elizabeth, and they were busy ones as stories of the past five years were retold, and possessions examined. Elizabeth and Mary Anne looked over each other's drawings, joined by the children. In turn, Elizabeth carefully studied the work of the four eldest and was very happy with what she saw. All four showed considerable skill at representation. As soon as she was settled in, she resolved to take them sketching in many picturesque places. Of her six children, Eliza and Francis seemed alike, inclined to tread lightly until they were certain of their ground. Caroline resembled them, in that she was small-boned and dark, but her personality was closer to Charlotte's and to that of their father. Harriet, too, tended to say what she thought without weighing the consequences, but none were as difficult for Elizabeth to manage as Sophia, who had not had the benefit of Mrs. Hunt's discipline. Almost from the outset, the older girls had a good effect on Sophia, as peer pressure brought her increasingly into line.

A few days after the Simcoes reached Wolford Lodge, the bulk of their baggage arrived from the *Pearl*, and they showed off the carriole and the stove bought in Quebec. Simcoe had the great canoe launched in the River Wolf by some servants, with many strictures to be careful not to puncture the birch bark. Most of all everyone admired the sleigh. The girls could hardly wait for some snow so that they could try it out.

Two weeks after the family had returned, Francis was sent to Honiton to board with Mr. Coplestone. Neither Elizabeth nor the general took seriously the difficulties mentioned by Mrs. Burges. On 19 November, Mrs. Gwillim wrote that she was pleased Elizabeth had found the family at Wolford well. The girls would make agreeable women, for they were sensible and good tempered. "You show fortitude leaving your Little man". Boys were better educated under men, and the Simcoe's choice of a clergyman was wise. Religion and the right morals were a safeguard against temptation.[6]

For a month Simcoe was content to regard himself as convalescent and to rest frequently. Elizabeth busied herself in strengthening the bond with the older girls, and with visits to and from Tracey, usually with the girls along, to be with Mrs. Burges and Julia. By late November Simcoe was writing letters to friends of influence who could secure him an appointment, and to government officials on the future of Upper Canada. He was receiving a stream of letters from Peter Russell, asking for advice. Russell was fearful of taking any initiatives himself, and he felt that Simcoe, who was still the lieutenant governor, should make all decisions, even minor ones.

Early in December, feeling much stronger, Simcoe left for London and stayed at the house in Wellbeck Street. On the sixth he wrote to the Duke of Portland, the home secretary, warning him that American ships of greater tonnage than agreed on were going to San Domingo, a former French colony which, since September 1793, had been a British protectorate. During a slave uprising their French masters had appealed for help to the governor of Jamaica, Lieutenant-General Sir Adam Williamson, who sent 1,000 men. Then the French joined the slaves' resistance and Britain ordered in more troops. Now a stalemate prevailed. Yellow fever was the worst enemy, and it had killed 7,530 British soldiers. On 10 December, the Duke of Portland

170

informed Simcoe that the King had a mission for him if his health was sufficiently improved — an appointment as governor and commander-in-chief at San Domingo.

Elizabeth was horrified when he came home and informed her that he had accepted it, but not taken by surprise. In her letter of 19 November Mrs. Gwillim had wished the general every success, and noted that he would be going at a good time of year and would probably return before the hot season. Nevertheless, Elizabeth wondered if she would see him again. He was no longer a robust man and easily fell prey to diseases.

Simcoe left for San Domingo early in 1797 and reached Port-au-Prince in March. As in Upper Canada, he found he could not obtain enough troops to conduct a proper campaign, and he was soon disheartened. In his letters to Elizabeth, he tried to appear cheerful, and his addresses were brimming with affection. In May, Elizabeth took the five girls to Mrs. Graves' in Bath for a fortnight. From there the girls returned to Wolford. Elizabeth went on to London, and Mrs. Hunt came from Bath, where she was living, to care for the girls. When Elizabeth returned she brought Francis from Honiton for a summer holiday.[7]

No one made any comments on how Francis adjusted to school. Since he was inclined to be diffident, he probably had too much sense to brag of his exotic life in Canada, to flaunt his Indian clothing or show off by dancing. The temptation to do so must have been strong but the need to conform may have held him in a more powerful grasp and saved him from bullying and ragging.

In August, Mrs. Gwillim was relieved to hear that Elizabeth had recovered from a fever, and that General Simcoe was in good health in San Domingo.[8] In fact, he was already on his way home, disillusioned and angry over the lack of support he had received, and unable to control the situation without adequate numbers of troops. He was back in London by 27 September, and in disgrace. Henry Dundas, now the secretary at war, refused to receive him, and the Duke of York, as commander-in-chief of the British army, only grudgingly allowed him an interview. The Duke tried to charge Simcoe with abandoning his post. Simcoe returned to Wolford Lodge and threw himself into improving the estate, his public career apparently over.

As the winter of 1797-98 approached, Elizabeth was ill. She had not minded the first winter home, but she was bothered by fevers frequently during the second. On 11 December Mrs. Gwillim, staying in Bath, advised her to get plenty of rest. She wished Elizabeth could come to Bath for the cold months, since that city was so much warmer than Wolford. Mrs. Graves was in good spirits despite her talk of "Republican mania", and going to plays every week, as well as attending and giving card parties. A mutual friend, Mrs. Clarke at Whitchurch, had had some deer poached. She had offered a reward of £50 for the culprit, but whoever had done it had not been caught, which indicated how common was lawlessness. Was the rumour that General Simcoe would not return to San Domingo true?[9] It was, for Britain had decided not to waste any more lives trying to rule the island, and to evacuate it. Later, the King gave Simcoe "two Brass Spanish guns" as he was the last British governor of San Domingo.[10]

In January 1798 a serious rebellion erupted in Wexford, Ireland at a time when British troops were already involved against France. In need of capable military leaders, the government warmed again towards Simcoe. Negotiations opened for him to succeed Robert Prescott as Governor General of Canada in the spring of 1799 when the latter's tour of duty would end. Meanwhile, the government had formally accepted Simcoe's resignation as lieutenant governor of Upper Canada.

Elizabeth was eager to return to Quebec, where she had so many friends. This time they would be able to take all five girls, since they would be living in the château, but Francis would have to stay behind to prepare for Eton. However, Simcoe had yet to assume the appointment, and he had made a peerage a condition of accepting it. Elizabeth felt that this was only fair, after all he had done for the Empire. He deserved at least a baronetage, and she would have the courtesy title that went with it. She was looking forward to becoming Lady Simcoe, or if the general became a baron, Lady Wolford or Lady Honiton, depending on what place name was chosen. The spring of 1799 would suit Elizabeth well as a time of departure. Her next child would be born in July 1798, which would leave her plenty of time to recuperate and make preparations for the long voyage and life in Quebec.

From Whitchurch, Mrs. Gwillim delivered more of her brand of common sense on 22 March. Mrs. Graves had reported that Elizabeth and the girls had been in Bath, where their niece had purchased a black wig to conceal a few wisps of grey. After enquiring whether Elizabeth's reunion with Francis had been joyous when she returned home, Mrs. Gwillim disapproved of false hair. "I should think with your fine dark hair you would not need a black wig." The softness of one's own hair was "much more becoming to the face". She was surprised to hear that Elizabeth was "in that way" and hoped it would be another boy. She was having surveys made at Whitchurch, and she wanted the magistrates to "settle with the surveyors & not let any Democrats come in". The Irish situation looked ominous, and many people disapproved of Pitt's proposed solution — union with Britain and Catholic emancipation. She thought that the Catholic Duke of Norfolk's influence was already making the country disloyal.[11]

On 21 May, Mrs. Graves wrote to Eliza that people in Bath were rejoicing over the escape from France of Sir Sidney Smith, a naval officer who had been taken prisoner near Le Havre while attempting to capture a French privateer. He had been in Bath for a week, and was much lionized. Whenever he appeared at the Pump Room or in the gardens, a crowd gathered. In June the Simcoes went to London and Eliza wrote Miss Hunt, asking her to stay at Wolford Lodge in their absence.[12] Later in the month the rebels were defeated in Ireland and the rebellion ended.

On 7 July, at Wolford, Elizabeth gave birth to a son, John Cornwall Simcoe. Mrs. Graves informed Eliza that she was pleased the girls had another brother even though she liked girls better than boys, who tended to be a "domineering set of beings". As Eliza had said, they had "girls enow".[13] Elizabeth was fussier than usual over the care of the new baby, and constantly aware of the small grave at York that held little Katherine.

August brought good news and bad news. Admiral Horatio Nelson had destroyed a French fleet off Aboukir in what people were calling the Battle of the Nile. Then, late in the month, a French force landed in Ireland, a belated reinforcement for the rebels. By the early autumn Napoleon was expected to invade Britain, and in October Simcoe was placed in command of all the forces along the southwest coast with the local rank of lieutenant-general. His territory comprised all the country of Dorset, Devon, Somerset and Cornwall. At first, Wolford Lodge was Simcoe's headquarters, and armies of visitors came and went, and carriages lined the drive to the house. Elizabeth was kept busy acting as hostess to this multitude, and the staff of servants and workers on the estate now numbered fifty. On 30 October Mrs. Graves wrote to Eliza thanking her for a pretty handkerchief she had embroidered. Her great aunt was pleased to hear that little John was strong and growing well.[14] Soon afterwards word arrived that the French had been defeated in Ireland.

As 1799 opened, Simcoe was again unhappy and disillusioned. The command in the southwest did not satisfy him. His troops were mostly militia embodied to guard the coastline. Pitt was promoting less able men for he disliked Simcoe's habit of demanding more troops and resources than the prime minister felt the country could afford. Besides, Simcoe was a supporter of Henry Addington, a Member of Parliament who was sometimes at odds with Pitt. As a consolation Simcoe organized his house along military lines. John Bailey, long a faithful employee, recalled:

> All the tradespeople assembled at the end of the Avenue and fell in there two deep according to their trades, those of the highest rank in trade going first. When all were mustered they were marched off to the house with drum and fife played before them, then all received their orders and were dismissed. When they left work all fell in again, and were marched off with drum and fife.[15]

Elizabeth paid little heed to such measures. She was preoccupied because baby John was sickly. As with the other children, John had been inoculated against smallpox, in his case when he was four months old. On 13 October 1798, Mrs. Gwillim wrote that she hoped "our little man" was safe from:

> all danger of the smallpox for his life, but as the Chicken pox is about who ever inoculated him ought to be particularly careful of mistakes ... but by your mentioning the ninth day it looks as to be the right sort the other drys away sooner.[16]

Mrs. Gwillim was wrong; the baby contracted a severe form of the disease. On 22 March 1799, John Cornwall Simcoe died at Wolford Lodge. At that time Elizabeth was also perturbed because Francis and Caroline were severely ill with whooping cough. On the thirty-first, Mrs. Graves commiserated with Eliza over the loss of her "amiable little brother John" who had been weakened by smallpox, but God's will be done. Alarmed over the report on Francis and Caroline, Mrs. Graves hoped they were improving. She was reading Moore's strictures on female education and recommended that Papa buy it for the girls as it made such good sense.[17]

Feeling that Elizabeth should get away from Wolford Lodge for a change of scene after losing John, Simcoe leased a house in Plymouth and moved his headquarters there. By June, Elizabeth was again pregnant, half joyful that there would be another baby, half fearful that it would follow the path of the last two. As usual, Simcoe was alarmed. Elizabeth was certain she would be fine, but she could not face losing another promising child.

When Simcoe resigned as lieutenant governor of Upper Canada, he recommended appointing Peter Russell as his replacement. In an unassuming way Russell had extended surveys and completed moving the capital to York. Pitt thought otherwise, as was almost to be expected. On 10 April he had appointed Lieutenant-General Peter Hunter, who would take up his duties as governor in the summer.

Eliza kept up a correspondence with her Great Aunt Margaret in Bath, whose letters to her great niece made her seem less erratic than Mrs. Burges' to Elizabeth. By the autumn Eliza had acquired a cottage as an investment. Mrs. Graves was delighted that Eliza was managing her own cottage and expected to make a profit from it. A woman ought to be taught the worth of things, which would "gain a husband's approbation". With the Simcoes still based at Plymouth, the girls must enjoy their excursions to visit them. She then lamented the superior status of males:

> By being brought up to professions they can acquire fortunes for themselves, or better those they have. Girls have none of those advantages and can scarce gain (with their utmost industry and pricking their finger to the bone) a single shilling a Day. Gentlemen's Daughters are too often an unfortunate set of beings. Brought up in affluence, . . in maturer age are often left to disappointment and distress.[18]

On 5 February 1800 the Act of Union with Ireland passed the British Parliament; it was to take effect on 1 January 1801. By that time Elizabeth was expecting her child any day. Henry Addington Simcoe was born on the 28 February 1800 at Plymouth. Mrs. Graves wrote to Eliza on 4 March offering her congratulations.[19] The Irish Parliament passed its own Act of Union on the twenty-eighth, viewed with mixed emotions by conservatives like the Simcoes; Union appeared to bring Catholic emancipation one step closer.

On the Wolford property were Cistercian ruins, where some monks had been buried before the dissolution of the monasteries which Henry VIII accomplished in 1539. Simcoe decided that the ruins would be the appropriate place for a chapel and the family burial plot, and a suitable way of greeting the new century. He hired skilled stonemasons and the project began. Although the chapel would not be ready to use for some time, the body of John Cornwall Simcoe was the first to be interred in the burial plot.

On 4 June to Eliza, Mrs. Graves was grieved that little Henry had been burned and relieved he would not be "marked" although scars would keep him from being vain — all too common in males who were "pretty". On 10 July, she warned Eliza that Mrs. Gwillim was near death and had been taken home to Whitchurch from Bath to spend her last days. Then Mrs. Graves complained that her stables had been robbed. Her servant William's livery had been taken, because he was too "indolent" to keep the clothes in the house. Elizabeth and the girls passed through Bath on their way to Whitchurch to be with Mrs. Gwillim during her last days. This sensible aunt died on 6 August 1800 and was buried in the family plot with her parents, sister and brothers, except for Elizabeth's father, Thomas. Mrs. Graves wrote Eliza that Mrs. Gwillim's death had been a release for she had suffered much pain "with Christian resignation".

Elizabeth's only surviving aunt was worried for her niece's health. Elizabeth had appeared thin and exhausted when she arrived in Bath en route to Whitchurch. She was weary because she was again pregnant, and Henry was only six months old. On her return, the younger children had come down with measles, which alarmed both aunt and niece. Mrs. Graves informed the Simcoes that Miss Hunt had been appointed governess to the four-year-old Princess Charlotte of Wales, which was a great honour.[20] (Charlotte was the only child of the Prince of Wales and Princess Caroline of Brunswick.)

An event of some importance to Elizabeth and to Mary Anne Burges was the publication in 1800, anonymously, of the latter's book *The Progress of the Pilgrim Good Intent*, a sequel to John Bunyan's popular *Pilgrim's Progress*. Good Intent was the great grandson of Christian's eldest son. The book ran to three editions before the year ended, and Sir James Bland Burges was urging Mary Anne to allow her name to be put on new editions slated for 1801.[21] Mary Anne blushed deeply at the very idea. She could not bear to have people staring at her, especially men.

The year 1801 arrived, and with it union with Ireland, which added the Cross of St. Patrick to the flag. Simcoe was made a lieutenant-general in the British army on 1 January.[22] A few days later a great masquerade was staged at Wolford Lodge, which Caroline Simcoe described in a letter to Mrs. Hunt.[23] Many guests dressed as characters from Shakespeare. Elizabeth, expecting her tenth child in March, was a spectator. General Simcoe, as Prospero, introduced everyone. Miss Burges was "the drollest figure in the room" as a witch from Macbeth. Julia Somerville was Moth with enormous wings; Eliza, Thisbe; Charlotte, Pyranus; Harriet, Wall; Sophia, Moonshine;

and Francis, Lion. Later they all changed costumes. Francis became Oberon King of the Fairies; Caroline was Titania the Queen; Sophia was Ariel. A band from Honiton played for dancing, and a "pedlar" distributed presents. "Henry is very well & I hope, will soon be able to walk alone." Among the guests were the four sons and one daughter of Captain James Coleridge of Ottery St. Mary, a brother of the poet Samuel Taylor Coleridge. The two eldest, James, twelve, and John, ten, acted as Oberon's attendants. Their sister, only four years old, was frightened by all the activity and went to bed. Julia represented Nimrod's ghost. On one side of the tomb of Nimrod the mighty hunter were a hare and hounds which Miss Burges had cut out, and on the other side was Semiramus.

By March 1801, Simcoe's career seemed about to take a turn for the better. Pitt resigned on the fourteenth over the issue of Catholic emancipation, and the general's friend Henry Addington, became prime minister. By that time Elizabeth was expecting her child daily, and on the twenty-third a seventh daughter was born at Wolford Lodge. She was named Katherine after the sixth daughter who had been buried at York, Upper Canada.

In June, Mrs. Graves paid a visit to Wolford Lodge, the first since her irate departure in 1792, and enjoyed herself. As summer of 1801 turned to autumn, Eliza Simcoe, now seventeen, was swept up in a social whirl such as her mother loved. Wolford Lodge was again her father's headquarters, with many entertainments there and at other houses. She was able to attend a ball almost every night and dance on into the dawn.

In the meantime, negotiations towards peace had begun, although Mrs. Graves was gloomy that Nelson's victory in Egypt might not deter "Bonaparte" for long. On 1 October a preliminary treaty was signed, instituting the temporary Peace of Amiens. The following day Mrs. Graves wrote exclaiming that Eliza had spent the autumn gaily, and was acquiring a taste for "military amusements". Chiding mildly she added, "you look on Soldiers as so many pieces in your chess board."[24]

Chapter 19

GENERAL SIMCOE'S LAST YEARS
1803~1806

Margaret Graves' letters to her great niece Eliza Simcoe show that the old lady had not mellowed with time. Apparently she was well-preserved, and she delighted in making snide remarks about contemporaries who were showing their ages more than she. She was still angry at the Richard Graveses; her favourite in-laws were now Thomas North 2nd Baron Graves and his wife. Lord Graves' father was Admiral Samuel Graves' first cousin. Her letters also show her resentment that men had more privileges than women, the reason why she did not like boys as well as girls. Independently wealthy, Margaret felt degraded because Admiral Graves took control of her fortune at the time of their marriage (as John Graves Simcoe had taken control of Elizabeth's wealth).[1]

At Wolford Lodge, Simcoe directed the festivities early in January 1802. Eliza, now eighteen, described the entertainment in letter to Miss Hunt. "Father" had written a play based on Joseph Addison's Roman tragedy *Cato*, for which all the cast was dressed by "Mother". Francis was Decius and his school friends acted other parts. Caroline spoke the prologue and Julia the epilogue, and Sophia was a senator. The house was full of company and everyone danced until 2.00 a.m. The epilogue is in the Devon Archives. Dressed as Britannia, ten-year-old Julia spoke thirty-six patriotic lines. They begin thus:

> Ye British youth, be worth like thus approved,
> And shew that you have Virtue to be moved
> From Greece, from Rome, your first Examples draw,
> And learn to reverence your Countries law,
> To their bright Precepts give your early day
> And mix instruction with your hours of play
> Such was tonight the Scene; a Scene that's dear
> To every English heart & English ear,
> For ever lov'd Monarch, in his youthful days
> In Cato's character obtain'd just praise
> Its worth admir'd & as He conn'd the past
> Stamp'd Cato's Image on his English Heart ...

The final two lines read:

> Kindle in all, a never dying flame
> And prove you worthy of your Countries fame.[2]

The record on Elizabeth is for the most part brief references in the replies Margaret Graves wrote to Eliza (whose letters to Mrs. Graves have not survived). Eliza sent a list of the Shakespearean plays she had seen, to which Margaret replied that she, too, had seen all of them. She approved of Shakespeare, but thought Sheridan paid no heed to morals.[3] On 27 March 1802 the Peace of Amiens became official. At the time Elizabeth was not well, Eliza informed Mrs. Graves. Her mother was worried about the military situation despite the peace that had been signed, and about Miss Burges, who was also ill. Mrs. Graves felt that Miss Burges' death would be a tragedy for Julia, who was coming to value her cousin as "an incomparable guardian". The peace was a blessed relief to Mrs. Graves, for among her friends were many officers.[4]

In late May General Simcoe went to London, taking Eliza and Charlotte as far as Bath. Both girls wrote to Miss Hunt (who was with Princess Charlotte of Wales) and both apologised for their untidiness, but they wanted to avert an inspection by Mrs. Graves. Charlotte wanted to put her letter in the post before "you know who" returned from visiting friends and impose "half- restraints". Eliza told Miss Hunt that she had avoided attending two "detestable card parties".[5]

Meanwhile, Simcoe had been acquiring more land, improving his holdings, and treating with the Enclosure Commissioners who were responsible for selling common lands. Assisted by John Scadding, who had returned from Canada, he had purchased the manors of Bywood and Windsor, and by purchasing, through the Enclosure Commissioners, the commons that separated them, he was able to link them and have about 10,000 acres "within a ring fence ... The three Manors and the hundred covers many miles and is the best partridge and woodcock country in Devon."[6]

Simcoe informed William Walcot that he would settle for a profit margin of four per cent, except that he needed five percent to support his family. His mention of the enclosures strikes a sensitive area in the history of farming in England. Enclosing land for sheep run or for crops, to replace the old open field system had been in process for some 300 years, and was the subject of much lament, yet it was also efficient. The land was more productive, and wool from sheep grazing on land formerly marginal brought higher returns. This meant dislocation for many agricultural workers. Fewer labourers were required on enclosed farms, which caused high unemployment and rural poverty. The hardship would be eased in time, through emigration and the Industrial Revolution, although wages in the factories would be very low. The Simcoes were among the most generous in contributions to alleviate conditions for the poor. As well, Simcoe was an important employer in the neighbourhood, having as many as fifty men working on the improvements to his estate.[7]

In order to pay for the two estates in Devon, Simcoe decided to sell Aldwinkle, Elizabeth's birthplace. She may have regretted the move, but she could still visit Northampton. William Walcot would always make her welcome at Oundle and at Titchmarsh, his country manor; she would still have the property at Whitchurch. Simcoe did not wish to deprive her of all her own manors. The Land Tax Assessment Records for 1799 show that Simcoe owned Manly, Shaptons (where Thomas Scadding was the occupant), "Woolford" Lodge, Marleshayne, Grange (a different one from The Grange that belonged to the Drewe family), and Bywood. The records for 1800 are the same; Simcoe's property in Dunkeswell was assessed at £58. 4. 0. Those for 1801 and 1802 are missing, but in 1803 he had added Mansels to his holdings.[8]

Working on the sale of Aldwinkle was William Walcot and ultimately the buyer was Thomas Powys, the 2nd Baron Lilford, already a friend of the Simcoes. During these negotiations, in July 1802, an invitation arrived from the Royal family for General and Mrs. Simcoe to attend the yacht races off Weymouth. A delighted Elizabeth selected ball gowns, riding habit, morning and afternoon dresses, and cloaks for joining friends on the esplanade. She kept a diary that echoed her Canadian one.[9] They left Wolford Lodge early on the morning of the eighteenth, a Sunday, and stopped in Bridport to attend church and dine, arriving at Weymouth at 8.00, the summer sun still shining.

On the following day a Captain and Mrs. Grey called at their hotel, and Miss Hunt, at Weymouth with Princess Charlotte of Wales, dined with the Simcoes. Elizabeth did not reveal any details of Miss Hunt's life in the Princess' household. (As one of the tutors she must have witnessed some of the battles between the Prince of Wales and his estranged wife, Caroline of Brunswick.) In the afternoon Elizabeth rode four miles from Weymouth to an ancient camp, and that evening she walked on the esplanade.

The race was staged on Tuesday the twentieth. They went aboard the Royal yacht *Charlotte* where the King joined his guests. After admiring the "crimson and gilt", the Simcoes and the Greys transferred to the yacht *Augusta* to watch the race. The contenders were *Defiance* and *Blanche*, the former outsailing the latter. As the Queen had not come, the King did not order the yachts into sheltered, calmer waters, and the *Charlotte* and *Augusta* stayed eighteen miles out to sea, bobbing up and down. Mrs. Grey became painfully seasick and Elizabeth developed a headache. Yet she enjoyed watching the other vessels; they were so picturesque. On the twenty-third she rode to Maiden Castle, a huge prehistoric hilltop fort encircled by rings of deep ditches. On the next day Simcoe rode with the King and the Duke of Gloucester, and in the evening with Elizabeth he attended a play, *The Iron Chest*, a "silly farce".

On their last day, 25 July, wet and rainy, they saw Miss Hunt's charge, seven-year-old Princess Charlotte, George III's only legitimate grandchild. They left in the evening, stayed the night at Bridport, and reached Wolford Lodge at 1.00 p.m. on Monday the twenty-sixth. The very next day they left home again, this time for a few days at Ugbrooke House, near Chudleigh, about fourteen miles southwest of Exeter.[10] Their host was Charles, 6th Baron Clifford of Chudleigh, whose wife was Eleanor Mary Arundell, a daughter of the 8th Baron Arundell of Wardour Castle, Wiltshire. The Cliffords and Arundells were both prominent Catholic gentry. (Ugbrooke

House is still owned by the Clifford family. Wardour Castle is now a girls' school.)

The Simcoes left Wolford at 8.00 a.m. and reached Ugbrooke at 3.00 p.m. "Lord and Lady Arundell" were there; Lady Arundell was Lady Clifford's elder sister, Mary Christine, and her husband was the 9th Baron. The next day Elizabeth rode in the park, and the Arundells went to Dawlish. On the twenty-ninth the Simcoes set out at 4.00 p.m. for the house of Sir John Northcote, near Newton St. Cyres, about fifteen miles northwest of Ugbrooke. (Sir John was a cousin of Sir Stafford Henry Northcote, another of the Simcoes' friends whose country seat was Pynes, four miles north of Exeter.) At Sir John's they supped under a tent with his "troop", danced in the "Grove" until 1.00, slept and returned to Ugbrooke on the thirtieth.

Meanwhile, Mrs. Graves arrived at Wolford Lodge for a visit. On Sunday 1 August, Simcoe rode into Exeter and returned to Ugbrooke after dinner. From Exeter he wrote William Walcot at Oundle, referring to the deeds to Aldwinkle and to plans for a monument to Mrs. Gwillim at Whitchurch. Wolford Chapel was now complete, and he wrote the vicar of Dunkeswell, the Reverend John Pratt, asking him to conduct the dedication ceremony "before our most valued Relation Mrs. Graves" wished to return to Bath. The family motto he had had inscribed in the chapel was "as for me and my house, we will serve the Lord" (Joshua 24:15). The Simcoes returned from Ugbrooke a few days later, and the dedication ceremony took place on Monday 23 August 1802.[11]

With the autumn, the general, Elizabeth and Eliza went touring. In London they had stayed with a Mrs. Miller because they no longer kept the house in Wellbeck Street. Mother and daughter shopped, and Simcoe leased a house in Somerset Street, Portman Square. The weather was stiflingly hot, and Elizabeth was "much deranged". Their business attended to, the three went on to Stowe to stay with the Buckinghams. Finding his gout flaring up, Simcoe went to Bath and on home, but Elizabeth and Eliza returned to London for a longer visit. Writing to William Walcot on 11 November, Simcoe told him that a Mr. Wood was going north and would make out an abstract of the title deeds to Aldwinkle. He was writing in a comfortable chair, and reading history as he waited for his gout to subside.

After purchasing and enclosing all the common land that was available, Simcoe had arranged with the Enclosure Commissioners to have roads laid out "agreeably to my wishes", which would be suitable for military use in case of invasion. Half of Devonshire was good cavalry country. The girls were constantly asking why Walcot did not come to see them. They were also missing Eliza, "an excellent girl" whose sisters depended on her. Cambridge was Walcot's "Alma Mater", but he hoped to send Francis to Oxford. For some years Simcoe had been collecting old armour, which he intended placing along the passage that led to the library. He wanted to tell his friend about conferences he had had with Addington, but he would not put anything in writing.[12]

At the close of 1802, the Queen's Rangers were disbanded, as an economy measure, to Simcoe's chagrin. The lieutenant-colonel was then

David Shank, who returned to England afterwards.[13] Samuel Smith, the major and John McGill, still the adjutant, were among the officers who intended to remain in Canada.

As 1803 opened, the older Simcoe girls were enjoying "routs". Eliza was nineteen, but nothing in the records suggested that her parents had any plans for her to be married. Eliza was acquiring her mother's taste for travel, and with a party of friends she was planning to visit Old Court, Whitchurch, the Gwillim home in Herefordshire and afterwards to tour in Wales. While Elizabeth and Eliza made plans, the threatening atmosphere on the Continent preoccupied Simcoe.

Peace with France had been short lived, and by March everyone knew that renewed hostilities were imminent. In May, as the war was about to be resumed, Simcoe wrote to his friend Henry Addington, now the prime minister, concerning the possibility of a command in Sicily, the topic the two had discussed the preceding autumn. This time the Dutch were aligned against Britain, and Addington put an embargo on all British ports for French and Dutch ships. Simcoe was again in his element as he organised the southwest for defence. According to Mrs. Graves, the General continued to be well because he was so busy.[14]

Eliza went off on her tour in July, and Mrs. Graves' friends in Bath were much entertained by the girl's account of her travels.[15] At Wolford Lodge Elizabeth was again playing hostess to Simcoe's many friends, fellow officers and useful politicians. Upper Canada was still much on her thoughts, and letters passed between Devon and the friends she had made in Quebec City, Montreal and York. Thomas Talbot had returned to the province. After purchasing several commissions, he had risen to be the lieutenant-colonel of the 5th Regiment. He sold that commission in 1800, and later he received 5,000 acres of land on the north shore of Lake Erie — in Simcoe's intended heartland of empire. This was the first of many grants Talbot acquired for settling pioneers.[16]

To Elizabeth, Talbot reported on how York had grown since she had last seen the muddy little capital. Castle Frank was empty and it had been vandalized when he had last seen the wooden Greek temple. Francis, for whom the castle had been named, was now twelve years of age, and ready for Eton. He left home in September for the old brick structure almost in the shadow of Windsor Castle, and seemed to adjust rapidly to the new situation. Mrs. Graves told Eliza that his liking "Eaton does him a great deal of credit". Francis was luckier than his father had been. John Foster, the headmaster in Simcoe's day had been despised, but when Francis entered Eton the headmaster was the popular Joseph Goodall, who could manage boys without frequent recourse to flogging.[17]

Few of Elizabeth's letters and diaries for this part of her life have been preserved, but later ones show that her friendship with Mary Anne Burges was as strong as ever. She was still busy as chatelaine of Wolford Lodge and in overseeing the upbringing of the younger children. And, as 1803 was ending, she was pregnant, at age forty-one, with her eleventh (and last) child. Much of the detail, outside the official record on General Simcoe, is found in Mrs. Graves' replies to Eliza's letters. Eliza was attending as many balls as ever, but Mrs. Graves warned her not to spend too much time writing and drawing. Stooping was bad for the lungs. Miss Hunt, Mrs. Graves reported, had had to leave Princess Charlotte's household because poor health had made her incapable of continuing as a tutor.[18] No doubt she had found the warring atmosphere an impossible strain.

There had been further troubles in Ireland, encouraged by the French. On 16 April Henry Addington resigned amidst furor over an Irish Militia Bill. The King accepted the resignation on the twenty-ninth, to General Simcoe's dismay, and Pitt was asked to lead a new government. Pitt formed his cabinet on 10 May, six days before Bonaparte was proclaimed Emperor Napoleon I by the French senate and tribunate. Over the next few months, Simcoe's mood was bleak for he had no hope of an appointment from Pitt. Elizabeth survived by being detached and enjoying her friends and children. She loved sharing the secret of the authorship of *The Progress of the Pilgrim Good Intent* with Mary Anne Burges, who, amidst wild speculation, was still too modest to admit she herself wrote it. On 31 July 1804, a daughter was born at Wolford Lodge, whom the Simcoes named Ann or Anne — Elizabeth spelled the name as often without the "e" as with it.[19]

Meanwhile, twelve-year-old Julia Somervile had acquired an admirer in her cousin Francis Bond Head, a year her junior, who wrote her doggerel. The precocious lad appeared already a little infatuated with his future bride.[20]

In October, Mrs. Graves was pleased with Eliza's good account of "little smiling, prating Catherine", and she asked Eliza to "kiss little Henry for me who was so good in church".[21] For once she did not comment on the war news, which was bad. The fault lay with Pitt's policy of never committing enough troops against the armies of Napoleon, and the poor quality of the training the British troops received, although the Duke of York had instituted reforms in 1795. Very much aware of the situation, Simcoe frequently stormed his discontent to Elizabeth, who tried to be patient. She had almost had enough of her husband's ambitions, which had brought him so little satisfaction. The authorities gave him impossible appointments, and then blamed him for not being able to carry them through.

On 2 December, in Paris, Napoleon had himself crowned emperor by Pope Pius VII. Ten days later Spain declared war on Britain, instigated by France. The outlook seemed bleak as 1804 ended. Simcoe conducted what John Bailey called "sham fights" as part of his training programme for the militia and regular troops:

> There was one very grand one; there were four thousand soldiers present, and, I should think, ten thousand lookers-on. The battle began at Fenny Bridges; the Militia and Regulars were the French, and the Volunteers, Yeomanry Cavalry and Volunteer Artillery, with their cannon were to be the English. So the French retreated to Hembury Fort,

owned by Admiral Graves, and on the lawns there was a very sharp attack. There was great fear the soldiers would get in earnest, so orders were given for the Regulars to retreat to Hembury Fort Hill ... where the battle ended, and the English gained a complete victory.[22]

The year 1804 brought an honour for Henry Addington: he was created Viscount Sidmouth as of January 1805. Simcoe's hopes for an appointment were raised when Pitt accepted Sidmouth into his cabinet. At home, Eliza went on a visit to Bath, and returned with a severe cold. Elizabeth blamed her daughter's illness on cold rooms at Bath, but Mrs. Graves maintained that cold rooms at Wolford Lodge were the cause. Miss Hunt, Mrs. Graves reported, had caught cold while attending a philosophical lecture in a room that was always like "Lapland". She was now tutoring a small boy, to prepare him to enter a Latin school.[23]

That month, Sidmouth left the cabinet, to Simcoe's dismay, because his own prospects again grew dim. His old complaints began to bother him, mainly because he had too much time to brood. Elizabeth wished he would consider retiring. He was now fifty-two, not truly old, but old for campaigning. She longed for him to be content with running the estates and travelling, visiting their many friends. She wanted to go to Oundle and to Whitchurch, but they stayed home waiting for orders from London.

Soon afterwards, Mrs. Burges and Julia moved to Ashfield, a house somewhat smaller than Tracey, which stood to the west of it. Wearied of paying rent, she purchased Ashfield, a property described on the Devon Land Tax Assessment Records, 1803, as "Joice Land and Slipper Close". (Ashfield is still there, but it has been enlarged and renamed Awliscombe House.)[24]

A letter dated 24 September from Mrs. Graves hinted of trouble for Harriet, now eighteen. Aunt Margaret was relieved to learn that "poor Harriet was not ruined", though she was convinced that Eliza had not told her the full story. Harriet's near "ruin" was financial. She had made some bad investments with money she possessed. All the daughters were encouraged to manage a sum of money, to educate them for the day when each would inherit a considerable sum. Mrs. Graves was pleased that General Simcoe had not been injured while riding with General Samuel Taylor Popham when the latter's carriage "broke".[25]

On 21 October Admiral Horatio Nelson was mortally wounded while defeating the combined French and Spanish fleet on the Atlantic off Cape Trafalgar. When the news arrived, Simcoe ordered an artillery salute fired, which his neighbours interpreted as the start of an invasion. As soon as they could make the arrangements, the Simcoes staged a celebration at Wolford Park, with fireworks and a great banquet to which all the gentry of South Devon were invited. The house was lit by 500 lamps, and the guests dined at a table sixty feet long. Meanwhile, Nelson's body was on the way home, preserved in a coffin filled with spirits. The funeral would take place in

January, and Simcoe left home just after New Years to be in the procession, his privilege as a lieutenant-general in the army. Elizabeth went for a short holiday to a cottage they had bought at Budleigh Salterton, near the mouth of the Otter River, about twenty-three miles from Wolford Lodge.

From London on 10 January, Simcoe wrote Elizabeth describing "Nelson's triumph" of the previous day at St. Paul's Cathedral. To his chagrin he had been "ranked as a squire because I came too late to town to go with the Commander-in-Chief" (then the Duke of York). At St. Paul's, "I deserted the low company I was in & got between two Highland Centinels." He found the ceremony impressive, but from a distance it seemed "too theatrical". He had seen Admiral Berkeley, the Duke of Kent, Lord Sidmouth, and Colonel William Spencer, who had agreed to assist with the "determinism about Francis". Spencer would help Francis, then fourteen, receive a commission in the army. Simcoe had decided not to have his elder son enter the navy.[26]

On 23 January, when Simcoe had returned home, Pitt died. The King called on Lord William Wyndham Grenville (a younger brother of the Marquis of Buckingham), to form a coalition from three factions that had opposed Pitt's government. What came to be known as the Ministry of all the Talents was formed on 10 February 1806. Lord Sidmouth became the Lord Privy Seal, and soon General Simcoe was being mooted as the man to replace Charles, 1st Marquis Cornwallis, as the governor general of India. (Cornwallis, the commander who had surrendered his army at Yorktown, Virginia, in 1781, had died in India on 5 October 1805.)[27]

Mary Anne Burges and the Simcoes were hosts to the Swiss geologist, Jean André De Luc in 1806. He stayed for a while at Ashfield, and Simcoe offered him the use of the seaside house at Budleigh Salterton. When De Luc published his three-volume *Geological Travels* in 1810 and 1811, he made several references to General Simcoe in the third volume.[28]

Britain declared war on Prussia on 1 April 1806, after that country had seized Hanover. Mrs. Graves informed Eliza that German plays were vulgar, because the language sounded so unattractive.[29] The young Simcoes were now excited as they anticipated seeing India, and Elizabeth's mood was buoyant, as it had been at the prospect of going back to Quebec. The viceregal residence in Calcutta was much more commodious than the Château St. Louis. They would be able to take the family, although Francis would have to remain at Eton. A journey to London would be necessary, to buy the many items they could not obtain elsewhere.

The news of Simcoe's appointment plunged Mary Anne Burges into a slough of despond. Again she would be denied the company of her dearest friend, and at a time when her health was deteriorating. She had long assumed that if she died, Elizabeth would take charge of Julia. Then a request from Lord Grenville and the Duke of York altered everyone's plans. They asked Simcoe to undertake a mission to Portugal, with Lieutenant-General Sir James St. Clair Erskine, the 2nd Earl of Rosslyn, to report on whether Britain should support that country by sending troops. Napoleon was threatening to invade Portugal. To Elizabeth's horror, Simcoe accepted the assignment. She had been contemplating the tour in India with pleasure, but she had a premonition that Portugal held dangerous portents for the general. Her Welsh clairvoyance had taken hold of her. Simcoe sailed from Plymouth with General Rosslyn in early August 1806, aboard the *Illustrious,* Admiral of the Fleet John Jervis Earl of St. Vincent in command of the ship and escort vessels.

Simcoe took Eliza, who was unwell, with him as far as Ubgrooke, near Chudleigh. Elizabeth thought a change of air would benefit her, and Lady Clifford had kindly invited her for a recuperative visit. To Miss Hunt, who was now working for a family near Warwick, Eliza described her mother's distress over the mission to Portugal, "to have a husband torn from her and sent on an expedition is hard". Her mother was ready to sink under the anxiety she experienced for her family when she most required consolation and support. The family felt that he was fit to go to India, but not to undertake the trip to Portugal. Eliza was the first person her father told when he thought he would be sent to India, and she had been flattered that he had confided in her.[30]

When the *Illustrious* entered the Tagus River in late August, Simcoe was too ill to go ashore. A physician who came aboard suggested he be sent straight home. Despite her premonitions, Elizabeth had taken Charlotte, and Eliza, now recovered and home from Ugbrooke, with her to London to complete the shopping for India. The *Illustrious* anchored in Tor Bay on 20 October, and Simcoe was taken to Exeter in a small boat and lodged at the home of Archdeacon George Moore. (This house was destroyed by bombs during World War Two.) A message was dispatched express to London, and Elizabeth and her daughters travelled by fast hired chaise to Exeter. They arrived just before John Graves Simcoe died on 26 April 1906 at the archdeacon's house, his wife and elder daughters by his bedside. According to John Bailey, the Simcoes' faithful servant, the *Illustrious* had been newly commissioned. The toxic smell of fresh paint so poisoned the general that even after he was taken ashore he did not recover.[31]

Mary Anne Burges arrived to comfort Elizabeth as the sorrowing family prepared to escort the coffin to Wolford Lodge. Simcoe's would be the second burial in the little cemetery outside his chapel, with its motto "as for me and my house, we will serve the Lord". His widow and children would take those words much to heart as the years passed, and devote most of their time to serving the Lord in practical as well as aesthetic ways. Elizabeth's immediate concern was the funeral arrangements, for, as Simcoe intended, they would require as much attention as a military operation.

The family remained in Exeter from Sunday 26 October until dawn on Tuesday 4 November, the day of the funeral. A commemoration worthy of so important a military man took time to organise. Many friends and colleagues had to be notified and some lived a distance away. Because an election was being held, to avoid intimidating the voters, no soldiers were in Exeter. The escort had to meet the cortège outside the city. Francis joined his mother and sisters from Eton, and Charlotte informed Miss Hunt that Miss Burges had probably injured her already indifferent health by coming to her mother's side.[32]

An account of the funeral appeared in the Exeter *Flying Post* on Thursday 6 November 1806:

> On Tuesday the remains of the late much lamented General Simcoe were removed from his appartments, at the rev. Archdeacon Hoore's, in this city, to his family seat at Wolford Lodge, for interment. The funeral was most respectably attended; three mourning coaches followed the hearse, in which were the chief mourners, the confidential friends of the late general, and his servants. After them came the general's carriage, attended by two servants in deep mourning on horseback. In succession we noticed the following gentlemen in carriages; Generals Thewles and Thomas, with the staff, lords Clifford and Graves, sir Stafford Northcote, sir Wm. Pole, sir John Kennaway, the High-sheriff, admiral Richard Graves, Mr. Baring, Mr. Morshead, colonel Chester, colonel Coleridge, major Dickinson, Mr Dalrymple, &c. All the troops having quitted this city on account of the election, the Exeter regiment of volunteers assembled at the three-mile stone on the Honiton road, to pay a compliment to the deceased general. From thence his remains were escorted by a squadron of dragoons, the volunteers assembling at various passes to line the road, whilst the procession passed on. At Honiton the troops were all drawn out, and minute guns fired. In short, every respect which could be paid to an esteemed and much-lamented commander was shown on this occasion. The body was interred by torch light, about six in the evening.[33]

John Bailey mentioned specific military units and their relationship to the general. The East Devon Yeomanry Cavalry were stationed at a battery on St. Cyres Hill, near Wolford, a regiment Simcoe had raised personally. Other cavalry was the Dunkeswell troop, of Simcoe's tenants. The militia was proceeded by a detachment of the 3rd Dragoon Guards, one of them leading Simcoe's horse, boots reversed in the stirrups, his arms on the saddle. When the procession reached Wolford Chapel, thousands were there:

> The church field was crowded. The Luppitt Company of Artillery [volunteers from the village of Luppitt raised by Simcoe] was there with the guns, which were fired when the body was put in the grave, which shook the very house of Wolford.[34]

Elizabeth had little time to be in seclusion. Before the end of November Eliza had a relapse, and her mother escorted her back to Upbrooke, where she had made such a good recovery in September, cared for solicitously by Lady Clifford.[35] Mrs. Graves, who did not attempt to attend the funeral, told Eliza that time was the best healer. She sent her best wishes to "Mother and her dear children" especially six-year-old Henry, who was too young to understand what he had lost.[36]

Chapter 20

FRANCIS AND MARY ANNE

1812~1813

A period of adjustment was inevitable once Simcoe's enormous presence no longer dominated Wolford Lodge. As Charlotte informed Miss Hunt, since the loss of Father, time was hanging heavy on her hands.[1] Yet Elizabeth could not afford to mourn long. She had the estate to run, and under Simcoe's will she was his sole Executrix. (The trustees were Simcoe's friends, William Walcot, John Pollexfen Bastard and Edward Welles.) Now Elizabeth rode with John Scadding in the early morning to inspect her property and to make decisions based on his recommendations. Scadding was newly married, to Melicent Triggs, and looking forward to the birth of their first child. Elizabeth owned property in Dunkeswell described as Mansells, Tenery and Cropfields, Little Southey, Southey plot, part of Daws, and Great Southey, and part of Sheldon Grange. She also owned a small plot of land in Awliscombe, known as Cleaves and Moors.[2] These were freehold properties, and she leased land from time to time. She was in touch with the Audit Office and with Whitehall; both wanted confirmation that Simcoe's accounts for public expenses in Upper Canada, San Domingo, Portugal, and for the2 2nd Regiment, of which Simcoe was the colonel,were in order.

Although Elizabeth missed the comings and goings associated with the military command, she found much to occupy her — the future of two sons, the company of seven daughters, and friends to visit and to entertain. She did not need as many servants and workers on the property, and she soon reduced the staff from fifty to seventeen. Letters in the decade after Simcoe's death are skimpy. Possibly Elizabeth was not in the mood to record her experiences, or diaries have been lost. She maintained her lively interest in Upper Canada, and in the successful defence of the province during the War of 1812. Material preserved in the 1830s shows that she studied reports on the rebellions, and she had been no less concerned over the news of the earlier time.

In January 1807, Britain began a blockade of France and her allies that aroused strong emotions in the United States, and might well endanger the Canadas. Another interest that grew stronger as time passed was her church. Whenever depression overcame her, or her daughters, they turned to the church for distraction. In March, Eliza asked Miss Hunt to pray for her.[3] On the thirty-first the Ministry of all the Talents fell because Lord Grenville refused to grant Catholic emancipation. Elizabeth was in agreement. She counted Catholics among her friends, but she was against their having any political power.[4] William Bentinck, 3rd Duke of Portland, who had been home secretary while Simcoe was in Upper Canada, succeeded Grenville as prime minister.

On 26 April 1807, Mrs. Graves wrote her last letter to Eliza from Bath.[5] She was failing by that time, and in July Eliza and Elizabeth were both in Bath, taking care of her. Eliza was distressed that her mother would be staying only a few days. Nursing Mrs. Graves by herself would be a heavy responsibility. Francis had spent a week of his holidays with them, dull for a sixteen-year-old, and Eliza felt sorry for him.[6]

Eventually Elizabeth heard that the Mohawk war chief, Joseph Brant had died at his home near Burlington Bay on 24 November 1807. In the meantime, the war in Europe continued. On 19 November, French troops invaded Portugal, as Lord Grenville suspected when he sent Simcoe to Lisbon. Towards the end of December the United States renewed its embargo against Britain and France, which Elizabeth thought boded ill for Upper Canada. A declaration of war might mean the annexation of Simcoe's empire by the United States.

Before 1807 ended, Francis Simcoe was commissioned an ensign in the 27th (Inniskilling) Regiment of Foot. His father's old colleague, Francis Rawdon-Hastings 2nd Earl of Moira, a full general in the army and the honorary colonel of the 27th, had used his influence. Elizabeth had to purchase the commission, which cost £400. While Simcoe was still alive, Francis had agreed to enter the army, rather than the navy. From Eton, he had written his mother on 28 June 1805 that he had no objection to going "in the Line, especially as Lord Moira has been so good as to offer me his assistance."[7] William Walcot wanted Francis to study law, but he would not abandon his plan for a military career.

On 9 January 1808, Elizabeth wrote to Lord Moira, thanking him for introducing Ensign Simcoe to the commander of the 27th, Lieutenant-Colonel Samuel Graham. At first, Francis was stationed in London, but by March he was on his way to Dublin before joining his battalion at Enniskillen (The Army List gives Inniskilling as the spelling but Francis used the usual form). He had travelled by way of Oundle and Holyhead, and had visited Mr. Walcot for a few days. That gentleman had given him £100 towards his expenses. Before he left Dublin he met Sir Edward Littlehales, Simcoe's onetime military secretary and now a baronet. Francis was alarmed that he was spending more money than he anticipated.[8] That did not deter him from wanting a promotion, even though it would again be by purchase. A lieutenant's commission cost £550. Elizabeth would have to supply an additional £150, for they would realise the other £400 from the sale of the ensign's commission.

In May, Eliza accompanied Elizabeth to Stowe. In London afterwards, Eliza informed Miss Hunt that the Marquis of Buckingham had taken her mother under his wing, and she seemed much better. Mrs. Graves was "tolerably well again". Eliza was looking forward to "darling Henry's" holidays. Then eight years old, Henry was attending Mr. Coplestone's school in Honiton.[9]

On 24 May, Francis wrote his mother that he longed to be in a grenadier company, and he was tall enough. "I measure 6 foot and a quarter in my boots. I think you will find me much altered when we meet again." He had attained a good height, for he would not turn seventeen until 6 June. When he wrote again, from a training camp near Kells, he had succeeded. They had been on a short march, and his feet were blistered, but "being in the grenadiers forbids talk of such trifles". His new status was costly, for he had to buy a second epaulette, a sabre, and a "handsome cap". Mary Anne Burges had worried that her letters to Canada might fall into enemy hands. Francis felt no such restraint, and he often told his mother details an enemy would find helpful. From camp he wrote that his battalion would soon embark from Cork for Spain or Portugal.[10]

By August the first detachments of a British expedition were on the way to Portugal, which reminded Elizabeth of her husband's last mission and its consequences. What she may not have foreseen was the omen war in the Peninsula held for her eager young Francis, larger than life in his red regimentals, two epaulettes and tall grenadier's cap and longing for a promotion. He embarked on 14 September, and arrived at Falmouth by the twenty-ninth. On 9 October the fleet sailed for Bilbao, arriving four days later, after a miserable voyage to an enthusiastic reception. Each Spanish soldier wore a red cockade and ribbon with the inscription VIVA FERNANDO VII. On the twenty-fourth they anchored in Corunna harbour. "I hope soon to amuse Miss Burges with some Spanish stories in the Spanish language."[11] Meanwhile, Lord Moira wrote Elizabeth on 26 November that a lieutenancy in the 27th Foot was for sale, and he had taken it upon himself to secure it for Ensign Simcoe. If Elizabeth approved, she should write to John Ridge, Esq., of 44 Charing Cross.[12] She did so, and Francis' commission as a lieutenant in the 27th Foot was dated 22 December 1808.

By that time Mrs. Graves' health had failed. She died in Bath during the last quarter of the year. Her will was probated in April 1809 at the Court of Canterbury, and William Walcot of Oundle was her sole executor. She left explicit instructions for her funeral — no pall or covered coffin, no hearse but her coffin was to be carried:

> by six poor men to the churchyard and there buried with-
> out entering the church which properly is a place of prayer
> for the living and not a receptacle for the dead and I think
> it profanation to introduce a putrid carcase into a place
> dedicated to the worship of the most high God. I desire that
> four guineas may be given to . . . each Bearer and my own
> three men may if they please be three of the Bearers.

Her estate was smaller than at the time of her marriage because some of her wealth had gone to Richard Graves through the admiral's will. To Elizabeth she left her two best pictures. After other bequests in furniture and personal effects, the house on Lansdown Crescent was to be sold and the money from it and other residue was to be divided amongst the five eldest

Simcoe girls — Eliza, Charlotte, Harriet, Caroline and Sophia. Each young woman inherited the sum of £1,000 from her great aunt's estate.[13] When he received the news in Spain, Francis replied:

> sorry to hear of poor Mrs. Graves' death although I believe it is a just relief to herself and my sisters. I am going to send Eliza a very account of my life since I left Middleton [barracks at Enniskillen] collected from my journal.

Jewellry was cheap, and he would send some.[14]

In 1809 the United States' Embargo Act expired, which relieved Elizabeth's mind over the threat to Upper Canada. But she was soon endeavouring to comfort Mary Anne Burges, whose sister, Frances Head, had died.[15] James Roper Head was abroad, everyone thought, to evade creditors.

Late in March, Major-General Arthur Wellesley left England for Lisbon to take command of the British army in Portugal. Wellesley pushed the French up the Tagus River and into Spain, winning the Battle of Talavera on 28 July, for which he would be created Duke of Wellington. During Wellington's campaign, Francis was safe in Lisbon, to Elizabeth's relief. By October, Francis was encamped outside Badajoz, which had been unsuccessfully besieged before his battalion arrived. The glorious battle of Talevera "will ever hold an high name in the annals of history," wrote Francis, adding,

> If you think Julia would like the ring I will find some-thing that shall please you just as well but my reason for not mentioning at first was that it was not so well set as it might be and I thought young Ladies were very particular about the setting.

Julia did not receive the the the ring, since Elizabeth thought it handsome and kept it.[16] In several letters the boy mentioned not having received any mail from home for some time, and he feared many of his family's letters were on ships that had been sunk.

On the 28 October, Charlotte, who was visiting Killerton, the home of Sir Thomas Acland, wrote Miss Hunt that the family had heard from Francis. They had read of the many skirmishes near Badajoz, and Mother and sisters were thankful that thus far Francis had survived the "dreadful carnage".[17]

By December, Eliza was at Stowe with the Buckinghams. She received a sad letter from Julia Somerville that the Chancellor of Exeter Cathedral, Nutcombe Nutcombe, a close friend of the family, had died.[18] Sixteen-year-old Julia had been assisting the failing Mary Anne Burges with her correspondence. The talk about the war was now centring on the seesaw operations in Spain and Portugal, and the gossip was about Napoleon's divorce from his Empress Josephine. On 11 December, Francis wrote that he had not received any letters for some time. He had dined with Lord Wellington (news of the dukedom had not reached Spain). Wellington was pleasant and agreeable, and kept a fine table.[19]

The possibility of war with the United States appeared to recede when in May 1810 that country reopened limited commerce with Britain and France. At home, a reform bill brought by the Whigs before the house was defeated, to the joy of conservatives like Elizabeth Simcoe. It called for a triennial parliament and a wider franchise. Like the late Elizabeth Gwillim, Elizabeth felt that allowing all sorts of irresponsible people to vote, whether male or female, was dangerous. While Napoleon annexed Holland, and the Mexicans revolted against Spanish rule, Elizabeth waited for news from Spain and Canada. Francis was in Lisbon in July, with a fever and swelling of his legs and thighs, receiving medical attention. He returned to duty in September and was encamped on a range of hills five or six leagues outside Lisbon.

As 1811 opened, the condition of George III caused concern. On 5 February Parliament passed a Regency Act empowering the Prince of Wales to act in his stead. That same month, the United States renewed a Non-Intercourse Act against British commerce, which brought more worries that Upper Canada might be attacked. By March Eliza was in London at the Buckinghams' town house. She no longer went driving and visiting on Sundays because she was influenced by the evangelical movement within the Church of England that advocated strict observance of the Sabbath.[20]

In Spain the second siege of Badajoz had begun. In the skirmishing, Captain John Pring, from Honiton, was wounded. Francis' brigade lost 500 men, and 49 were wounded. He himself had been hit on the back by a splinter but he was unhurt as its force had been spent. In a letter dated 22 May, he wrote out the army's line of battle — a grave breach of security.[21]

As reports of the successes of the Duke of Wellington poured in, work began on a memorial of John Graves Simcoe for the south choir aisle in Exeter Cathedral, paid for through a subscription among his friends. The sculptor was John Flaxman, and the design comprised a bust of Simcoe in the centre with what purported to be a Queen's Ranger on the left (with the wrong cap) and an Indian warrior (scantily clothed) on the right. The inscription would read: "To the memory of John Graves Simcoe, Lieutenant-General in the Army and Colonel of the 22nd Regiment of Foot". Since it lacked any reference to his time in North America, many who viewed it must have pondered the inclusion of the near-naked "savage".

At that time Mary Anne Burges' health was continuing to fail. In July, Miss Harriet Bowdler of Exeter, now a close friend of Eliza's, wrote from Rhyddings, Swansea, that she was worried about Mrs. Burges. Eliza went to stay at Ashfield to help Julia care for her, and Elizabeth was alarmed that she might lose her dearest friend.[22]

Letters from Canada warned Elizabeth of American frontiersmen demanding that Congress and President James Madison declare war on Britain because of interference with United States' maritime rights. The situation was all too familiar to her. Major-General Isaac Brock, the administrator in Upper Canada and commander of forces, was calling for more troops and being ignored. Brock, another lively, inventive officer, was enduring the same frustrations that had so impeded Simcoe's efforts to protect the infant province from predatory Americans.

By early 1812, more letters informed Elizabeth of President Madison's recommendation that Congress prepare the United States for hostilities. Undoubtedly Upper Canada would be the first objective. Meanwhile, letters from Francis were still edged with bravado. He wrote to Caroline from the encampment two leagues from Badajoz, describing the actions that had taken place. His regiment had performed magnificently.[23] He was again hoping for a promotion. He had been a subaltern for four years, but field promotions were not being handed out. His only hope for a captaincy was through purchase at a cost of £950, or an additional £400 after his lieutenant's commission was sold. He told Charlotte he might be a grey-haired old man before obtaining a captaincy, although his lieutenant-colonel, John Maclean, had spoken highly of him. He was out of luck. A clerk from Horse Guards informed Elizabeth's agent, Mr. Flood, that too many subalterns in the 27th had seniority over Francis, and he would have to wait his turn.[24]

Amidst worries for Francis' safety, Elizabeth was saddened to hear that Mary Elizabeth the Marchioness of Buckingham, had died on 16 March.[25] Then late April brought disastrous news from Badajoz about Francis. He survived until almost the end, for the siege was lifted on 6 April 1812. Shortly before the city surrendered, Francis was killed in action. The Reverend George Jenkins, chaplain to the forces 4th Division, Badajoz, wrote to Elizabeth on 9 April:

> I am aware yr. anxiety must be gr. respecting the fate of my most esteemed friend your Son — sincerely lamented by all who knew him, he fell on the night of the 6th in the midst of several others his Brother Officers & hundreds of his fellow Countrymen, while storming th town of Badajoz — to state the details of this circumstance would be needless ... I was so fortunate as to find him lying in the breach ... I performed those last offices over him, & got him as decently interred as the confusion of our most melancholy situation wd. admit.[26]

Elizabeth would not have the comfort of receiving his body for burial outside Wolford Chapel near his father. When word reached Wolford Lodge, the family was plunged into despair. That the third siege of Badajoz succeeded was cold comfort. Elizabeth resolved that Henry should not enter the army when he was old enough. Equally worthy would be devotion to the church. Henry would be schooled to become a clergyman and serve the Lord. In that way he would fulfil his father's purpose for the family. To General Simcoe's monument in Exeter Cathedral, an inscription on the death of Francis at Badajoz was added.

For a while the war clouds beyond the Atlantic seemed scarcely to matter. Almost unnoticed were reports that the United States militia was preparing to attack Canada. Also almost unnoticed was word that Prime Minister Spencer Perceval had been assassinated on 11 May, shot by a demented man in the lobby of the House of Commons. Eliza summed up the atmosphere at Wolford Lodge in a letter to Miss Hunt on 29 May. It was the longest she had been able to write since word of Francis' death had arrived, and she did not know how she would ever banish the "melancholy sensation". Her mother's spirits were very low, and yet she did not withdraw into her immediate family. Miss Hunt had offered to come for a visit, bringing her sister Caroline, and Eliza assured her that Mama would be happy to see them. Eliza herself would find their visit a great comfort.[27]

Happily, Mary Anne Burges was in better health, and Jean André De Luc came for another visit. Eliza informed Miss Hunt in August that Caroline and Sophia were staying with Miss Burges at Ashfield, and they were expecting Mr. Walcot at Wolford Lodge. Sir James Bland Burges was to marry for the third time on 27 May, a widow, Lady Margaret Fordyce. (His second wife had died in 1810.) In closing, she enquired "What Milner's church History can Emily Powys mean?" Emily was a daughter of Lord Lilford, Simcoe's friend, who had purchased Aldwinkle, Northamptonshire.[28]

On the Continent, Wellington's armies were doing well, and everyone had hopes he would soon defeat Napoleon. If he were successful, Elizabeth decided, Francis' sacrifice had not been in vain. General Simcoe's life would have been shortened for far less, if Upper Canada, the empire of his dreams, were swallowed by the aggressive republic south of it. In the summer she learned that the United States had declared war on Britain. The news added to Elizabeth's dismay, until the report of Major-General Brock's capture of Detroit arrived in the autumn. Brock had shown the dash of a John Graves Simcoe. With scarcely 300 regulars, 1,000 militia (disguised in red coats) and Indian allies, Brock had made prisoners of 2,400 Americans.

By January 1813, Wellington had entered France, and there seemed hope that the long struggle with Napoleon would end. About the same time Elizabeth learned of Brock's success at Queenston Heights, on the exact spot where she had camped during hot spells at Newark. Brock had been killed, but with a force of scarcely 1,000 regulars, militia and Indians, his second-in-command, Major-General Roger Sheaffe, had vanquished an American force nearly three times that strength, and taken 925 prisoners. Capturing Upper Canada would not be a mere matter of marching as former President Thomas Jefferson had predicted; the United States was not going to take Simcoe's infant empire without a fight.

Elizabeth was bereft when she received word that the Marquis of Buckingham had died on 11 February 1813.[29] Another link to Simcoe was gone. On 3 March, she wrote to Eliza of her concern that Catholics might soon be enfranchised. She was surprised that "serious persons should approve of voting for the Roman Catholics", who were "never distinguished for liberality". Catholics, she maintained, did not know the meaning of the word.[30]

The next news from Canada suggested that the Americans were doing much better. In April they captured York and burned many of the public buildings before withdrawing. The hero of the invasion had been the new Anglican clergyman in York, John Strachan, who had stood up to the American general, Henry Dearborn. Strachan stormed into his headquarters and demanded the right to succour the British and Canadian wounded in his church (named St. James' in the 1820s). By the summer the news was even worse. The Americans had captured Fort George at Newark, and the British had abandoned the entire Niagara frontier. Elizabeth was too worried to take much notice and spending most of her time at Ashfield.

On 6 August, Charlotte wrote Miss Hunt that Miss Burges was sinking slowly and the end would not be long in coming. Miss Frances Anne Elliott, who now lived in Egland House, Honiton, had moved into Ashfield to help twenty-one-year old Julia keep house. Charlotte hoped that "Mamma" would let her return to Ashfield, because she was the strongest. All the others were in low spirits. On Tuesday the tenth at 4.00 p.m. Mrs. Burges died in the arms of a broken-hearted Julia. Sir James was expected from Beauport, his country seat in Sussex, on Friday.[31]

On the twentieth Charlotte told Miss Hunt that Julia, Miss Burges' executrix, was as well as could be expected. Fanny Head, the daughter of Mary Anne's deceased sister, Frances, had arrived shortly before her aunt died. (James Roper Head had returned from the Continent and was living in Southampton.) Sir James Bland Burges had stayed with Miss Elliott at Egland, and had behaved handsomely towards Julia. Lady Margaret, Sir James' new wife, had invited the bereft young woman to come to Beauport but she did not want to leave yet and would stay for the present with Miss Elliott. Fanny Head's situation was "lamentable", Charlotte reported. The dictatorial James Roper Head had only reluctantly given her permission to come to Devon, and the poor girl did not want to return to him at Southampton. With Eliza and Julia, Charlotte had spent Saturday at Egland comforting Fanny. Charlotte had never seen her mother so depressed, and she wondered how the family could ever help her recover her spirits. Never had any of her daughters known her to feel a loss so deeply.[32]

The war in Europe was going well, but Upper Canada seemed in great danger as 1814 began. The United States had recaptured Detroit and had won naval supremacy on Lake Erie. The outcome might have been different had Dorchester allowed Simcoe to build his naval station, Elizabeth lamented. In March some of the allied troops entered Paris, and on 11 April the Treaty of Fontainebleau was signed. Napoleon abdicated and was banished to the Isle of Elba. On 3 May, the rightful king, Louis XVIII, reached Paris after seven years in exile in England. To Elizabeth's satisfaction, Britain now prepared to pour into the Canadas sufficient troops to prevent an American takeover.

That spring of 1814, Elizabeth and her daughters all went visiting, in pairs or singly. All returned to Wolford Lodge in July, for a great celebration of peace that was worthy of Simcoe's own entertainments. Charlotte informed Miss Hunt, who was living in the Cathedral Close in Exeter, of a fête at Dunster, while a "Thanksgiving Day" was held at Wolford with arches of flowers. School children sat on the grass, and John Scadding, who had helped Elizabeth with the arrangements, carried a flag with "Peace, thank God" on it. A band played "God Save the King" and "Rule Britannia", and Scadding led the singing.[33]

During the summer Francis Bond Head, now a lieutenant in the Royal Engineers and serving on the Continent, became engaged to Julia Somerville. About the same time his father, James Roper Head, died, which was something of a relief to the Head family and their friends.[34]

By September, Eliza was at Stowe and having a pleasant visit with the Marquis of Buckingham's daughter, Lady Mary, who was three years younger and the wife of the Honourable James Everard Arundell, heir to Lord Arundell of Wardour. Charlotte was at Monmouth, and Eliza told her she was angry with Richard Lord Buckingham, the late marquis' heir, for insisting that she drink too much champagne. Otherwise Eliza, now thirty, was happily renewing her acquaintance with "old haunts". At that time Elizabeth was at Hinckley, and she would be joined by Harriet and Mrs. John Fownes Luttrell of Dunster Castle, Somerset. She was the former Mary Drewe, sister of the late Reverend Edward Drewe (who died in 1810) who had been appointed chaplain of the Upper Canada garrison in the 1790s. With Harriet and Mrs. Luttrell, Elizabeth would go to Clapham. Caroline and Sophia were already there, sharing a rented room which they had made look like the chambers of the young men at Cambridge. Elizabeth planned to be at Wolford Lodge over Christmas.[35] Eliza would accompany Lady Mary to Wardour Castle, and join the family at Wolford Lodge for Christmas, where Mr. Walcot was also expected. From home on 2 December, Elizabeth wrote to Harriet, who was with friends in Bath, replying to a query. The mouth of the St. Lawrence River did not freeze though ice floated down from the Great Lakes. Ships usually left Quebec by 10 October, and the *Triton*, which did not leave Quebec until 13 November 1791, had been the exception.[36]

The Christmas celebration in 1814 was not quite as lavish as in Simcoe's day, but there were entertainments, especially to please the youngest children. Henry was now nearly fifteen and at Eton; Katherine was thirteen; Ann was ten. Before Elizabeth set out visiting again in the new year, she learned that the Treaty of Ghent, signed on 24 December, ended the war with the United States. Upper Canada had been saved. She had scarcely time to rejoice before word reached her that Napoleon had escaped from Elba and landed in France on 1 March. Again she wondered whether Francis had been sacrificed in vain. She was relieved that, should Henry be overcome by patriotism, he could do little because he was was too young for a commission. In March she again left Wolford to visit friends. Eliza remained there in order to be hostess to Miss Harriet Bowdler, who was coming to visit at several houses in the neighbourhood.[37]

Napoleon's "Hundred Days" had begun, and Britain and her allies formed two armies, one of Prussians and Saxons, the other, of Britons, Dutch and Germans under the Duke of Wellington. The contest was decided at Waterloo, Belgium, on 18 June 1815. The allies agreed to banish Napoleon to the more remote South Atlantic Island of St. Helena, where he arrived on 17 August. By that time Eliza was planning a grand tour, in common with many English people who had not been able to travel on the Continent for two decades.

Her travelling companions would be friends of her fathers', Mr. and Mrs. John Pollexfen Bastard, whose family seat was Kitley, about ten miles southeast of Plymouth. Bastard had been a Member of Parliament for Devon since 1784. The Bastards were childless, and the heir to Kitley was their nephew, Edward Rodney Pollexfen, elder son of John's brother Edward. The Edward Bastard family home was at Buckland in the Moor, on the River Dart. The Simcoes had often visited both homes.

Eliza went shopping in London in September, in preparation for the tour, but she forgot to buy a small Spanish dictionary. She asked Miss Hunt to purchase one in Exeter, because her large dictionary was not practical for touring. Mrs. Hunt, she wrote, was probably right in complaining that her Catholic friends were influencing her. Yet Eliza thought her opinions had been more influenced by the Protestant books she had read, as were Caroline's, which were similar.[38]

For their mother, the pain and sorrows of the Napoleonic Wars were no easier to bear, but she was becoming reconciled to the era that saw the deaths of husband, eldest son and dearest friend. Many of the Simcoe papers are still in good condition. But Francis' letters are among the most faded, as though they had been read and reread as Elizabeth and his sisters sought to feel him near them.

PART IV

HEAD OF THE FAMILY
1813-1850

Chapter 21
FRESH INTERESTS

The letters in the Devon Archives do not indicate that any of the Simcoes other than Eliza ever went travelling on the Continent, although they travelled extensively in England and Wales. Elizabeth continued her pursuit of the picturesque to sketch and paint, and she may have taken to heart what Mary Anne Burges had written while she was in Canada, that having seen the ultimate, she would find the Continent dull by comparison.[1]

Eliza was to sail from Plymouth on the *Camel*, and accompanied by Charlotte and Harriet, she went in the carriage to Kitley, the Bastard family seat.[2] The Bastards and Eliza sailed on 26 October for Boulogne. From that port of entry they went to Paris, Lyons on the Rhône and Marseilles, and to Leghorn, Italy. Eliza wrote Caroline to expect her journal from Florence, but they never got there. Mr.Bastard died suddenly at Leghorn on 4 April 1816, perhaps suffering from tuberculosis. She wrote Charlotte: "We have lost one of the few remaining who are really interested in us. Losing our own friends is a loss, but losing Father's is far worse."

They would be returning, with the embalmed body, through Genoa, Geneva and Paris.[3] Elizabeth was shocked when she received Eliza's letter from Leghorn, and deeply sorry that her daughter found herself in such a situation so far from home.[4]

Back in England, the public was rejoicing in May because on the second, Princess Charlotte of Wales married Leopold of Saxe-Cobourg. The match was a popular one for Charlotte was warm-hearted and loved by the populace. A second wedding of interest to the Simcoes was that of Julia Somerville to her cousin Francis Bond Head on 20 May. Elizabeth felt saddened, recalling that Julia might have been a suitable bride for their own Francis. Frank Head was now a 1st lieutenant in the Royal Engineers, stationed at Valenciennes, France, where the couple took up housekeeping. Elizabeth rather liked Frank, who was short and wiry, with a gift of both the spoken and written word. Hyperactive, he reminded her of a small mammal, constantly in motion and constantly searching for food. Frank, too, could not sit still, and was always nibbling.

No letter indicates when Eliza finally reached home. During the summer she spent considerable time at Kitley, to help Mrs. Bastard adjust to being without her husband, and to cope with the many sympathisers who came to stay for a few hours or days. By the autumn Eliza was again at Wolford Lodge, and Elizabeth, accompanied by Harriet, had gone to Clapham, where a group of Evangelical Anglicans had formed.[5]

Elizabeth was becoming more caught up in the Evangelical Movement within her church, which she saw as an answer to the Wesleyans, who were making inroads among the common people in the West Country. The establishment ought to be reformed, not overthrown. Her patriotism now led her to work towards improving the Church of England to make it worthy of its role as the established one, relevant to everyone. She had been denied a father and had lost a son through patriotism to the nation, and her husband had died prematurely from the same cause. Now her entire family would serve the nation by serving the Lord.

In Elizabeth's opinion, much work needed to be done before the affairs of her church were in good order. There were not enough church buildings so that all people could attend. More parishes were needed, and each should have a resident clergyman. The church required more clergymen, and these should be better educated. There should be a national system of education. The notion popular with the gentry that the poor should be kept ignorant was dangerous, one that could lead to anarchy. The Sabbath should be strictly kept, and no clergyman should go hunting on the Lord's day. Ideally each parish should have a philanthropic squire who would support the clergyman both morally and financially, hand out charity, provide facilities for a social life, and ensure that well maintained cottages were available for employees on the estate. Elizabeth became the model squire, and she called on her daughters to assume responsibility for parish work. To Eliza she assigned Dunkeswell Abbey, Caroline to Luppitt, and when she was older Anne cared for Dunkeswell.[6]

The faithful John Bailey, who had entered the Simcoes' service in 1802, at age twelve, left in 1808 to go to sea. Tiring of seafaring in 1816, he returned to Elizabeth's service, as a footman. (After twenty years he became her coachman.) He told how indefatigable Elizabeth and her family, sick or well, were in setting a good example:

> I have known when the snow has been up level with the hedges and no horse or carriage able to go, the ladies and servants all set off, the men in front one after another to tread down the snow, then the ladies and maid-servants in our tracks. We had no cause to think that the deepness of the snow would prevent Mr. Clarke from coming to church, as I never remember him, not once, for the cause of bad weather to miss coming.[7]

John Clarke, later named one of Elizabeth's executors, was the rector of Dunkeswell and for many years her good friend.

199

Writing to Eliza, who was at Oundle early in 1817, Elizabeth hinted that she was finding twelve-year-old Anne less than agreeable. Anne had been willing to accompany her to Sidmouth for an excursion but Elizabeth preferred to go alone. She hoped that Eliza would visit Mrs. Bastard on her return from Oundle because her spirits were low, and then go on to Killerton; Elizabeth always considered her letters from the Acland household to be so interesting. "If you call at Escott, thank Sir John [Kennaway] for giving me the force of truth". It was delightful. Eliza and her sisters also paid visits to Mr. Thomas Walcot, another distant cousin, whose address in April 1817 was Elton Hall, Oundle, although it was closer to Peterborough. Elton Hall was a seat of the Proby family. Apparently Thomas Walcot was leasing the house.[8]

Britain now had a new policy for Upper Canada that pleased Elizabeth. Settlement was to be encouraged as a way of accommodating the many disbanded and unemployed troops from the Duke of Wellington's army. Since, to everyone's astonishment, Upper Canada had not been captured by the Americans in 1812-1814, the government wanted to fill the empty land with British settlers, to counteract the influence of the many Americans who had taken up land there. Simcoe's dream of a new empire in the heartland of North America might yet become a reality. Elizabeth thought that the policy did not go far enough. Emigrants were expected to pay their own passage, which put the scheme beyond the reach of the truly poor.

Among those who left Devon in 1817 was John Scadding, who came to Wolford to tender his resignation. He wanted to develop his 200 acres at York so that his sons could become men of property. In Devon they would have to go into service. He was going alone, and would send for Mrs. Scadding and his three boys when he had a decent place for them to live. Elizabeth wished him every success. If he wanted to send any of his sons home to school, she would contribute to the cost, because Upper Canada needed men of education.

In May, Julia Somerville Head gave birth to her first son, Frank Somerville, at Cambrai, France. Soon afterwards the Prince of Wales announced that his daughter, Princess Charlotte, would be having a baby about November. Miss Hunt's former charge, living at Marlborough House, was happy for the first time in her short life.[9]

Eliza spent most of the summer of 1817 at Oundle with Mr. Walcot, enjoying the the company of Miss Emily Powys and other friends in the neighbourhood, and visiting Walcot's country estate at Titchmarsh, close by. One of Elizabeth's letters showed that Eliza was still overly shy and sensitive. Elizabeth was afraid to state her opinion because Eliza took everything personally. She had not meant to accuse Eliza of doing wrong, and she apologised to her eldest daughter. "I should always write and speak with deliberation". Around Wolford, she reported, a collection was being taken to build a cathedral for the Kishnagan mission in Calcutta, India. The movement to reform the Church of England also encompassed foreign missions to spread the gospel abroad.[10]

The entire country was soon plunged in to mourning with the death on 5 November of Princess Charlotte, after she gave birth to a stillborn son. Miss Hunt was particularly crushed, as she had always found the Princess amiable, though she never felt kindly towards either parent.

Henry Simcoe finished at Eton in 1818 and matriculated at Wadham College, Oxford, probably in September.[11] By December Sophia was with Mr. Walcot at Oundle. (Eliza claimed that Sophia was his favourite Simcoe sister.) As 1819 began, Charlotte was at Oundle. To Miss Hunt, on 18 February, she reported that Walcot was suffering from lumbago and was not able to take exercise, which was so necessary for good health.[12] Meanwhile, the loss of Princess Charlotte had sent the Prince of Wales' brothers scrambling to contract suitable marriages and produce heirs to the throne. Most of the Royal dukes had been prolific through their mistresses, but they had failed to sire legitimate children. The Simcoes' old friend, Prince Edward Duke of Kent, bade Mme. St. Laurent farewell, and married a German princess. On 24 May 1819, their daughter and future Queen, Alexandrina Victoria, was born.

Elizabeth's efforts on behalf of church reform were redoubled when news of the Peterloo massacre, in Manchester, reached her. On 16 August, when a large crowd had assembled to hear reform speakers, some militia who had been called out to keep order charged the crowd with resulting loss of lives. She believed that more had to be done to bring the word of God to everyone, to end the social unrest that was too widespread.

On 8 December 1819, Charlotte was sympathising with Miss Hunt because their dear friend Miss Harriet Bowdler was seriously ill. Miss Bowdler was lucky to have Miss Hunt to care for her. "Mamma" and Harriet Simcoe had enjoyed a visit to Oundle, and had spent a night at Titchmarsh, Walcot's country estate. Charlotte rejoiced in Miss Hunt's news that Mr. James Duke Coleridge, was now ordained, and she wanted to see copies of his sermons. (As a child Coleridge had often spent Christmas at Wolford Lodge, and had been one of Francis Simcoe's attendants at the masquerade in 1801.) Charlotte asked Miss Hunt to send her some religious tracts; Harriet would write her which ones when she reached home.[13]

In January 1820 Simcoe's friend from Quebec days, the Duke of Kent, brought his Duchess and the tiny Princess Victoria to Sidmouth for a holiday. There the Duke died of pneumonia on the twenty-third, an event that saddened the Simcoe family. Just six days later, on the twenty-ninth, King George III, whom people had long been considered insane, died, and the Prince of Wales succeeded him as George IV. The new King had a bill introduced in Parliament to deprive his wife Caroline of titles and dissolve her marriage, after having accused her of infidelity. For the Simcoe ladies, this surely was the pot calling the kettle black, and they wondered what Aunt Margaret Graves would have had to say had she been alive. When the bill against Caroline was dropped in November, Elizabeth felt only indifference. She admired neither King nor Queen. George IV, like Elizabeth, had been born in 1762. Otherwise they had nothing in common in lifestyle or beliefs. Now in her fifty-eighth year, she was extremely fit, and riding daily on a favourite black pony. His Majesty, who had led a debauched life, was grossly overweight, and an old man who would not reign long.

That autumn she was detecting signs of sentiment in twenty-year-old Henry, still at Oxford. He had a lovesick mien while on holidays. The object of his regard was Anne, a daughter of the Reverend Charles Palmer of Moseley, Warwickshire and Stogumber, Somerset. The Palmer family were friends of Harriet's.[14] The Palmers paid a visit to Wolford Lodge in early November, after which Elizabeth went to explore Biddulph, in North Staffordshire. Eliza went on a sketching holiday to Tor Abbey, near Torquay, with Lord and Lady Clifford's daughter, Lucy.[15]

In the spring of 1821, Mrs. Scadding and her sons left Devon to join John at York. Elizabeth sent a servant to help them pack and close their house, and Mrs. Scadding came to pay her last respects before they left by wagon to join a ship at Plymouth. When Elizabeth told her guest that she would like to help educate the three Scadding sons, the other demurred, but to Elizabeth this was not charity. She wanted to help Upper Canada, where men of learning, especially men in holy orders, were too few. Assistance to the Scadding boys, she believed, would be a service to God.

Elizabeth was gratified to learn that Napoleon died at St. Helena on 5 May. Now England, looking forward to the coronation of George IV in July, need not fear another escape from exile. On Coronation Day, the tenth, the King and Caroline left their separate abodes, but Caroline arrived to find Westminster Abbey locked against her, and she retreated in a rage. She died in August, ending an era rich in gossip that she had had many lovers.

By October, Elizabeth wanted a seaside holiday. Sidmouth was not acceptable because recent storms had devastated the beach there. She had had a large party at Wolford Lodge, and with much influenza about she needed a change of air. She rented a house at Seaton, on the coast near the mouth of the River Axe below Axminster, from a Miss Parker. It had three bedrooms, five beds, and a servant's room. Located on a path leading to the beach, Elizabeth thought it was "ridiculously ornamented" with trellises. Eliza, Charlotte and Sophia were at Oundle with Mr. Walcot. In the party that left Wolford Lodge by carriage for Seaton were Katherine and Miss Luttrell, one of four daughters of John Fownes and Mary Drewe Luttrell of Dunster Castle. Caroline had been left at home, in bed with a cold. On 25 October Katherine wrote Eliza that Henry, still at Oxford, had had a letter from Miss Anne Palmer, which, had put him in good spirits.[16] The year ended satisfactorily for Elizabeth, when Henry received his Bachelor of Arts degree on 17 December, at age twenty-one.

In 1822 Sir James Bland Burges brought out an edition of his sister's work *The Progress of the Pilgrim Good Intent* with Mary Anne's name on it. Again the book was well received, with many comments on the learnedness of Mrs. Burges. Elizabeth enjoyed basking in her late friend's reflected glory, yet aware that if Mary Anne had lived she would have gone into seclusion, too embarrassed to face her admirers.[17]

Now that Henry had completed his studies at Oxford, nothing needed to delay a marriage with Anne Palmer. Elizabeth was well able to see that he had a good income until he could qualify for an appointment as a curate. The meagre salary would barely keep a family, but for Henry that did not matter. In time he would be his mother's principal heir, with generous legacies to his sisters. The marriage ceremony took place on 8 February 1822 at Moseley, performed by the Reverend Charles Palmer, father of the bride. Their first home was the Simcoes' seaside house at Budleigh Salterton.[18] Elizabeth hired a local clergyman to tutor Henry, and he pursued his study of theology. After tutoring, apprenticeship under a rector of a church would follow, with opportunities to preach, for experience, until he qualified for ordination as a deacon by the Bishop of Exeter.

Henry was the only one of Elizabeth's children to marry during her lifetime. This led John Ross Robertson to conclude that she refused to allow any of her daughters to marry. One daughter was believed to have been in love with Sir Thomas Acland whom Elizabeth discouraged, and one story suggests that Anne tried to elope with one of the footmen. There may be some truth in this, but again there may have been many other reasons why none of the daughters married. As head of the family Elizabeth controlled all funds, and was in a position to cut off any daughter who disobeyed her. At the same time, Charlotte, Sophia and Anne had their father's temperament, and had they been determined, Elizabeth would hardly have been able to stop them. Of all the daughters, Eliza and Caroline seemed to have the best business sense, and these two may have been more help than the others with the finances of the large estates. Under her will, Elizabeth bequeathed to Eliza and Caroline, all her real estate, whether freehold or leasehold. (This did not include Wolford Lodge and lands, or property at Hemyock.)[19]

The Simcoe women's extensive circle of unmarried friends implies a shortage of eligible men. Although the Napoleonic Wars were not as costly for men who served in the ranks, brightly dressed officers were excellent targets, and the enemy took a high toll of them. As Francis Simcoe had been shot down at Badajoz, so died many of the officers that upper class women would otherwise have married. Furthermore, if a woman had money in her own right, she had reason not to marry, to avoid surrendering it, as the law required, to a husband's control. The Simcoe girls had all heard their late Great Aunt Margaret Graves deplore that injustice. Childbirth, the greatest hazard to women, was another reason for remaining single, to avoid the risk. All seven daughters led active lives, caring for friends, sketching and painting, designing stained glass windows in a workshop at Wolford Lodge, and learning stone carving to decorate the interiors of churches.

The daughters had been schooled to be serious-minded, dedicated women, sincerely interested in the Church of England and in furthering good works. They resembled not only their mother in her preoccupation with parish work, but their father, who had planned an established church in Upper Canada. After Simcoe's death, Elizabeth or one of the daughters, and occasionally Henry, conducted family prayers. All agreed that Henry needed the practice, since he had a slight hesitation in his speech. To these prayers Elizabeth added one for a safe arrival before setting out on any of her journeys, and repeated the 121st Psalm.[20] Called the traveller's psalm in the King James version of the Bible, it ends, "The lord shall preserve thy going out and thy coming in."

(John Ross Robertson also assumed, because Elizabeth's daughters did not sit down in her presence until she gave them permission, that they stood in awe of their mother. Rising when an older person entered a room, and remaining standing until invited to sit, was at the time, merely a matter of correct manners.)

Meanwhile, Henry was turning out to be a model son, trying to satisfy his mother, studying hard with his tutor. In June 1822, Henry informed Elizabeth that his wife, Anne, would be presenting her with her first grandchild early in the new year. A son was born, and baptised at Moseley on 31 January 1823.[21] They named him Henry Walcot Simcoe, mindful of the wealthy bachelor cousin in Oundle on whom Elizabeth's seven daughters lavished attention.

Chapter 22
THE NEW GENERATION
1824~1826

Early in 1824 John Scadding wrote Elizabeth describing how York had grown. Some 1,000 people now lived on the town plot, and a row of farms stretched along Yonge Street all the way to Lake Simcoe. A stagecoach ran regularly from Kingston to Montreal, and occasionally one went to Burlington Bay and Newark. Steamboats operated above the Galops Rapids in the St. Lawrence and on Lake Ontario. The Duke of Wellington, now in Lord Liverpool's cabinet, advocated a canal along the Ottawa and Rideau Rivers to bypass the St. Lawrence route, which was vulnerable to attack from the United States. William Dummer Powell was now the chief justice, and Thomas Talbot was opening up vast acreages on the north side of Lake Erie, in Simcoe's heartland. Elizabeth's onetime genial riding companion had become dictatorial with the settlers, and complaints flowed to the government offices in York.[1]

Disturbing to John Scadding, and to the Tory government, was the arrival at York of the radical Scotsman William Lyon Mackenzie. He had started the newspaper *Colonial Advocate,* and was pressing for a democratic republic with a constitution on the American pattern. So, Elizabeth thought, there were radicals in Upper Canada similar to misguided liberals demanding reforms in Britain. Simcoe would be most unhappy by this turn of events since he had tried to plant only the purest forms of the British constitution. Much more satisfactory was Scadding's report on the progress of the Anglican Church. Reverend George Okill Stuart, a son of the Kingston rector, had been rector of York until 1812. Then Mr. Stuart succeeded his father at Kingston and was replaced at York by Reverend John Strachan. Occasionally Elizabeth sent donations for improvements to St. George's church in Kingston, and to St. James' Church at York, at first a wooden building completed in 1807.

In the summer of 1824, Henry and Anne Simcoe were expecting their second child. The baby was a girl, whom they named Anne Eliza. She was baptised at Wolford on 7 September.[2]

Louis XVIII of France died in September and was succeeded by his brother as Charles X. The following month, on 25 October 1824, Sir James Bland Burges died at Beaufort, cutting a precious tie with the past. At that time Eliza was at Oundle with Mr. Walcot, and Elizabeth had recently returned from a rented house in Seaton. At Wolford Lodge she found Harriet in charge of five men who were tearing up lead and pulling off timber because a pipe to the stove they had bought in Canada had become so hot that it set fire to a partition. The danger was soon past, but the house had narrowly escaped serious damage. If the fire had moved one foot more, it could have ignited a beam and might have caused the roof to collapse. Elizabeth blamed the servants, who were not used to stoves and had put too much fuel in theirs. She advised Eliza not to travel alone when she wanted to leave Oundle, lest bad weather detain her anywhere.[3]

In October Elizabeth visited London. She was charmed by Westminster Abbey, and at the British Museum she saw a drawing of the Hudson River by Major John André (who had served under Simcoe in his first Queen's Rangers and been hanged as a spy for his part in the defection of Benedict Arnold). She thought André's drawing "a counterpart of my own". She had never seen the Hudson, but had copied someone else's drawing. She met a Monsieur Mallandet, who had invented a piano forte that never went out of tune. He had high hopes for it, and the Duke of Gloucester was a patron. Elizabeth thought it sounded like a combination of harp and harmonica. With a friend she visited Newport, and hoped to cross to Calais — the only time she mentioned contemplating going to the Continent — but "contrary winds" prevented them.[4]

Katherine was on a visit to Cornwall, and she wrote from Launceston, describing the woods and rocks, which pleased her mother enormously. Fanny Head, Elizabeth wrote Katherine, was in Edinburgh, visiting Julia and Frank Head, who had been posted there when the army of occupation in Europe was reduced. Elizabeth had been to the Grange, where John Rose Drewe, an older half-brother of the late Reverend Edward Drewe, was now the owner. The electric machine arrived; it worked well, and Anne had learned to use it quickly.[5] What Elizabeth meant was an induction coil or Leyden jar, or perhaps something Jean De Luc had devised. Electricity was still a novelty, since as yet it had no practical applications. The Simcoes had acquired it because they found it intriguing, and were interested in anything new. After Christmas, Elizabeth spent a few days with Henry and family at Budleigh Salterton. On Christmas Day there had been considerable confusion when a group of singers arrived at Wolford Lodge to brighten the celebration. Just as they were starting, Cook fell and dislocated her shoulder. The arm was not broken, but Elizabeth felt annoyed over the inconvenience. She decided to dismiss her since, she reasoned, Cook would not have fallen had she not been drinking. Elizabeth had hired a new footman of noble mien who looked "ridiculously" like General Sir Ralph Darling. (Could this have been the man who turned Anne's head?)[6]

Towards the end of the year sad news arrived from Upper Canada. John Scadding had been killed when a tree he was felling landed on him. Mrs. Scadding resolved to remain on the farm since John Junior, now seventeen, was old enough to take over, with some help from his younger brothers, Charles, fifteen, and eleven-year-old Henry.[7]

Francis Bond Head was promoted to captain in the 5th Regiment of Foot; his commission was dated 23 March 1825. He was something of a hero in Edinburgh, following a fire in November 1823, when many buildings around Parliament Square were badly damaged. Lieutenant Head of the Royal Engineers had been in charge of demolishing the ruins before they could collapse upon the tenements close to them. This won him praise from the Duke of Wellington, now commander-in-chief of the army, and led to a promotion. Head had been offered a position by the Rio Plata Mining Association, and he was about to go on half-pay in order to supervise mines in South America. Julia and their family of four young children, Frank Junior, Henry, George and Julia, would reside in Buenos Aires while Frank was in the field.

In March, learning that Mr. Walcot was unwell, Elizabeth and Charlotte went to stay with him at Oundle. At the same time Eliza was visiting Arundells at Wardour Castle. From Oundle, Elizabeth went with some friends to see a paper mill, which she thought a dirty, disagreeable place. The machinery fascinated the others, but she could not escape fast enough from the noise. She had been sketching and had found some picturesque scenery at Titchmarsh. As was customary at this stage in her life, her letter became a sermon. Special grace was nothing more than a general grace, for God was not partial.[8]

By May, Elizabeth was appealing to Eliza to intervene with Charlotte, who was teasing Mr. Walcot by contradicting him, especially over what he wanted to eat. With friends and two carriages Elizabeth had taken him for a drive, which he enjoyed the more because Charlotte had not been along to "hammer" him. In closing she told Eliza that she was helping Walcot make decisions over his will, but he was extremely depressed, and fearful that he might never see Eliza again. Of course he would, she replied. Eliza was an excellent traveller, and would come whenever he asked her.

Walcot remained gloomy. "If Lord Clifford should die, Lady Clifford would claim her completely."

"Oh, no," Elizabeth said quickly. "If Eliza went to live with Lady Clifford she would soon become a Catholic."[9]

That summer of 1825, Elizabeth made her first known visit to Cheltenham to take the waters at the spa that was becoming more fashionable than Bath. With her were Caroline, Anne, Miss Mary Graves of Woodbine Hill, and the Reverend and Mrs. Clarke. Eliza remained at Wolford Lodge with Henry's son, two-year-old Henry. Twenty-one-year-old Anne had been taking lessons in the riding house, and was to jump on a spirited horse soon. After some discourse on religion, Elizabeth, now sixty-three, admitted to feeling her age:

> I take the waters but do not walk as others do; but I take
> some turns in my own parlour with the window open, I
> should be exhausted if I walked half as much as the people
> do & Miss Graves walks twice as much as the other people,
> she is much better —[10]

In July Francis Head applied for his half-pay, and with Julia and the four children set sail for Buenos Aires. On 3 September Julia wrote to Charlotte and Sophia, who were at Oundle, describing her new life. Frank had ridden off to visit the miners, one of many rides that would earn him the nickname "Galloping Head". He had thoroughly enjoyed his expeditions. Meanwhile, Julia was settling herself and the four children in a small country house they had rented from a Spanish family. Near the house peons earned a living herding cattle. She thought the English in Buenos Aires were drinking far too much brandy because it was so cheap. All the Heads were well and happy. [11]

In November, Henry Simcoe became a Master of Arts, as was customary after having been graduated from Oxford for three years. At that time one of his sisters was in London, and Eliza was again at Wardour Castle with the Arundells. [12] Elizabeth was at Wolford until after the Christmas and Twelfth Night celebrations, and Eliza went from Wardour Castle to Oundle to spend the season with Mr. Walcot, now seventy-three and in failing health.

In January 1826 the weather was bitterly cold, but despite the freezing temperatures Elizabeth was having a coffee ice every day. The sun was so dazzlingly bright and reminded her of a winter day in Quebec City that she was transported back to Canada. In such cold she was concerned that her evergreens might be harmed. She was pleased to hear from Eliza, that Mr. Walcot seemed some better. [13]

She was surprised to receive a letter from Julia Head, at Cathedral Yard, Exeter. Frank had gone on to Chile, and he did not want to leave Julia and the children in Buenos Aires because of the threat of war with Brazil. Julia hoped to rent a small house near Honiton and put the three boys in school. Elizabeth sent her an invitation to Wolford Lodge, but Julia wanted to stay at first with Frank's sister Fanny at Ashfield, her home while Mrs Burges was alive. Elizabeth wrote Eliza, enquiring whether she could recall the name of Aunt Elizabeth Gwillim's youngest sister, who had died of smallpox at Aldwinkle, aged seventeen years, after riding from Herefordshire. Her name was not "in the Pedigree which I wonder at". [14] (This was Anne Jemima, 1736-1757, who was actually twenty-one, not seventeen, at the time of her death.)

Elizabeth was also coping with a defaulting creditor, a draft for £160 from one Bromage that had been returned marked "won't be paid" in red ink. She had received another draft for £100 on Ross Bank payable in London, which she trusted would be made good.

Pondering how best to accept illness, she wondered how much longer Mr. Walcot would survive. [15] She was sending Frank Head's new book *Rough Notes from the Pampas* that had just been published in London, which she thought would entertain Mr. Walcot. [16] By April 1826, Eliza had returned home and Elizabeth was at Oundle, seeing for herself how Mr. Walcot fared, and she had brought Caroline, Sophia and Anne with her. Mr. Walcot's legs had been so swollen of late and a great deal of "flegm" troubled him. "Would Eliza please relay to Henry how much [she was] enjoying the preaching of the evangelical divine, Mr. Legh Richmond?" [17]

Elizabeth and Eliza again changed places, with mother returning to Wolford and daughter to Oundle. Fanny and Julia Head and three of the latter's children had called to report that Frank had turned up unexpectedly at Ashfield after landing at Plymouth. He had departed at once for London in quest of a settlement from the Rio Plata Mining Association for unpaid wages and expenses. The government in Buenos Aires, Elizabeth explained in a letter to Eliza on 20 April, had deceived the company in England; the minerals could not be extracted without great expense. Fanny complained about the briefness of his visit. All he could talk about was a lasso, and he insisted on showing her how to toss it round a cow's neck. Elizabeth was not surprised. Frank never could think of more than one thing at a time.

Henry's little Anne Eliza now had seven teeth, Elizabeth's letter continued. She was pleased to hear that Sophia had joined Eliza at Oundle. Elizabeth had caught one Levi Richards, and some other Dunkeswell men building a house on the Turbury, less than a mile from Wolford Lodge, on her manor, without her permission. She agreed to let Richards build some distance farther away, but she did not want a dishonest man living so close to her fences. A tenant, Mary Hill, was ill with gallstones, and Elizabeth was giving her red onions to cure them.[18] A new storeroom had been finished at Wolford Lodge, but the smell of iron and oil "kept me a prisoner in my Room". Elizabeth sent Eliza £30, of which £10 were already owed for her expenses, and the rest so that she would not run short.[19] A few days later when Eliza suggested coming home because Mr. Walcot seemed better. Elizabeth, then at Henry's house in Budleigh Salterton, agreed to send her a £60 bill she happened to have on hand. Eliza was to keep £20 for her own use and leave the rest with Sophia. A former woman servant, Hodge, was looking for employment at Bath or Bristol. If Eliza stopped in either city, she might find a way to help her. Hodge's worthless husband, suspected of cutting down someone else's apple trees and of writing threatening letters, might soon be transported to a penal colony.[20]

Elizabeth referred to the escape, over a garden wall, of a Mr. Daly from the platform of a Bible meeting when a mob of "gentlemen" threatened to attack him. She thought this might help William Wilberforce's "cause" (and her own) since he could hardly vote in favour of emancipation when Catholics openly opposed the distribution of the Bible. She had heard that Wilberforce's motive in supporting the Catholics lay in his hope for a general emancipation "to detach people from their priests who have persuaded them that Protestants use them so ill". (Like Elizabeth, William Wilberforce was influenced by the Evangelical Movement within the Church of England. Although he had retired from Parliament in ill health in 1825, he was still promoting emancipation of all people to advance the cause of abolishing slavery.) Elizabeth admitted she was confused by so much controversy, and she did not understand what people were arguing about. She only knew that she was Protestant, and doing right by adhering to the "Articles of Religion". The greatest compliment she could pay was to wish someone dead — through with this life of toil and sickness.[21]

The Simcoes had received some 5,000 acres of land in Upper Canada, which had been deeded to Henry. When John McGill wrote that taxes were mounting up and the family was not receiving any revenue, Henry had sold some of the land. Elizabeth, on holiday at Seaton with Katherine in May 1826, wrote Eliza that she had been in touch with one of Dr. Macaulay's friends about appointing a reliable agent to collect what was still owing. She was worried about Anne, who was taking Iceland moss and bitters, and having difficulty walking, and if she did not hear soon that Anne was on the mend she would send Katherine to be with her at Wolford Lodge. Her favourite black pony had been ill with distemper, and she hoped it could be cured.[22]

Henry's wife Anne was expecting their third child in late June. A son was born at Budleigh Salterton on the twenty-sixth, and named John Kennaway Simcoe.[23] At the time Henry was nearly ready for his ordination as a deacon. He had an appointment, as a curate for the charge of Egloskerry and Tremaine, in Cornwall, ten miles east of Launceston, on condition of his being ordained. He had rented the manor of Penheale, half a mile north of Egloskerry village, where Anne and the children were settled, but he was keeping on the house at Budleigh Salterton. Eliza wrote a detailed description of Henry's ordination, at Exeter Cathedral, to her sisters at Wolford Lodge. Family members were not usually present, and Eliza attended only because Henry felt ill.

Brother and sister had been staying at the Budleigh Salterton house when Henry received a letter from the Bishop of Exeter, William Carey, ordering him to come to Exeter to be examined by Dr. John Bull, a canon residentiary. Henry had already met with Bishop Carey, who informed him that success would depend on Dr. Bull being satisfied. Henry developed a blinding headache from nerves, and Eliza felt that he was in no condition to go alone. They set out in a gig on Saturday 28 October 1826, and took rooms at the Old London Inn. At 8.00 a.m on Sunday morning the twenty-ninth, Eliza accompanied Henry to see Dr. Bull at the house of Chancellor James Carrington, the officer of the See of Exeter, where she kissed him and gave him her blessing. She went the home of her friend, Miss Frances Nutcombe, a daughter of the late Chancellor Nutcombe, in Cathedral Yard, to ask for breakfast. At ten o'clock she heard Henry's voice at the door and hurried from the parlour to hear how he had fared with Dr. Bull. To her joy, Henry had passed the examination.

Back at the inn she repaired his gown in time for the ceremony. Still in great pain, he asked her to stay with him. When they arrived at the cathedral at eleven o'clock they found Bull and twenty-three young men. Eliza was much embarrassed to be the only lady present. The actual service she found very affecting, seeing Henry in the long, solemn procession to the alter. She heard every word the bishop said, he sounded very sincere, and she was thrilled to see it all. When they returned to the inn she made Henry lie down until six o'clock, at which time he was expected for dinner at the bishop's palace. Then Eliza went to see Miss Hunt, where Henry called for her at nine and escorted her to the inn. Neither could sleep; the events of the day were too vivid. The next morning they drove the gig to Budleigh Salterton, and set out in a coach for Penheale, where Henry would take up his duties as curate.[24]

As the year 1826 ended, Britain agreed to send troops to Portugal in support of the Portuguese Queen Marie, if Spain attacked. For Elizabeth this was a sad reminder of the purpose of her husband's last journey abroad on a similar mission. On a happier note, Henry was well settled in Penheale, and his parishioners seemed to like him. His wife Anne was expecting their fourth child sometime in the summer. Elizabeth was pleased, but she hoped four grandchildren would suffice. She saw no need for Anne to wear herself out childbearing as so many women did. Elizabeth knew she had been luckier than most. To have reached age sixty-four, after having eleven children, and to be fairly free of complaints, was indeed remarkable. Placing herself in God's hands, she believed, accounted for her well-being.

Chapter 23

MORE JOY IN HEAVEN

1827~1837

The Simcoe letters show that the Simcoe women continued travelling and visiting friends. Eliza was often at Ugbrooke with the Cliffords, or with the Arundells at Wardour. Elizabeth wrote from such seats as the Northcotes' at Pynes, the Misses Elliotts' at Egland, or the Kennaways' at Escot. In 1827 all the ladies were preoccupied with William Walcot, who was failing quickly. Eliza spent most of the year at Oundle, with one or more of her sisters to help her, and Elizabeth was there several times. To Eliza at Oundle, Elizabeth wrote that she did not know where her great great grandmother, Mrs. Steward, had been buried. Her grave was most likely wherever she died. Since she had no money, and her daughter was raising six children on £600 a year, they could not afford to "send a corpse traveling about".[1]

Elizabeth's fourth grandchild, Mary Northcote Simcoe, was baptised at Penheale on 4 August 1827; Henry now had two boys and two girls.[2] Soon afterwards William Walcot died at Oundle. No documents refer to his passing or his funeral. Elizabeth and her eight offspring must have attended since Henry inherited the properties at Titchmarsh, and Elizabeth and her daughters the proceeds from the sale of other holdings. Eliza stayed at Oundle for some time, attending to the deceased's affairs and disposing of personal effects and any furnishings Henry did not want.

Elizabeth went to Escot in November to visit Sir John Kennaway and his family. In 1797 he had married Charlotte Amyatt, and they had seven sons and five daughters.[3] Sir John had gone riding alone and had fallen from his horse. He said nothing until after dinner, when he took some strong medicine. She told of a frightened cart horse that broke out of a gig and knocked a lady off her pony, which fell on her. The lady "behaved with coolness & propriety".[4]

The most important event of 1828 was the ordination of Henry Simcoe as a priest, although he remained a curate of Egloskerry and Tremaine and did not become the vicar until 1846. No letter describing this ordination, at Exeter Cathedral, has survived. (In 1846, Henry acquired the advowson to his two-point charge, probably through purchase. The advowson was the right to appoint a clergyman to a living, and was sometimes retained by one family for generations. By 1850, Henry was shown on The Clergy List as the Perpetual Curate of Egloskerry.)[5]

On 25 January 1828 the Duke of Wellington became the Prime Minister. His was a Tory ministry, and Elizabeth had every hope that he would suppress all talk of Catholic emancipation. She made her feelings clear in a letter to Eliza:

if Romanists had the upper hand, tythes would be abolished, which would appeal to many, and that Ionians should see nothing to alter in a Religion that invites multitudes of mediators..., is not surprising, for they do not believe in the atonement, but that independents and Methodists, if they are not too illiterate to know the doctrines of the Reformed Churches, can support them is very unlikely ... as Mr. Clarke told me, there were abundance of falsehoods, which he repeated. At a meeting in Exeter there was a most excellent letter printed by a dissenter against Catholic Emancipation.

She had a better opinion of an illiterate man than of Members of Parliament who supported enemies of their civil and religious government. She was helping equip a local school and taking a great interest in it, but she mentioned a radical preacher in the neighbourhood from whose school she thought children should be removed.[6]

Julia Head visited Wolford Lodge in February. Writing on the twelfth her husband Francis told a friend that she was in the west country "and is probably at this moment talking broad devonshire with Katherine Simcoe".[7] Other events of 1828 were the birth of Henry's fifth child, Elizabeth Lethbridge Simcoe, who was baptised on 28 September, and Francis Head's promotion to Major of the Royal Wagon Train.[8] Since he was on half-pay, he could not have performed some service to deserve the honour.

In 1829, Castle Frank burned down. By that time the Simcoes no longer owned any property in Canada, but the rustic Grecian temple of logs had many memories for Elizabeth, especially of young Francis. The average price paid for the land was two dollars an acre, not enough for a location so close to York. The agents who sold it had not acted in the Simcoes' best interests.[9] To Elizabeth's chagrin, the Catholic Relief Bill passed the House of Commons on 4 March, and she was furious with Wellington. Her only hope lay with the House of Lords, but that body passed the bill on 13 April and Catholics were granted full rights. The only offices they could not hold were Regent of the United Kingdom, the Lord Chancellor, and the Lord Lieutenant of Ireland. On a happier note, Lieutenant Governor Sir John Colborne opened Upper Canada College, the equivalent of a grammar school, at York. The first pupil enrolled was seventeen-year-old Henry, the youngest son of the late John Scadding.[10]

Henry Simcoe purchased Penheale in 1830, and set about enlarging it, and Elizabeth had to find a tenant for the house at Budleigh Salterton.[11] During Elizabeth's early visits to Penheale, she spent her days with her grandchildren, and John Bailey drove her five miles to an inn at Launceston for the night, as Henry had no rooms for guests. Sometimes Elizabeth brought her favourite black pony from Wolford Lodge, and she rode, with a grandchild in front, along the lanes and into nearby hills.[12]

She made contributions to the school in Dunkeswell, and some people from Hemyock applied to her to pay for their children, who were being taught by a woman named Collins. Elizabeth planned to inspect the Hemyock school and if satisfied, she would give Collins some patronage and books.[13] The residents of Hemyock had had a claim to her philanthropy since 1816, when the trustees of Simcoe's estate purchased the ruins of the old castle and considerable acreages around it. The largest properties were Castle Farm and Millhays, the first rated at £14. 18. 11 and the second at £9. 17. 9.[14]

Miss Harriet Bowdler, a friend of Eliza's as well as of Miss Hunt and Miss Nutcombe, contracted smallpox early in February 1830, in what Katherine Simcoe said was "the natural way", meaning she had not been inoculated, and the attack proved fatal.[15] In April, Elizabeth became a grandmother for the sixth time with the birth of Samuel Palmer Simcoe, who was baptised on the twelfth. To Eliza, who was at Ugbrooke, Elizabeth wrote, "Tell Lord Clifford I intend to have a bridge made in hopes he will pass over it towards the chase and pass by it to go to the garden". A friend had lent her *Oriental Customs or an Illustration of the Scriptures* by Bander which she found interesting. It was a compilation of well chosen passages for all travellers in the East.[16] On 26 June, George IV died, and his brother the Duke of Clarence succeeded him as William IV. In September the new King created Francis Bond Head a Knight of the Royal Guelphic Order, apparently for demonstrating the properties of the lasso.[17]

Elizabeth recounted a "beautiful anecdote" about Bernard Gilpin, who was on his way to London in 1558 to be burnt at the stake when he broke his leg. The delay in his journey saved his life; while he was still recovering Queen Mary died and he escaped the fire.[18] Gilpin (1517-1583), a church reformer nicknamed the "Apostle of the North", was Archdeacon of Durham when Bloody Mary succeeded Henry VIII in 1553.[19]

Another link with the past was broken when the Simcoes' dear friend Lord Clifford died on 29 April 1831. In the autumn Elizabeth went on a journey to Wales and kept a diary.[20] With Anne, Eliza and a Lady French, and John Bailey as the coachman, she left Wolford on Friday 7 October and reached Welshpool on the eighth. There they stayed over Sunday, and Elizabeth enjoyed an excellent sermon on the text "there's more joy in heaven over the sinner that repenteth". In the afternoon the service was in Welsh. On Monday they passed through Merioneth — flat country, not picturesque enough to tempt them to stop and sketch. Elizabeth bought a pair of socks of Welsh wool. By the eleventh the scenery had improved. They stayed near Snowdon, and on 12 October, Lady French and Anne went into Bangor. Eliza rode part of the way, but Elizabeth sat drawing.

On Thursday the thirteenth Elizabeth rose early and went by herself to find a picturesque view of Snowdon. As she sat on a rock, an immense black greyhound put his nose into her hand. Because the path was steep, and slippery from rain that had fallen during the night, she followed the dog home. It led her to a picturesque cottage on a rock where a Welsh woman said nothing, and set a table with milk and oatcakes, butter, hot crumpets and bread. Then a girl escorted her down the hill.

After breakfast, Eliza and Anne left with a guide to climb Snowdon. At two o'clock Elizabeth set out over the greatest rocky scenery she had ever beheld, and she thought her walk must be similar to ascending the Alps. The day turned windy and rainy, and she met Eliza and Anne, who had only gone half way to the top. The guide advised against proceeding, for the slippery ground made walking hazardous. (Attached to the diary is a note Elizabeth added, that a handsome inn was built near the spot in 1832.)

On Friday they drove to Carnarfon before breakfast. Elizabeth thought the castle ruins very grand. Before they left she bought a Welsh woollen petticoat and some Welsh shoes. They passed on to Beddgelert for the night. Elizabeth pretended that the hound she had met the day before was descended from the heroic Gelert of Welsh lore. John Bailey recalled how the village earned its title:

> [Beddgelert] gets its name from the story of Llewellyn, who came here during the hunting season with his child and his greyhound, Gelert. The child, left unprotected in a hut, was attacked by a wolfe. On Llewellyn's return he met Gelert wagging his tail, but covered with blood. Alarmed, and thinking that the dog had injured the child, the impetuous prince slew the hound. He entered the hut, to find the dead body of a wolfe lying near his sleeping child. In grief for his dog the prince erected a tomb and called the spot Beddgelert for Bedd, the grave, and Gelert, the dog.[21]

At Dolgellau on 17 October they admired a fine waterfall, and the following day they rode towards Bala, where the girls went climbing (Eliza was now forty-seven and Anne twenty-seven). The inn at Machynlleth, twelve miles from Dolgellau, was so vile they kept going. On the night of the nineteenth they slept at Newtown, at a dirty place. They went to Montgomery on the twentieth, and to Ludlow the next day where they walked about the historic castle. They were at Hereford by Saturday the twenty-second, the weather very cold. At St. Peters Church on Sunday, the preacher had a dismal voice.

On Monday they stopped at Old Court, the Gwillim family manor, and the twenty-fifth they rode from Whitchurch amidst scenery so glorious that all the ladies were busy with sketchbooks and pencils. They went on to Coleford, and from there took a steamer down the Severn River and up the Avon to Bath, where they arrived on the twenty-ninth and stayed at the Clifton Hotel. Meanwhile, John Bailey brought the carriage the long way round, crossing the Severn on a bridge and taking a ferry across the Avon above Bristol.

To Eliza, at Wardour Castle in May 1832, Elizabeth described a new gallery in the Dunkeswell parish church. The "simplicity" of the church was so "Protestantlike", and Mr. Clarke had no need to march backwards and forwards in going to and from the communion table, as he had been doing before the gallery was finished. He had preached a good sermon with less "perambulation".[22]

On 7 June, Elizabeth faced the defeat of her principles. Coerced by the King, the House of Lords passed the great Reform Bill. The Lords bent to His Majesty's will when he threatened to create enough Whig peers to outvote the Tory majority in the Upper House. News from Upper Canada depressed Elizabeth further because friends sent copies of the *Colonial Advocate*. The editor, William Lyon Mackenzie, had written vile gossip about the members of the legislative and executive councils, many of them the sons of loved friends. She heard regularly from the rector of St. James Church in York, Dr. John Strachan. Like Mackenzie he was a Scot, but of a different stripe.

In November, Fanny Head was visiting her Somerville relations who lived in Musselburgh. She wrote that cholera was rampant nearby in Edinburgh, but not where she was. "Cholera," Elizabeth told Eliza who was visiting Miss Nutcombe in Exeter, "has done more to change worldly thoughts of people than preachers could in years".[23] By that time, Henry Scadding had arrived in England to continue his education. Elizabeth was pleased that she would not have to contribute as much money as she anticipated, for Henry came as a King's scholar to Cambridge university. He would be at St. John's College, and he promised to visit Devonshire during his summer holidays. Elizabeth preferred Oxford, but Henry had done well to be accepted at Cambridge, since Upper Canada College was too new to have established a good reputation. At an unspecified date in 1832, Elizabeth's seventh grandchild, Lydia Hannah Simcoe, was born at Penheale; "Simcoe", as she often called Henry, could be careless about record-keeping.

Not much happened to the family in 1833. Elizabeth visited Cheltenham, and she was now bothered by rheumatism. To Eliza, again at Ugbrooke, she discoursed on the origin of gypsies and why they were tolerated, based on Ezekiel. A local girl who had got into a scrape with a worthless man was not to blame. Her mother had been selfish; the girl had many good offers, but because she was so useful at home her mother had put them off, and now "this inconsiderate step has happened."[24]

The year 1834 began on a buoyant note, for slavery was abolished throughout the British Empire, which would complete the phasing out John Graves Simcoe had begun in Upper Canada. Then on 5 February, the eighth grandchild, Philip Francis Simcoe, was born. In March, York was incorporated as the City of Toronto, news that infuriated Elizabeth, for a pack of republicans had rejected her husband's choice and restored the ugly Indian word. Suddenly she felt old; at seventy-three she had outlived the lifespan of three score and ten set down, in Psalm 90:10, in her Bible.

On 21 June, Lord Arundell died at Wardour Castle, and Eliza went there to comfort his widow, and from there to Penheale where Elizabeth joined her. Eliza went to Fowey with "Simcoe".[25] The old port had fond memories for the Simcoe women, of their friend Susan, a daughter of a naval surgeon,

Captain Thomas Mein. Susan had spent her childhood at Fowey, and at a boarding school in Bath. After the captain retired, the Mein family moved to their ancestral home, Eildon Hall, near Melrose, in the Scottish borders. By 1807, Susan had married Lieutenant-Colonel William Sibbald of the 15th Regiment. Two of Susan's sons, William and Charles, were in Upper Canada, employed on a farm near Orillia, acquiring the skills needed to work land of their own which they intended to purchase.[26]

Elizabeth described a missionary meeting at Bude, Cornwall, where a delegate sustained an injury while riding under an archway. His horse reared so that he struck the arch, which "took part of the top of his head off". Yet he attended the meeting, although he could not speak much.[27] The air of Penheale agreed with Elizabeth, and she was often riding on her black pony. She attended a confirmation ceremony where "Simcoe" preached a "beautiful exhortation" to the young people, and a christening he performed was not the "hasty business common to country churches". Henry was dignified and setting a good example to others. He had ridden home with some parishioners to ensure they did not stop at an ale house.[28] Henry had paid part of the cost of restoration on the church at Egloskerry, as well as enlarging his own manor house. Like his father he made wholesale alterations to the land, with planting and new roads. He had a printing press at Penheale, on which he ran off religious material, including *Epistle of the Apostle Paul to the Ephesians*, and he edited a magazine, *Light from the West*.[29]

From Penheale, Elizabeth went again to Wales, with Anne and Harriet. There she received a letter, forwarded from Wolford Lodge, from Dr. John Strachan in York (she refused to say Toronto). She wondered if the £50 Strachan suggested was enough to support his son at university in England and asked for more particulars. Strachan sent three sons to England in the 1830s to complete their education, and Elizabeth probably helped all of them.[30] As 1834 came to an end, Sir Francis Bond Head was appointed an Assistant Poor Law Commissioner for East Kent.[31]

In 1835, Elizabeth visited close to home, at Egland with the Elliotts, and at the Grange, which Edward Simcoe Drewe, son of the late Reverend Edward Drewe, had inherited from his father's elder half-brother, John Rose Drewe.[32] She went again to Penheale and enjoyed many outings there with her grandchildren. On a Wednesday holiday, she set out, the three smallest in a tiny cart pulled by a pony, the older boys "conducting" it. Anny rode behind Elizabeth, and they stopped at a plantation below Killy Crop. Near a brook they picnicked on Cornish pasties. Anny was a sweet child though she had "a lot of wind" and was not strong. Mary was a sensitive, agreeable girl. Elizabeth was a very pleasant child, and Lydia the dearest entertaining little thing. The baby (Philip Francis) resembled Lydia. Samuel was the least of the children in their grandmother's opinion. Henry's wife Anne was expecting her ninth child, who would be named Paul Creed Gwillim Simcoe, in September.[33]

Elizabeth took the same interest in the progress of Henry's children as she had her own. While she was at Penheale, Henry Scadding came to visit.

She hoped he was less indolent than he appeared to be, for doing poorly at Cambridge would not help his future prospects.[34] She was saddened on 24 November, when Lady Clifford died at Upbrooke at age sixty-nine. Fifty-one year old Eliza, of course was grief-stricken. Her friendship with the Cliffords continued, but she was not a close to the younger members as she had been to their mother.

Meanwhile, Sir Francis Bond Head was appointed the sixth lieutenant governor of Upper Canada, with orders from the colonial secretary, Lord Glenelg, to mediate between the warring Tories and Reformers. The choice bewildered many, but not Elizabeth. Sir Francis had the right ideas and would soon put stop to all the talk of reform in John Graves Simcoe's province! However, Head's administration of the poor laws had caused a riot in East Kent, and when the magistrates did not protect the poor law officers, he resorted to the army to quell the disturbance.[35] He was foreordained to make a bad situation in Upper Canada worse.

He sailed from Liverpool on 8 December 1835, accompanied by an aide-de-camp and a secretary, but not Julia or their children. Frank Junior was employed by the East India Company. Henry would soon be commissioned in the 15th Regiment then in Montreal. Once Sir Francis was settled, he would send for Julia and the two youngest, George and Julia.[36] In February 1836 Elizabeth heard that Sir Francis had reached Toronto.

In the summer, Susan Sibbald, whose husband had died, emigrated to Upper Canada with three of her sons.[37] On an earlier visit, she had purchased a property in Georgina Township on Lake Simcoe — with no church near it — a situation she intended to remedy with the Simcoes' help.

Late in December, Ensign Henry Bond Head sailed for Canada, and Julia followed on 7 January 1837. Elizabeth was relieved to hear that she had reached Toronto by late March, as she tried to picture how it must look after forty years. She might soon have a more vivid impression, for Fanny Head had invited her to Ashfield to meet a guest who had recently come from there.[38]

Chapter 24

SIR FRANCIS AND THE REBELS OF 1837

If Elizabeth wrote a letter after her visit to Ashfield to meet the guest from Toronto, it has not survived. In any event, she was more preoccupied with Henry Scadding's poor performance at Cambridge. He had passed his examinations but was nearly at the bottom of the list. He was going to Penheale, but he had promised to call at Wolford Lodge en route. To Katherine, Elizabeth admitted that she was distressed at Henry's low standing, and she had written "H.B." of Montreal about it.

She was astonished at the progress the Indians of the Western District in Upper Canada had made, as reported by the Reverend Richard Flood, their Anglican missionary. "We often forget," she wrote Katherine who was in Exeter, "is anything too hard for the Lord". Then she turned to events closer to home. Mr. Roberts, the Methodist preacher at the Honiton chapel, had found so many smart ladies attending that he dwelt on vanity and dress.[1]

Meanwhile, Sir Francis Bond Head, now a baronet, was making his everlasting mark in the capital of Upper Canada. He dissolved the assembly in April and called an election in which he personally campaigned for the Tory candidates. A vote for the established government was proof of a man's loyalty. With no secret ballot, and with each vote recorded in the poll clerk's book, a man's politics were public knowledge. As a result, the Tories won a substantial majority. The Reformers — disloyal republicans to Head — had held sway in the former house. To Mrs. Simcoe, following events eight weeks after they occurred, the election result was fortunate. Sir Francis was a great success.

While the Upper Canada elections were being held, Elizabeth was at Pynes visiting the Northcotes. On her return she wrote to Katherine, who was in Winchester. She saw Miss Nutcombe on her way home, who told her the chapel at Torquay might close as the preacher was "going to a place that will agree with him." Sophia had bought Blunt's *Trial of the Spirits*, which she thought was an excellent book. She hoped Katherine had enjoyed her journey by steamer.[2]

A less than pleasant scene must have occurred at Wolford Lodge when twenty-four-year-old Henry Scadding arrived and faced a disappointed Mrs. Simcoe. Possibly the dressing down he received placed him in what was reported as a more sober and industrious mood by the time he had returned to Toronto.

On 20 June 1837 a great new era dawned with the death of King William IV and the accession to the throne of his nineteen-year-old niece. Victoria was the daughter of Edward Duke of Kent, who had been sympathetic to both the Simcoes at the time of their arrival in Canada in 1791. Elizabeth did not state her opinion of the new monarch. In the letters that have survived she seemed more concerned with developments in Upper Canada.

Lady Head (Julia) wrote from Toronto on 26 June that they had heard Henry Scadding preach his first sermon at St. James' Church. "Your young charge ... is considered a young man of considerable talents," she informed Elizabeth. Archdeacon Strachan was pleased with him. And, Mrs. Scadding was so proud of Henry, she had cut a hole in the door of his bedroom so he would never be out of her sight. Henry was to preach at Newmarket on Sunday 2 July, where John, his eldest brother, lived. Julia mentioned Reverend William McMurray, who had an Indian wife. He was the missionary to the Ojibway Indians at Sault Ste. Marie, but he had a home in Toronto. Julia had seen Mrs. James Givins the morning she wrote, and that lady loved talking about Mrs. Simcoe. James Givins, a lieutenant in the Queen's Rangers in Upper Canada, was now a colonel in the militia and a superintendent of Indian Affairs. When Mrs. Givins asked after Sophia, Julia showed her Sophia's drawing of Wolford Lodge. Mrs. Givins said she was glad the Simcoes had such a pretty house. Colonel Givins, Samuel Jarvis and Sir Francis all sent greetings.[3]

Julia was unaware of the effect the recent election had had on the reform-minded residents of the province. William Lyon Mackenzie decided that only open rebellion would convince the government to change the province's constitution. He formed a committee and adopted a Declaration of Independence. From June until late September, Mackenzie travelled through the rural areas of the Home District, organizing political unions. In the London District (formed by dividing the former Western District), another rebel leader, Dr. Charles Duncombe, had resolved that only an uprising would bring into being a government responsible to the electorate. Meanwhile, Sir Francis was not being a mediator, as Lord Glenelg intended. When Head suspected George Ridout, a Toronto lawyer, of reform sympathies, he dismissed him from several public offices he held. Then Lord Glenelg ordered him to reinstate Ridout, and to appoint a leading reformer, Marshall Spring Bidwell, a judge. Sir Francis refused to agree to appeasement, and in September he resigned. However, he could not relinquish office until his successor arrived in Upper Canada.[4]

Such were the events of the summer and autumn of 1837 in the province Simcoe had founded. When Sir Francis' letter of resignation reached London, the government appointed Sir George Arthur, a Plymouth man, to succeed him. Meanwhile, Eliza was at Wardour Castle with the Dowager Lady Arundell, and Elizabeth wrote that Mr Clarke's sermon of Sunday 2 July had been excellent but she had not spoken with him afterwards. He was busy watching nine men, all strangers in Dunkeswell, because two of them seemed drunk. She had found fuller's earth in her ground at Hemyock, a valuable asset. The soft, absorbent earth was used for removing grease from material to be fulled (cleaned and thickened) in the finishing of woollen cloth.[5]

Eliza went to Cheltenham to drink the waters, as an excuse for not going to Penheale. From Cheltenham she went on to the Edward Bastards at Buckland-in-the-Moor. Elizabeth told Eliza that the Clarkes had arrived on their way to Sidmouth, and they brought Eliza's seaweeds, neatly packed. The August weather was very hot, and Elizabeth had slept in the parlour, which was cooler than the upstairs bedrooms. The air on the common, though, was fresh and fine. Instead of Eliza, Elizabeth would go to Penheale, taking a useful servant, "better ... than Anne & I do not in the least wish for her". Her favourite black pony had finally died, to her sorrow. A servant Samson had bled it with Caroline's pen knife, but that did not save the old animal.[6]

In the meantime, in Upper Canada, Sir Francis Bond Head remained sublimely unaware of smouldering resentment in some parts of his province. Sir John Colborne, Head's predecessor and now the commander of forces in both the Canadas, had contributed his share to the discontent, by endowing forty-four Church of England rectories. This caused a furor among the members of the more numerous denominations and sects.[7] When rebellion threatened to break out in Lower Canada in October, Colborne asked Head to send what troops he could spare from Upper Canada. Sir Francis, confident in the loyalty of his militia, sent what amounted to his entire force of British redcoats — the 24th Regiment — to Montreal. This greatly unnerved a Toronto civil servant and militia colonel, James FitzGibbon, a half-pay captain from the 49th Regiment who had fought on the Niagara peninsula during the War of 1812. When FitzGibbon begged Head to retain the half-company of the 24th from Penetanguishene that arrived in Toronto after the rest of the regiment was gone, Head refused.[8]

December saw the two risings in Upper Canada, that led by Mackenzie from the fourth to the seventh, and Duncombe's the following week. As soon as the presence of Mackenzie and his rebels, at Montgomery's Tavern, north of Toronto, was confirmed, Sir Francis sent Julia and the two children aboard a steamer in the harbour for safety. On 7 December, with militia Colonels James FitzGibbon and Allan MacNab, and two brass bands playing, Sir Francis rode up Yonge Street at the head of some 700 volunteers. Without difficulty they dispersed Mackenzie's poorly-armed rebels. Afterwards MacNab went on to the London District with more volunteers and put Duncombe's men to flight before they actually formed up to attack anywhere. Sir Francis' opinion that Upper Canadians did not want their government reformed seemed confirmed. In fact, the majority did want a government responsible to the electorate, but they disapproved of a minority taking matters into its own hands.

While the militia searched for rebels, both Mackenzie and Duncombe fled to the United States. Mackenzie reached Buffalo, New York, on 11 December, and by the thirteenth he had enlisted the help of American sympathisers. With some escaped Canadian rebels and American friends, he had set up a provisional government on Navy Island, in the Niagara

221

River above the Falls. The scene was vivid to Elizabeth once she heard of these developments, and she knew many of the people involved. She remembered that Allan MacNab's parents had come to Newark in 1793. His father, Allan MacNab Senior, had been a lieutenant in Simcoe's first Queen's Rangers during the American Revolution.

Just how badly the Heads were taken by surprise was revealed in a letter dated 25 November from Lady Head that arrived at the beginning of January 1838. Julia wrote that "nothing alarming or terrific had taken place"[9] She was replying to enquiries from the Simcoe ladies about the rumours rampant in England of trouble brewing in Upper Canada. By the time Julia's letter reached Wolford Lodge, the rebellions were over, but ahead lay border raids by American sympathisers. Most declared that they wanted to help liberate the Canadians, but annexation was their real goal as far as the British authorities were concerned. While many half-pay officers among Elizabeth's friends felt that Sir Francis had handled the situation badly, Elizabeth remained steadfast. Sir Francis had resigned before the rebellions broke out, because Lord Glenelg wanted him to appoint disloyal democrats to public office. Prime Minister Melbourne and all his Whig ministers were behaving as though they cared nothing at all for Upper Canada, and precious little for England either.

Writing to Eliza at Buckland on 22 January 1838, Elizabeth was waiting for news from the Heads at Ashfield before posting her letters, in case there was more word from Toronto. Mr. Clarke, who had as usual preached an excellent sermon, had called, and discussed arrangements for the services at Dunkeswell and the fees for them. He had told her about one of his parishioners who had taken ill in Taunton, and who had died the next day without speaking. She saw this as a warning that one should always be prepared for the end, for the good of one's soul.[10]

On a Monday in February, Fanny Head sent word to Wolford Lodge that she had news, and Elizabeth took the letters she had written with her to Ashfield. Lady Head had sent three Toronto newspapers. Some carried the story that Sir Francis was going to attack Navy Island, which Elizabeth thought must be false, as indeed it turned out to be. She approved of his speech to the assembly which she thought "admirable", containing all one wanted to know and in good language.[11] Fanny Head was relieved that her brother would soon be coming home. Sir George Arthur, his successor, was welcome to the thankless task. Thankless was an appropriate word. At least Sir Francis had been in the province only one year, not long enough for his health to be undermined.

Major-General Sir George Arthur was a well-known local man, born in Plymouth in 1784 and a contemporary of Eliza's. His last tour of duty had been as the lieutenant governor of Van Diemen's Land (now Tasmania), a colony wherein half the residents were convicts transported from Britain. Arthur had governed there from 1824 until 1836, and he received his appointment to Upper Canada in November 1837, before the rebellions had occurred. By January 1838 the home government felt that an experienced military man was needed more than ever, now that a faction in the province had risen. Not long after Elizabeth's visit to Ashfield, local newspapers were reporting on an international incident, but happily Sir Francis was not being blamed for it. The initiative lay with Colonel Allan MacNab, who authorized a party to capture the American steamer *Caroline*.

The *Caroline* had been carrying supplies and reinforcements to Mackenzie's men on Navy Island, and MacNab resolved to put a stop to this activity. While Sir Francis had ordered only defensive action, an angry MacNab disobeyed. MacNab sent some men in small boats across the Niagara River into American waters, where they found the steamer tied up at Fort Schlosser, near the very place where Elizabeth had sat and sketched during her time at Newark. They took the *Caroline* out into the river, but when they could not start her engine, they set her afire. The steamer grounded above the Falls, although American reports, and even a picture in a Fleet Street newspaper, showed her going down the huge cataract. The home government was embarrassed by this destruction of the property of a foreign nation in peacetime. A capture might have been smoothed over, but entering another nation's waters and destroying a ship was an act of war.

Fanny Head told Elizabeth that she was happy Sir Francis would not have to cope with many more such incidents. A governor of more military experience was required in Upper Canada. Sir George Arthur's talents were needed, they soon learned, not against the people of the province, but against marauding Americans. In fact, their depredations kept the Upper Canadians on edge all through 1838 as badly organized bands of American sympathisers and Canadian exiles staged raids on border communities. In the course of that year, what amounted to nine full regiments of British regular troops poured into Upper Canada, on a scale that would have astonished John Graves Simcoe, who had had to make do with his 400 Queen's Rangers and two small regular regiments, the latter at border points.[12]

Mid April brought more alarming news. A pitched battle had been fought on Pelee Island, in Lake Erie, between Canadian militiamen and regulars of the 32nd Regiment, sent to reinforce the 24th, and some 500 American and Canadian exile invaders boastfully calling themselves Patriots. The brigands were speedily put to flight, but four regulars and one militia cavalryman had been killed in action, and more than thirty regulars were wounded. Elizabeth shuddered over the newspaper account, and remembered her terror at the sound of musket fire.

By the end of May, the home government had sent Lord Durham to the Canadas to investigate the causes of the unrest in both provinces. Elizabeth disliked Durham because his views, even more liberal than those of most Whigs, had earned him the sobriquet, "Radical Jack." The Heads were back in England before Durham landed in Quebec. They had left Toronto in late March 1838, one day after Sir George Arthur arrived to assume his duties. Sir Francis leased a house at Atherstone, near Birmingham. At the time

Elizabeth was in Cheltenham taking the waters. Soon after their return, Julia brought her son George and daughter Julia to Ashfield for a holiday.[13] Elizabeth, eager to hear first hand about the shocking events still taking place in Upper Canada, invited them to dine at Wolford Lodge. Julia told the Simcoes that Sir Francis did not attack Navy Island after all; that wretch Mackenzie evacuated it after Sir John Colborne sent the 24th Regiment back to Toronto. Sir Francis took it to the Niagara frontier, and Mackenzie and his brigands hurried back to Buffalo. Sir Francis inspected the island afterwards, and found a truly shocking mess — appallingly dirty little huts, and filthy clothing littered about. Elizabeth hoped that was the end of the border troubles, but Julia was pessimistic. There had been many incidents, most of them small, but Pelee Island was not. There were also rumours that secret societies were forming in the border states, to create an army to capture Upper Canada. Sir George Arthur would have his hands full coping with the border crossings. As reports of other outrages trickled to England, Elizabeth told Katherine she was feeling the weight of her seventy-six years. Katherine was staying at the home of Reverend William Oxenham in Modbury, Devon, twelve miles east of Plymouth. Writing on Sunday 4 November, Elizabeth as usual praised Mr. Clarke's fine sermons, but she was not at all pleased to hear that Katherine had set up some work for her to do each day. "I do less & less in every way, eat less, work less, read less", everything except sleep less. She took no medicine but Miss Salter's, which was made of dandelions. She had not seen Robert Booth's book about gypsies, nor did she want to buy a subscription to the magazine *Gypsy Advocate*. Elizabeth had read an amusing anecdote, about a French lady who had a goat as nurse for her two babies.

Eliza, who had been visiting a Miss Richey, returned earlier than Elizabeth wished, which disturbed her. From Eliza, she heard that Katherine was reading the new biography of the Duke of Wellington, which Elizabeth, too, had received. The book did not impress her; she wished that the part on his promoting the Emancipation Bill had been deleted. Also, the conclusion was "shocking" for not enough credit was given to the "superior power".[14] By 23 November, Katherine was back at Wolford Lodge, and Elizabeth and Eliza were in Leamington and going to Campden for a few days. She walked till her back ached, and was distressed when she went to fetch something from another room and forgot what she came for. She disliked being annoyed now, but she should be thankful that she was free of any painful illness.[15]

Elizabeth and Eliza were at Cheltenham. By 29 November, Elizabeth was having "fits of debility". They would spend a few hours at Whitchurch on their way to Wolford Lodge. She wrote Katherine that she had been invited to Penheale but had decided the journey and Henry's lively family were too much for her. For the most part Elizabeth was happy *listening*, but writing, thinking and action were fatiguing. She could write about the characters she was meeting daily, but Katherine knew enough of human nature that she did not need the information. Reverend Francis Close had recommended a widow as a mistress for the infant school at Dunkeswell. Eliza was to interview her, and if she found her satisfactory, they would keep her in mind in case of an opening. Eliza was reading a curious book, *Deane in the worship of so Universal in any part of the World.*[16]

As the holiday season was at its height more news came from Upper Canada. Lord Durham had resigned and sailed for home on 1 November, because he had not received the support he needed from the home government. That had a familiar ring for Elizabeth Simcoe, whose husband had had the same problem for five years, not five months! After Durham sailed away, the Canadian militia and British regulars had fought a bloody battle at Windmill Point, just west of Johnstown. In the major encounter, two regulars had been killed and nineteen wounded, while Canadian militia losses were fourteen killed and forty-eight wounded. Americans calling themselves members of Hunter's Lodges, and a few Canadian exiles, staged this outrage.[17] Elizabeth heard that Durham was writing a report, but he would not find a solution to the unsatisfactory situation in the Canadas. The only way to bring about peace and order, she reasoned, was through the church and the constitution. If something was not done, the Canadians might become godless republicans like their southern, interfering neighbours.

Chapter 25

The Church Builders

To Elizabeth Simcoe, an event of importance was the creation of the diocese of Toronto, that took effect on 1 January 1839, with John Strachan consecrated as the first bishop. The diocese covered the whole of Upper Canada. Formerly, Bishop Mountain's diocese included both the Canadas, and he had ordained Henry Scadding a deacon soon after that young man's return from Cambridge.[1]

By February, Parliament was debating Lord Durham's Report on conditions in the Canadas. Sir Francis Head was living by himself in the house he leased at Atherstone, ten miles northeast of Birmingham, while Julia stayed on at Ashfield. He was writing his *Narrative of Recent Events in Canada* and being vociferous in his criticisms of Durham. At Atherstone he was joined by the Chief Justice of Upper Canada, John Beverley Robinson, who was as opposed to Durham's notions as Head himself. Robinson had brought his family to England with him while he pleaded with Tory opponents of the Melbourne government to defeat "Radical Jack's" proposals. Emily Robinson, the chief justice's wife, had relatives in Cheltenham with whom the family was staying.

Durham had recommended granting responsible government to the Canadas, a suggestion that raised Elizabeth Simcoe's hackles as well as those of Head and Robinson. The constitution so admired by her late husband should not be altered. Nor did Durham's other suggestion please her. He advocated uniting Upper and Lower Canada, so that the French-speaking majority of Lower Canada could be outvoted by the overall English-speaking majority the union would bring about. She approved of two separate provinces, one where the French could have their established church, the other for the English with the Anglican church as the established one. Durham's contention that uniting the provinces would make the French assimilate was nonsense; their language and religion were far too deeply engrained. When the Melbourne ministry declined responsible government, but agreed to unite the Canadas, she was somewhat relieved. At least, some aspects of the constitution John Graves Simcoe treasured would remain untouched.

Katherine was on a visit to the Reverend William Oxenham at Modbury. Writing to her on 2 March, Elizabeth thought the troubles in Ireland were never-ending, and she wondered whether "Mr. Buller", who was to go there, might not make matters worse. She may have meant James Buller of Downes, in north Devon, a former Member of Parliament, or his cousin, Charles Buller, a liberal politician who had accompanied Lord Durham to Canada. (James' son, Redvers Buller, born at Downes in 1839, would be an under-secretary in Ireland in the 1880s.)

Elizabeth admired immensely the preaching of Mr. James Temple Mansel, the new Dunkeswell curate,[2] but she thought him not "energetic" enough for the poor. She had promised money to Mr. Oxenham's church, but could not recall whether she had sent any, and she enclosed an extra five shillings with her letter. When Katherine was ready to come home, Sir John Kennaway had asked that she stop at Escot and escort Lady Kennaway, who was to go to Wolford Lodge for a change of air.[3]

Soon after Lady Kennaway's visit, Elizabeth set out for Coleford with Eliza and Anne, planning to visit Whitchurch. At Monmouth she came down with a cold and stayed at the Beaufort Arms to recover. Eliza went on ahead to Coleford while Anne remained with her. When Elizabeth felt fit enough to proceed, she drove with Anne first to the old church in Monmouth to see a Saxon monument, where she sketched a "singular font". She told Katherine not to quarrel over the sum to be paid to a carpenter working at Wolford Lodge since in "Borows" (Joseph Burrows) opinion the man was efficient. Burrows may have been her manager who succeeded John Scadding. After their visit to Coleford, Eliza and Anne expected to spend some time in Seaton, while Elizabeth returned home.[4]

She remained at home for the summer, while Katherine went to Penheale to visit Henry and his family. Elizabeth wrote Katherine that Mr. Edward Simcoe Drewe of the Grange had been riding with his eldest girl, eight-year-old Adele Caroline, when her horse tried to crush her. Drewe acted promptly, whipping the horse until it released her and she was not badly hurt. Elizabeth had told Blackmore that if he wanted any handbills they could be printed at Penheale on Henry's press. Harriet was with Miss Powys in Northamptonshire. Her mother was pleased with Katherine's account of the children at Penheale, while "our baby" was somewhat better when she had been at Budleigh Salterton. She did not keep a tenant in the house all the time, for Henry and other members of the family liked to have the use of it. Elizabeth had decided to defer a bazaar she was planning until 26 June, after the Honiton fair, to avoid competing with it.[5]

On 5 July 1839, Elizabeth Lethbridge Simcoe, Henry's third daughter who would be eleven years old on 28 September, wrote her Aunt Caroline. "Papa" would be going to Birmingham on the ninth to "marry Aunt Beny". She meant that her father would be performing the ceremony for his wife's sister. The child thanked Caroline for the basket and mentioned alterations to the house at Penheale, which had a new schoolroom.[6] At that time John Strachan was on his way to England, to be consecrated Bishop of Toronto by the Archbishop of Canterbury. The ceremony took place on 4 August at Lambeth Palace, with Chief Justice John Beverley Robinson in attendance.[7] Apparently neither man was in touch with Elizabeth during their visits.

In Upper Canada, Susan Sibbald had donated sixty-five acres of her land on the shore of Lake Simcoe for the church and a glebe — an attractive point that now bears her surname. The house she had bought had been called Penn Range, but she renamed it Eildon Hall, after the Sibbald family seat in the Scottish borders. With the cooperation of a close neighbour, John

Mills Jackson, she had started a subscription for the building, contributing the largest amount — £50 — herself. Another neighbour, Commander James O'Brien Bourchier, late of the Royal Navy who had settled in the area in 1835, contributed a raft of lumber valued at £10 towards the church's construction. The first clergyman, Reverend John Gibson, arrived from England on 20 June with his wife and son, and stayed with Mrs. Sibbald until a log building had been renovated for a parsonage. The church was dedicated on 26 August 1839, although only the walls were up and it had neither roof nor pews.[8] It was named St. George's Church because Susan admired the warrior saint. She had proved a warrior herself during the rebellions. When Godfrey Wheeler, a rebel leader in the neighbourhood, arrived with a party to search her house for arms:

> Mrs. Sibbald appeared with the members of her household armed with pitchforks and swords, and stoutly refused admission to the rebels, who eventually retired. Subsequently one of them, a half-pay naval lieutenant, who was about to be arrested, came to Mrs. Sibbald, and going down on his knees begged her to intercede for him, but she replied, "Get up, Mr. _____. Kneel to your God, and not to me," and ordered him from her house.[9]

Word of Susan's success as a builder prompted Elizabeth to think about the state of Dunkeswell parish church. A new and larger building was needed, and the Simcoe women would follow in the footsteps of Susan Sibbald by rebuilding it. There was plenty of cut stone since the ruins of Dunkeswell Abbey that had long provided a source of building material to the local people. Her daughters had a workshop which Susan Sibbald's son Hugh visited in September 1844:

> I was welcomed by Mrs. Simcoe and four daughters — unmarried and of mature age — after luncheon three of the sisters took me to a long room called the 'workshop,' where they all devote much of their time to carving oak and stone for an ancient church which is being restored on the property.[10]

In September 1839 Elizabeth and Eliza were in Wales again, touring the area she loved so. They had come through Whitchurch, where Henming the blacksmith and a tenant was now clerk of the parish. Henming had given her an account of the influence of the "Plymouth party", a sect founded in 1830, and under its influence the village apothecary had become decidedly new light. Henming heard the Brethren once, and would never go again for their opinions were "unscriptured". They were immoral in calling themselves saints and Elizabeth had advised some Whitchurch people against hearing them or reading what they wrote. A Miss Herbert was in one of the "cottages" as she preferred to call them, for she disliked the name "Alms Houses".

They found the church in Abergavenny disgracefully dirty, its monuments neglected, and the new part in poor taste. The free seats for the poor were so far behind they could not hear the preacher. Eliza's delight in the scenery gratified Elizabeth, although she was disappointed that a wall obscured the view of Sugar loaf, a mountain north of the town. They were all leaving for Coleford the next day to be in time to hear Mr. Guerensey, a clergyman and good friend, preach in his own church in the Forest (of Deane) near Whitchurch.[11]

In the autumn, with Eliza and Anne, Elizabeth went to Leamington, as fashionable a spa as Cheltenham, to take the waters. From there they continued on to London, and she wrote to Katherine from a house on Portland Street. The weather was very foggy, and had been since they were in Leamington. Elizabeth was staying inside, but the other ladies went "dripping" in it. A physician who examined her recommended that she walk more.

"You have legs to walk and a tongue to talk and the more you use them the better," he told her.[12]

By 1840, her 78th year, Elizabeth was making shorter journeys. Sidmouth was a favourite destination, sometimes just for the day. On 23 July 1840, Parliament passed an act to unite the Canadas, to take effect on 1 January 1841. Elizabeth took little notice since she had wearied of politics. As autumn approached, she was more and more worried by reports from Penheale, and she made that long, exhausting journey to see the situation for herself. Henry's wife Anne was in failing health, and Elizabeth thought she had done wrong by not telling him how ill she was. At her advanced age, Elizabeth took command of Henry's household, and among her concerns were young Anny's teeth, which were very bad, and her face ached constantly.[13]

Anne Palmer Simcoe died on 6 December 1840, and for much of the year that followed Elizabeth was at Penheale overseeing the welfare of the nine children, aged five to seventeen. Her other preoccupation was with plans for the new church at Dunkeswell, for which she made sketches. Some excavation work was also started that season.[14] In 1841 she wrote Anne, visiting in Twiston, claiming that the head of a criminal was shaped differently from that of a normal man, and included a drawing to support her conviction.[15] Gratifying was the resignation of Lord Melbourne, and the formation under Robert Peel of a conservative ministry. Now there would be fewer changes to upset people who had faith in the old ways.

In May, Sir George Arthur's tour of duty as Upper Canada's seventh lieutenant governor ended, and with his family he sailed for England. Soon after they landed the Arthurs journeyed to Penheale, where Elizabeth was still staying. She was delighted to receive first hand news of Upper Canada, which she sent at once to Katherine. That daughter took a lively interest in the welfare of the Anglican church in the province even though she was destined never to go there. On 30 June one H. Exeter had written her from Torquay that he honoured her feeling about the church in Canada, and hoped that the church's head office would help out.[16]

Elizabeth asked Sir George for details on the border raids of 1838, and listened intently to his descriptions before turning to the matter of the union of the Canadas. Privately, Sir George did not agree that the provinces should be united. Union would bring together in one assembly the Reformers of both provinces, and they might be strong enough to form a majority in the house. That would not make them the government, for the power would still rest with the governor, but as soon as a Whig ministry replaced the present Tory one, Arthur suspected it would make the councils responsible to the legislature. The governor would become solely the Queen's representative in the Canadas. To Elizabeth that meant mob rule, as in the United States. Arthur thought the province might follow the same path as Texas. The substantial American element in Upper Canada would no doubt demand annexation, as the Texans had done.

Yet not all Sir George's news was gloomy. He brought word of Henry Scadding, who had been ordained a priest that year by Bishop Strachan. Henry was a classics master at Upper Canada College, and the assistant minister at St. James' Church under Strachan. Katherine sent him a warm letter of congratulations. Scadding's reply was dated 4 December 1841, from the College. He was pleased that the Arthurs had been to Penheale, so that the Simcoes could hear from Sir George's own lips about Canadian affairs, whose account would be "just and favourable". He was sorry that Katherine had not been at Penheale to meet Arthur's daughters, because they were acquainted with Miss Harriet Baldwin, who had recently become Mrs. Henry Scadding.[17]

During 1842, work began in earnest on the restoration of the Dunkeswell parish church. Elizabeth worried that time might be running out for her. If she wanted to see the church completed she would have to devote considerable effort to the task, despite her concern over the situation at Penheale. While her daughters did some wood and stone carving, Elizabeth made drawings for the stained glass windows. The site required much clearing because the ruins of the old abbey buildings were strewn about on it. While some of the abbey stones had been carted off to use for houses, there were also people living in the ruins for whom other housing had to be arranged.[18]

She was also worried that Charlotte seemed unwell. In June she sent her, accompanied by Eliza, to Leamington Priors, in the hope that a visit to the spa would revive her. Then she sent Katherine and Anne to Leamington, so that Katherine and Eliza could have a holiday on the Isle of Wight while Anne cared for Charlotte. She sent £20 for Eliza and Katherine's expenses, wishing she could go to the Isle of Wight, but she had used ill health as an excuse for not going to Penheale.[19]

On 1 July 1842, H. Exeter wrote to "Miss Simcoe", admitting that he saw little hope for the church in Canada. He thought that Britain was not particularly interested in governing colonies, and much less concerned about religion.[20] By that time Elizabeth was at Leamington Priors at Charlotte's side. The end came on the eighteenth, a bitter blow, for this daughter, then aged fifty-seven, most resembled her father, both in stature and personality. Yet Charlotte's death did not depress Elizabeth as much as those of the first Katherine, her husband, Francis, and Mary Anne Burges. She had the work on the church to occupy her. Katherine, who was deeply depressed over Charlotte's passing, went to stay with friends at Budehaven.[21]

Katherine was still absent in early December when Elizabeth was planning Christmas celebrations. The meeting would be smaller than usual, she wrote Katherine, mainly a puppet show for the Dunkeswell children. She was upset that no one had invited some visiting deputations to dinner after a service at the church. Next year, "if I live so long, Mr. Willisford and I must give the dinner". "Simcoe" would bring Mary to Wolford when he went to Oxford, but he had to leave Anny at Penheale. Elizabeth would not "bewail her being left behind for she must find satisfaction her father wants her as his deputy". She continued, "debility drives one oftener to a throne of grace", and trifles of the world occupied the mind through Satan's devices. On the twentieth, Mary's visit was over and she wrote from Penheale that Henry Junior, now nineteen, had finished his examinations at Oxford.[22]

A few days later Elizabeth was relieved of the responsibility she felt towards Penheale when Henry married Emily Mann, a daughter of the Reverend H. Mann of Mawgan/St. Martin, Cornwall.[23] About the same time, Holy Trinity Church, on the site of the old abbey church, was dedicated, although work on it would not be completed for another three years.[24] The first rector was Theodore Miller; John Clarke had died shortly before, to Elizabeth's sorrow since they had worked well together.[25]

The Simcoe ladies continued working on the carving and windows, and visiting to their many friends. Elizabeth was surprised and gratified to receive a letter dated 21 April 1844 from Silvanus Miller Junior in New York. He wrote at the request of a publisher, Dr. Scoresby, to acknowledge the indebtedness of the history of the American Revolution to John Graves Simcoe's Journal of 1777-1781 that had been published in 1787. Miller had first learned of the existence of the book in the autumn of 1843. Dr. Scoresby had reprinted the journal, with annotations from local people who remembered Simcoe and the war. He asked Mrs. Simcoe to send him any relevant papers in her possession, and informed her that great sympathy existed among Americans for Major John André who had been hanged as a spy. Miller was sending a copy of the reprint to Wolford Lodge.[26]

When the Simcoe daughters had completed the stained glass windows for Holy Trinity Church, Dunkeswell, they began painting one for St. George's Church at Sibbald Point. In the design were thirteen crosses, one for each member of the Simcoe family — eleven children and their parents.[27] The window would not be sent immediately to Canada. They had to find some reliable person to carry it and take care of it during the long voyage.

No matter how carefully it was packed, it could not be trusted to the hold of a ship along with other baggage.

As 1845 began, Harriet's health was failing fast. She died at Wolford Lodge on 16 March, aged fifty-eight. Hers was the fourth burial at Wolford Chapel. As Elizabeth stood with Eliza, looking at the graves of her husband, baby John, Charlotte and now Harriet, she thought of Katherine's little one at York, of the stone Mrs. Hunt had sent, and of Francis in his unmarked resting place near Badajoz. Elizabeth longed for God to call her before He claimed any more of her children. Still, she admitted, His will be done.

In April 1845, the Peel ministry passed a free trade budget that repealed export duties and limited import duties, news that depressed Elizabeth. Colonies seemed of little value, even to a Conservative government, which boded ill for the future of Upper Canada. As the year was ending, Elizabeth was both gratified and alarmed. On 22 December, Emily Simcoe, the first child of Henry and his second wife Emily, was baptised at Egloskerry — her tenth grandchild, and all ten were alive and well.[28] About the same time, the United States completed the annexation of Texas, and again her thoughts for Upper Canada were gloomy. John Graves Simcoe's five year struggle to retain the province for Britain might yet be for nothing.

Chapter 26

THE BEST CHRISTIAN

For Elizabeth Simcoe, the most important event of 1846 occurred on 4 July, when her son Henry became the vicar of Egloskerry and Tremaine, nearly twenty years after his ordination as a deacon when he had already begun serving in the Cornwall parish.[1] However, she was depressed about Canada. As Sir George Arthur had warned her, the united province would soon be granted responsible government when the Conservatives were out of power. Sir Robert Peel had resigned, and Lord John Russell formed a Liberal government.

At Wolford Lodge, in late June, the ladies played host to Susan Sibbald, on a visit from her home on Lake Simcoe. While she was there she inspected the window for St. George's Church. In her diary she recorded, "27th June 1846. — Went to Honiton with Miss Simcoe to see the painted Georgina Window."[2] Simcoe had named the township where she had built the church Georgina in honour of George III. That season, the window was taken apart, packed with great care, and entrusted to someone, possibly Susan herself, for the long journey to Sibbald Point. It arrived in good condition, and was placed in the wooden church that had been dedicated in 1839. (Susan Sibbald died in 1866, and in 1877 her sons opened a stone church on the site of the former wooden one. The Simcoe window was removed from the old structure and built into the new.)

In January 1847, a new governor arrived in Canada, and Elizabeth's fears for the fate of her husband's constitution were realized. Lord Elgin, a son-in-law of Lord Durham, had orders to act only as Her Majesty's representative, an event bemoaned by both the Head and Simcoe families. Julia and Sir Francis, the latter still scribbling, were now living in Duppas Hall, at Croydon, outside London, where his favourite sport was foxhunting.[3] Both families were worried that Sir Francis' sister Fanny was in failing health, although their older sister Mary was fit.

From Escot where she was visiting the Kennaways, Elizabeth reported to Eliza on 21 January that Fanny Head was more comfortable since the Simcoes had loaned her the eiderdown. Sir John Kennaway, however, was much better than on her last visit.[4] A friend of both Fanny and the Simcoe daughters was Mme. Antoinette de Milanges, who had moved to England because of the French Revolution. Mrs. Burges had befriended her and she had continued visiting friends around Honiton after Mary Anne's death in 1813. Madame had returned to France in 1838. Nine years later, upon hearing how ill Fanny Head was, she journeyed from Paris to be a comfort to her old friend, and she remained until after Fanny's death.[5]

Fanny lingered until August, visited often by the ladies from Wolford Lodge. Among other members of her family who arrived for the funeral were Sir Francis Head's brothers, Sir George and Henry. Sir George had been a deputy knight-marshal at the coronation of King William IV, and knighted afterwards.[6] He had hoped to thank Katherine personally for the comfort she had given Fanny, but at Ashfield he had found the drawing-groom empty. A servant told him Katherine and Mme. de Milanges had left.[7]

The month before, an event gratifying to the Simcoes occurred at Hemyock. Since June 1846, an extensive renovation had been under way at St. Mary's, the parish church. Elizabeth had contributed generously towards the cost of the rebuilding, which amounted to £900. By July 1847 the work was completed, and Henry was invited to preach the first sermon, to his mother's delight.[8]

As 1847 ended, the family was worried that Henry Junior, Elizabeth's eldest grandson, was unwell. His father sent him, accompanied by his second sister, twenty-one-year-old Mary Northcote Simcoe, to the Island of Madiera to recuperate away from the damp cold of England. The mild climate did no good; on 31 January 1848, the twenty-fifth anniversary of his baptism, Henry Walcot Simcoe died on Madiera.[9] His body was sent to Penheale, and there Elizabeth journeyed for the funeral. She was nearly eighty-six, and travel was hard on her. She went because a heartbroken Henry needed her. Even his second wife Emily was not enough comfort for him.

As soon as he received the sad news, Henry Scadding, ten years young Henry's senior, wrote his condolences to Katherine. Scadding had heard of Henry's indisposition, but he had no idea how ill he was. He had expected Henry to visit Toronto one day, and he hoped Mary had recovered from the shock. "She had been early made to taste of trial." He mentioned a confusion over funds, a hint that Elizabeth was paying John Scadding's widow a pension after his years of faithful service to the Simcoes.[10]

Elizabeth was soon distressed that Sir George Arthur's suspicions were confirmed. The Reformers in the two Canadas joined forces and formed a majority in the legislature in Montreal, then the capital. The Reform government, led by Robert Baldwin and Louis LaFontaine, had drafted the Rebellion Losses Bill, to compensate everyone, those who had stayed loyal and those who had rebelled! Elizabeth agreed with Sir Francis Head that this was lunacy. Violence soon erupted. On 25 April 1849, after Lord Elgin gave Royal assent to the bill, his carriage was pelted with rotten eggs by angry Tories. That night the Parliament Building was gutted after the mob set it on fire. Elizabeth took no comfort because the mob were Tories; mob rule was not acceptable for either party.

Elizabeth was slowing down. She no longer wrote diaries or letters as her hands were so stiff and she was having great difficulty rising each morning because of rheumatism in her limbs. The vicar, Mr. Miller, made frequent calls as the summer and autumn of 1849 passed, to pray with her.

The end came on 17 January 1850, an occasion for mourning throughout South Devonshire. John Bailey described the funeral at Wolford Chapel, at which her six surviving children, her tenants, household servants and estate workers, as well as the clergy and landed gentry were present.

> A beautiful escutcheon was placed over the front door, done by Mr. Ward of Honiton . . . the whole funeral procession went from the front door, and went slowly round the front of the house and up the garden walks . . . The funeral service was read by Mr. Muller [sic] in the chapel. The body was then taken to the grave close to General Simcoe's. When it was let down into the grave I thought what a wonderful thing it was that I should have been present at General Simcoe's funeral, then only a boy of fifteen years of age, and now an old man of sixty to be present at Mrs. Simcoe's funeral, forty-four years later.[11]

Her will came up for probate on 19 March 1850. Made in 1840, it had three codicils. By the first, dated 30 March 1841, she left all her lands and real property, both freehold and leasehold, of Dunkeswell Abbey, to Eliza and Caroline as joint tenants. The second, of 9 October 1843, added the Honourable Sir John Taylor Coleridge, by that time a Judge of the Court of Queen's Bench, to her other executors, her son Henry and Reverend John Clarke. By the third, of 7 January 1848, she appointed Francis George Coleridge, Sir John's son, as executor to replace Reverend Clarke "who has departed this life, and to act in conjunction with her son, Henry Addington Simcoe, and Sir John Taylor Coleridge".

Elizabeth did not delete Charlotte and Harriet from the will, although both had died by the time of the third codicil. To each of her five eldest daughters, Eliza, Charlotte, Harriet, Caroline and Sophia, she left £5,000. To Katherine and Anne she made the sum £6,000, because the five older sisters had each received £1,000 from their great aunt, Margaret Graves. All the daughters were entitled to shares in their late great aunt Elizabeth Sophia Gwillim's estate on the death of their mother. Under Simcoe's will, Elizabeth was empowered to pay each child a sum not to exceed £5,000. To Eliza she left her prints, pictures, plate, books, china, linen, wine, horses, cows, carts, carriages, household goods and other furniture, bank notes, and cash in Biddulph's Bank. All the rest went to Henry. Among the witnesses was James Temple Mansel, Clerk Curate of Dunkeswell.[12]

She favoured Eliza and Caroline with the Dunkeswell lands, perhaps because these two had more ability to manage land and money than the others. Their parents' bequests, and those of the two great aunts, were not the full extent of the Simcoe offsprings' wealth. William Walcot had left each daughter £2,000, and Mrs. Simcoe £100 and all his lands and houses in Norfolk, Huntingdon and Northampton, to be sold and the proceeds divided "share and share alike" amongst the seven daughters. His estates at Titchmarch, Northampton, went to Henry Addington Simcoe, who inherited the Gwillim properties at Whitchurch, Herefordshire, as well as Wolford Lodge and other lands.

The five sisters soon took up residence in Bath, at 11 Royal Crescent, where they could have a busier social life than at isolated Wolford Lodge. Henry put a tenant in the lodge since he had no use for it. At Penheale, early in 1851, his wife Emily gave birth to his eleventh child, Catherine Louisa Beatrice Simcoe, and she was baptised on 30 March.[13]

A startling event occurred in 1854, probably to the chagrin of Eliza, Caroline, Sophia and Katherine. Their youngest sister Anne did what she either lacked the opportunity — or had been forbidden — to do by their mother. In the London suburb of Paddington, she married William Allford, whose surname was a common one in Devon. The record suggests she married below her station, and to a man somewhat younger than she:

When Married:	12 January 1854	
Names:	William Alford [sic]	Anne Simcoe
Ages:	Both of full age	
Condition:	Bachelor	Spinster
Rank/Profession:	servant	
Residence of Mu.	Parish of Paddington	
Father's Name:	John Alford	John Simcoe
Rank/Profession of Father:	Farmer	General in the Army

The witnesses were William Hogg and Harriet Winter.[14] None of Anne's sisters attended, suggesting they disapproved. The bride was forty-nine (she turned fifty on 31 July 1854).

The Simcoe ladies' interest in Canada did not end with their mother's passing. In the autumn of 1859 they received a letter from Bishop Strachan warning them that the Indian Department might be closed down. Since the department had rendered assistance to the missions, these would need an alternate source of funds. The situation was serious because there were not enough missions to the Indians, and more were needed. The sisters agreed to send £100.

Bishop Strachan replied on 27 March 1860, and signed in a bold, legible hand, "John Toronto". "You are aware of the poverty of the Society for the Propagation of the Gospel in Foreign Parts". It paid nothing to the Diocese of Toronto except a small allowance for "Catechists & partial salary to Rev. P. Jacobs on Manitoulin Island". Peter Jacobs was an Anglican clergyman and son of the Methodist preacher also called Peter Jacobs. The father was an Ojibway Indian known as Pahtahsega, who married an Ojibway of the Mississauga of the Credit River band, near Toronto.[15]

Strachan wanted to have three missions in the north, a second one on Saint Joseph Island and the third at Sault Ste. Marie. The Church of England had made astonishing progress since the turn of the century. Sixty years ago there were only four clergymen in Upper Canada, and Strachan had been the fifth. Now there were between 400 and 500. The eighty-two-year-old Strachan thanked the Simcoes for their liberal donation, and he hoped others would follow their example. The memory of their parents was much cherished in Upper Canada, where their names were "household words". While the bishop had never met either of them, they had been the cause of his coming to Canada, and he took pleasure in addressing the daughters of such respected persons.[16]

The letters bearing the most recent dates pertain to papers Governor Simcoe had left in Canada. Henry Simcoe asked George Coventry, an Englishman then residing in Cobourg, Canada West, to look for these papers. On 31 May 1861 Coventry wrote Henry that he had found some and was arranging to send them to England. Then on 9 June one Alpheus Todd informed Henry that he had forwarded a box of his father's papers by steamer. George Coventry wrote again on 23 September that he was looking for more documents.[17]

Of the six Simcoes who outlived their mother, Eliza died on 12 August 1865, aged eighty-one; Caroline on 21 September 1858, then nearly seventy; Sophia on 18 February 1864, aged seventy-four; and Katherine on 14 February 1861, at not quite sixty. All four died at Bath and their bodies were taken for burial to Wolford Chapel. Henry passed away on 15 November 1868, nearly sixty-nine years old, while Anne, the youngest, survived until age seventy-three, in 1877, although little is known of her after her marriage. Because none of the Simcoe daughters married while they were of child bearing age, all the descendants of John Graves and Elizabeth Posthuma Simcoe were from Henry's daughters. Five of the six married, but of his four sons who were living when he died, only one, John Kennaway Simcoe, married, and he had no children.[18]

Eliza Simcoe's will was proved on 12 August 1865. Her estate was valued at £30,000, and she was the owner of 11 Royal Crescent, Bath, which she willed to her nephew, Samuel Palmer Simcoe. The residue, after bequests to schools at Dunkeswell Abbey and Hemyock, the Dunkeswell Abbey Missionary Society and to assist the poor, went to her eldest surviving nephew, John Kennaway Simcoe, for the upkeep of Wolford Lodge, the chapel and burying ground.

Henry Addington Simcoe's estate was valued at £8,000, which indicates that he had disposed of most of his property to his children just before his death. What Henry did with the property he inherited from William Walcot is not clear. In his will Henry mentioned only manors and other property in Devon, Cornwall and Herefordshire. Eliza, however, refers to her shares in Bythorne estate, near Titchmarsh, and to other holdings in parishes in the counties of Northampton and Buckingham. Henry bequeathed the advowson to Egloskerry and Tremaine to his son, Philip Francis Simcoe, on condition that he take holy orders. Philip, who had obtained his Bachelor of Arts degree from Oxford in 1858, ten years before his father's death, did not enter the church. He had assisted his father in parish work, for which Henry left him £1,000. Since Philip did not "qualify", the will empowered the trustees to appoint the next rector.

The other Simcoe sisters left estates that were smaller than Eliza's. Both Caroline's and Katherine's were valued at £18,000.[19] The wealth originated for the most part with their mother, who had inherited the properties at Aldwinkle and Whitchurch, but their father had improved the Wolford estate and added to its value.

The tangible reminders of Elizabeth and John Graves Simcoe in Devonshire are Wolford Chapel, Hembury Fort, Hembury Fort House, Little Hill House in Budleigh Salterton (once called Simcoe House), Holy Trinity Church, Dunkeswell, and St. Mary's Hemyock. A plaque in a third church shows their influence on their children:

> The church of St. Nicolas Dunkeswell was restored by the incumbent, the Rev'd Richard Croly M.A. The restoration was planned with the aid of Miss [Eliza] Simcoe of Wolford Lodge in 1865, & completed after her decease with the help of the Rev'd Henry Addington Simcoe, the parishoners & friends in the year of our Lord 1868. To the glory of the Lord & as a memorial to the departed sisters of Wolford Lodge whose memory hallows the scene of their labours.

> Their names are recorded here. Eliza Simcoe, Charlotte Simcoe, Henrietta Maria Simcoe, Caroline Simcoe, Sophia Jemima Simcoe.

Wolford Lodge, which stands downslope with its view of the sea, is not the building Elizabeth Simcoe knew. It was erected after 1923 when the property was sold to Brigadier-General Gordon Kemball, who tore down the house and used the stone to build a smaller one. On the death of Henry Simcoe in 1868, Elizabeth's only surviving son, the heir to Wolford was his second son, John Kennaway Simcoe, like his great grandfather a captain in the Royal Navy. With the help of the bequest from his Aunt Eliza, John Kennaway Simcoe took up residence in the house, but he was not interested in maintaining it. He died childless in 1891 and was buried outside the chapel. His widow, Mary, a daughter of Colonel Basil Jackson of Glewstone, Herefordshire, died in 1920 and was buried beside her husband.

The heir was Arthur Henry Linton, a grandson of Henry Addington Simcoe's eldest daughter, Anne Eliza, the one Elizabeth called Anny. Anne Eliza married Sedley Bastard Marke, of Woodhill, Cornwall, in June 1847, and one of her daughters married a Linton. Their son added Simcoe to his name in order to inherit the arms of his great grandfather, John Graves Simcoe. The family fortune, so substantial at the time of Elizabeth's death, had been dissipated. Wolford Lodge was partly destroyed by fire before Arthur Linton Simcoe sold it.

Brigadier Kemball sold Wolford Lodge in 1926 to Alfred Le Marchant, a descendant of a one time lieutenant governor of Newfoundland (1847-

1852) and of Nova Scotia (1852-1857). The purchase did not include Wolford Chapel and the Simcoe burying ground. To preserve the chapel and its grounds, the English publisher, Sir Leicester Harmsworth, bought them and he offered them to the people of Ontario. At the time of his death, the Ontario government was still debating whether to commit funds for the upkeep of the chapel and grounds.[20]

By 1966, the government of Ontario had become conscious of its heritage. In a ceremony held at Wolford Chapel, Sir Geoffrey Harmsworth, Sir Leicester's son, presented the title deeds for the chapel and grounds to the premier of the day, John Robarts. At the same time Mr. Le Marchant guaranteed access over his property to visitors to the chapel. More recently, the Ontario government and the John Graves Simcoe Association of Toronto organised a Simcoe Weekend in May 1989. Lunch was served at Wolford Lodge, now owned by Mrs. Pamela Le Marchant Mitchell, whose husband, Reverend Patrick Mitchell, the Dean of Wells Cathedral, conducted a rededication ceremony in the chapel.

Within Ontario, tangible memorials are few; the best are the Simcoe window in St. George's Church, Sibbald Point on Lake Simcoe, and the colours of the Queen's Rangers at Fort York armouries. At Niagara-on-the-Lake (Simcoe's Newark) a building reputed be one of the four that comprised Navy Hall stands encased in Queenston squared limestone to preserve the wood. Heavily travelled Yonge and Dundas Streets are other tangibles. If objects are few, Governor Simcoe's names are numerous. Of the nineteen counties he established, seventeen remain, although some now form regional municipalities. Many townships within counties bear names bestowed by Simcoe — Bastard, Burgess, Kitley, Wolford, Oxford, Leeds, Lansdowne, Yonge, and Escott in Eastern Ontario. In York County (now York Region) are Pickering, Uxbridge, East and West Gwillimbury, Georgina, York and Scarborough.

The town of Simcoe, the seat of Haldimand County, and Simcoe County, between Lake Simcoe and Georgian Bay, were named later, in honour of the first lieutenant governor. In Toronto, now a sprawling metropolitan area, a road, drive and subway station are named Castle Frank, a reminder of the dark-haired boy who played about with the Shaw children, and who fell at Badajoz before his twenty-first birthday. Simcoe, John and Elizabeth Streets are reminders as well as Woodbine Avenue, named for Woodbine Hill, the seat of Admiral Thomas Graves. The exact spot where lie the remains of the first Katherine Simcoe is not known. She was buried in the military cemetery, east of Fort York, which is now Victoria Square Memorial Park on Portland Avenue. Such stones as have survived have been placed in the centre of the square, but if one of them is Katherine's the carving is no longer legible.

In England, while the original Wolford lodge is gone, many of the homes the Simcoes visited are there, such as Pynes, Escot, Woodbine Hill, Tracey, the Grange, Henbury Fort House and Ashfield (renamed Awliscombe House) in Devon. Penheale in Cornwall, and Fitzhead Court, Somerset, remain. Stowe, Buckinghamshire, the home of the 1st Marquis of

Buckingham, is a boys' school. William Walcot's house in Oundle is the Water Board Offices. Elizabeth Posthuma Gwillim's birthplace, The Hall of All Saints, was pulled down in 1826.[21] The manor house where John Graves Simcoe is thought to have been born is still standing at Collerstock, although of late whether he was born there has become a matter of debate.

Three houses open to the public during the summer are Killerton, once the seat of the Aclands and now managed by the National Trust, Ugbrooke, still owned by the Clifford Family, and Elton Hall, which belongs still to the Proby family. The ruins of Old Wardour Castle, in Wiltshire, are also open to the public. New Wardour Castle, where Eliza Simcoe often stayed, is now a girls' school and open to the public during the summer holiday. The title Baron Arundell of Wardour has been extinct since World War Two when the heir was killed in action.[22]

In Toronto, Civic Holiday, celebrated the first Monday in August, is now known as Simcoe Day. The energetic imperialist John Graves Simcoe and his tiny observant wife are remembered, although not necessarily understood. Imperialists are often ridiculed, and Elizabeth herself has been portrayed as Lady Simcoe, an incongruous figure in the wilderness of Upper Canada with her good china and ball gowns. At each phase of her life she was the typical gentlewoman of her time — in her younger days the amused lady of the Age of Reason in quest of the picturesque who left a valuable collection of sketches and watercolours. In later life she found meaning in service to her church. Like other Evangelical Anglicans, she believed that the best Christian made the most loyal subject.[23]

NOTES

Abbreviations
DCB   Dictionary of Canadian Biography
DNB   Dictionary of National Biography
NA   National Archives of Canada
OA   Ontario Archives
PRO   Public Record Office, London

Introduction
1. Mary Quayle Innis, *Mrs. Simcoe's Diary* (Toronto, 1965) p. 21.
2. Jane Austen, *Jane Austen's Letters to her Sister Cassandra and Others,* R.W. Chapman ed. (London, 1964), pp. 47-8, 79.
3. James Morris, *Heaven's Command: An Imperial Progress* (Harmondsworth, Middlesex, England, 1973), p. 20.
4. Ibid., pp. 24-5.

Chapter 1: A Very Special Child
1. Hilary Arnold. Hilary Arnold genealogy, see Appendix A.
2. DNB, biography of Mrs. Elizabeth Montagu; NA Reel A606, F29, letter dated Wolford 14 Dec. 1791. The entire folder 29 is letters from Mary Anne Burges to Elizabeth Simcoe.
3. Ibid., Reel A607 F35, 65th letter in folder, Elizabeth to Eliza, 31 Jan. n.yr., refers to Anna Jemima having smallpox.

Chapter 2: Early Life
1. NA Reel A606, F28, Mrs. [Elizabeth] Gwillim to Elizabeth Simcoe, 22 Mar. 1789, refers to the black wig over her own dark hair.
2. Ibid., Reel A607, F39, journal of a trip to Wales. Elizabeth mentioned attending a service in Welsh.
3. John Ross Robertson saw this grave and assumed it was that of Elizabeth's father, which gave rise to the wrong date of birth. Proof that Elizabeth's grandmother, Mrs. Jemima Spinkes, played an important role in raising the child comes from a letter to William Walcot Jr. at school, 6 May, n. yr., from his mother. Mrs. Walcot wrote of Mrs. Spinckes, "She went yesterday into Herefordshire and took your little cousin with her who grown a fine girl." (West Country Studies Library, Exeter, microfilm A-4-1, item 22, sent by Hilary Arnold.) William Walcot comes later in the biography, at the appropriate time.
4. Arnold genealogy.
5. NA Reel A607 F30, Margaret Graves to Eliza, 8 Apr. 1794.
6. DNB, biography of Admiral Samuel Graves; card index, Devon Record Office, Exeter, item 63/5/19, 30 Aug. 1770, 10 Geo III.
7. NA Reel A606, F29, letter dated 5 June 1793 refers to vigils.
8. Sir James Balfour Paul, CVD LLD, Lord Lyon King of Arms, *The Scots Peerage,* vol. 8 (Edinburgh 1911), p. 37.
9. DNB, biographies of Mary Anne Burges and Jean André de Luc.

Chapter 3: Hembury Fort House
1. DNB, biography of Admiral Thomas Graves; Arnold genealogy.
2. Ibid.
3. NA Reel A605 F23, poem by William Bowcawen [sic] Esq. to Colonel Simcoe on his return from San Domingo.
4. DNB, biography of John Graves Simcoe. He entered Merton on 4 Feb. 1769.
5. The Army List 1772; the commission was dated 27 Apr. 1770.
6. DNB, biography of Admiral Thomas Graves.
7. *Newcastle Current,* death notice, supplied by Hilary Arnold.

8.   Mary Beacock Fryer, *King's Men: the Soldier Founders of Ontario* (Toronto, 1980), p. 17.
9.   Marcus Van Steen, *Governor Simcoe and his Lady* (Toronto 1968) p. 24.
10. Pamphlet, *A Short History of Dunkeswell Abbey,* by the Dunkeswell Abbey Preservation Fund, n.d., pp. 10-11.
11. NA Reel A 605, F7, Simcoe to Walcot, 11 Nov. 1802.
12. Van Steen, *Governor and his Lady,* p. 26.

Chapter 4: Wolford Lodge
1.   NA Reel A606, F29, 5 June 1793. Miss Burges recalled how despairing Simcoe was at each confinement.
2.   T.A. Reed, "The Scaddings", Ontario Historical Society *Papers and Records* 1944, vol. 36, p. 7; Devon Record Office, Exeter, Land Tax Assessments, 11 June 1793.
3.   Arnold genealogy.
4.   Devon Record Office, Exeter, Land Tax Assessments 1794, when the owner was Thomas Jenkins Esq. The records for 1783-1794 are missing, but in the Ontario Archives, Simcoe Collection B- 1-2 is Miss Burges' letter of 1 Sept. 1793, in which she said she had moved to Tracey seven years before, in 1786.
5.   Van Steen, *Governor and his Lady,* pp. 35-6.
6.   Arnold genealogy.
7.   Devon Record Office, Exeter, Land Tax Assessments. The records do not indicate that the Richard Graves lived at Hembury Fort House until 1800, but according to Mary Anne Burges' letters he was there by 1791.
8.   Rev. John Swete, "Tour Through Devon 1792-1801". Unpublished manuscript, vol. 9, p. 38, description of Wolford Lodge.
9.   Ibid., p. 35, description of Dunkeswell.
10. DNB, biography of Sir James Bland Burges.
11. Ged Martin, "The Simcoes and their Friends", *Ontario History,* vol. 69, no. 2 (June 1977), p. 102.
12. DNB biography of Sir George Yonge; NA Reel A606, F29, letter, 14 Apr. 1792.
13. Ibid., letter of 30 June 1793, written from Hermitage.
14. Martin, "The Simcoes", pp. 102-3.
15. NA Reel A607 F 32, Mrs. Hunt to Miss Hunt, C/O Mrs. Graves, Lansdown Cres., Bath, 26 Apr. 1793; F32, Charlotte to Miss Nutcombe C/O Rev. [Edward] Hunt, Benefield, 15 Sept. 1818; OA, Simcoe Non-Canadian Collection, Reel 10, fragment of letter by Simcoe dated 14 Apr. 1791 refers to Mrs. Hunt being old and to her salary.

Chapter 5: Departure for Upper Canada
1.   DCB, vol. 5, biography of Henry Caldwell.
2.   NA Reel A606 F29, letter, 29 Aug. 1792. Miss Burges frequently mentioned plans for sending letters.
3.   Ibid., Miss Burges made several references to the annuity in the few letters in the folder.
4.   Innis, *Diary,* p. 85, entry for Sun. 17 Feb. Elizabeth mentions hanging the tapestry in a hut.
5.   E.A. Cruikshank, *Simcoe Correspondence* (Toronto, 1923-1931), 5 vols., vol. 1, p. 71, Yonge to Simcoe, 20 Dec. 1791 from the War Office.
6.   Marian Fowler, *The Embroidered Tent.* Toronto 1982. In her short biography Fowler includes the miniature, supposedly in Welsh dress. The picture is C-81931 NA collection, attributed to "Mrs. Burgess".
7.   NA Reel A606 F29, 3rd in folder, undated.
8.   Cruikshank, *Simcoe Correspondence,* vol. 1, p. 84, Simcoe to Dundas, Quebec 19 Nov. 1791.
9.   NA Reel A606 F29, 4th letter in folder, undated.

Chapter 6: Winter at Quebec
1.   Innis, *Diary,* p. 142.

2.	Ibid., p. 43; DCB, vol. 6, biography of François Baby.
3.	E.A. Cruikshank, *Simcoe Correspondence.* vol. 1, p. 71, Yonge to Simcoe from the War Office, 20 Dec. 1791.
4.	Innis, *Diary*, p. 92.
5.	Ibid., p. 58, Elizabeth to Mrs. Hunt, Quebec, 26 April 1792.

Chapter 7: News From Home
1.	NA Reel A606, F29, first four letters, undated.
2.	Ibid., 5th letter, undated and out of sequence.
3.	Ibid., undated precedes one dated 14 Dec. 1791.
4.	Ibid., 2nd letter, out of context.
5.	Ibid., letter, 8 Jan. 1792.
6.	Ibid., letter, 28 Jan. 1792.
7.	Ibid., letter, 25 Jan. 1792.
8.	Ibid., letters, 8 and 12 June 1792.

Chapter 8: Nature Untamed
1.	Thad. W. Leavitt, *History of Leeds and Grenville* (Brockville, 1879), pp. 32-33.
2.	Innis, *Diary*, p. 72,
3.	Fryer, *King's Men,* pp. 131-5, 333.
4.	Cruikshank, *Simcoe Correspondence*, vol. 1, p. 205.
5.	The Army List 1792; genealogy of the Drewes of Broadhembury and the Grange, courtesy of Mr. Francis Drewe of Ticehurst, Sussex, England.
6.	Innis, *Diary*, p. 77.
7.	Ibid., p. 79.
8.	NA, Reel A605, F2, Simcoe to Eliza, Aug. 1792.
9.	Ibid., Reel A606, F24, Simcoe to Charlotte, 23 Aug. n.yr.
10.	Ibid., F29, letter, 20 Nov. 1792.
11.	Innis, *Diary*, p. 80.

Chapter 9: Winter in the Wilds
1.	Innis, *Diary*, pp. 85, 109.
2.	NA Reel A606, F29, letter, 30 Nov. 1792.
3.	Innis, *Diary*, p. 83.
4.	NA Reel A606, F24, section with poetry.
5.	Innis, *Diary*, p. 14, from NA, William Jarvis Papers.
6.	Ibid., pp. 84-7.
7.	Van Steen, *Governor and his Lady*, pp. 80-1; DNB, biography of Hugh Percy, 2nd Duke of Northumberland.
8.	Innis, Diary, p. 91.
9.	OA, Robertson-Mackenzie Collection. Elizabeth to Miss Hunt, Navy Hall, 19 Apr. 1793.
10.	NA Reel A606, F29, letter of 26 Sept. 1792.

Chapter 10: Miss Burges Reports
1.	Innis, *Diary*, p. 89.
2.	NA Reel A606 F29, letter of 19 July 1792.
3.	Ibid., letter, 15 Jan. 1793.
4.	Ibid., letters, 26 Sept. and 25 Oct. 1792.
5.	Ibid., letter, 22 Oct. 1792.
6.	Ibid., letter, 29 Dec. 1792.
7.	Sydney W. Jackman, *Galloping Head: A Biography of Sir Francis Bond Head 1793-1875.* (London, 1958), p. 153.
8.	NA Reel A606, F29, letters from 9 Jan to 1st dated 20 Apr. 1793.
9.	Ibid., letter, 8 Apr. 1793.
10.	Innis, *Diary*, pp. 89-90.

11. NA Reel A606 F29, 2nd letter, 20 Apr. 1793.
12. Ibid., letter, 19 May 1793.
13. Drewe genealogy.
14. NA Reel A606 F29, letter of 2 Sept. 1795; Balfour Paul, *The Scots Peerage*, vol. 8, p. 37.
15. OA, Simcoe Collection, Reel 7-531, Simcoe-Burges B-1-2 are the missing pages, 542-815. There are small gaps in both the Devon and Ontario collections because some packets of letters were lost in transit.

Chapter 11: The Move to York
1. Innis, *Diary*, p. 95.
2. Arnold genealogy.
3. Innis, *Diary*, p. 10, from "Journal of a treaty held in 1793..." Massachusetts Historical Society, Collections, 3rd series, vol. 5 (1936) pp. 123-4.
4. Ibid., p. 10, from William Jarvis Papers.
5. Ibid., p. 96.
6. Ibid., p. 99.
7. Ibid., p. 105.
8. Ged Martin, "Simcoes Friends", pp. 104-5.
9. DNB, biography of Sir George Yonge.
10. Henry Scadding, *Toronto of Old*, F.H. Armstrong ed. (Toronto, 1987), p.xiii.
11. Innis, *Diary*, p. 15.
12. Ibid., pp. 111-2.
13. Ibid., p. 113.
14. Van Steen, *Governor and his Lady*, p. 108. The letter is quoted in full, dated York, May 1794.
15. Martin, "Simcoe Friends", p. 109 and fn. 26; NA Reel A606 F30, last letter in folder, Elizabeth Gwillim to Eliza, n.d.; OA Simcoe Collection, Reel 7-531, Simcoe-Burges B-1-2, the missing pages are 668-77.

Chapter 12: Miss Burges and Mrs.Graves
1. OA, Simcoe Collection, Reel 7-531, Simcoe-Burges B-1-2, Aug. 1793, opening is missing.
2. Balfour Paul, *The Scots Peerage*, vol. 8, p. 37.
3. OA, Simcoe Collection, Reel 7-531, Simcoe-Burges B-1-2, letter of 18 Aug. 1793.
4. Ibid., 26 Aug. 1793.
5. Ibid., 6 Sept. 1793.
6. Ibid., 10-13 Sept. 1793.
7. Ibid., 15 Sept. 1793.
8. Ibid., 15 Sept. 1793.
9. Ibid., 26 and 29 Sept. 1793.
10. Ibid., 3 Oct. 1793.
11. Ibid., 27 Dec. 1793.
12. Ibid., 30 Dec. 1793; 1 Jan. 1794.
13. Ibid., Clifton 3 Jan. 1794.
14. Ibid., 15 and 18 Jan. 1794.
15. Ibid., 16 Feb. 1794; Innis, *Diary*, p. 127.
16. Ibid., 28 Feb., 5 Mar., 4 May 1794.
17. Ibid., 8 Mar. 1794.
18. Ibid., 25 Mar. 1794.
19. Ibid., 14 Mar. 1794.
20. NA Reel A607 F33, letters of Harriet Bowdler.
21. OA, Simcoe Collection, Reel 7-531, Simcoe-Burges B 1-2, 30 Mar. 1794.
22. Ibid., Tracey, 12 Apr. 1794.
23. Ibid., 26 Apr. 1794.
24. Ibid., 20 Apr. 1794.
25. Ibid., 26 Apr. 1794.

26. Ibid., Kittery and Exeter, 2-16 Apr. 1794.
27. Ibid., 19 June 1794.

Chapter 13: War Clouds

1. Innis, *Diary*, pp. 120-1.
2. Ibid., p. 124.
3. Ibid., p. 127.
4. Ibid., p. 129.
5. Ibid., p. 131.
6. Ibid., p. 134.
7. DCB, vol. 6, biography of John McGill; The Army Lists 1793-1796.
8. Innis, Diary, p. 139.
9. Ibid., p. 146; The Army List 1792.
10. Innis, *Diary*, p. 21.
11. NA Reel A608. F39, Simcoe to Charlotte, 22 Oct. 1794.
12. Ibid., Reel A606, F24, Simcoe to Charlotte, 8 Nov. 1794.
13. Innis, *Diary*, p. 21.
14. Ibid., p. 146.
15. Ibid., p. 148.

Chapter 14: Mrs. Burges' "Commissions"

1. OA, Simcoe Collection, Reel 7-531, Simcoe-Burges B 1-2, 30 Aug. and 1 Sept. 1794.
2. Ibid., 5, 17 and 22 Sept. 1794.
3. Ibid., 10 and 15 Sept. 1794.
4. Ibid., 22 Sept, 18 Dec. 1794, and 21 Apr. 1795.
5. Ibid., 25 and 28 Sept. 1794.
6. Ibid., 10 Nov. 1794.
7. Ibid., 5 and 9 Nov. 1794, 5 June 1795.
8. Ibid., 18 and 19 Dec. 1794.
9. Ibid., 25 Dec. 1794.
10. Ibid., 2 Jan. 1795.
11. Ibid., 24 Jan. 1795.
12. Ibid., 28 Feb. 1795.
13. Ibid., 11 Mar. 1795.
14. Ibid., 17 Mar. 1795.
15. Ibid., 27 Mar. 1795.
16. Ibid., 27 Mar. to 8 Apr. and 17 Apr. 1795.
17. Ibid., 18 Apr. 1795.
18. Ibid., 18 and 21 Apr. 1795.
19. Ibid., 23 Apr. 1795.
20. Ibid., 15 May 1795; Balfour Paul, *Peerage*, vol. 8, p. 37.
21. OA, Simcoe Collection, Reel 7-531, Simcoe-Burges B1-2, 22 and 25 May 1795.
22. Ibid., 22 May and 5 June 1795.
23. Ibid., Letter of 5 June, Tracey.
24. DNB, biography of Sir James Burges; NA Reel A606 F29, 18 Sept. 1795.

Chapter 15: The Season of 1795

1. Innis, *Diary*, p. 149.
2. Ibid., p. 151.
3. Ibid., pp. 152-3.
4. Ibid., p. 155.
5. Ibid., p. 158.
6. Hon. William R. Riddell, *The Life of John Graves Simcoe* (Toronto, 1926), p. 276.
7. Cruikshank, *Simcoe Correspondence*, vol. 5, p. 147, Dorchester to Simcoe, 6 July 1795.
8. Innis, *Diary*, p. 160.
9. DCB, vol. 6, biography of William Dummer Powell.

10. Innis, *Diary*, p. 161.
11. NA Reel A606 F24, letter dated night of 25 Oct. n.yr.
12. Innis, Diary, pp. 163-5.
13. OA, Robertson-Mackenzie Collection, Elizabeth to Mrs. Hunt, York, 6 Jan. 1796; Alumni Oxiensis (1715-1886).

Chapter 16: Julia
1. OA, Simcoe Collection, Reel 7-531, Simcoe-Burges B 1-2, 5 June 1795.
2. Ibid., 8 June 1795.
3. Ibid., 12 June 1795.
4. Ibid., 18 June 1795.
5. Ibid., 27 June 1795.
6. Ibid., 30 July but should be 3 July; and 31 July 1795.
7. Ibid., précis of August letters.
8. NA Reel A606 F29, 20 Oct. 1795.
9. Ibid., 14 Jan. 1796.
10. Ibid., Letter on p. 824, date illegible.
11. Ibid., 10 Nov. 1795.
12. Ibid., 31 Jan. 1796.
13. Ibid., 7 Jan. 1796.
14. Drewe and Arnold genealogies.
15. NA Reel A606 F29, letter dated 29 Apr. 1796.
16. Ibid., 9 Feb. 1796.
17. Ibid., 28 Feb. 1796.
18. Ibid., 2 Mar. and 6 and 27 May.
19. Ibid., 6 May.
20. Ibid., 3 Apr. 1796.
21. Ibid., 18 and 28 Apr. 1796.
22. Ibid., 7 Apr.,7 and 15 May; Paul, *Peerage*, vol. 8 (Somerville), p. 37.
23. NA Reel A606 F29, 20 May 1796.
24. Ibid., 27 May 1796.

Chapter 17: End of the Tour of Duty
1. Cruikshank, *Simcoe Correspondence,* vol. 2 pp. 3, 123, 137, 154, 165, 203; vol. 3 p. 278; vol. 4 pp. 25, 36, 37, 230, 242-3.
2. NA Reel A607 F39, Simcoe to Charlotte, 12 Feb. 1796.
3. Innis, *Diary*, p. 178.
4. Ibid., p. 182.
5. Ibid.
6. Ibid., p. 184.
7. DNB, biography of Samuel James Ballard.
8. Innis, *Diary*, p. 195.
9. Ibid., p. 191.
10. Ibid., p. 193.
11. Ibid., p. 194.
12. Ibid., p. 198.
13. Ibid., p. 200.
14. Ibid., pp. 134, 204.

Chapter 18: Return to Wolford Lodge
1. NA Reel A607 F39, Miss Hunt to Harriet, 3 June 1796.
2. Ibid., Reel A606 F28, E. Gwillim to Elizabeth, 17 Oct. 1796.
3. Innis, Diary, p. 206.
4. NA Reel 606 F28, E. Gwillim to Elizabeth, 22 Oct. 1796.
5. Innis, Diary, p. 207.
6. NA Reel A606 F28, E. Gwillim to Elizabeth, 19 Nov. 1796.

7. NA Reel 607 F31, three letters from Eliza and Charlotte to Miss Hunt, June 1797.
8. Ibid., Reel A606 F28, E. Gwillim to Elizabeth, 29 Aug. 1797.
9. Ibid., E. Gwillim to Elizabeth, 11 Dec. 1797.
10. The information about the brass guns is from Eliza Simcoe's will, Devon Record Office, #337B/30/1; DNB biography of Sir Adam Williamson.
11. NA Reel A606 F28, E. Gwillim to Elizabeth, 22 March 1798.
12. Ibid., Reel A607 F30, M. Graves to Eliza, 21 May 1798; F31, Eliza to Miss Hunt, ? June 1798.
13. Ibid., Reel A606 F30, M. Graves to Eliza, ? July 1798.
14. Ibid., M. Graves to Eliza, 30 Oct. 1798.
15. John Ross Robertson, *The Diary of Mrs. John Graves Simcoe.* (Toronto: William Briggs, 1911), Coles Facsimile Edition 1973, p. 407.
16. OA, Simcoe Non-Canadian Collection, Reel 10, E. Gwillim to Elizabeth, 13 Oct. 1798.
17. NA Reel A607 F30, M. Graves to Eliza, 31 Mar. 1799.
18. Ibid., M. Graves to Eliza, 25 Oct. 1799; M. Graves to Eliza, 12 Dec. 1799.
19. Ibid., Reel A606 F30, M. Graves to Simcoe, 4 Mar. 1800.
20. Ibid., Reel A607 F30, M. Graves to Eliza, 4 June 1800; M. Graves to Eliza, 23 Aug. 1800.
21. DNB, biography of Mary Anne Burges.
22. The Army List 1802.
23. NA Reel A605 F7, Caroline to Mrs. Hunt, 9 Jan. 1800 (should be 1801; Henry was not born until 28 February 1800).
24. Ibid., Reel A607 F30, M. Graves to Eliza, 3 June 1801; M. Graves to Eliza, 2 Oct. 1801.

Chapter 19: General Simcoe's Last Years
1. NA Reel A607 F30, M. Graves to Eliza, 8 Apr. 1801, is one of several letters where Mrs. Graves criticised the Richard Graveses.
2. Ibid., F31, Eliza to Miss Hunt, 23 Jan. 1802;   Reel A606 F24, Julia's epilogue.
3. Ibid., Reel A607 F30, M. Graves to Eliza, 23 Feb. 1802.
4. Ibid., M. Graves to Eliza, n.d., but precedes one dated 23 Feb. 1802.
5. Ibid., F31, Charlotte to Miss Hunt, 3 June 1802; Eliza to Miss Hunt, 2 June 1802.
6. Riddell, *Simcoe*, p. 320, Simcoe to Walcot, 1 Aug. 1802.
7. Robertson, *Diary*, p. 409.
8. Devon Record Office, Exeter, Land Tax Assessment Records for Dunkeswell, 1799 and 1803.
9. NA Reel A606 F24, journal 18-26 July 1802.
10. Ibid. Follows journal of July 1802.
11. Riddell, *Simcoe*, p. 319; Macdonald-Stewart Foundation, Montreal, Simcoe Collection, Simcoe to Rev. Pratt, 19 Aug. 1802.
12. NA Reel A605, F7, Simcoe to Walcot, 11 Nov. 1802.
13. The Army List 1803.
14. NA Reel A607 F30, M. Graves to Eliza, 29 Oct. 1803.
15. Ibid., M. Graves to Eliza, 29 July 1803.
16. DCB, vol. 8, biography of Talbot.
17. NA Reel A607 F30, M. Graves to Eliza, 12 Dec. 1803; Sir Henry C.M. Lyte, *A History of Eton College, 1440-1875* (London, 1875) , pp. 332-3, 355.
18. Ibid., M. Graves to Eliza, 29 Jan. 1804.
19. Arnold genealogy.
20. Jackman, *Galloping*, p. 154, poem.
21. NA Reel A607 F30, M. Graves to Eliza, 23 Oct. 1804.
22. Robertson, *Diary*, p. 406.
23. NA Reel A607 F30, M. Graves to Eliza, 1 May 1805; M. Graves to Eliza, 24 July 1805 (1806?).
24. Devon Record Office, Exeter, Land Tax Assessment Records, Awliscombe; references in letters of Miss Burges living in Ashfield, which her niece Frances Head inherited in 1813.
25. NA Reel A607 F30, M. Graves to Eliza, 23 Sept. 1805.

26. Ibid., Reel A605 F7, Simcoe to Elizabeth, Fri. night, 10 Jan. 1805. The year is wrong; he meant 1806. Nelson's funeral was Thurs. 9 Jan. 1806.
27. Ibid., Moira to Simcoe, 8 Mar. 1806.
28. *Devon and Cornwall Notes and Queries,* p. 230, supplied by J. Bastin.
29. NA Reel A607 F30, M. Graves to Eliza, 23 May 1806.
30. Ibid., F31, Eliza to Miss Hunt, 6 Sept. 1806.
31. Robertson, *Diary,* p. 412.
32. NA Reel A607 F31, Charlotte to Miss Hunt, 30 Nov. 1806.
33. Exeter *Flying Post,* 6 Nov. 1806.
34. Robertson, Diary, p. 404.
35. NA Reel A607 F31, Charlotte to Miss Hunt, 30 Nov. 1806.
36. Ibid., F30 n.d., between letters dated Oct. 1804 and Dec. 1803, Margaret Graves to Eliza, 20 Nov. 1806.

Chapter 20: Francis and Mary Anne

1. NA Reel A607 F31, Charlotte to Miss Hunt 30 Nov. 1806.
2. PRO London, Will of J.G. Simcoe, PROB 11/1458; Devon Record Office, land Tax Assessment Records, Dunkeswell 1807 and Awliscombe 1806.
3. NA Reel A607 F31, Eliza to Miss Hunt, 18 Mar. 1807.
4. Ibid., F35, Elizabeth to Eliza, 31st letter in folder; F39 same to same, 3 Mar. n.yr., 39th letter in folder.
5. Ibid., F 30, Mrs. Graves to Eliza, 26 Apr. 1807.
6. Ibid., F31, Eliza to Miss Hunt ?, July 1807.
7. OA, Simcoe Non-Canadian Collection, Reel 14, F.G. Simcoe to his mother, Eton 28 June 1805.
8. Ibid., F.G. Simcoe to his mother, 5, 17 and 27 Mar. 1808.
9. NA Reel A607 F31, Eliza to Miss Hunt, 24 May 1808.
10. OA Simcoe Non-Canadian Collection Reel 14, F.G. Simcoe to his mother, 24 May, 2 June and Thurs. June n. day.
11. Ibid., F.G. Simcoe to his mother, 9, 13, 24 Oct. 1808.
12. Ibid., Moira to Elizabeth, London, 26 Nov. 1808.
13. PRO London, Will of Margaret Graves PROB 12/193 Reel 1495, p. 441,probated 21 Apr. 1809; Robertson, *Diary,* pp. 384-5, will of Mrs. Simcoe.
14. OA, Simcoe Non-Canadian Collection, Reel 14, F.G. Simcoe to his mother,n.d., precedes a letter from Cadiz, 9 Feb. 1809; NA Reel A607 F39, Elizabeth to Harriet C/O Rt. Hon. and Lady I. King, Bedford St., Bath, 2 Dec. 1814.
15. Jackman, *Galloping,* p. 14; Robertson, *Diary,* p. 382.
16. OA, Simcoe Non-Canadian Collection, Reel 14, F.G. Simcoe to his mother, Badajoz, 8 Oct. 1809.
17. NA Reel A607 F31, Charlotte to Miss Hunt, 20 Oct. 1809.
18. Ibid., Eliza to Miss Hunt, 1 Dec. 1809.
19. OA, Simcoe Non-Canadian Collection Reel 14, F.G. Simcoe to his mother, 11 Dec. 1809.
20. NA Reel A607 F31, Eliza to Miss Hunt, 5 Mar. 1811.
21. OA, Simcoe Non-Canadian Collection Reel 14, F.G. Simcoe to his mother, 22 May 1811.
22. NA Reel A607 F33, Harriet Bowdler to Eliza, 5 July 1811; F31, Eliza to Miss Hunt, 11 Aug. 1811.
23. Ibid., F39, F.G. Simcoe to Caroline, Camp near Badajoz, n.d.
24. OA, Simcoe Non-Canadian Collection, Reel 15, F.G. Simcoe to Charlotte, 19 Sept. 1811; C. Flood to George ? at Horse Guards, n.d., follows F.G. Simcoe's letter of 25 Mar. 1812.
25. DNB, biography of George Nugent-Temple, 1st Marquis of Buckingham.
26. OA, Simcoe Non-Collection Collection, Reel 15, George Jenkins to Elizabeth, Badajoz, 9 Apr. 1812.
27. NA Reel A607 F31, Eliza to Miss Hunt, 29 May 1812.

28. Ibid., Eliza to Miss Hunt, ? Aug. 1812.
29. DNB, biography of George Temple-Nugent, 1st Marquis of Buckingham.
30. NA Reel A607 F35, Elizabeth to Eliza, 3 Mar. n.yr., 39th letter in folder.
31. Ibid., F31, Charlotte to Miss Hunt, 11 Aug. 1813.
32. Ibid., F31, Charlotte to Miss Hunt, 20 Aug. 1813.
33. Ibid., Charlotte to Miss Hunt, 11 July 1814.
34. Jackman, *Galloping*, p. 34.
35. NA Reel A607 F39, Eliza to Charlotte, Stowe, 18 Sept. 1814; F31, Eliza to Miss Hunt, Stowe, 4 Oct. 1814.
36. Ibid., F39, Elizabeth to Harriet, C/O Rt. Hon. Mr. and Lady I. King, Bedford St., St. James Sq., Bath, 2 Dec. 1814.
37. Ibid., F32, Eliza to Miss Hunt, 23 Apr. 1815.
38. Ibid., Eliza to Miss Hunt, 20 Oct. 1815.

Chapter 21: Fresh Interests

1. NA Reel A607 F35, Elizabeth to Eliza at Oundle, 20 Oct. 1816. Elizabeth wanted to go to Calais, but could not because of "contrary winds". This was the only reference to a plan to go to the Continent.
2. Ibid., Reel A608 F39, Eliza to Caroline from Kitley, 24 Oct. 1815.
3. Ibid., Reel A607 F36, Eliza from Plymouth to her sisters, 8 Nov. 1815; F34 Eliza from Boulogne to Charlotte 24 Nov. 1815; F32, Eliza from Hotel de l'Europe, Lyons to Miss Hunt, 7 Dec. 1815; F34, Eliza to Elizabeth from Marseilles, 27 Dec. 1815; two letters dated 6 Jan. 1816, Eliza to Charlotte; F32, Eliza to Miss Hunt from Marseilles, 15 Jan. 1816; F34, Eliza from Livorno to Caroline, 1 Apr. n. yr; Eliza from Leghorn to Elizabeth, 4 Apr. 1816; Reel A608 F39, Dundas aboard *Tangiers* to Eliza, 29 Apr. n.yr.
4. Ibid., F32, Harriet to Miss Hunt 9 Apr. 1816.
5. Ibid., F35, Elizabeth from Clapham to Eliza, 3 Oct. 1816.
6. Robertson, *Diary*, p. 366.
7. Ibid., p. 393.
8. Ibid., F35, Elizabeth to Eliza at Oundle, n.d.; F33, Miss Bowdler to Miss Simcoe, C/O Thomas Walcot Esq., 16 Apr. 1817.
9. DNB, biography of Princess Charlotte Augusta.
10. NA Reel A607 F35, Elizabeth to Eliza at Oundle, 8 July n. yr.
11. DNB, biography of Henry Addington Simcoe.
12. NA Reel 607 F32 Sophia from Oundle to Miss Hunt at Exeter, ? Dec. 1818; Charlotte from Oundle to Miss Hunt at Exeter, 18 Feb. 1819.
13. Ibid., Charlotte from Oundle to Miss Hunt at Exeter, 11 Dec. 1819.
14. Ibid., F39, Anne Palmer from Moseley to Harriet, 21 Oct. 1820.
15. Ibid., F32, Eliza from Tor Abbey to Miss Hunt in Exeter, 22 Nov. 1820.
16. Ibid., F35, Elizabeth from Seaton to Eliza at Oundle, 25 Oct. The year seems to be 1824; this is too late for Henry was married in 1822.
17. DNB, biography of Mary Anne Burges.
18. NA Reel A607 F35, Elizabeth to Eliza C/O Miss Nutcombe, Cathedral Yard, Exeter, n.d. The letter refers to Henry having lived in the house.
19. Robertson, *Diary*, p. 386
20. NA Reel A607 F37, Elizabeth to Katherine, C/O Church House, Bromley, Kent, readdressed to the Fanshawes nr. Godstone, Surrey, n.d.
21. Arnold genealogy.

Chapter 22: The New Generation

1. DCB, vol. 8, biography of Thomas Talbot.
2. Arnold genealogy.
3. NA Reel A607 F35, Elizabeth to Eliza at Oundle, n.d.
4. Ibid., Elizabeth to Eliza at Oundle, 20 Oct. 1824.
5. Ibid., F38, Elizabeth from near Launceston to Katherine, 13 Nov n.yr.
6. Ibid., F35, Elizabeth to Eliza at Oundle, 25 Dec. n.yr.

7. T.A. Reed, "The Scaddings", p. 13.
8. Ibid., F35, Elizabeth to Eliza at Wardour Castle, 1 Apr. 1825; F37, Elizabeth at Oundle to Eliza at Wardour Castle, 19 Apr. n.yr.
9. Ibid., Elizabeth at Oundle to Eliza at Wardour Castle, 5 May n.yr.
10. Ibid., Elizabeth at Cheltenham to Eliza, Sun. 6? 1825.
11. The Army List. Head went on half-pay on 18 Aug. 1825 by which time he was already in South America; NA Reel A608 F39, Julia Head to Charlotte and Sophia, 3 Sept. 1825.
12. Ibid., F39, from ? Post, Grosvenor Sq., to Miss Simcoe; F36, Eliza from Wardour Castle to her sisters, 23 Nov. n.yr.
13. Ibid., Reel A607 F35, Elizabeth to Eliza at Oundle, 19 Jan. 1826.
14. Ibid., Elizabeth to Eliza at Oundle, 31 Jan. n.yr.
15. Ibid., Elizabeth to Eliza at Ondle, 22 Feb. n.yr.
16. F.B. Head, *Rough Notes taken during some rapid journeys across the pampas and among the Andies* (London, 1826); NA Reel A607 F35, Elizabeth to Eliza at Ondle, 22 Feb. n. yr.
17. Ibid., Elizabeth from Oundle to Eliza, 5 Apr. n.yr.
18. Ibid., Elizabeth to Eliza at Oundle, 20 Apr. n.yr.
19. Ibid., Elizabeth to Eliza at Ondle, 2 Dec. n.yr.
20. Ibid., Elizabeth to Eliza at Oundle, n.d., 50th letter in folder.
21. Ibid., Elizabeth to Eliza at Oundle, 6 Dec. n.yr.
22. Ibid., Elizabeth to Eliza at Oundle, 3 May n.yr.
23. Arnold genealogy.
24. NA Reel A607 F36, Eliza from Salterton to her sisters n.d., postmarked Penheale. The date of Henry's ordination was sent by Peter Thomas, Assistant Librarian at the Exeter Cathedral Library.

Chapter 23: More Joy in Heaven

1. NA Reel A607 F35, Elizabeth to Eliza at Oundle, Feb. n.yr.
2. Arnold genealogy.
3. DNB, biography of Sir John Kennaway.
4. NA Reel A607 F35, Elizabeth from Escott [sic] to Eliza at Oundle, 26 Nov. 1827.
5. DNB, biography of Henry Addington Simcoe; notes on H.A. Simcoe in The Clergy List 1850, Exeter Cathedral Library, and in Crockford's Clerical Dictionary 1846; Devon Record Office, will of H. A. Simcoe.
6. NA Reel A607 F35, Elizabeth to Eliza, n.d., no place.
7. Martin, "The Simcoes", p. 110.
8. The Army List 1826.
9. Robertson, *Diary*, p. 338.
10. Richard B. Howard, *Colborne's Legacy: Upper Canada College 1829 - 1979* (Toronto, 1979), p. 14.
11. NA Reel A607 F35, Elizabeth to Eliza, C/O Miss Nutcombe, Cathedral Yard, Exeter, n.d.
12. Robertson, *Diary*, pp. 397-8.
13. NA Reel A607 F35, Elizabeth to Eliza, 12 Jan. 1830.
14. Devon Record Office, Land Tax Assessment Records for Hemyock, 1816-1832; Public Record Office, London, PROB 11/1485, will of John Graves Simcoe.
15. NA Reel A607, Katherine to Miss Nutcombe, Cathedral Yard, Exeter, n.d.
16. Ibid., F35, Elizabeth to Eliza, 2 letters, the first to Ugbrooke, n.d.
17. DCB, vol 10, and DNB, biographies of Sir Francis Bond Head.
18. NA Reel A607 F35, Elizabeth to Eliza, n.d., 25th letter in folder.
19. DNB, biography of Bernard Gilpin.
20. NA Reel A607 F39, Elizabeth to Eliza at Wardour, 23 May, n. yr.
21. Robertson, *Diary*, p. 399.
22. NA Reel A607 F35, Elizabeth to Eliza, n.d. or place, 3rd letter in folder.
23. Ibid., Elizabeth to Eliza, C/O Miss Nutcombe, Cathedral Yard, Exeter, 29 Nov. n.yr.
24. Ibid., four letters from Elizabeth to Eliza at Ugbrooke, 21 to 24 in sequence n.yr. or place.
25. Ibid., F37, Elizabeth from Penheale to Katherine, 30 July n.yr.

26. Francis Paget Hett, *Georgina*, Facsimile edition (Sutton West, Ont.: Paget Press, 1978) p. 13.
27. NA Reel A607 F37, Elizabeth from Penheale to Katherine, 30 July n. yr.
28. Ibid., F38, Elizabeth from Bude to Katherine at Pynes, 9 Sept. n.yr.
29. DNB, biography of Henry Addington Simcoe.
30. Silvia Boorman, *John Toronto* (Toronto, 1969), p. 157; NA Reel A607 F35, Elizabeth from Beddgelert to Eliza at Penheale, n.d.
31. Ibid., Elizabeth to Eliza, Sat. night, n.d.
32. Ibid., Elizabeth from Egland to Eliza, n.d.; Drewe genealogy.
33. Arnold genealogy.
34. NA Reel A607 F37, Elizabeth from Penheale, postmark Launceston, to Harriet C/O Sir Stafford Northcote at Torquay.
35. Jackman, *Galloping*, pp. 67-8.
36. Ibid., p. 72.
37. Hett, *Georgina*, pp. 15-6.
38. NA Reel A607 F37, Elizabeth to Katherine, C/O Rev. Archdeacon Harris, Winchester, 12 Apr., postmarked May, Honiton, n. yr.

Chapter 24: Sir Francis and the Rebels of 1837

1. NA Reel A607 F37, Elizabeth to Katherine at Exeter, apparently dated 1839, but the context indicates 1837, the year Henry Scadding left England to begin his ministry in the Canadas.
2. Ibid., Elizabeth to Katherine C/O Rev. Archdeacon Harris, Winchester, postmarked May, Honiton, n.yr.
3. Ibid., F39, Lady Head to Elizabeth, 26 June 1837.
4. Jackman, *Galloping*, pp. 102-3.
5. NA Reel A607 F35, Elizabeth to Eliza at Wardour, 3 July, n. yr.; Elizabeth to Eliza, 8 July Sat. n.yr.
6. Ibid., Elizabeth to Eliza at Buckland, near Ashburton, Sat. n.d.
7. Colin Read, *The Rising in Western Upper Canada: The Duncombe Revolt and After* (Toronto, 1982), p. 59.
8. James FitzGibbon, *An Appeal to the People of the Late Province of Upper Canada* (Montreal, 25 May 1847), p. 10.
9. NA Reel A607 F35, Elizabeth to Eliza, C/O Mrs. Bastard, Buckland, Thurs., n.d.
10. Ibid., Elizabeth to Eliza at Buckland, 22 Jan. n.yr.
11. Ibid., Elizabeth to Eliza, Mon. morning, n.d., 2nd letter in folder. One newspaper referred to the appointment of Sir George Arthur as Head's successor.
12. Mary Beacock Fryer, *Volunteers and Redcoats: Rebels and Raiders* (Toronto, 1987), p. 142.
13. NA Reel A607 F37, Elizabeth from Cheltenham to Katherine at Godstone, 27 May n.yr.
14. Ibid., Elizabeth to Katherine, C/O Rev. Oxenham, Modbury, 4 Nov. n.yr.
15. Ibid., Elizabeth from Leamington to Katherine, 23 Nov. n.yr.
16. Ibid., Elizabeth from Cheltenham to Katherine, 29 Nov., Thursday, n.d.
17. Fryer, *Volunteers*, pp. 103-13.

Chapter 25: The Church Builders

1. Henry Scadding, *Toronto of Old*, F.H. Armstrong, ed. (Toronto, 1987), p.xiv.
2. Robertson, *Diary*, p. 383.
3. NA Reel A607 F37, Elizabeth to Katherine at Modbury, C/O Rev. Oxenham, 2 Mar. n.yr.
4. Ibid., Elizabeth from Coleford to Katherine, Thurs. n.d.
5. Ibid., Elizabeth to Katherine at Penheale, 2 July n.d.
6. Ibid., F39, Elizabeth L. Simcoe to Aunt Caroline, 5 July 1839.
7. Patrick Brode, *Sir John Beverley Robinson: Bone and Sinew of the Compact* (Toronto: The Osgoode Society,1984), p. 217.
8. Hett, *Georgina*, pp. 14, 46-50.
9. Ibid., p. xxi.
10. Ibid., p. 48, quoted from Hugh Sibbald's diary.

11. NA Reel A607 F37, Elizabeth to Katherine from Abergavenny, 16 Sept. n.yr.
12. Ibid., Elizabeth to Katherine from Portland Street, 2 Nov. n.yr.
13. Ibid., F39, Elizabeth from Penheale to Caroline, Sunday n.d.
14. *A Short History of Dunkeswell Abbey*, p. 9.
15. NA Reel A607 F39, Elizabeth to Anne, C/O J. Dumtze Esq., Hemby, Twiston, Thursday evening n.d.
16. Ibid., H. Exeter to Miss Simcoe, from Torquay, 30 June 1841.
17. Ibid., F38, Henry Scadding to Katherine, from the College, Toronto, 4 Dec. 1841.
18. *Short History of Dunkeswell Abbey*, p. 11.
19. NA Reel A607 F35, Elizabeth to Eliza, 19 June n.yr.
20. Ibid., Reel A608 F39, H. Exeter to Miss Simcoe, 1 July 1842.
21. Ibid., Reel A607 F38, Vigil of St. James 1842 to Katherine at Budehaven from Arthur H. Shebeland.
22. Ibid., F37, three letters from Elizabeth to Katherine, 10, 10 and 20 Dec. n. yr.
23. Arnold genealogy.
24. Hett, *Georgina*, p. 48, quoted from Hugh Sibbald's diary.
25. William White of Sheffield, *White's 1850 Devon* (New York, 1968), with a new introduction by W.E. Minchinton, p. 393.
26. Ontario Archives, Robertson-Mackenzie Collection, Correspondence 1798-1944, letter dated 21 Apr. 1844.
27. Hett, *Georgina*, pp. 46, 48. Hett mentioned seven crosses, but the author found thirteen.
28. Arnold genealogy.

Chapter 26: The Best Christian

1. DNB, biography of Henry Addington Simcoe.
2. Hett, *Georgina*, p. 48.
3. DNB, biography of Sir Francis Bond Head.
4. NA Reel A607 F35, Elizabeth from Escot to Eliza, 21 Jan. n. yr; Jackman, *Galloping Head*, Appendix A, p. 153.
5. NA Reel A607 F38, Antoinette de Milanges to Katherine, 22 Feb. n. yr; same to same Sat. 30 June, n. yr. Note, the 30th did not fall n a Saturday in 1847 and Mme de Milanges may have made a mistake.
6. DNB, biography of Sir George Head.
7. NA Reel A607 F38, George Head from Feneton parsonage to Katherine, 16 Aug. 1847.
8. Chris Dracott and Brian Clist, *Hemyock, a village history* (Culm Valley Dairy Company Limited of Hemyock, 1986), p. 8.
9. Arnold genealogy.
10. NA Reel A607 F38, Henry Scadding from Toronto to Katherine, 17 May n.yr.
11. Robertson, *Diary*, p. 404.
12. Ibid., pp. 381, 383-5, 386.
13. Arnold genealogy.
14. Hilary Arnold, from Public Record Office, London.
15. DCB, vol. 11, biography of Pahtahsega (Peter Jacobs Sr., the Clergyman's father.
16. NA Reel A608 F39, John Toronto to Miss Simcoe, 11 Royal Cres., Bath, 27 Mar. 1860.
17. Ibid., Reel A605 F20, letters of Alpheus Todd to Henry Addington Simcoe, 9 June 1861; letters of George Coventry of 31 May and 23 Sept. 1861.
18. Arnold genealogy.
19. Devon Record Office, wills of Eliza and Henry Simcoe; probate data supplied by Hilary Arnold.
20. Queen's York Rangers, *The Colours of the Queen's Rangers*, (Toronto: Fort York Armoury, n.d.) pp. 11-3.
21 Rev. Henry Ward, "A Popular History of Aldwincle [sic]", Northamptonshire Architectural Society, *Reports and Papers of the Architectural Societies in 1864*, p. 251, courtesy of Hilary Arnold.
22. Pine, *The New Extinct Peerage*, Arundell of Wardour.
23. Derek Beales, *From Castlereagh to Gladstone 1815-1885* (Norton Library, New York, 1969), p. 71.

BIBLIOGRAPHY

PRIMARY SOURCES

Unprinted

Drewe Family Genealogy.
     Mr. Francis Drewe of Ticehurst, Sussex, and Broadhembury, Devon, England, sent information that was most useful in identifying the many Drewes mentioned in the letters of Elizabeth Simcoe and Mary Anne Burges.
Simcoe Collection, Devon Archives, Devon Record Office, Exeter.
     Copies are on microfilm in the Public Archives of Canada, Ottawa, Reels A605, A606, A607 and A608.

Simcoe Collection, Ontario Archives, Toronto.
     Part of the collection is on microfilm. The letters from Mary Anne Burges to Elizabeth Simcoe in these archives are B-1-2, microfilm reel 7-531. These pages are missing from Folder 29 of the Devon Archives collection.
     The letters by Francis Simcoe, and some by Elizabeth Gwillim, have been culled from the portion of the Simcoe Collection that does not pertain to Upper Canada. Uncatalogued at the time of writing, the collection is on reels 10 through 16.

Printed

Cruikshank, Brigadier E.A. (ed.). *Simcoe Correspondence.* 5 vols. Toronto, 1923-
    1931.
Exeter *Flying Post.* 6 Nov. 1806.
FitzGibbon, James, *An Appeal to the People of the Late Province of Upper Canada.*
    Montreal, 25 May 1847.
Innis, Mary Quayle (ed.). *Mrs. Simcoe's Diary.* Toronto, 1965.
Robertson, John Ross. (ed.). *The Diary of Mrs. John Graves Simcoe.* First published
    in Toronto, 1911, by William Briggs. Coles' facsimile edition, 1973.

SECONDARY MATERIALS

Austen, Jane. *Letters to her Sister Casandra and Others.* R.W. Chapman (ed.).
    London, 1964.
Beales, Derek. *From Castlereagh to Gladstone 1815-1885.* New York, 1969.
Boorman, Silvia. *John Toronto.* Toronto, 1969.
Brode, Patrick. *Sir John Beverley Robinson: Bone and Sinew of the Compact.* Toronto
    1984.
Burke's *Peerage and Baronetage.* London, 1980 edition.
Devon and Cornwall Notes and Queries. Sent by J.W. Bastin from Devon.
Dictionary of Canadian Biography. Frances G. Halpenny and Jean Hamelin (eds.).
    Toronto, 1966-82.
Dictionary of National Biography. Sir Leslie Stephen and Sir Sidney Lee (eds.)
    London, 1917.

Dunkeswell Abbey Preservation Fund. *A Short History of Dunkeswell Abbey*. Undated pamphlet.

Fowler, Marion. *The Embroidered Tent*. Toronto, 1982.

Fryer, Mary Beacock. *King's Men: the soldier founders of Ontario*. Toronto, 1980.

-----. *Volunteers and Redcoats, Rebels and Raiders: a Military History of the Rebellions in Upper Canada*. Toronto, 1987.

Hett, Francis Paget. *Georgina*. Facsimile edition by Paget Press. Sutton West, Ontario, 1978.

Howard, Richard B. *Colborne's Legacy: Upper Canada College 1829- 1979*. Toronto, 1979.

Jackman, Sydney W. *Galloping Head: a biography of Sir Francis Bond Head 1793- 1875*. London, 1958.

Leavitt, Thad. W. *History of Leeds and Grenville*. Brockville, Ontario, 1879.

Lyte, C.M. *A History of Eton College 1440-1875*. London, 1875.

Martin, Ged. "The Simcoes and their Friends." *Ontario History* vol. 69, no. 2. June 1977.

Morris, James. *Heaven's Command: an Imperial Progress*. Harmondsworth, Middlesex, England, 1973.

Neville, William. *Chronology of the Modern World: 1763-1965*. Harmondsworth, Middlesex, England.

Paul, Sir James Balfour, Lord Lyon King of Arms. *The Scots Peerage*. Edinburgh, 1911.

Pine, L.G. *The New Extinct Peerage* 1884-1971. London: Heraldry Today, 1972.

Queen's York Rangers. *The Colours of the Queen's Rangers*. Pamphlet. Fort York Armoury, Toronto, undated. Ceremony 18 April 1975.

Read, Colin. *The Rising in Western Upper Canada: the Duncombe Revolt and After*. Toronto, 1982.

Reed, T.A. "The Scaddings." Ontario Historical Society *Papers and Records*, vol. 36. 1944.

Riddell, the Hon. William. *The Life of John Graves Simcoe*. Toronto, 1926.

Scadding, Henry. *Toronto of Old*. F. H. Armstrong (ed.) Toronto, 1987.

The Memoirs of Susan Sibbald. Facsimile edition by Paget Press, Sutton West, Ontario, 1980.

Van Steen, Marcus. *Governor Simcoe and his Lady*. Toronto, 1968.

Ward. Rev. Henry. "A Popular History of Aldwincle." Northamptonshire Architectural Society. *Reports and Papers of the Architectural Societies in 1864*.

White, William of Sheffield. *White's 1850 Devon*. With a new introduction by W.F. Minchenton. New York, 1968.

APPENDIX

GENEALOGY OF ELIZABETH POSTHUMA GWILLIM SIMCOE BY HILARY ARNOLD

HER GRANDPARENTS AND THEIR CHILDREN

Paternal

Thomas Gwillim, Elizabeth Simcoe's father, was born at Cotterstock Hall, Northamptonshire, the home of his mother's parents, and baptised at Cotterstock Church on 11 April 1726. Soon afterwards his family removed to his father's ancestral home, Old Court, Whitchurch, in Herefordshire. Thomas had an older sister, Elizabeth Sophia, the "Mistress Gwillim" of Elizabeth Simcoe's Canadian diary to whom she likened the Mother Superior of the convent at Quebec. Another sister, Henrietta Maria, lived until age fifty-eight and died in 1785. These were the two Gwillim aunts who helped to rear Elizabeth Posthuma. Two brothers, Richard Elmes and Jasper, died young. There is a memorial to Jasper who died at age twelve endeavouring to save a friend from drowning in the River Wye. Another sister, Anna Jemima, died on a visit to her Spinckes cousins at Aldwinkle, and was buried in the Spinckes chapel of All Saints' Church there.

Thomas Gwillim Senior inherited the manor of Whitchurch, Herefordshire, from his father, also Thomas Gwillim. The younger Thomas and his wife built a walled enclosure in the churchyard of St. Dubricius' Church to hold their family tombs. How he met his wife, Elizabeth Steward, who lived so far from Herefordshire, is not known. St. Dubricius' Church is still in use, but the inscriptions on the Gwillim graves are now barely legible. Old Court is an hotel.

Thomas Gwillim Sr. of Old Court, Whitchurch, Herefordshire: mar. Elizabeth Steward at Cotterstock, 5 Aug. 1721; died at Whitchurch in 1766; bur. St. Dubricius' Church, Whitchurch.

Elizabeth Steward of Cotterstock Hall, Northamptonshire; (sister of Jemima, mother of Elizabeth Spinckes); mar. Thomas Gwillim Sr. at Cotterstock, 5 Aug. 1721; died in July 1767; bur. St. Dubricius' Church, Whitchurch.

Children of Thomas Gwillim Sr. and Elizabeth Steward

1.   Elizabeth Sophia: bap. at Cotterstock 15 Oct. 1724; died at Whitchurch 6 Aug. 1800.

2. Thomas: bap. at Cotterstock Hall, Northamptonshire, his mother's home, 11 Apr. 1726; died in Germany probably in late January 1762.

3. Henrietta Maria: no records of her birth or baptism have been found, but she died unmarried at Whitchurch on 25 June aged 58, suggesting she was born in 1727.

4. Richard Elmes: bap. 23 Feb. 1729 at Whitchurch and died young.

5. Jasper: bap. 22 Feb. 1731 at Whitchurch; drowned at age 12 trying to rescue a friend from drowning in the River Wye 24 June 1743.

6. Anna Jemima: bap. 3 Feb. 1736 at Whitchurch; died of smallpox on a visit to Aldwinkle and was bur. there on 28 Nov. 1757 aged 21. (Note: NA Reel A607 F35, 65th letter in folder. In this letter to Eliza, 31 Jan. n.yr., Elizabeth wrote that she thought Anna Jemima was 17.)

Maternal

Elizabeth Spinckes, Elizabeth Simcoe's mother, was baptised along with her twin sister Jemima on 15 April 1723. Twins were usually baptised at birth, as their chances of survival were not great and the parish register records the burial of Jemima two days later. Her younger brother Elmes and sister Catherine also died in infancy. Margaret Spinckes, baptised on 24 February 1727, was the only sister to survive. Elizabeth gave birth (to Elizabeth Posthuma) at age thirty-nine sometime around 20 September 1762, and was buried on the 23rd. Her tomb slab still lies in the Spinckes chapel with those of her parents and grandparents in All Saints' Church, Aldwinkle.

Elmes Spinckes and Jemima Steward were the parents of Elizabeth Spinckes. Elmes inherited the manor of All Saints' Aldwinkle from his father of the same name in October 1721. Elmes Spinckes Senior was baptised at Orton Longueville (two miles southwest of Peterborough, in Huntingdonshire) in 1661 but his father soon retired to the Elmes ancestral home at Warmington, three miles northeast of Oundle. Elmes inherited £150 at age eight on his father's death. The money would have been useful in paying the premium for his apprenticeship, in 1677, to Henry Lamb, a London goldsmith. Elmes completed his seven-year apprenticeship and was admitted as Freeman of the Goldsmiths' Guild in 1686. He joined the firm of J. Spink and son (who claimed him as a "cousin" but no relationship has been established). He had enough money to be able to buy the manor of All Saints at Aldwinkle in 1699.

Elmes Junior married Jemima Steward, youngest daughter of the Steward family of Cotterstock Hall. On his death in 1749 he bequeathed his property to his widow, and on her death in May 1776 it was divided between his daughter Margaret Spinckes Graves and granddaughter Elizabeth

Posthuma Gwillim (later Simcoe). All Saints Aldwinkle, the latter's birthplace, was demolished, probably by the next owner, Lord Lilford, but the beautiful medieval church still stands although it is no longer in use. All saints' is now in the care of the Redundant Churches Fund. Inside is a plaque to John Dryden, poet laureate, who was born in the Old Rectory opposite the church in 1631.

Elmes Spinckes: born ca. 1697, just before his father moved to the manor of All Saints' Aldwinkle; bur. Aldwinkle, 14 May 1749, aged 54.

Jemima Steward of Cotterstock Hall, bap. 25 Feb. 1698 (sister of Elizabeth, mother of Thomas Gwillim Jr.); bur. Aldwinkle, 31 May 1776, aged 78.

Children of Elmes Spinckes and Jemima Steward

1. and 2. twin daughters, Jemima and Elizabeth; Jemima bap. Aldwinkle 15 Apr. 1723; bur. 17 Apr. 1723. Elizabeth bap. Aldwinkle 15 Apr. 1723; mar. her first cousin, Thomas Gwillim Jr., 14 Jan. 1750 at St. Dubricius' Church, Whitchurch; bur. at Aldwinkle, 23 Sept. 1762, aged 39.

3. Elmes: bap. Aldwinkle, 24 Feb. 1724; bur. 19 Mar. 1724.

4. Margaret: bap. Aldwinkle, 16 Mar. 1727; mar. Admiral Samuel Graves (1713-1787), 14 June 1769, at Aldwinkle; died at Bath, Nov./Dec. 1808 (Plymouth Navy Records).

5. Catherine: bap. Aldwinkle, 24 Nov. 1728; bur. 8 Aug. 1731.

Parents and Brothers of John Graves Simcoe

The early records on the Simcoe family are much sketchier than on the Gwillim-Spinckes familles. John Graves Simcoe's parents were married in Bath Abbey on 8 August 1747 by licence

Father: Captain John Simcoe R.N.; bap. 28 Nov. 1710; lived at Cotterstock 1748-1756; shown in Bath Abbey marriage records as commander of His Majesty's ship *Prince Edward*; was commander of the *Pembroke* when he died off Anticosti in May 1759 while serving with Wolfe's expedition to capture Quebec.

Mother: Katherine Stamford; described in the Bath Abbey marriage records as a spinster of the parish of Walcot (or Walcott), Bath, Somerset; died in Aug. 1776, probably in Northumberland while visiting some of her in-laws.

Children of Captain John Simcoe and Katherine Stamford

1. Pawlett William: bap. at Cotterstock 29 May 1750; but. 28 Apr. 1750.

2. John: bur. 1751.

3. John Graves: born at Cotterstock 25 Feb. 1752; bap. at St. Andrew's Church, Cotterstock, 5 Mar. 1752; mar. Elizabeth Posthuma Gwillim at Buckerell, Devon, 30 Dec. 1782; died at Exeter 26 Oct. 1806; bur. Wolford Chapel.

4. Percy William: born at Cotterstock 1754; drowned in River Exe near Exeter in 1764.

Marriage of EPG to JGS — 30 Dec. 1782 at Buckerell, Devonshire.

Elizabeth Posthuma Gwillim: bap. 22 Sept. 1762 at Aldwinkle, Northamptonshire; died at Wolford Lodge, Devon, 17 Jan. 1850; bur. Wolford Chapel.

John Graves Simcoe: born 25 Feb. 1752 at Cotterstock, Northamptonshire; bap. Cotterstock 5 Mar. 1752; died at Exeter, 26 Oct. 1806; bur. Wolford Chapel.

Children of John Graves Simcoe and Elizabeth Posthuma Gwillim

1. Eliza: born at Exeter, 28 Jan. 1784; bap. at Dunkeswell, 1 Sept. 1784; died at Bath. 12 Aug. 1865; estate valued at £30,000 when proved at Honiton by her nephew Samuel Palmer Simcoe and Sir John Taylor Coleridge.

2. Charlotte: born 18 Aug. 1785; bap. at Dunkeswell, 3 Sept. 1785; died at Leamington Priors, 18 July 1842

3. Henrietta Maria (Harriet): bap. at Dunkeswell, 24 Apr. 1787; died at Wolford Lodge, 16 Mar. 1845.

4. Caroline: bap. at Dunkeswell, 27 Nov. 1788; died at 11 Royal Crescent, Bath, 14 Sept. 1858; estate valued at under £18,000; no executor named.

5. Sophia Jemima: bap. at Dunkeswell, 23 Oct. 1789; died at Bath, 11 July 1864; estate valued at less than £16,000; all her executors may have died by then; letters of administration were granted to her brother Henry Addington Simcoe.

6. Francis Gwillim: born at Wolford 4 June 1791; bap. at Dunkeswell, 17 July 1791; killed in action at Badajoz, Spain, 6 Apr. 1812.

7.   Katherine I: born at Newark (Niagara-on-the-Lake, Ontario) Canada, 6 Jan. 1793; died at York (Toronto) Canada, 19 Apr. 1794.

8.   John Cornwall: born at Wolford Lodge, 7 July 1789; bap. at Dunkeswell, 2 Aug. 1798; died at Wolford, 20 Mar. 1799; bur. Wolford Chapel, 23 Mar. 1799 (Reel A607 F30, Mrs. Graves to Eliza, 31 Mar. 1799, condolences on the loss of her "amiable little brother").

9.   Henry Addington: born at Plymouth 28 Feb. 1800; bap. at Dunkeswell, 2 June 1801; mar. 1st Anne, daughter of Rev. Edward Palmer of Moseley, Worcestershire, 8 Feb. 1822; 2nd Emily, daughter of Rev. Horace Mann of Mawgan/St. Martin, Cornwall, 4th quarter 1842; Henry purchased the manor of Penheale and inherited Wolford in Devon and Old Court, Herefordshire. He died at Penheale, 15 Nov. 1868.

10.   Katherine II: born at Wolford, 23 Mar. 1801; bap. at Dunkeswell, 3 June 1801; died at Bath, 14 Feb. 1861; estate valued at £18,000; will proved at Bristol by Mary Vowler, her niece and wife of John Nicholson Vowler of Leawood, Bridestowe, Devon, and her nephew Philip Francis Simcoe of Penheale House, Cornwall.

11.   Anne (sometimes written Ann): born at Wolford 31 July 1804; "received into church" 30 July 1805; mar. at Paddington, 12 Jan. 1854 William Allford; lived in Herefordshire, died in 2nd quarter of 1877; will never proved, and she may have left everything to her husband.

Elizabeth Simcoe's Grandchildren
Children of Henry Addington Simcoe and Anne Palmer Simcoe

1.   Henry Walcot: born at Moseley, Worcestershire, 31 Jan. 1823; B.A. Oxon. 1845; died unmar. on Madeira, 31 Jan. 1848, aged 25.

2.   Anne Eliza: bap. 7 Sept. 1825 (Dunkeswell Parish Register); mar. 22 June 1847 Sedley Bastard Marke of Woodhill, Cornwall; died 24 Apr. 1869; left issue. Note: Olive Ann, daughter of Anne Eliza and Sedley Marke Bastard, m. Rev. George Linton. Their eldest son, Arthur Henry Linton, inherited Wolford Lodge from his uncle, Capt. John Kennaway Simcoe. A.H. Linton Simcoe was the last owner of the original Wolford Lodge which was sold in 1924.

3.   John Kennaway: born 26 June 1825; bap. 10 Nov. 1825; captain in Royal Navy and J.P.; mar. Mary, daughter of Colonel Basil Jackson of Glewstone Court, Herefordshire, 13 Mar. 1867; inherited and lived at Wolford Lodge; died 20 Mar. 1891.

4.   Mary Northcote: bap. at Egloskerry 4 Aug. 1827; mar. John Vowler of Parnacott, Devon, 16 Apr. 1850; died 6 Oct. 1890; left issue.

5.　Elizabeth Lethbridge: bap. at Egloskerry, 28 Sept. 1828; mar. 1st Lt.-Gen. Willoughby Trevelyan of Neufaigue, Perth, Scotland, 20 Sept. 1859; Trevelyan died in 1871; mar. 2nd. Rev. John Burton, Provost of St. Ninian's Cathedral, Perth, Scotland; died 8 July 1885; no issue.

6.　Samuel Palmer: born 5 Apr. 1830; bap. at Egloskerry, 12 Apr. 1830; attended Wadham College, Oxford, settled at Penheale; died 1899.

7.　Lydia Hannah: born 1832; mar. Rev. Francis Charles Cole, vicar of Sutton Greywell, Hampshire, 3 Oct. 1861; left issue.

8.　Philip Francis; born 5 Feb. 1834; bap. Egloskerry, 22 June 1834; B.A. Oxon. 1858 (Wadham College), J.P. for Cornwall; died 12 Oct. 1885.

9.　Paul Creed Gwillim: born 30 Sept. 1835; bap. Egloskerry, 25 Feb. 1837; attended Wadham College, Oxford; died 17 Feb. 1875.

Children of Henry Addington Simcoe and Emily Mann Simcoe

1.　Emily: bap. at Egloskerry, 22 Dec. 1845; became a Church of England nun and Mother Emily Clare, Mother Superior of the Wantage Sisterhood at Poona, India.

2.　Catherine Louisa Beatrice: born 1st quarter 1851, registered at Launceston, Cornwall; mar. 1st General Henry Edward Doherty, who died 15 Sept. 1885; 2nd. on 14 Dec. 1887 John Canning Doherty, J.P. of Newstown, Co. Carlow, Ireland.

Other Antecedents: The Creeds, Pickerings and Montagus

The Stewards and the Creeds

Elmes Steward, Elizabeth Simcoe's maternal great grandfather, married Elizabeth Creed. Elmes was a wealthy hunting squire who inherited Northamptonshire estates at Pattishall from his father and Cotterstock Hall from his uncle, William Elmes. His wife, Elizabeth Creed, was probably born in London before her parents moved to Oundle. She became a lady-in-waiting at the court of William and Mary. The couple may have met at court, as they were married in London at the fashionable church of St. Margaret's, Westminster, on 26 July 1693. Like most young women, Elizabeth went to her mother's home for her first confinement. Her eldest daughter, also Elizabeth, was born at Oundle in August 1694, but her two younger daughters, Ann and Jemima, were born at her own home, Cotterstock Hall, in 1696 and 1698.

Elmes Steward acted as Sheriff of Northamptonshire in 1700. He died in 1724, and in his will he ordered that all of his estates had to be sold. His widow, unmarried daughter Anne Steward, married daughter and her husband (Elizabeth and Thomas Gwillim Senior) with their two children, removed to Old Court, Whitchurch. Elizabeth Steward died on 17 January 1743 and was buried in a finely carved tomb in the centre of the Gwillim enclosure in St. Dubricius' churchyard. The inscription setting out her genealogy, of which she was inordinately proud, reads:

In Memory of that excellent Lady Mrs. Elizabeth Stuart, who died on 17th January 1743 aged 71 years. She was widow of Elmes Stuart Esq. Daughter of John Creed Esq., secretary of Tangiers to King Charles II, Grand-daughter of Sir Gilbert Pickering, Bart., Great Grand-daughter of Sir Sidney Montague, Knt., Master of Requests to King Charles I who was father of Edward, Earl of Sandwich and of Lady Pickering.

Spelling varied in the eighteenth century, so that Steward was sometimes written "Stuart" (like the Royal family). Cotterstock Hall has not been greatly altered since the Stewards' time. It is in private hands and not open to the public. St. Andrew's Church, Cotterstock, where Thomas Gwillim and John Graves Simcoe were baptised, contains a carved memorial to Captain John Simcoe, R.N. The church is locked, but the key may be obtained in the village.

The Creeds and Pickerings

Little is known of the origins of John Creed, Elizabeth Simcoe's great-great grandfather. Samuel Pepys paints a vivid picture of him in his Diary when both men worked at the Admiralty. He was "as shrewd and cunning a man as any in England", and "not to be too much trusted". John Creed replaced his brother, Richard, who had been one of Cromwell's civil servants, and who deemed it safer to disappear from public life after Cromwell's death. In March 1660, Samuel Pepys was appointed Secretary and John Creed Treasurer to the Generals of the Fleet in succession to Richard. They accompanied Edward Montagu to The Hague in May 1660 to bring back Charles II at the Restoration of the Monarchy. Pepys spent a long time helping Creed out of a financial scrape when Creed had been making a profit for himself. Pepys believed that Creed was worth £10,000, but that must have been an exaggeration. However, he was in a position to lend money to the Montagus (now Lord and Lady Sandwich) to help pay for the remodelling of Hinchingbrooke House. Pepys recorded the vain efforts of John Creed to find a wife until he made his addresses to Lord Sandwich's niece, Mistress Betty Pickering. "To think that he should have this devilish presumption to aim at a lady so near to my Lord!" (Pepys was a distant relation of Lord Sandwich.)

Elizabeth (Betty) Pickering was the daughter of Sir Gilbert and Lady Elizabeth Pickering. Pepys recorded the parents' efforts to find a wife for their son John to gain a dowry which would "make a portion for Mistress

Betty." Pepys described her as being "a very well bred and comely lady but fat", and "she is not over-handsome, though a good lady and one that i love." Despite Pepys' objections the couple were married at Titchmarsh in September 1668 and lived first in London, but later moved to Oundle, Northamptonshire, to the house now known as Cobthrone. They had ten children, only five of whom survived to maturity. Two of them married — Elizabeth who married Elmes Steward, and John Creed Junior whose last descendant was William Walcot of Oundle, a friend and distant relative of the Simcoe family. When Walcot died unmarried in 1827, Walcot made Henry Addington Simcoe his heir.

Mrs. Elizabeth (Pickering) Creed is believed to have learnt to paint in the studio of Sir Peter Lely, Court Painter. A small sketch of her hangs on the wall of Canons Ashby, home of a relation, Sir John Dryden. She is credited with decorating one room of Canons Ashby with *trompe d'oeuil* marble columns and panelling, and other work is ascribed to her there and in the house and the church. Her work also survives in the chapel at Ashton near Oundle, and she painted many memorial inscriptions to members of her family in Titchmarsh Church. She may also have painted the picture of ships at Cobthorne as a reminder of her husband's time at the Admiralty and the part he played in the Restoration of Charles II. Cobthorne is in private hands and not open to the public, but Canons Ashby, where so much of Elizabeth Creed's work is to be seen, belongs to the National Trust, and can be visited. Her memorials also survive at Titchmarsh Church. The Walcot family home in Oundle is now the Water Board Offices.

The Gwillim - Walcot Link

William Walcot of Oundle also owned an estate at Titchmarsh, and both were often visited by Mrs. Simcoe and her daughters. Walcot was a second cousin of both Mrs. Simcoe's parents, Thomas Gwillim Junior and Elizabeth Spinckes. Their common ancestors were John Creed and Elizabeth (Betty) Pickering.

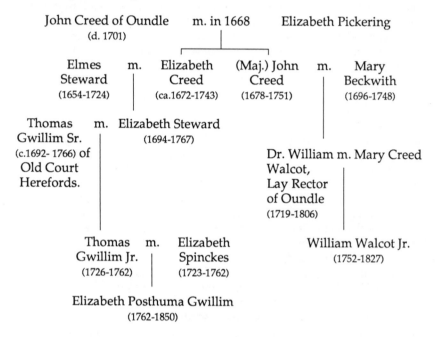

John Creed of Oundle   m. in 1668   Elizabeth Pickering
(d. 1701)

Elmes   m.   Elizabeth   (Maj.) John   m.   Mary
Steward   Creed   Creed   Beckwith
(1654-1724)   (ca.1672-1743)   (1678-1751)   (1696-1748)

Thomas   m.   Elizabeth Steward
Gwillim Sr.   (1694-1767)
(c.1692- 1766) of
Old Court   Dr. William m. Mary Creed
Herefords.   Walcot,
                 Lay Rector
                 of Oundle
                 (1719-1806)

Thomas   m.   Elizabeth   William Walcot Jr.
Gwillim Jr.   Spinckes   (1752-1827)
(1726-1762)   (1723-1762)

Elizabeth Posthuma Gwillim
(1762-1850)

The Pickerings and Montagus (Elizabeth Simcoe's Great Great Great Grandparents)

Sir Gilbert Pickering inherited the manor of Titchmarsh, Northamptonshire, from his father. Like many of the local gentry, he was a keen supporter of Parliament during the Civil War, and he was one of the judges appointed in 1648 to try King Charles I. He was astute enough to attend only two sittings, and he did not sign the death warrant. By 1655 he was appointed Lord Chamberlain to Oliver Cromwell, and he continued in that office; later, John Dryden served as his secretary. Pickering married Elizabeth Montagu, a sister of Edward Montagu, and together they had twelve children, including Mistress Betty. By December 1659, Sir Gilbert's political career was over. At the Restoration of Charles II his close involvement with Cromwell led to the likelihood of his being condemned to death. His brother-in-law (now Lord Sandwich) spoke up for him in the House of Lords. He was pardoned but banned from public office, and he rusticated to Titchmarsh.

Mrs. Simcoe makes one reference to Sir Gilbert in her Canadian Diary, in May 1793. By that time the Gwillims seem to have been pretending ignorance of their ancestors' strong support of Parliament and claiming relationship to the Royal Stuarts. Margaret Graves wrote to her great-niece Eliza Simcoe about a Miss Penderell, descendant of the family who helped hide Charles II after the battle of Worcester:

Miss Pendrille is a great favourite with your aunt Gwillim and used, when your mother and Miss Smith was at Ross with your two aunts, to walk out with them and guard them through the woods and over rocks, but I never heard that she did it merely on account of your mother's being a descendant of the Stuarts and that therefore she looked upon herself to have an hereditary right to protect all the line of Stuart. (NA Reel 607 F30, Mrs. Graves to Eliza n.d.)

Elizabeth Montagu was the only daughter of Sir Sydney Montagu, who married Paulina Pepys (great aunt to Samuel Pepys). Sir Sydney lived at Barnwell Manor until 1625, when his three-year-old son and heir drowned in the moat of the old castle and the grieving parents accepted his brother's offer of Hinchingbrooke House, Cambridgeshire (recently bought from the Cromwells). Later another son, Edward Montagu, was born and he inherited Hinchingbrooke House. Edward married Jemima Crew, and thus introduced the name "Jemima" into the family, which continued in use until Mrs. Simcoe's fifth daughter was given it. One of Edward Montagu's grandsons, also Edward, married Elizabeth Robinson who became the famous Mrs. Montagu who invited intellectual ladies to her "bluestocking" parties. In 1793, Mrs. Simcoe wrote asking Mrs. Montagu to be a godmother to her baby Katherine, born in Canada.

Hinchingbrooke House is now a school and open to the public on certain summer afternoons. Boughton House, the ancestral home of the Montagus, remains in the hands of their descendants, and is sometimes open to the public in the summer. In Devon, Wolford Lodge was pulled down in the 1920s; Hembury Fort House is now a home for elderly people. The Dunkeswell and Buckerell parish churches continue in use. The house where General Simcoe died was hit by a German bomb during World War II, but a memorial plaque marks its position in the Close at Exeter.

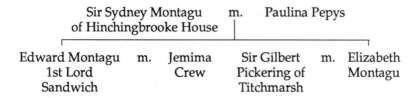

Sir Edward Montagu of Boughton House

Sir Sydney Montagu   m.   Paulina Pepys
of Hinchingbrooke House

Edward Montagu m. Jemima   Sir Gilbert m. Elizabeth
1st Lord   Crew   Pickering of   Montagu
Sandwich   Titchmarsh

Relationship of John and Elizabeth Creed to the Stewards

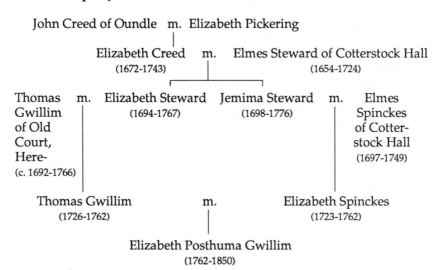

John Creed of Oundle m. Elizabeth Pickering

Elizabeth Creed m. Elmes Steward of Cotterstock Hall
(1672-1743)   (1654-1724)

Thomas m. Elizabeth Steward Jemima Steward m. Elmes
Gwillim   (1694-1767)   (1698-1776)   Spinckes
of Old   of Cotter-
Court,   stock Hall
Here-   (1697-1749)
(c. 1692-1766)

Thomas Gwillim   m.   Elizabeth Spinckes
(1726-1762)   (1723-1762)

Elizabeth Posthuma Gwillim
(1762-1850)

Knowing the part her ancestors had played in affairs of state must surely have contributed to Elizabeth Simcoe's self-confidence. She had only to read the inscription on her great grandmother's tomb at Whitchurch to see her pedigree. Yet her wealth no doubt reinforced this feeling of confidence, too.

SOMERVILLE - BURGES GENEALOGY

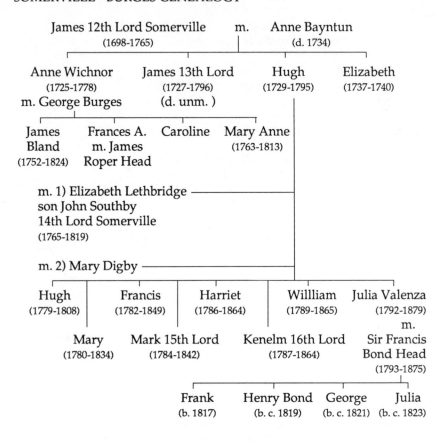

James 12th Lord Somerville   m.   Anne Bayntun
(1698-1765)   (d. 1734)

Anne Wichnor	James 13th Lord	Hugh	Elizabeth
(1725-1778)	(1727-1796)	(1729-1795)	(1737-1740)
m. George Burges	(d. unm.)		

James Bland	Frances A. m. James Roper Head	Caroline	Mary Anne
(1752-1824)			(1763-1813)

m. 1) Elizabeth Lethbridge
son John Southby
14th Lord Somerville
(1765-1819)

m. 2) Mary Digby

Hugh	Francis	Harriet	Willliam	Julia Valenza
(1779-1808)	(1782-1849)	(1786-1864)	(1789-1865)	(1792-1879)
				m.
Mary	Mark 15th Lord	Kenelm 16th Lord		Sir Francis
(1780-1834)	(1784-1842)	(1787-1864)		Bond Head
				(1793-1875)

Frank	Henry Bond	George	Julia
(b. 1817)	(b. c. 1819)	(b. c. 1821)	(b. c. 1823)

HEAD-BURGES GENEALOGY

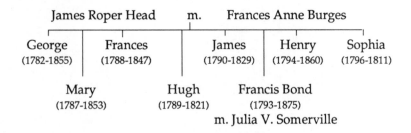

James Roper Head   m.   Frances Anne Burges

George	Frances	James	Henry	Sophia
(1782-1855)	(1788-1847)	(1790-1829)	(1794-1860)	(1796-1811)

Mary	Hugh	Francis Bond
(1787-1853)	(1789-1821)	(1793-1875)
		m. Julia V. Somerville

INDEX

Numbers in **boldface** indicate illustration.

Abergavenny, church at, 229
Acland, Sir Thomas, 191, 203
Addington, Henry, see Lord Sidmouth
Addison, Rev. Robert, 64
Aitken, Alexander, surveyor, 90, 157
Agricultural Society, at Newark, 157
"Ague", at Newark, 85; at Kingston, 141; at Queenston, 147
Aldwinkle, Northamptonshire (birthplace of EPS), manor at, 9, 10, 12, 13, 15, 16, 24; sale of, 178, 179, 180; 208, 238; EPS' birthplace demolished, 240
Allford, William, marriage to Anne Simcoe, 236
American Revolution, 20-22
Amiens, Peace of, 176, 178
André, Major John, 206, 231
Anglican Church (Church of England), 10, 13-14, 36, 60, 64, 76, 90, 157; evangelical movement within, 19, 209, 240; interest of Simcoe women in, 203; progress of in Upper Canada, 205, 219, 236-7; Simcoe daughters' interest in, 229, 236
Arthur, Sir George, 7th lieutenant governor, 220, 222, 223; at Penheale, 229, 230; 233, 234
Arundell, James E., 9th Lord, 133, 180, 196, 207, 208, 212; death of, 216
Arundell, Mary Christine, Lady, 133, 180, 196. 207, 208, 212, 220
Ashbridge family, 157
Ashfield (now Awliscombe House), M.A. Burges purchases, 183; 184, 192, 194, 195, 208, 218, 219, 221, 223, 224, 226. 234. 239
Austen, Jane, 7-8
Awliscombe Parish, Devonshire, 27, 76

Baby, Dell Marie-Anne, 48, 49, 50, 110, 164
Baby, François, 48, 49, 50, 164
Baby, James (Jacques), 39, 62

Badajoz, Spain, sieges of, 191, 192, 193, 203, 232
Bailey, John, EPS' servant, 173, 182; account of JGS' funeral, 186; 199, 214, 215, 235
Baldwin, Robert, 234
Ballard, Capt. Samuel James, R.N., 161, 165, 166
Barnard, Mr., and the Enclosure Commission, 150; 155
Bastard, Edward, 155, 197, 221
Bastard, Edward R.P., 197
Bastard, John Pollexfen, 188; JGS' trustee, 188; 197; death of, 198
Bastard, Mrs. John P., 197, 199, 200
Bateaux, description of, 51; 53, 59, 108, 162
Bath, Somerset, 16, 22; Mrs. Graves moves to, 75, 76; 79, 81, 96, 97, 98; 99, 169, 180, 183, 215; Simcoe sisters move to, 236
Beckwith, Col. George, 110, 111
Belmont House (Caldwell home), 34, 109, 110, 111, 112, **116**, 138, 163
Berczy, William, and settlers, 106, 147-8
Black bass, in Lake Simcoe, 158
Black Prince, tomb in Canterbury Cathedral
Border raids, see Upper Canadian Rebellions, 1837
Boston Tea Party, 20
Bouchette, Capt. Joesph, 88
Bourchier, Commander James O'Brien, 228
Bowdler, Harriet, 97, 101, 192, 196, 201; death of, 214
Brant, Joesph, Mohawk war chief, EPS' describes, 69; 71-2; Simcoe visits home of, 72; 161; death of, 189
Brant, Mary (Molly), 86, 106, 141
British Museum, 206
British North America, provinces of, 34
Broadhembury, Devonshire, 64
Brock, Gen. Isaac, 192-3; captures Detroit, 194
Bruyere, Capt. Ralph H., 168
Buckerell, Devonshire, 19, 24, 27, 57, 78
Buckingham, George Grenville, 1st Marquis of, 30, 50; tapestry donated by, 67; 72, 142; donates instruments to Queen's Rangers band, 74; befriends EPS, 189; death of, 194
Buckingham, Elizabeth, Marchioness of, 35; death of, 193
Buckingham, Richard Lord, 196

Buckland in the Moor, 197, 222, 222
Bude, Cornwall, EPS at missionary meeting, 217
Budleigh Salterton, Simcoes' cottage at, 184, 203, 206, 209, 210, 213, 217
Buenos Aires, Heads at, 208, 209
Bull, Dr. John, canon residentiary, 210
Burges, Frances Anne, see Frances Anne Head
Burges genealogy, 264, 265
Burges, Sir James Bland, 17, 30, 32, 35; JGS' letter to, 63; 79, 90, 94, 100, 101, 102, 131, 137, 152, 154, 155-6, 175, 194; at M.A. Burges' funeral, 195, 202; death of, 205
Burges, Mary Anne, 6, 16-18, 22, 24, 26, 27; moves to Tracey House, 27; 28, 31, 32, 35; miniature of EPS by, 37, 169; journals of to EPS, 38, 39, 53-5; fear of Mrs. Graves, 56-7; on North American silkworm, 58; 65-6, 71, 73, 74-5; reports to EPS, 76-84; comments on mosquitoes, 77; pleased to receive installment from EPS, 78; sells stories, 79; on high-waisted gowns, 80, 130, 153; holds vigil, 83; part of journal in Ontario Archives, 84; on death of Katherine Simcoe, 94 ; reports to EPS, 95-102; identifies trilium, 95; visits Mrs. Graves, 97-8, 100-01, 131; plants seeds, 100; author, *Cavern of Death*, 100, 102; as "Mrs." Burges, 101; quarrel with Mrs. Graves, 101; orders clothes for Simcoes, 129-31; becomes Julia Somerville's guardian, 135-7; sends marmalade to EPS, 133, 135; letter from JGS, 134; difficulties with Julia, 149, 152; suitor, 149; has etchings made of EPS' sketches, 150; severe headaches of, 152; EPS sends fur tippet to, 154; grave robbing story, 155; inheritance from 13th Lord Somerville, 156; 167, 169; book *The Progress of the Pilgrim Good Intent* printed anonymously, 175, 183, with M.A. Burges' name on it, 202; 176, 181, 184, 185, 190, 191; health failing, 192; 194; death of, 195, 233
Burlington Bay, 69, 71, **121**, 142
Burrows, Joseph, "Borows", 227

Butler, Col. John, 63, 68; death of, 159
Butterfly, 127
Bythorne, manor of, 237
Bywood, manor of, 178, 179

Calais, EPS tries to visit, 206
Caldwell, Ann, Mrs. Henry, 34, 48, 104, 106, 109, 163
Caldwell, Henry, 34, 49, 110, 131, 163
Cambridge University, 180, 196, 216, 219
Campbell, Lady Charlotte, 80, 99
Campbell, Maj. William, 106, 142-43
Campbell, Mrs. William, 143
Canada Act, or Bill, 33, 34, 48, 49
Canoe, gift of Northwest Company, 91; from York to Newark in, 142-3; 162; at Wolford Lodge, 170
Canise, the Ojibway, 89, 91
Canise, the younger, 91
Canvas houses, 35; erected at Newark, 67; at York, 142, 147
Capital, see London, Upper Canada
Carey, William, Bishop of Exeter, 210
"Carioles",113, 139, 157, 170
Carleton, Sir Guy, see Lord Dorchester
Carleton Island, 61, 89
Carleton Thomas (Dorchesters' son), death of, 110, 111
Carleton, Miss (Dorchesters' daughter), 111, 112
Caroline of Brunswick, see Princess of Wales
Cartwright, Richard, 61, 62, 64, 141
Carey's house, 140
Cascades Rapids, 59, 108
Castle Frank, 90, 92, 127, 142, 158-9, 161; vandalised, 181; burnt down, 213
Catholic emancipation, 172, 174, 176, 188, 194, 209, 212-3; Catholic Relief Bill of 1829, 213; 224
Cedars Rapids, 59, 138, 162
Charlotteville, Lake Erie, JGS' intended naval base, 147
Chastellux, Marquis de, JGS' anger over, 28
Château de Ramezay, Montreal, 52
Château St. Louis, Quebec City, 48, 110, 111, 163, 164
Cheltenham, spa, EPS visits, 207, 216, 221, 224; and the J.B. Robinsons, 226
Chimney Island, 60, 61

Chippawa, 64, 104, 145, 146
Christie, Gen. Gabriel, 163
Cistercian order, 23, 175
Clarence, Duke of (William IV), 214
Clarke, Gen. Alured, 47
Clarke, Rev. John, rector of Dunkeswell, 199, 207, 213, 216, 220, 221, 222, 224; death of, 231, 235
Clarke, Mrs. John, 207, 221
Clifford, Eleanor Mary, Lady, 133, 179, 185, 187, 207, 212; death of, 218
Clifford, Charles, 6th Baron of Chudleigh, 133, 179, 207, 212; death of, 214
Clifford, Lucy (daughter of Lord and Lady C.), 202
Clifton, Somerville house at, 99, 130, 134, 135
Close, Rev. Francis, 224
Colborne, Sir John, 5th lieutenant governor, 213, 221, 224
Coleridge, Francis George, EPS' executor, 235
Coleridge, Capt. James, 176
Coleridge, James Duke, 176
Coleridge, Sir John Taylor, 176; EPs' executor, 235
Collins, childrens' nurse, 52, 103, 108, 112, 138, 142
Colonial Advocate, newspaper, 205, 216
Cook, Capt. James, 35
Coplestone, Rev. John, 95, 140, 155, 170, 188
Cornwallis, Lord Charles, 21, 184
Coteau du Lac, 59
Cotterstock, Northampton-shire, birthplace of JGS, 19, 240
Coventry, George, looks for Simcoe papers, 237
Credit River, 161
Crookshank, Rachel, 157, 161

Darling, Lt. Henry, 69, 90
Darling, Gen. Sir Ralph, 206
Davison, George, 154
De la Pole, Sir John, 150, 155
Delaware Indians, 60, 73
De Luc, Jean André, 17-18; and Geological Travels, 184; 194
Deseronto Mohawk village, 61
Despard, Col. John, 110
Detroit, 63, 68, 89, 93, 105, 106, 107, 143; Brock captures, 194; Americans recapture, 195
Digby, Mary, see Mrs. Hugh Somerville
Digby, Miss, 78, 99, 130, 136
Districts in Upper Canada, 63-4; local government by, 87

Domville, Maj. Charles, 154
Don River, 89, 90, 91, 142, 157, 161
Dorchester, Lady Maria, 8, 110, 111, 112, 135, 164
Dorchester, Lord, 8; JGS angry with, 25; 31, 32, 33, 36, 37; on leave of absence, 47; 61; returns to Quebec, 90; 93, 102, 106; EPS admires his "Dormeuse", 111; 112, 143, 154, 157; resigns, 161; ship-wrecked, 164; 195
Dover, Simcoes visit, 167-8
Drewe, Adele, Caroline, 227
Drewe, Charles, 154
Drewe, Rev. Edward, 64, 82, 102, 196, 206, 217
Drewe, Edward Simcoe, 217, 227
Drewe, Herman, 82, 150, 152, 155
Drewe, John Rose, 206, 217
Drewe, Mrs. Herman, 82, 96, 150, 151
Drewe, Mrs. Mary, 82
Duke, Maj. George, 109
Duncan, Richard, 60; lends EPS a horse, 68
Duncombe, Dr. Charles, 220, 221
Dundas, Henry, Home Secre-tary, 92, 103, 147, 171
Dundas Street, 92
Dunkeswell Abbey, Devon-shire, 23, 24; window, Holy Trinity Church, 128, 199, 228
Dunkeswell Parish, 24, 27; poverty in, 29; 55; EPS' property in, 188; 199; school, 214, 215; parish church, 215, 228, 229, 230; St. Nicolas Church, 223
Dunster Castle, 196,202
Durham, Lord, 223; resigns, 225; Narrative of Recent Events in Canada, 226

Eastern District, 64
Eden, Hon. Emily, 8
Edinburgh, Heads in, 206; 207
Edwardsburgh Township, 140
Egland House, Honiton,195, 212, 217
Egloskerry and Tremaine, Henry Simcoe's two point charge, 210; H.S. buys advowson to, 212, 237; H.S. helps restore church at, 217; H.S. becomes vicar of, 233
Eildon Hall, Mein seat, Scotland, 217
Eildon Hall, Sibbald home in Upper Canada, 217
Elba, Isle of, 195; Napoleon escapes from 196
Electric motor, 8, 206

Elgin, Lord, and responsible government, 233; 234
Elliott, Admiral, 79, 131, 150
Elliott, Frances Anne, 79, 150, 195, 212, 217
Elliott, Mary, 79, 150, 212, 217
Elton Hall, seat of Probys, 200, 240
Enclosure Commissioners, 150, 178; of common lands,180
England, Col. Richard, 73, 165
Escot (Escott) House, 153; seat of Kennaways, 200; 233, 239
Eton College, 20; Francis Simcoe at, 181; headmasters, 181; Henry Simcoe at, 196
Exeter, 133; Honiton rioters sentenced, 150; 180; death of JGS at, 185; election in, 185; *Flying Post* account of JGS' funeral, 186
Exeter Cathedral, monument to JGS in, 192; inscription on Francis, 193; ordination of Henry Simcoe in, 210
Exeter, Mr. H., 230-31

Fairfield brothers, 108
Fallen Timbers, Battle of, 106
Finlay, Hugh, postmaster general, 112, 138, 139, 164
Fisher, Capt. John, R.A., 132
FitzGibbon, James, 221
Fitzhead Court, Somerset, 17, 27, 54, 55, 77, 78, 83, 96, 239
Flamborough Head, Upper Canada, 159
Flood, C. (JGS' bookeeper), 76, 133, 152
Flood, Rev. Richard, missionary to Indians, 219
Fort Erie, 145
Fort George at Newark, 195
Fort Miamis, 93, 103
Fort Niagara, 61, 63, 64, 66, 69, 72, 85, 91, 104; to be vacated, 159
Fort Oswegatchie, 89
Fort Rouillé, 88
Forty Mile Creek, Simcoes' journey to, 105
Fraser, William, 140
French Revolution, 33; execution of Louis 16th, 79; refugees from, 80, 81; execution of Marie Antoinette, 93; Eliza Simcoe's interest in, 151
Frobisher, Joseph, 51, 59, 109, 163

Galops Rapids, 109
Gananoque, EPS' sketch of mill at, 60, 81, 124; 108
Gananoque River, 60, 140
Genealogy of EPS, paternal, 255; maternal, 256-7; children of, 258-9; grandchil-

dren of, 259-60; Steward-Creed line, 260-61; Creed and Pickering connection, 261-2; relationship to William Walcot, 262; Pickerings and Montagues, EPS' great great great grandparents, 263-4
Genealogy of JGS, 257-8
Genet, Citizen Edmond Charles, French ambassador to the U.S., 89-90
Georgina Township, 218, 233
German settlers, 92,
Gibson, Rev. John, 228
Givins, James, 90
Givins, Mrs.James, 220
Glenelg, Lord, colonial secretary, 218, 220, 222
Glengarry House, 59, 104, 108
Gloucester, Duke of, 179, 206
Grant, Alexander, 39, 51
Grange, Drewe seat, 82, 206, 217, 239
Graves, Caroline, Mrs. Richard, 54, 102, 150, 151
Graves, Thomas North 2nd Baron, 177
Graves, Margaret (aunt), 9, 10-12, 13, 14; marriage of, 16; 19, 20, 22, 23, 24, 26, 28; moves to Wolford Lodge, 29; 31, 32, 35; turns against Simcoes, 37-9; 53-4, 55; has JGS' journals published, 55; jealous of M.A. Burges, 56; on education of girls, 56-7; leaves Wolford Lodge, 75, 76; destroys will, 77; 80, 81, Simcoes back in favour, 83; 95-6, 97; writes "violent letter" to JGS, 98-9; accuses M.A. Burges, 101; invites girls to Bath, 102; 130, 134; again invites girls to Bath, 150; 154; Simcoes visit, 169; 171; prefers girls to boys, 173, 174, 177; grieved Henry burnt, 175; visits Wolford Lodge, 176; letters to Eliza Simcoe, 177, 182, 187, 188; 178, 180, 181, 183; death, funeral in Bath, 190; bequests to Simcoe daughters, 190-91; 201; influences Simcoe daughters against marriage? 203; 235
Graves, Mary (daughter of Thomas), 56, 57, 154, 155, 207
Graves, Mary, Mrs. Thomas, 56, 81, 151; death of, 152
Graves, Capt. Richard, 19, 27; inherits Hembury Fort House, 29; 35, 53, 54, 57, 77, 79, 81,150, 151; snubbed by King, 152; 190

Graves, Admiral Samuel, 16, 19, 20, 22, 23, 24; death of, 27; monument to, 78; 177
Graves, Samuel (Richard's son), 81, 151; spoiled, teased at school, 154-55
Graves, Capt. Thomas, 19, 20, 56, 77, 79, 81, 154, 155
Gray, Maj. James, 59, 139
Gray, William Henry, 109, 111, 138, 163
Great Sail the Ojibway, 91, 92, 120; EPS' etching of, 156
Green, Adam, 160-61
Grenadier Island, 60
Grenville, Lord William Wyndham, prime minister, 184, 188-89
Grey, Lieut. Thomas, 52, 66, 92
Grinfield, Gen. William, 167
Guernsey, Rev. Mr., church in the Forest of Deane, 125; 229
Gwillim, Anne Jemima, dies of smallpox, 208
Gwillim, Elizabeth Posthuma, see Elizabeth Posthuma Simcoe
Gwillim, Elizabeth Spinckes (mother), 9, 10-11; death of, 12
Gwillim, Elizabeth Sophia (aunt), 9, 10-11, 12, 14, 16, 22, 24, 26, 83, 85; on death of Katherine Simcoe, 94; 100, 130, 131, 167, 168, 170, 171, 172, 173, 174; death of, 175; monument to, 180; 192, 235
Gwillim, Elizabeth Steward (paternal grandmother), 9, 11, 13; death of in 1767, 14
Gwillim, Henrietta Maria (aunt), 9, 10-11, 13, 14, 16, 22, 24; death of, 27
Gwillim, Col. Thomas Jr (father), 9; death of in 1762, 10-12; 34, 48; Caldwell recalls knowing, 119, 131
Gwillim, Thomas Sr. (grandfather), 9; death of in 1766, 14
Gypsies, EPS on, 216; *Gypsy Advocate*, 224

Hamilton, Col. and Mrs., escape from the Terror, 99
Hamilton, Catherine Askin, Mrs. Robert, 64, 67, 68, 72, 68, 67, 86, 87; house at Queenston, 119; 144; EPS bids farewell to, 159
Hamilton, Capt. James, 145
Hamilton, Robert, 62, 64
Hammond, George British ambassador to U.S., 68-9; 143
Harbour Boat Scene, 126
Harmsworth, Sir Geoffrey, presents title deeds to Wolford Chapel, 239

Harmsworth, Sir Leicester, offers Wolford Chapel to Ontario, 239

Haynes, Mr., Methodist preacher, 78, 95; his school, 96, 129; 151

Head, Frances Anne Burges, 17, 30, 58, 78, 79, 101, 131-32; death of, 191

Head, Frances (Fanny), 79, 132, 195, 206, 208, 215, 222, 223; death of, 233-34

Head, Sir Francis Bond, 78, 79, 182, 196; marries Julia Somerville, 198; 206-7; writes *Rough Notes from the Pampas*, 208; knighted, 214; 6th lieutenant governor, 218; baronet, 219; makes bad situation worse, 219, 221; resigns, 220; EPS approves of conduct, 222; house at Atherstone, 223; 226, 233, 234

Head, Frank Somerville (son of F. B. Head and Julia), birth of, 200; 207, 208, 209, 218

Head, George (son of F. B. Head and Julia), 207, 208, 209, 218, 224

Head, Sir George (brother of F. B. Head), 79, 98, 234

Head genealogy, 264, 265

Head, Henry Bond (son of F. B. Head and Julia), 207, 208, 209, 218

Head, James Roper (father of F. B. Head), 30, 58, 78, 79, 101, 131-2, 191, 195; death of, 196

Head, Julia (daughter of F.B. Head and Julia), 207, 208, 209, 218, 224

Head, Julia Lady, see Julia Valenza Somerville

Head, Mary, 79, 132

Hembury Fort, 16, 19; sham battles at, 182

Hembury Fort House, 16, 17, 19, 20, 22, 23, 27, 28; Richard Graves inherits, 29, 190; 53, 239

Hemyock, Devonshire, Simcoe property in, 203, 213; 220; parish church at, 234

Hennepin, Louis, 144

Holland, Samuel, Surveyor General, 50, 74

Holy Trinity Church, Dunkeswell Abbey, Simcoe window 128; 229; dedicated, 231; 238

Home District, 64, 220

Honiton, Devonshire, 16, 57, 135; riots in, 150; assembly, 151; politics, 156; 170

Honywood, Dr. magistrate, 34

Howe, Admiral Richard, Lord, 106-7, 166

Humber River, Upper Canada, 157, 158, 161

Hunt, Mrs. Ann, salary of, 32; 39, 50, 54, 57, 71, 73, 76, 77, 79, 81, 82; EPS letter on death of Katherine, 93-4; 95, 96, 98, 101, 135, 136, 148; takes girls to Seaton, 149, 150; 153, 154, 167, 171, 175, 197, 232

Hunt, Caroline, 32

Hunt, Rev. Edward, 32, 133

Hunt, Mary, tutor to Simcoe girls, 32; 37, 39, 54, 55, 57, 58, 73-4, 76, 80, 81, 83, 96, 98, 101, 129, 130, 167, 172; a governess to Princess Charlotte of Wales, 175; 178, 179; leaves Princess Charlotte's service, 182; 183, 185, 186, 188, 191, 194, 195, 197, 201, 214

Hunter, Gen. Peter, 2nd lieutenant governor, 174

Ile aux Soeurs, 162

"Inchbrooke House", 126

Indian Dept., 86, 157; missionaries, 219; 220; missions to natives, 236

Indian ladder, Niagara Falls, 145

Ireland, 172, 173, 182; Act of union, 174, 175; 182, 226

Jack Sharp, Newfoundland dog, 67, 73, 91, 100

Jackson, John Mills, 228

Jacob, a Mohawk, 158

Jacobs, Rev. Peter, 236

Jarvis, Hannah Peters, Mrs. William, 39, 51; opinion of EPS, background of, 70-71; 86, 91

Jarvis, Samuel Peters, 220

Jarvis, William, 39, 52

Jay, John, U.S. chief justice, 143; treaty, 143, 159

Jefferson, Thomas, 194

Jessup, Capt. Joseph, 140

Johnson, Ann (daughter of Sir John), 112

Johnson, Mary Lady, 112

Johnson, Sir John, 36, 112

Johnstown, 60, 139

Jones, Augustus, surveyor, 74, 142, 143, 160

Jones, Ephraim, 140

Jones, Dr. Solomon, 140

Junk, children's nurse, 103

Kembell, Gen. Gordon, buys, rebuilds Wolford lodge, 238

Kennaway, Charlotte A., Lady, 212, 227, 233

Kennaway, Sir John, 153, 200, 212, 227, 233

Kent, Prince Edward, Duke of,

31, 47, 48, 50, 64; visits Niagara, 65-6; 184; death of, 201; 220

Killerton House, Acland seat, 191, 200, 240

King George III, 38, 80, 152, 192; death of, 201

King George IV, see Prince of Wales

King William IV, 214; death of, 219

King's Head Inn, 159; description of, 160; 161

Kingston, not suitable for capital, 61; 107-8, 110; Simcoes second visit, 140-42; 162

Kitley, Bastard seat, 197, 198, 199

Lachine Rapids, 59

LaFontaine, Louis, 234

Lake Erie, 89, 103, 145, 146

Lake Ontario, 62, 69

Lake St. Francis, storm on, 108; 138

La Tranche River, see Thames River, Upper Canada

Leamington spa, 224, 229; Leamington Priors, 230, 231

Le Marchant, Alfred, gives access to Wolford Chapel, 238-39

Le Marchant, Pamela, Le M. Mitchell, 239

Leopold of Saxe-Cobourg, marries Princess Charlotte, 198

Leveson Gower, Capt., R.N., 165, 166

Lévis, Lower Canada, 50

Liancourt-Rochfoucault, Duke of, description of EPS, 143

Lilford, Thomas Powys, 2nd Baron, buys Aldwinkle, 179; 194

Lincoln, Gen. Benjamin, U.S. Army, 85, 86

Littlehales, Sir Edward, 59, 66, 68, 71, 139; Francis Simcoe visits in Dublin, 189

London, England, 16, 23; JGS leases house in, 27, 31; 32, 34; JGS leases 2nd house in, 169; EPS summoned from, 185; EPS visits, 1824, 206, in 1840, 229

London, Upper Canada, 36; site of JGS' intended capital, 63, 74; plan of site, 121

London District, 220, 221

Long Point, Lake Erie, 147

Long Sault Rapids, 60, 108; Bateaux running, 161; 162

Longueuil, Baronne de., 59

Lowe, Capt. Hudson, 99, 130, 135, 152

Lower Canada, 31, 32, 33, 34, 143, 157; Durham proposes union with Upper Canada, 226; act of union, 229

Loyalists, American, during and after the revolution, 28, 31, 34, 39, 60, 87

Luttrell, Mary Drewe, Mrs. John F., 196

Macaulay, Elizabeth, Mrs. James, 62, 67, 69, 144, 148

Macaulay, James, surgeon, 62, 93-4, 105, 141

Macaulay, John Simcoe, 62, 157

Macdonell, Hugh, adjutant general of militia, 108

Macdonell, John, Speaker, 59, 104

Macdonnell, Alexander, surveyor, 90

Mackenzie, Alexander, explorer, 107, 130

Mackenzie, William Lyon, 205, 216; leads rebellion, 220-21; escapes to Buffalo, 221

MacNab, Allan, 221, 222; *Caroline* affair, 223

Maiden Castle, Dorset, prehistoric fort, 179

Malcolm, Lieut. James, 165

Mansel, Rev. James T., 227, 235

Mann, Emily, see Emily, Mrs. Henry Simcoe

Maumee River, 93, 106

Mayne, William, 55, 86, 87, 105, 112, 138, 139

McCord, John, 163

McGill, John, injured, 51; adjutant, 107; 108, 110, 157, 162, 181, 209

McGill, Mrs. John, 147, 157, 161

McKee, Col. Alexander, Indian Dept., 86

McMurray, Rev. William, 220

Mecklenburg District, 64

Melbourne, Lord, 299

Methodists, 76, 213

Miami Chief, 120

Midland District, 64

Milanges, Antoinette de, 233, 234

Military Units:
3rd Dragoon Guards, 186
5th Foot, 71, 145, 181
7th Royal Fusiliers, 9, 31-2, 50, 109, 110, 154
22nd Foot, JGS full colonel of, 188
24th Foot, 50, 73, 106; in 1837 Rebellions, 221, 223
26th Foot, 109
27th Foot, Francis Simcoe's commissions in, 189, 190
32nd Foot, 223
35th Foot, 20, 21
40th Foot, 21
49th Foot, 221

50th Foot, 9, 10, 99
60th Foot, 108

Butler's Rangers, 63, 66
East Devon Yeomanry Cavalry, 186
Dunkeswell troop of cavalry, 186
King's Royal Regiment of New York, 36, 60, 62
Luppitt company of artillery, 186
Queen's Rangers, 1st American Regiment, 21, 22, 23, 24, 25; JGS publishes journal on, 28; 34, 39, 51, 52; colours of, 239
Queen's Rangers, Upper Canada, 15, 24; strength of, role of, 35-6; 39; on regular establishment, 49; 51, 55; at Kingston, 61; at Queenston, 64; 65, 71; band of, 74, 87; 86, 87-8,89; build roads, Dundas and Yonge Streets, 90, 92; officers' land grants, 91; detachment for Fort Miamis, 106; barracks at Queenston, 118; 157; disbanded, 181-82; 206, 220, 223

British regular soldiers, 35; during 1837 Rebellions, 223

Miller, Silvanus Jr., 231

Miller, Rev. Theodore, 231, 234; conducts EPS' funeral, 235

Ministry of All the Talents, 184, 188

Mitchell, Pamela Le Marchant, 239

Mitchell, Rev. Patrick, Dean of Wells, 239

Mohawks' chapel at Grand River, 72

Mohawk Indians, 59, 61; village at Grand River, 71, 72, 120; 161

Moira, Francis Rawden-Hastings, 2nd Earl of, 134, 189, 190

Monmouth, Saxon monument in, 227

Montagu, Mrs. Elizabeth, 10, 53, 77, 80

Montmorency Falls, Lower Canada, 50, 113

Montreal, 36, 50, 52; Simcoes at, 59; EPS visits, 109; 163

Moore, Archdeacon George, JGS dies at his house, 185

Moravian missionaries, 60. village for Delaware Indians, 73-4

Mosquitoes, EPS' dread of, 52, 64

Mount Dorchester,144

Mountain, Bishop Jacob, 90; visits Newark, 105-6; 111, lends Simcoes his house, 163; house catches fire, 164; 165, 226

Mountain, Rev. Jehosophat, 105, 163

Munroe, John, 60

Murray, Capt. George, 38, 46, 47

Napanee River, 141

Napoleon I, 173, 176, 182, 184-5, 191, 192, 194; abdicates, 195; 196; defeat of, 197; death of, 202

Native peoples, U.S. at war with, 67-8; allies of Britain, 68; muskets frighten EPS' horse, 160; missions to, 236

Navy Hall, JGS' description of, 63; 64, 74, 85, 86, 87, 103; rattlesnakes near, 104; 105, 143

Navy Island, 221, 223, 224

Nelson, Admiral Horatio, battle of the Nile, 173; death of, 183; JGS attends funeral, 184

Newark (Niagara-on-the-Lake), JGS renames, 62; description of, 63, 68; winter isolation, 70; 85-6, 88, 89, 103; sessions of legislature, 104, 144; 107, 142; Somcoes leave, 159

Niagara, see also Newark, 61; JGS renames, 62; camp at, 119

Niagara Escarpment, 103; red colouring of Queenston shale, 159

Niagara Falls, 63, 64; whirlpool below, 74, 144; 132; "Fort Schlosser" (American) Falls, 145; 222

Niagara Gorge, 118

Niagara River, 61, 63, 64, 86, 221-22

Nooth, Dr. Merwyn, 111

Norfolk, Duke of, 172

Northcote, Sir John, 180

Northcote, Sir Stafford Henry, 180, 212, 219

Northwest Company, presents JGS with a canoe, 91

Nutcombe, Frances, 210, 219

Nutcombe, Nutcombe, Chancellor of Exeter Cathedral, 191, 210

Ojibway Indians, 89

Old Court, New Court, Whitchurch, 10, 181, 215

Osgoode, William, 38, 39, 62, 71, 72, 88, 90; moves to Quebec City, 105; 112, 144, 164

271

Ottawa River, 138
Oundle, Northamptonshire, 24, 178, 183, 189, 200, 207, 212
Oxford University, 20, 180; Henry Simcoe enters Wadham College, 201

Pacific Ocean, 107
Paine, Thomas, *Rights of Man*, 99, 130, 167, 168
Palmer, Anne, see Anne, Mrs. Henry Simcoe
Palmer, Rev. Charles, 202
Payne, Thomas, bookseller, 130
Peel, Robert, 229; ministry passes free trade budget, 232
Penheale, manor in Cornwall, 210; Henry Simcoe purchases, 213; 216, 221; printing press at, 217; 224, 227, 229, 230, 234, 236, 239
Peterloo massacre, 201
Petroleum, 73
Pickering, Sir Gilbert, 85
Pickering, Thomas, U.S. Postmaster General, 85, 86
Pitt, Prime Minister William, 38, 39, 47, 58, 176, 182; death of, 184
Pilkington, Lieut. Robert, R.E., 103, 145
Playter's Bridge, 122, 161
Playter, George, 161
Plymouth, Devonshire, 58; JGS' headquarters at, 174; birth of Henry A. Simcoe at, 174; Eliza sails from, 198
Plymouth Brethren, EPS' opinion of, 228
Pointe au Baudet, 59, 138, 139
Popham, Gen. Samuel Taylor, 183
Port au Prince, Haiti, 171
Porter, Capt. Richard, 108
Portland, William Bentinck, Duke of, 103, 143; discourages aristocracy, 147, 169, 170-71; prime minister, 188-9
Powell, William Dummer, 144, 205
Powell, Anne, Mrs. Wm. D., 144, 146
Powys, Emily, 194, 200, 227
Pratt, Rev. John, dedicates Wolford Chapel, 180
Prescott, Gen. Robert, 161, 163, 172
Princess Charlotte of Wales, Miss Hunt governess to, 175; EPS sees, 179; Miss Hunt leaves, 182; marriage of, 198; death of, 201
Prince of Wales (George IV), 56, 58, 79, 80; marriage of, 132, 179; Regent, 192; King, 201; coronation, 202; death of, 214

Princess of Wales (Caroline of Brunswick), 132, 179, 201; death of, 202
Princess Elizabeth, 80, 152
Proby family, 200
Prussia, declares war on Britian, 184
Pynes, Northcote seat, 180, 212, 219, 239

Quebec Act, 34
Quebec City, 31-2, 34, 36, 38, 46; EPS arrives at, 47; celebrations in memory of defence in 1775, 49; 57, 58, 103, 163; fire in, 164; 196
Queen Charlotte, 38
Queen Victoria, birth of, 201; accession , 219-20
Queenston, lower landing, 64, 72, 74, 86, 88, 118, 144
Queenston Heights, battle of, 194
Quinte, Bay of, 36, 141

Randolph, John, U.S. emissary, 85, 86
Rapide Plat, 60, 139
Recollect Church, Protestant services in, 48; burnt, 164
Rebellion Losses Bill, 234
Rebellions of 1837, see Upper Canadian Rebellions, 1837
Reform Bills, 192, 216
Responsible government in the Canadas, 226; EPS' view of, 230,233
Rice Lake, 92
Richardson, Madeleine, Mrs. Robert, 87, 144
Richmond, Legh, 208
Richmond Hill, England, 127
Ridout, George, 220
Rio Plata Mining Association, 207, 209
Robarts, Premier John, accepts title deeds to Wolford Chapel, 239
Roberts, Methodist minister, 219
Robertson, William, 39
Robinson, John Beverley, 226, 227
Rock bass, 127
Rocky Mountains, 107
Roman Catholics, EPS' attitude towards, 48-9, 194-5, 207; 60, 212-13
Rousseau, Capt. Jean Baptiste, 88
Russell, Elizabeth, 39, 51, 63, 67, 91
Russell, Peter, 38, 39, 51, 62, 63; to be administrator, 161; 170, 174
Russell, Lord John, 233

St. George's Church, Kingston; Simcoe sworn in at, 62; 205
St. George's Church, Sibbald Point, Lake Simcoe, 124; Simcoe window in, 128, 228, 231, 233; dedicated, 228; second church, 233
St. Helena, Island of, 197, 202
St. James' Church, York, 195, 205, 216; Henry Scadding preaches in, 220; 230
St. John's Hall, Johnstown, 139
St. Laurent, Mme., 48, 201
St. Lawrence River, 35, 46, 51, 60-1, 63; Bend in, 124; at Pointe aux Trembles, 115; raft on, 162; 163, 196; canal to bypass, 205
St. Mary's Church, Hemyock, 234, 238
St. Nicolas Church, Dunkeswell, Simcoes help restore, 238
San Domingo (Haiti), JGS' mission to, 170-71
Sandusky, Ohio, 86, 87, 89, 105
Scadding, Charles (John's son), 200, 202, 206
Scadding family, 26, 206
Scadding, Harriet Baldwin, Mrs. Henry, 230
Scadding, Rev. Henry, 26, 200, 202, 206, 213; at St. John's College, Cambridge, 216; indolence of, 217-8; poor showing of, 219; 220; ordained deacon, 226; ordained priest, 230; 234
Scadding, John, 26; leaves for Canada, 56, 74; land at York, 90; cabin destroyed by fire, 92; 93; Scadding's cabin, 122; farm, 161; returns from Canada, 178; marriage, 188; 196; returns to Canada, 200; describes York, 205; killed, 206
Scadding, John Jr., 200, 202, 206
Scadding, Melicient Triggs, Mrs. John, 188, 200; moves to Canada, 202; 206; proud of Henry, 220; EPS' pension to, 234
Scadding, Thomas, 26, 110
Scarborough Bluffs, 89
Seneca Indians, 105
Shank, David, 49, 51, 52, 157, 158, 181
Shaw, Aeneas, 49, 51, 52; brings family to Niagara, 74; 107
Shaw, Mrs. Aeneas, 147
Sheaffe, Gen. Roger, 194

Ships:
Active, 163, 165
Bonita, 21
Brook Watson, 165

Caldwell, 93, 104
Camel, 198
Gov. Simcoe, 104, 147
Henneken, 51
Illustrious, JGS ill aboard, 185
Liberty, 47
Mississauga, 89, 104, 107, 142
Mohawk, launch of, 142; 159
Monarque, 19
Onondaga, 62, 88, 89, 142, 162
Pearl, 161, 163, 164, 165; menaced by French, 165; 167, 170
Pembroke, 19, 35
Prince Edward, 19
Thunderer, 79
Triton, 37, 38, 40, 46, 47, 165, 196

Sibbald, Hugh (Susan's son), visits Simcoes, 228
Sibbald, Susan Mein, Mrs. William, 216-7; sons, 217, 218; donates land for St. George's Chruch near Lake Simcoe, 227; 228, 233
Sibbald, Col. William, 217, 218
Sidmouth, Devonshire, 16, 26, 96, 202, 229
Sidmouth, Lord (Henry Addington), 30, 173; prime minister, 176, 181; resignation, 182; in Pitt's cabinet, 183, 184
Simcoe, Anne (daughter), birth of, 182; 196; parish work of, 199; tries EPS' patience, 200; electric motor, 206; 207, 208, 210, 214, 217, 221, 227, 229, 230; inheritances, 235; marriage, 236; death of, 237
Simcoe, Anne, Mrs. Henry, 202, marriage, 203; 210, 211; death of, 229
Simcoe, Anne Eliza (Henry's daughter), birth of, 205; 209, 217, 229, 231
Simcoe, Arthur Henry Linton, sells Wolford lodge, 238
Simcoe, Caroline (daughter), birth of, 30; 33, 37, 50, 53-4, 55, 57, 77, 81, 82, 83, 84, 96, 134, 150, 167, 170, 174; describes masquerade, 175; 193, 194, 198; parish work of, 199; 202; and marriage question, 203; 207, 208, 227; inheritances, 235; death of, 237; estate of, 238
Simcoe, Catherine Louisa Beatrice (Henry's daughter), birth of, 236
Simcoe, Charlotte (daughter), birth of, 27; 30, 33, 37, 53-4, 55, 56, 57, 65, 76-7, 78, 79, 82, 83, 84; makes shirt for JGS,

96; 97, 110, 129, 134, 148, 150, 154, 158, 169-70, 178, 185, 186, 188, 191, 193, 195, 198, 201, 202; and marriage question, 203; 207; last illness, 230; death of, 1842, 231, 232; 235
Simcoe, Eliza (daughter), birth of, 26, 27; 30, 33, 37; and miniature of EPS, 53; 54-5; misses parents, 56; 57-8, 65, 74-5, 76, 78, 79, 82, 83, 94, 96, 97, 99, 129, 134, 148, 150, 153, 154, 158, 169-70, 172, 174; attends many balls, 176; Margaret Graves' letters to, 177; 178; to Stowe, 180; tours Wales, 181; 185, 187, 188, 189, 191; observes Sabbath, 192; 194, 195, 197; tours Continent, 198; parish work of, 199; sensitive, 200; and marriage question, 203; at Oundle, 205; 206, 207, 208, 209, 212, 214, 218, 221, 224, 227, 228, 230, 232; inheritances of, 235; death of, 237; will and estate of, 237
Simcoe, Elizabeth Lethbridge (Henry's daughter), birth of, 213; 227
Simcoe, Elizabeth Posthuma, 6; birth of, 11-12; Canadian diary, 7, 18, 38; appearance of, 14; education, 15-16; artistic ability, 15, 22; marriage, 24; as a parent, 28; social work of, 29; miniature of, 37; voyage to Canada, 46-7; tries strange foods, 49; sketches Quebec, 49; enjoys social life, 51; to Montreal, 51, 59; to Kingston, 59-61; love of nature, 62; embarks for Niagara, 62; studies local animals, china broken, 65; at opening of Parliament, 66; pets of, 67; on local foods, 68; all-night vigil, 69, 83; Trojan destroys map, 69-70; balls at Newark, 71; sketch of Niagara, 78; "Sovereign Lady of Upper Canada", 82; 86; studies loons, 88-9; sends map to James B. Burges, 90; to Quebec City for safety, 107-10; rents house, 110; 111; return to York, 138-42; loves bright sun, 138, 169; on harvest foods, 146; spring in York, 158; journey, Newark to York, 159-61; on local food, 160; depressed at leaving York, 181; beds soaked, 163; sails home, 165-66; reunited with older girls, 169-70; on JGS' mission to

San Domingo, 171; buys black wig, 172; diary of yacht races, 179; diary on Ugbrooke visit, 179-80; to London and Stowe, 179; on JGS' mission to Portugal, 184; makes JGS' funeral arrangements, 185; JGS' executrix, 188, 189; death of Francis, 193, 194; Henry to be clergyman, 193; mourns M.A. Burges, 195; 198; as Evangelical Anglican, 199; model squire, 199; finds Anne disagreeable, 200; foreign missions, 200; at Oundle, 201; black pony, 202, 210, 213, death of, 221; and marriage question, 203; 121st Psalm, 204; in London in 1824, 205; Christmas 1824, 206; at Cheltenham, 207; 208; as Protestant, 209; cure for gallstones, 209; health at 64, 211; with grandchildren, 213, 217,; contributes to schools, 213, 214; visits to Wales, 214-15, 217, 228; approves of F.B. Head's performance; 219; disappointed in Henry Scadding, 219; newspapers from Lady Head, 222; feels her age, 225; belief in church and constitution, 225; at Monmouth, 227; helps Henry at Penheale, 229; on head of criminal, 229; Christmas, 1842, 231; death of, 235; will of, 235; descendants of, 237; misunderstood, 240; genealogy of, see Genealogy of EPS
Simcoe, Emily Mann, 2nd Mrs. Henry, 231, 234
Simcoe, Emily (Henry's daughter), birth of, 232
Simcoe, Francis Gwillim (son), birth of, 33; 37, 46, 52, 58, 67, 76, 86, 88, 89; land at York, 90; Castle Frank, 90; 92, 93-4, 99, 100, 103; third birthday, 104; 105, 108, 109, 110-11, 139, 145, 146; school, near Tice's 146; 147, 148, 153, 157, 158, 159; fifth birthday, 159; 161, 163, 166, 169; school in Honiton, 170; 171, 174, 180; at Eton, 181; 184, 185; commissioned in 27th Foot, 189; cost of commissions, 189; promoted, 190; tall enough for grenadiers, 190; 191; ill, 192; killed in action, letter from chaplain, 193; letters of, 197, 198, 203, 213, 232

Simcoe, Harriet (daughter), birth of, 28; 30, 33, 37, 53-4, 55, 56, 57, 65-6, 77, 81, 82, 87, 95, 96; buys gloves for M.A. Burges, 97; 99, 129, 134, 150, 167, 169-70, 196, 198, 199, 201, 202; and marriage question, 203; 217, 227; death of, 232; 235

Simcoe, Henrietta Maria, see Harriet Simcoe

Simcoe, Henry Addington (son), 17; birth of, 174; 175, 176, 182, 187, 189, 193, 196; enters Oxford, 201; B.A. Oxford, 202; first marriage, 203; model son, 204; 206; M.A. Oxford, 208; sells land in Upper Canada, 209-10; curate of Egloskerry and Tremaine, 210; leases manor of Penheale, 210; ordained a deacon, 210; ordained a priest, 212; 217, 227; second marriage, 231; vicar of Egloskerry and Tremaine, 233; EPS' principal heir, 235; William Walcot's heir, 236; death of, 237; estate of, 237

Simcoe, Henry Walcot (Henry's son), birth of, 204; 207; death of, 234

Simcoe, Capt. John, R.N. (father of JGS), 19, 35, 166

Simcoe, John (brother of JGS), 19

Simcoe, John Cornwall (son), birth of, 172-3; smallpox, 173; death of, 174, 232

Simcoe, John Graves (husband), 17; early life, 20; early military career, 21-2; meets EPS, 22-3; marriage, 24; anger at Dorchester, 25; as a parent, 28; publishes journal on Queen's Rangers 1st American Reg't, 29, 231; M.P., 31; colonel in British army, 32; dream of empire, 37; commission reaches Weymouth, 40; to Montreal, 50; 58; sworn in, 62; ill after cannon fired, 66; succours natives, 68; verses by, 70; to Detroit, 71, 73; levee at Newark, 86; fear of Russia, 90; wounded finger, 105, 106; 110; major-general, 111; ill in Kingston, 141; ill at Chippawa, 146; frustrations of, 157; granted leave of absence, 161; souvenirs to take home, 162; saves houses in Quebec City, 164; reunion with older girls, 169; London house, 170; mission to San Domingo, 170-2;

mooted governor of Canadas, peerage a condition, 172; in command of West Country, 1783; lieutenant-general in army, 175; directs Cato, 177; acquires two more manors, 178; leases third London house, 180; to Portugal, 184-5; death of, 185; funeral of, 185-6; burial of, 186; accounts settled, 188; 232; descendants of, lack of male heirs, 237; reminders of in Devon, 237; places he named in Canada, 237

Simcoe, John Kennaway (Henry's son), birth of, 210; 237; inherits Wolford Lodge, 237

Simcoe, Katherine I (daughter) birth at Newark, 71; 82, 83; death at York, 93-4; 94, 99, 103; grave at York, 239

Simcoe, Katherine II (daughter), birth of, 176; 182, 196, 202, 210, 213, 219, 224, 226, 227; interest in church in Upper Canada, 229; inheritances of, 235; death of, 237; estate of, 238

Simcoe, Katherine Stamford (mother of JGS), 19-20

Simcoe, Lydia Hannah (Henry's daughter), birth of, 216; 217

Simcoe, Mary Jackson, Mrs. John Kennaway Simcoe, 238

Simcoe, Mary Northcote (Henry's daughter), birth of, 212; 217, 231, 234

Simcoe, Paul Creed Gwillim, birth of, 217

Simcoe, Pawlett William (brother of JGS), 19

Simcoe, Percy William, (brother of JGS), 19, 20

Simcoe, Philip Francis (Henry's son), birth of, 216; 217; and advowson to Egloskerry and Tremaine, 237-8

Simcoe, Samuel Palmer (Henry's son), birth of, 214; 237

Simcoe, Sophia Jemima (daughter), birth of, 30; 33, 37, 46, 52; EPS' difficulties with, 67, 78; 80, 86, 109, 132, 152; put in school, 110; 111, 134, 161, 166, 169-70, 194, 196, 202; and marriage question, 203; 207, 208, 220; inheritances of, 235; death of, 237

Slavery, JGS phases it out, 87; abolished in British Empire, 216

Smallpox, disease and inoculation, 76, 173-4, 208

Smith, Anne, Mrs. David William, 85, 105

Smith, David William, 71, 72, 85, 89, 91, 157, 158

Smith, Maj. John, 64, 66, 71

Smith, Samuel, 49, 51, 90, 103, 181

Smith, Miss, governess to EPS?, 14

Smith, Sir Sidney, escape from France, 172

Somerville family, 17, 27, 54, 83, 96, 135

Somerville genealogy, 264, 265

Somerville, Harriet, 96

Somerville, Col. Hugh, 17, 54, 81, 96, 130; death of, 135; 136

Somerville, James, 13th Lord, 81; dies intestate, 155-6; funds for natural children, 155-6

Somerville, John Southby, 17, 54, 136; 14th Lord Somerville, 156

Somerville, Julia Valenza, birth of, 77-8; 95, 130; to live at Tracey, 135-6; appearance of, 137; first visit to Wolford Lodge, 150; obstinate, 152; 155, 169; recites epilogue, 177; 178, 182; moves to Ashfield, 183; 184, 191; M.A. Burges' executrix, 195; engagement, 196; marriage to F.B. head, 198; birth of son Frank, 200; 201, 207; in Argentina, 207, 208; back in England, 208-9; 213; reaches Toronto, 218; writes EPS, 220; sends newspapers to EPS, 222; 226

Somerville, Kenelm, 95, 129, 135

Somerville, Mark, 95, 96, 129, 135

Somerville, Mary Digby, Mrs. Hugh, 54, 77-8, 95; death of, 129

Somerville, William, 95, 136

Spain, declares war in Britain, 182

Spencer, Capt.-Lieut. George, 49, 51; ill, 97, 98, 133

Spinckes, Jemima Steward (maternal grandmother), 9, 12-13, 14; death of in 1776, 16; 24

Spinckes, Elizabeth (mother), see Elizabeth Spinckes Gwillilm

Spinckes, Margaret, see Margaret Graves

Stevenson, Capt. Charles, 39, 48, 49, 68

Steward, Mrs. (EPS' great great grandmother), 212
Stone, Joel, 60, 108
Stoney Creek, Upper Canada, plunge pool near, 160
Stowe (house, later school), Buckinghamshire, 30, 35, 189, 191, 196, 239
Stove from Canada for Wolford Lodge, 170
Strachan, Rev. John, 195, 205, 216; EPS helps son study in England, 217; 220; Bishop of Toronto, 226; consecrated at Lambeth Palace, 227; ordains Henry Scadding, 230
Stuart, Rev. George Okill, 205
Stuart, Rev. John, 62, 141, 205

Talbot, Thomas, 50, 51, 52, 61, 66, 68, 86, 92, 129, 130, 181
Texas, annexed to U.S., 230, 232
Thames River, Upper Canada, 36, 60, 63, 71, 72, 73, 74
Thousand Islands, 123
Tice, Christian, Mrs. Gilbert, 87; house of, 124; EPS rents rooms from, 144-7; 151
Titchmarsh, W. Walcot's manor at, 178, 200; EPS visits, 201; EPS sketching at, 207; 212, 235, 237
Todd, Alpheus, looks for Simcoe papers, 237
Tor Bay, Devonshire, 166, 185
Toronto Carrying Place, site for naval base, 74, 85; description of site, 87; York renamed Toronto, 1834, 216; Lady Head arrives in, 218
Toronto Islands (EPS' peninsula), 87, 89
Toronto, city of, 216; diocese created, 226
Town meetings, 87
Tracey House, 27, 30, 37, 38, 39, 54-5, 75, 81, 95, 98, 102, 133; holiday celebrations at, 153-4; 170; M.A. Burges leaves, 183, 240
Trafalgar, Battle of, JGS orders artillery salute, 183
Trois Rivières, 52, 109, 138
Trojan, 67; chews map, and JGS' verses, 69-70, copy of map, 123; death of, 74

Ugbrooke House, Clifford seat, 133; Simcoes visit, 179-80; Eliza ill at, 185, 187; 212, 214, 216, 218; still owned by Clifford family, 240
United States, hatred of British, 85; embargo acts, 189, 191; Non-intercourse Act, 192; declares war on Britain, 194

Upper Canada College, founded 1829, 213, 216, 230
Upper Canada, province of, 15; description of, 31; 32; potential of, 33; 34, 36, 39; local government, 63-4; first election, 66; first Parliament, 66; second session, 85; third session, 104; U.S. threatens, 104; costly to defend, 157; EPS retains interest in, 181; Rebellion of 1837, 188; resists capture by U.S., 194; unemployed soldiers to settle in, 200; lack of clergy in, 202; progress of Anglican Church in, 205, 237; sale of Simcoe land in, 209, 213; Durham proposes union with Lower Canada, 226; act of union, 229; JGS' papers left in, 237
Upper Canadian Rebellions, 1837, 220, 221; Pelee Island raid, 223; 224; Battle of Windmill Point near Johnstown, 225; border raids, 230; Rebellion Losses Bill, 234
Ursuline Convent, Quebec City, 48, 164; Mother Superior, 48, 164

Walcot, Thomas, 200
Walcot, William (distant cousin), 24, 77, 178, 180, 189; Margaret Graves' executor, 190; 196, 200, 201, 202, 205, 207, death of, 212; EPS' children his heirs, 212, 235-6; house in Oundle, 240
Wales, Eliza Simcoe tours, 181; EPS' visits to, 214-15, 217, 228
War of 1812, 188; U.S. declares war, 194; Battle of Queenston Heights, 194
Wardour Castle, Arundell seat, 133, 179-80, 196, 207, 215, 220; girls' school, 240
Washington, President George, 86, 89-90
Waterloo, Battle of, 197
Wayne, Gen. Anthony, 86, 105, 106
Wellington, Duke of, as Arthur Wellesley, 191; as duke, 192, 194; at Waterloo, 197; proposes canal to bypass St. Lawrence, 205; 208; prime minister, 212; EPS disapproves of role in Catholic emancipation, 224
Wesley, John, 76
Western District, 64
Weymouth, Dorset, 37, 40; yacht races at, 179

Wheeler, Godfrey, 228
Whitchurch, Herefordshire, manors at, 9, 10, 12, 13, 14, 15, 64, 94, 171, 181, 215, 224, 227, 228, 229; Henry Simcoe inherits, 235-36
White, John, 39
Whitefish, 127
Wilberforce, William, 87, 209
Wildflower, 127
William V, Prince of Orange, 131
"Williams", childrens' nurse, 28
Williamsburgh Township, 139
Windsor, manor of, near Wolford Lodge, 178
Wolfe, Gen. James, 9; bust of, 134
Wolfe's Cove, Cascade in, 115
Wolford Chapel, 125; Cistercian ruins, work begun on, 175; dedication of, 180; motto in, 180, 185; burial of JGS, 186
Wolford Lodge, family prayers at, 25; building of, 26-7; description of, 29; 36, 37, 38, 39, 46, 53, 54, 55, 58, 75, 76, 78, 79, 81, 89, 94, 110, 129, 148, 153; French lesson at, 154; 166; Simcoes return to, 169; 171; JGS' military headquarters, 173; masquerade at, 175; JGS directs play at, 177; celebrations after Trafalgar, 183; celebrations of peace in 1814, 196-7; stove catches fire, 205-6; new storeroom, 209; Sophia's drawing of, 220; workshop at, 228; Henry Simcoe inherits, 236; Arthur H.L. Simcoe sells, 238; torn down, 238
Wolford, manor of, purchased, 24; 26
Woodbine Hill, home of Thomas Graves, 152, 154, 239

Yonge, Sir George, 30, 90, 153
Yonge Street, 90, 157-8
York, Duchess of, 56, 80
York, Duke of, 56, 80, 171
York, Toronto Carrying place renamed, 89; 142, 147, 157; civil servants ordered to move to, 159; burnt by Americans, 195; renamed Toronto in 1834, 216

Acknowledgements

No biography of Elizabeth Simcoe would have been possible without the many letters and diaries of two people. One was Mrs. Simcoe herself; the other was her dearest friend, Mary Anne Burges. In the quotations from their writings, the original spelling and punctuation have been retained. Both help to recapture the cadence and the flavour of English usage of the time, and so does the retention of certain archaic words and phrases.

Many people, on both sides of the Atlantic, have given generously of their time and shown great interest in the project. In England are Keith Taylor, a trustee of Dunkeswell Abbey; the Reverend Nicholas Wall, rector of Holy Trinity Church, Dunkeswell; Peter Thomas, assistant librarian of the Exeter Cathedral Library; and Francis Drewe of Ticehurst, Sussex, and Broadhembury, Devon, who supplied the genealogy of the Drewe family. Chris Dracott of Hemyock, Devon, who is working on the life of General Simcoe in Devonshire, shared his discoveries. Correspondence with John Vowler of Parnacott, Devon, was of particular interest as he is descended from Mary Northcote Simcoe, Elizabeth Simcoe's granddaughter. Others who shared their knowledge were Paul Dixon of Cotterstock, and Alice Thomas of Oundle. Hilary Arnold of York contributed useful information, in addition to the extensive genealogy in the Appendix. The staff at the Devon Record Office in Exeter, and at the Public Record Office in London, were always obliging.

Closer to home, Bruce Wilson of the National Archives of Canada in Ottawa sent reference numbers and read the manuscript as did Barbara Smith; Leon Warmski, reference archivist at the Archives of Ontario, was most supportive; Allan Macdonald, manager of special collections at the Archives of Ontario, made available Simcoe material that had not been catalogued; Jan Rollins and Paul Thomas at the Archives of Ontario were patient during the selection, for reproduction, of Mrs. Simcoe's sketches and watercolours. The staff at the Metropolitan Toronto Library were helpful as always. Last, and most important, are publisher Kirk Howard, editor Boyd Holmes, and designer Andy Tong, of Dundurn Press.

All illustrations including the cover are courtesy The Archives of Ontario, with the exception of the frontispiece portrait of Elizabeth Simcoe which is courtesy of the National Archives of Canada, and the photographs of stained glass windows on page 128 which are courtesy of the author.